ENCYCLOPAEDIA OF MILITARY MODELS

CLAUDE BOILEAU HUYNH-DINH KHUONG THOMAS A. YOUNG

ENCYCLOPAEDIA OF MILITARY MODELS

1/72

AIRCRAFT · MISSILES · SCIENCE-FICTION
VEHICLES · ARTILLERY · FIGURES · WARSHIPS

First English language edition published 1988 by Airlife Publishing Ltd.
This U.S.A. edition published 1988 by Tab Books Inc.

Library of Congress Cataloging-in-Publication Data
Boileau, Claude.
(Encyclopédie des maquettes 1/72. English)
The encyclopedia of military models by Claude Boileau, Huynh-Dinh Khuong, Thomas A. Young.
Translation of: Encyclopedie des maquettes 1/72.

1. Airplanes—Models—Catalogs. 2. Airplanes, Military—Models—Catalogs. 3. Military miniatures—Catalogs. 4. Airplanes—Models—Collectors and collecting. 5. Airplanes, Military—Models—Collectors and collecting. 6. Military miniatures—Collectors and collecting. I. Huynh, Dinh Khuong. II. Young, Thomas A. III. Title.
TL770.B53713 1988 88-6298
629.133'1'074—do19
ISBN 0-8306-8283-X $28.95 (Hardback)
ISBN 0-8306-8383-6 $19.60 (Paperback)

Printed in Hong Kong.

CONTENTS

INTRODUCTION

The definition of the word "model" in some dictionaries reads like this: "a miniature representation of some existing object, such as a machine or a theatre scenery, which is accurate in its proportion and aspect". More generally, it can be said that the expression is used to cover all three dimensional reduction of an object.

The idea of creating a reduced version of reality stems from manifold aspirations. Architecture makes use of models, and so does shipbuilding for hydrodynamic tests. Models are again used in the field of aeronautics for aerodynamic research but, apart from technical or industrial requirements, private reasons for building models do exist.

A good model is rather like a work of art that amateurs handle with care or indeed content themselves with inspecting it from all angles. It can be said to be real in its presence and unreal insofar as it conjures up different places or periods. Models can represent any subject, be it a historical event or the brainchild of fiction; technical or human feats, passions, wars or even fancy rank among those multiple subjects that can be conjured up by models.

Modellers will often devote a lot of time to making models of what they like and what they may never be able to afford. That accounts for the universal and growing appeal of modelling.

Broadly speaking there are three ways of building a model:

- Straight from the box. The assembly of such a model can be very quick and some of them will look quite satisfactory, even with simplified assembly and painting.

- Using a kit as a basis, with improved or modified parts, or even conversions, to achieve greater realism.

- Scratchbuilding, using the best available documents and "raw materials" ranging from plastic card to copper wire.

These procedures should enable a modeller to assemble all the aeroplanes of an aerobatic team in a day or, in the case of the opposite extreme, to spend months or even years to portray that prototype whose rakish lines took his fancy.

Experienced modellers will not content themselves with assembling their models properly, they will try to analyse kits and to understand the "whys" and "hows". They will not hesitate to leave aside a poor model and build up their own masterpiece from scratch, so as to evoke the history of the original as accurately as possible.

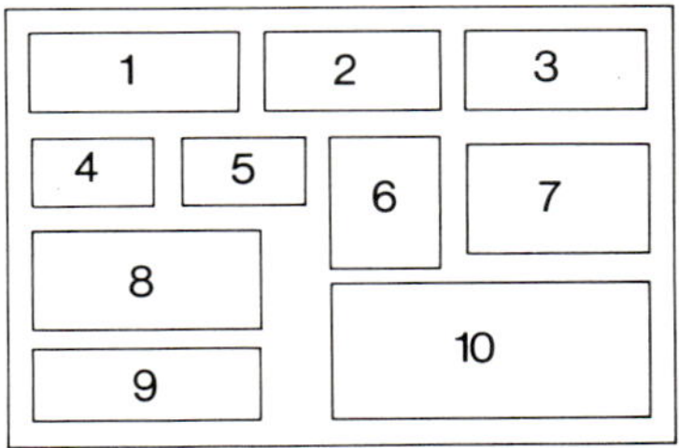

1*	AVRO *CF-100 Mk.IV Canuck*	**(Aurora)**
2	B.A.C. *Lightning F-6*	**(Frog)**
3*	ADER *Eole*	**(Brifaut)**
4*	AERMACCHI *M.B.326*	**(Cunarmodel)**
5	AICHI *M6A1 Seiran*	**(Aoshima)**
6*	BELL *X-1*	**(Airvac)**
7	AGUSTA-BELL *AB-205*	**(Esci)**
8	B.A.C. *TSR-2*	**(Contrail)**
9	ANTONOV *An.2 Colt*	**(VEB)**
10	AVRO *Vulcan*	**(Rareplane)**

ADER *Eole* — **Brifaut**

The French name "Avion", meaning a heavier-than-air machine fitted with wings and designed for flight, was invented by Clément **Ader** in 1890 who made his childhood dream come true that year, when he built his "Avion I", better known as *Eole*. That flying machine was probably the first to actually leave the ground under its own power. Witness accounts are not unequivocal but Charles **Dollfus**, a historian and flyer who personally knew **Ader,** wrote the following lines in the spring 1974 issue of *Icare* magazine (No. 68) devoted entirely to **Ader**:

> "On October 9th, 1890, Clément **Ader** clearly demonstrated the possibility of leaving a flat surface, and making a progress of 50 yards in a straight line, no more, for lack of power and stability."

That is one of the reasons why any mention of the *Eole* will raise the greatest interest among a group of modellers. Produced more than 20 years ago by **Brifaut**, the *Eole* plastic kit was one of the first to bear the "Made in France" label. In spite of its age it remains one of the best models of old aircraft in the 1/72 scale series.

Pierre **Brifaut** aimed at several objectives when he designed his kits:

— he wanted his boxes to look better than the others and had the box arts painted by Bernard **Brenet**, a famous pre-war artist;

— he wanted to improve the culture of those who purchased his models; that is the reason why he added a historical account of the *Eole* and a biography of **Ader**;

— he wanted his models as accurate as possible and the *Eole* must have been the first plastic model to be supplied with a template, fabric, nylon thread and liquid cement for covering and rigging; this new method made assembly much more difficult. So as to encourage the average modeller to succeed in spite of the difficulties, **Brifaut** included two *Eole* models in each box. Pierre **Brifaut** planned to make no less than 100 models of French aeroplanes to 1/72 scale. That scheme was a way for him to convey his views by telling the history of aeroplanes, their manufacturers and their pilots. He hoped thus to urge modellers to go beyond their normal abilities. Unfortunately, he died before his schemes could materialise. He was buried at Presles, a pretty village in the Val d'Oise near Paris. A tribute in his memory is a must, should you happen to go there.

AVRO *CF-100* — **Aurora**

This kit was eagerly sought after by Canadian modellers, although the packaging contains a slightly oversized model whose moulding quality is not up to present-day standards, but was reasonable when it was released. Purists may prefer to work out a *CF-100* from the **Hosey Craft** model, which is a more accurate kit and still available.

AERMACCHI *M.B. 326* — **Cunarmodel**

The **Gualdoni** brothers mainly manufacture desk-models for **Aermacchi** at Cunardo, near Varese, **Italy**. On request of local modellers, they develop very unique aircraft kits to 1/72 and 1/100 scale for them. These planes, released in small batches under the **Cunarmodel** label, are eagerly sought after throughout the world . . .

BELL *XS-1* — **Air Vac**

On October 14th, 1947, Captain Charles E. **Yeager** was the very first in the world to break, the sound barrier with his **Bell** *XS-1* named "Glamorous Glennis" to honour his wife. After an outstanding service, this aircraft performed his 59th and last flight on May 12th, 1950. On that day, Charles **Yeager** flew it again in spurious Soviet markings, for the shooting of a short sequence of the *Jet Pilot* film.

Retired Brigadier General Charles E. **Yeager** appeared recently in the film *The Right Stuff*, not as himself (Sam **Shepard** did), but as Fred, the bartender at Pancho's bar, the only meeting-place in the Mojave desert for all those famous test pilots who were pioneering supersonic flight.

The *XS-1* number one is now displayed in the **National Air and Space Museum** in Washington DC.

The **Air Vac** vacuformed kit is very crisply made and enables the building of an excellent model, even if decals are not included. However, a very fine **Microscale** decal sheet is provided with the *X-1E* made by the same manufacturer. The assembly instruction sheet provides a good plan and quotes the source references used for the design of the kit, particularly the remarkable book *Supersonic Flight* written by Richard P. **Hallion**. Congratulations to **Air Vac** for the choice of this plane and their good results.

▲
ADER *Eole* — Didier **Palix**

ADER *Eole* — Didier **Palix**

The *Eole* is difficult to cover with fabric, following the procedure recommended by Pierre **Brifaut**, because of its flexible structure. Indeed, after gluing, the fabric has a tendency to blistering. One of the tip developed for covering this kit consists of inserting thin sheets of plastic cards tailored to the proper dimensions between the ribs, and wrap and glue the whole with **Renwal** *Aero-Skin*. François **Portier**, a member of the friendly **MKSB** (Model Kit Static Boulonnais), used carbon paper protection sheets to replace the *Aero-Skin*.

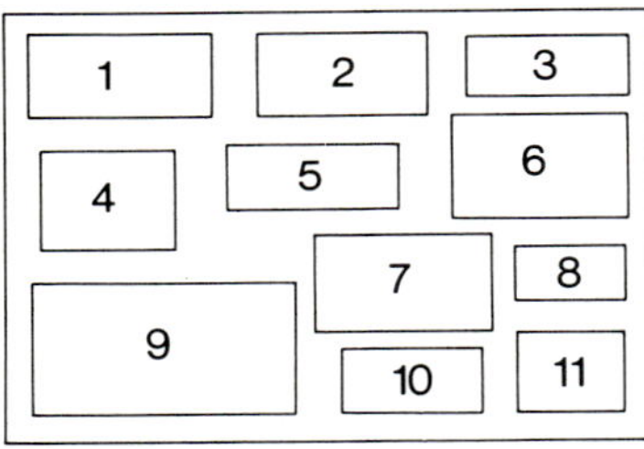

1*	AICHI *E13A1 Jake*	**(Hasegawa)**
2	AVRO *Triplane MkI*	**(Renwal)**
3*	AERO COMMANDER *Jet Commander*	**(Aurora)**
4*	BEDE *BD-5*	**(299 Models)**
5	BAC *Canberra PR7*	**(Triang)**
6	BELL *AH-1S Tow Cobra*	**(Fujimi)**
7*	AVRO *Canada CF-100*	**(Alpha)**
8	AERO *L.29 Delfin*	**(Kovozavody)**
9	BERIEV *Be.6 Madge*	**(VEB)**
10	BRISTOL *138A*	**(Frog)**
11	BAC *Jet Provost Mk.3*	**(Airfix)**

AICHI *E13A1 Jake* — **Hasegawa**

Ross **Abare** owns one of the finest collections of models in the world. He moulded hundreds of Japanese catapults for the sheer pleasure of improving his dioramas of Japanese aircraft. Some of those catapults were sold for $3 each by **Unique Scale Accessories** from Springfield, Massachusetts, USA. **Hasegawa** eventually bought up the mould and now includes Ross **Abare's** catapult in the **Aichi** *Jake* and **Kawanishi** Alf kits, thereby increasing their price and making a handsome profit.

AERO COMMANDER *Jet Commander* — **Aurora**

No **Aurora** *Jet Commander* will ever be re-issued. As a matter of fact, Rick **Waldorf**, the Marketing and Sales Manager of **Monogram Inc.**, has confirmed that the mould (bought from **Aurora**) was broken up when the train that was carrying it, derailed.

BEDE *BD-5* — **299 Models**

The *BD-5* is the smallest existing 1/72 scale aircraft kit. This one is made by Terry **Elmore**, a dynamic American who successfully used a press whose injection load limit does not exceed ¾ oz. The bagged kit shown here is of the first release and only offers the jet-powered version, but, with some modifications, may also be worked-out into a prop-driven version. The last release of the *BD-5J* includes a decal sheet.

AVRO CANADA *CF-100* — **Alpha**

André **Longchamps** is an orthopaedist-podologist in Liege, **Belgium**. Fortunately, he is also a modeller. When one of his models is particularly well-made, he moulds it and installs the mould on the machine he currently uses for vacuforming the prothesis of his patients.
The result lies before your eyes: one must confess that this pair of **Alpha** prothesis will not help you if you are suffering from sore feet, but surely you'll jump with pleasure if you love the *CF-100.*

▲
AIRSPEED *AS.51 Horsa* — Jacques **Niot**

The military transport glider *Horsa* was built during WWII. It was designed as a troop-carrier and a freighter. Two versions were made: the *Horsa I (AS.51)* which accommodated from 20 to 25 troops and the *Horsa II (AS.58)* with a hinged nose for the loading of vehicles and heavy equipment. Roughly 3700 *Horsa* were built.
This **Italaeri** kit depicts the *Horsa I* version. No criticism can be formulated about this model.

AMIOT 143 — Jacques **Niot**

AMIOT 143 — Jacques **Niot**

The all-metal **Amiot 143** was a Recon/Bomber. Its double-deck fuselage was its most characteristic feature.
The **Heller** kit is to be ranked in the NTB (not too bad . . .) category as the shortcomings can be corrected without any major difficulty.
As a matter of fact, Jacques **Niot** modified the vertical fin, engine cowlings and propellers of his **Amiot 143.** Markings are those of aircraft No. 112, 35th Bomber Wing, 4th Flight, of the French Air Force.
When he assembled his model Jacques had no vacuform machine to mould the transparencies. That is why he used to sand those provided in the box with finer and finer grain sandpaper and then polished them with some kind of car wax.

▲
ARMSTRONG-WHITWORTH *Siskin* — Paul **Goujon**

The **A.W.** *Siskin* was selected by the British Air Ministry as a day fighter in 1926. It was produced by **Gloster, Blackburn, Bristol** and the parent company — **Armstrong-Whitworth**. Over 350 aircraft of the type were delivered until 1931.
The **Matchbox** kit is well moulded, easy to assemble and offers scope for intricate rigging. The checkerboard markings of No. 43 Squadron come from a **Modeldecal** sheet. *Aircraft of the RAF* **(Putnam)** is a useful — indeed indispensable — reference for lovers of British military aircraft.

▲
BELL *XP-77* — Claude **Boileau**

Compared to its contemporaries, this prototype fighter was rather tiny (the *P-47* was three times heavier). Its simplified construction and wooden structure would have made it possible for the USA to mass-produce it with lower costs and a quicker rate of delivery than were required for conventional fighters.
Moreover, from an operational point of view, the reduced size and weight of the *XP-77* would have bestowed upon it a higher manoeuvrability and superiority over its opponents. These hopes were unfortunately dashed.
Two *XP-77s* were built *(SN 43-34915* and *916).* The first flight *(915)* took place on April 1st, 1944. 916 crashed on October 2nd, 1944 following a spin but the pilot successfully baled out and escaped unscathed.
The performances of the *XP-77,* particularly its climbing speeding and its service ceiling turned out to be lower than the **Bell** Company estimated and the programme was shelved in December 1944.
The **Airframe** model is generally accurate but the fuselage section is about 3mm too narrow at the bottom. The 3 view drawing included in the kit is good though slightly over-scale. The canopy was vacuformed with a **Mattel** machine. The landing-gear was almost entirely made from copper wire, aluminium tubes and foil. Painting was carried out with **Liqu'a Plate**. **Microscale** decals were used. A very detailed account of the *XP-77* with about 20 photographs and a 3 view plan can be found in *AAHS Journal* (Winter 1981). *Air Pictorial* and *Le Fanatique de l'Aviation* have also published short articles on the same subject with three or four photographs along with a plan, respectively in April 1960 and March 1971. Finally, Bob **Archer** described the assembly of the **Airframe** model and added photographs of the prototype and of his model in *Scale Aircraft Modeler,* Summer 1975 and January 1979.

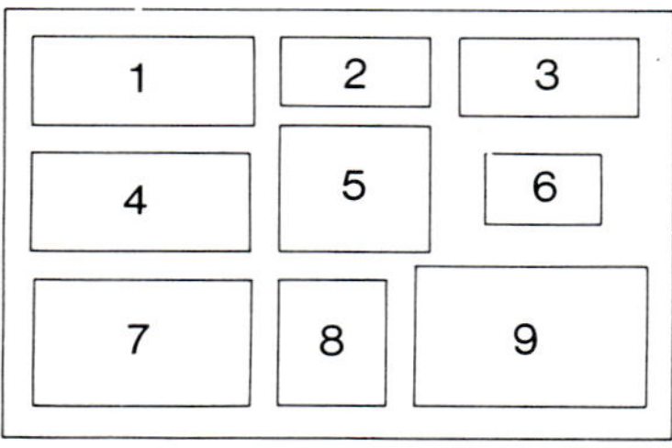

1. BELL *AH-16 Huey Cobra* **(Monogram)**
2. BACHEM *Ba.349A Natter* **(Heller)**
3. ANTOINETTE *Monoplan 1908* **(Brifaut)**
4. BRISTOL *170 Superfreighter Mk.31* **(Airfix)**
5* BELL *X-5* **(Dragon)**
6. ALBATROS *D.V* **(Renwal)**
7. AVRO *Lancaster « Dam Buster »* **(Revell)**
8. AUSTER *Antarctic* **(Airfix)**
9* CANADAIR *CL.215* **(Heller)**

NORTHROP *X-4* and BELL *X-5* — **Dragon Model Works**

US prototypes of the fifties and sixties are fascinating, yet no plastic injection kit manufacturer shows any real interest in these planes at present. **Dragon Model Works** had the good idea to provide us with a **Northrop** *X-4* and a **Bell** *X-5* on the same plastic sheet.

CANADAIR *CL.215* — **Heller**

This model was widely acclaimed by modellers and aircraft modelling magazines when it was released. **Heller** is to be congratulated for this handsome achievement.

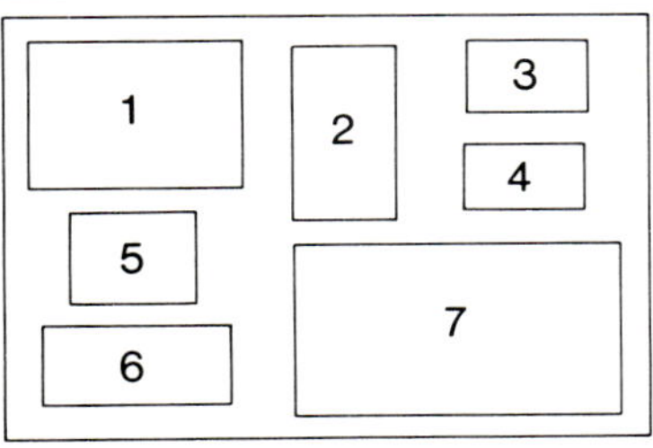

1	ARMSTRONG-WHITWORTH *Whitley*	**(Frog)**
2	BELL *XV-3* *collection P. Legrand*	**(Eagles Talon)**
3	BREWSTER *Buffalo F2A*	**(Aoshima)**
4	BEDE *BD-5/BD5-J* *collection D. Palix*	**(L.S.)**
5*	DASSAULT *Mystère IVA*	**(Rudel)**
6	DASSAULT *Mirage F.1C*	**(Hasegawa)**
7	AVRO *Vulcan B.2*	**(Airfix)**

DASSAULT *Mystère IV* — Bernard **Rudel**

Already at the age of 12, Bernard **Rudel** had started making models carved from wood. Three years later, his collection included no less than 50 models built to 1/50 scale. But, probably like many other collectors, he got worried about the lack of space. Finally he decided to carry on making models to the less cumbersome 1/72 scale. Soon his new collection grew to 300 models but, in spite of that, Bernard **Rudel** could not find his favourite aeroplanes in hobby shops.
In 1968, he discovered **Rareplanes** vacuforms and a small machine for producing vacuum formed objects, sold as a toy by **Mattel**, all these at the **Camouflage Air Club**, a society no longer existing today but almost every member now belongs to **IPMS France**. He started on a few conversions with the **Mattel** machine but the latter showed its limitations. So Bernard **Rudel** decided to invest his savings, amounting to some $350, in a new machine he built himself from an old gas cooker, an electric resistor, three empty bottles of camping gas, a small vacuum pump, a pressure switch, an electric valve, some elbow grease and . . . sweat. His first efforts produced crude models but nowadays, thanks to the experience he gained by producing some twenty different kits, **Rudel's** vacuforms have become products that are appreciated by those modellers who wish to get off the beaten track.
Bernard **Rudel** is thus the father of French vacuform and, in 1984, he was still the only exponent of the technique in **France**.

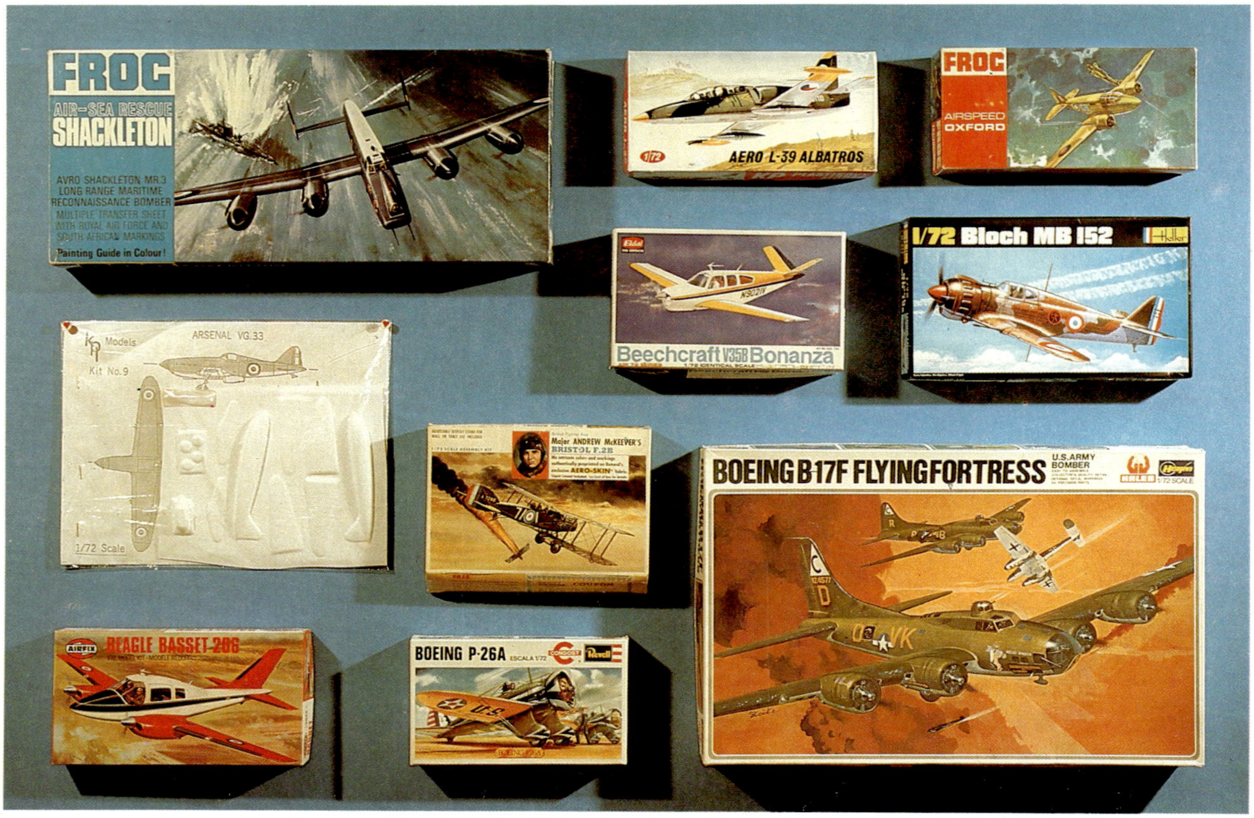

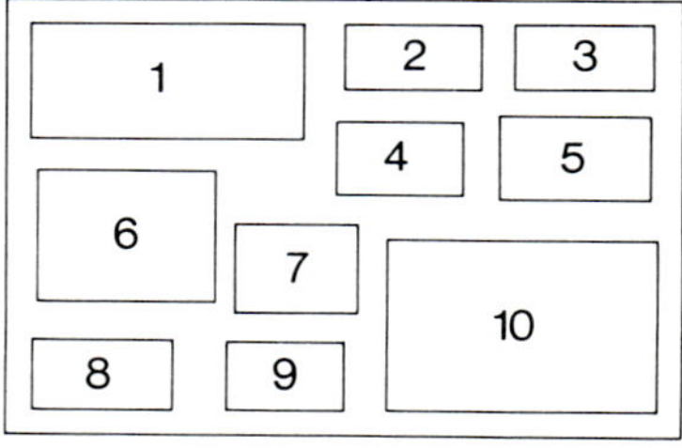

1	AVRO *Shackleton Mk.3* collection *P. Legrand*	**(Frog)**
2	AERO *L.39 Albatros*	**(Kovozavody)**
3	AIRSPEED *Oxford*	**(Frog)**
4*	BEECHCRAFT *Bonanza*	**(Eidai)**
5	BLOCH *M.B.152*	**(Heller)**
6*	ARSENAL *VG.33*	**(K.P.L.)**
7	BRISTOL *F2B*	**(Renwal)**
8	BEAGLE *B.206 Basset*	**(Airfix)**
9	BOEING *P-26A Peashooter*	**(Revell)**
10	BOEING *B-17F Flying Fortress*	**(Hasegawa)**

BEECHCRAFT *Bonanza* — **Eidai**

The line of **Eidai** civil lightplanes is of such high standards that it is an absolute must for modellers who like Flying-Clubs. It is really a pity that manufacturers show so little interest for that category of aeroplanes.

ARSENAL *VG.33* — **K.P.L.**

Bernard **Rudel**, the French pioneer in vacu-formed kits, and Ken **Lasala**, the founder of **K.P.L Models**, have both focused their interests on the **Arsenal** *VG.33.*
The American model shown above is very crude and its accuracy is questionable, but at least it is easily available. The French model is better, but can only interest collectors as it has not been re-issued.

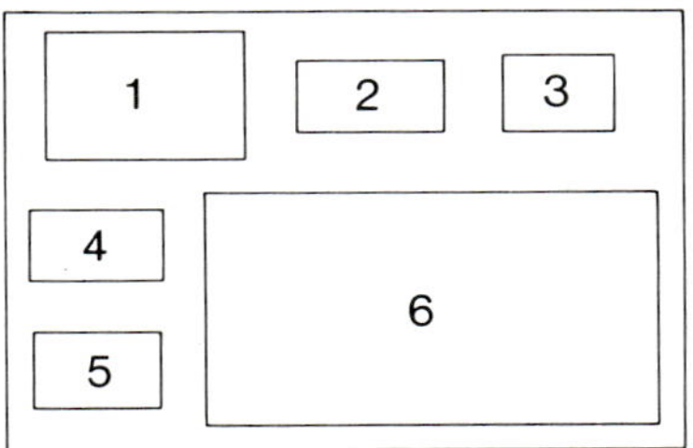

1* CAPRONI *Campini* (Delta)
2* CONVAIR *XF-92A* (Hawk)
3 CESSNA *O-1 Bird Dog* (Airfix)
4* CESSNA *Skymaster* (Aurora)
5 CESSNA *172 (With Floats)* (Grip)
6 BOEING *B-52 Stratofortress* (Monogram)

CAPRONI-*Campini N.1* — **Delta**

Delta kits mean tidings of joy : they conjure up historical achievements and on top of the usual instruction and decal sheets, each box includes a well-produced colour booklet about the aircraft. Curiously enough, some mouldings of the **Caproni-***Campini N.1* are pistachio green.

CESSNA *337 Skymaster* — **Aurora**

Thanks to a *KCI* (Kit Collectors International) interview published in their *Vintage Plastic* bulletin, we all know that the mould of this **Cessna** *Skymaster* by **Aurora** was destroyed at the same time as that of the *Jet Commander*. Although it was not broken when the train derailed, it sunk into the marshes of Upstate NY, where the accident occurred.

CONVAIR *XF-92A* — **Hawk**

The box is not upside down — the aircraft is in inverted flight! This model of 1966 vintage includes no landing gear, but oddly enough offers four US Navy Sparrow I missiles, although the *XF-92A* was an experimental US Air Force aircraft that carried no armament.

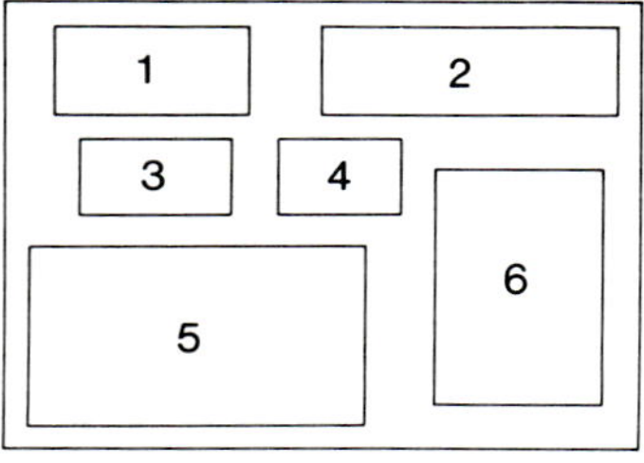

1 BLERIOT *XI* **(Brifaut)**
2 BOEING *B-737* **(Monogram)**
3* BLOHM UND VOSS *BV.141* **(Airfix)**
4 BOEING *P-12E* **(Matchbox)**
5 BOEING *B-47E Stratojet* **(Hasegawa)**
6 BELL *XP-83* **(K.R.)**

BLOHM UND VOSS *BV.141A* — **Airfix**

This observation aircraft featured an extraordinary asymmetrical layout that was meant to provide the crew with excellent visibility. It first flew in 1938 but never achieved mass production status.
Jacques **Niot**, who specialises in WWII German aircraft, claims that the **Airfix** offering is quite accurate but unfortunately marred by the poor quality of the transparencies.
Good references about the various versions of the *BV.141* are to be found in the July and August 1964 issues of *Flying Review International.*

BLOHM UND VOSS *BV.138MS* — Jacques **Niot**

This **Supermodel** moulding is rather crude and the fit of the parts is inferior to today's standards. However, the general outline is quite accurate.
This *MS* version (Minensuche, ie, mine-searcher), fitted with a large magnetic field generator hoop, was nicknamed, literally, "mouse-catcher" (Mausi Flugzeuge).

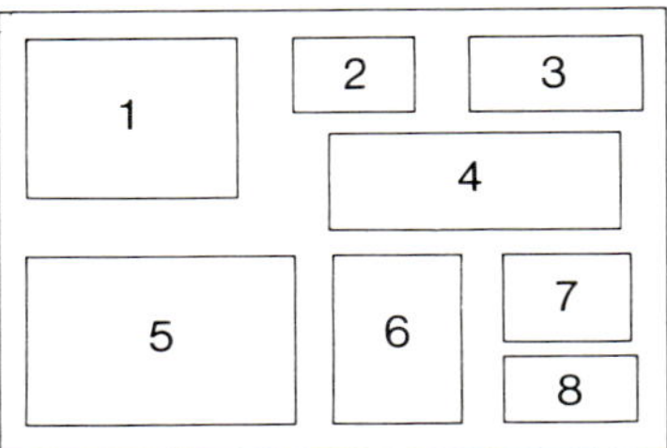

1	CONSOLIDATED *PB4Y Privateer*	**(Matchbox)**
2	BELL *P-63 Kingcobra*	**(Aoshima)**
3	BLACKBURN *Buccaneer S2B*	**(Frog)**
4*	CONVAIR *B-58 Hustler* *collection B. Macaire*	**(Aurora)**
5	BLOHM UND VOSS *BV. 138*	**(Supermodel)**
6	BELL *P-59 B Airacomet*	**(Rarejets)**
7	BEECHCRAFT *17*	**(Rareplane)**
8	BOEING *Vertol 107*	**(Airfix)**

BLOHM UND VOSS BV. 138 MS

CONVAIR *B-58 Hustler* — **Aurora**

Until the release of the **Italaeri Convair** *B-58*, this **Aurora** *Hustler* was much sought after. Being the only plastic injection moulded kit close to 1/72, it allowed the non-specialists of vacuforms to build-up a satisfactory model of this well-known bomber.

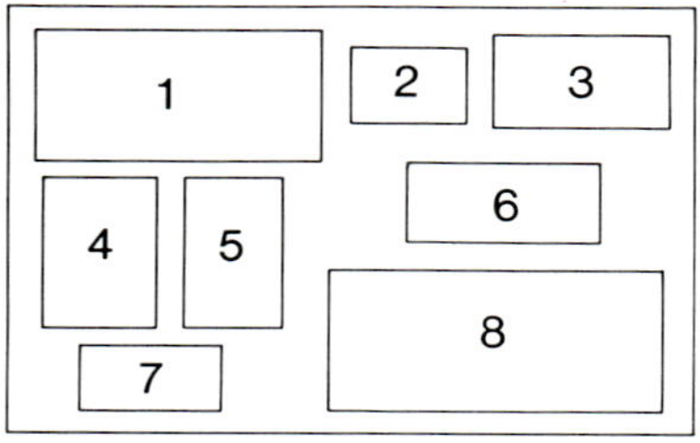

1 BOEING *B-29 Superfortress* **(Airfix)**
2 BELL *P-39Q Airacobra* **(Airfix)**
3* GENERAL DYNAMICS *F-16XL* **(Monogram)**
4 BLOHM UND VOSS *BV40* **(VP Canada)**
5* BUGATTI *100 Racer* **(Projekts)**
6* DASSAULT *Mirage IIIC* **(Central)**
7 BLACKBURN *Shark* **(Frog)**
8 BOEING *KC-97G Stratocruiser* **(Rareplane)**

GENERAL DYNAMICS *F-16XL* — **Monogram**
In spite of some minor imperfections, this **Monogram** *F-16XL* is an interesting kit, since it portrays the brightly coloured first prototype built by **General Dynamics** from the fifth *F-16A*. This model is one of the few (among others such as **Hasegawa's Lockheed** *S-3A Viking*, **PZW Siedlce's** *SZD Jantar Standard*, **Monogram's** *B-1B* and *F-16 Thunderbirds Team)* to include a tinted canopy. This is not a novelty, since 20 years ago, **Aurora** for instance, already supplied a green-tinted canopy for its quarter-inch scale **Lockheed** *XFV-1*.

BUGATTI *100 Racer* — **Projekts Model Company**
Who on earth was original enough to produce a **Bugatti** *Model 100* (a French racer that did not even fly, and was the brainchild of Louis **De Monge** under an Air Ministry contract to try to win the 1938 Deutsch de la Meurthe Cup)? You guessed! That was the American Matt **Hargreaves**. This **Projekts Model Company** kit was introduced for the first time at the **IPMS** National Convention in Salt Lake City, Autumn 1979. 600 kits — all of them numbered — were issued. Collectors still have a chance, if . . .

DASSAULT *Mirage IIIC* — **Central**

Trying to show off a model to its best advantage with top-quality box-art is a praiseworthy practice, but depicting it with accessories that are not included in the box can be misleading. Thus **Heller** saw it fit to represent their *Javelin* (box reference No. 346) or their *Lansen* (box reference No. 343) with an external fuel tank without including those parts in the kits.
Conversely, why did **Central** fail to picture the **Matra** *R.530* missile on their box-art, since it is supplied with their model?

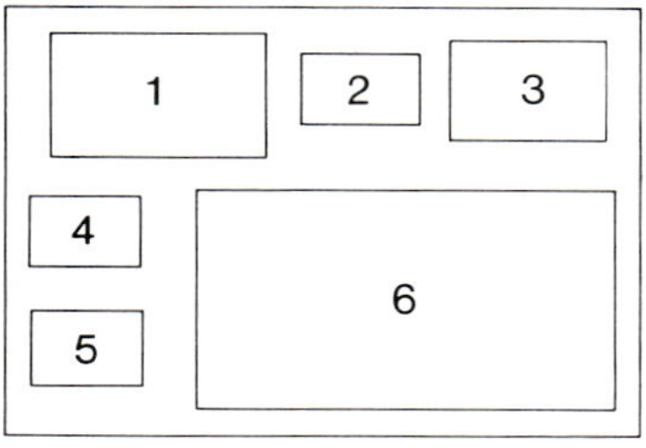

1* CONSOLIDATED *PBY-6A Catalina* **(Revell)**
2 CESSNA *172* **(Eidai)**
3 CURTISS *BF2C-1 Goshawk* **(Gunze Sangyo)**
4 CURTISS *P-36 A* **(Monogram)**
5 CESSNA *O-2A* **(Airfix)**
6 CONVAIR *B-36 Peacemaker* **(Monogram)**

CONSOLIDATED *Catalina Cousteau* —
Revell

We have chosen to show the *Catalina* in its **Calypso** packaging to honour the memory of Philippe **Cousteau** who was killed while flying this aeroplane over **Portugal** for the shooting of a film dealing with marine life. No one will ever forget those wonderful moments spent watching him and his *PBY-6A* on TV. Thanks to the **Cousteau** team, the deltas of **Costa Rica**, the jungles of **Nicaragua,** and the rivers of **Senegal** seem so much closer to us.
The **Cousteau** kit includes two frogmen, a fine **"Zodiac"** dinghy and beautiful decals picturing the nymph **Calypso**.
Revell moulded their *Catalina* in three versions: the *PBY-5* flying boat with detachable undercarriage, the *PBY-5A* amphibian with retractable landing gear and *PBY-6A* amphibian with retractable landing gear, taller fin and rudder and modified nose.
At least two documents will facilitate the task for those modellers who wish to assemble a *Catalina:*
— *PBY Catalina in Action* published by Squadron/Signal,
— *Scale Aircraft Modeler* Volume 2, No. 6, Spring 1974 that includes good drawings and some black and white photographs.

▲
BOEING *B-737* — Jean-Frédéric **Boullier**

1/72 scale airliners are such a rarity that **Aurora's** *B-737* is eagerly sought after by civil airplanes patrons.
Jean-Frédéric **Boullier** told us about his method of applying **ABT's** Argental powder on the metal panels, when we took this picture:
— He cleaned all surfaces thoroughly with washing up liquid and told us it was essential to avoid touching the model with one's bare hands. If it was absolutely necessary to handle the model, cotton gloves (similar to those that are used by photographers to hold negatives or prints) had to be worn.
— Then he applied the powder with a cotton or paper pad and buffed it up with a compact drill fitted with a felt pad revolving at high speed to force the metallic powder into the plastic.
— Then he applied more powder with a cloth and polished it with another cloth until a satisfactory finish was obtained.
Jean-Frédéric resorts to this technique for all his models now and considers it as second to none.
The tail assembly of this **Royal Air Maroc** *B-737* shows off the result to perfection. The metallic glint which is so typical of new airliners can also be found on the same modeller's **Air France** *Constellation.*

BREGUET *XIV* — Francis **Nicole**

Francis **Nicole** built this **Breguet** *XIV* from Bernard **Rudel's** vacuformed kit and was awarded a silver medal, an **IPMS** first prize and the President's prize at a contest held during the 4th modelling exhibition which took place in the "Palais du CNIT" at **Paris-La Defense** from April 2nd to 10th, 1983.
The **Breguet** *XIV* was used mainly as a postal aircraft. An interpreter often flew with the pilot. This was quite useful in case of a forced landing in the desert among the Moors.
Francis **Nicole** carried out extensive research to build his model and consulted

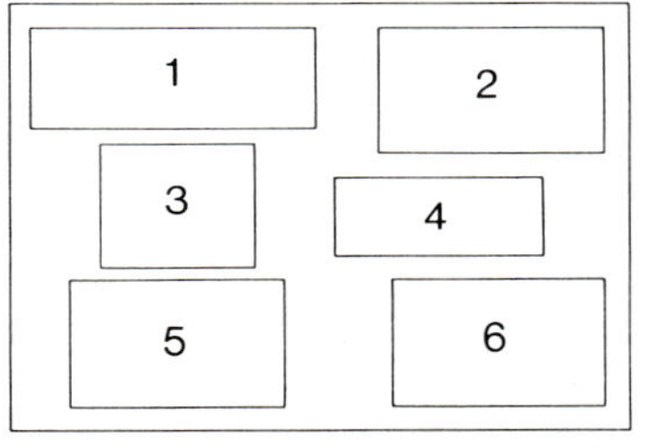

1 CONSOLIDATED *PBY-5A Catalina* **(Aurora)**
2 CONSOLIDATED *PBY-5A Catalina* **(Toho)**
3* CAUDRON *R.11* **(Cramer)**
4 CONSOLIDATED *PBY-5A Catalina* **(Airfix)**
5 CONSOLIDATED *PBY-5A Catalina* **(Revell)**
6 CONSOLIDATED *PBY-5 Catalina* **(Revell)**

the pioneers who made the first commercial flights.
He thus benefited from the knowledge and advice of Marcel **More**, the author of *J' ai vécu l'épopeè de l'Aéropostale* (My life with Airmail).
Among the solutions put forward for the reproduction of the wheel spokes of these "old crates" one can use the following techniques:
— stretched sprue,
— nylon or metal wires,
— transparent disks on which the spokes are engraved and painted,
— printed circuits (photograph etching).
Francis had his own technique, which was to use his hair for exquisite detailing of rigging and spoke wheels.

CAUDRON *R.11* — **Cramer**
Ken **Cramer** is one of those manufacturers who specialise in vacuformed kits. It is only thanks to people like him that the *R.11* in particular can be part of the *Encyclopedia of Models.*
A three-seater biplane, the *R.11* deserves to be better known, as it proved to be an excellent fighting machine. Its two engines gave it very good performances for the period, but unfortunately, it came into service late, towards the end of 1917. The model portrayed here bears the following mention: "Kit No. 2013".

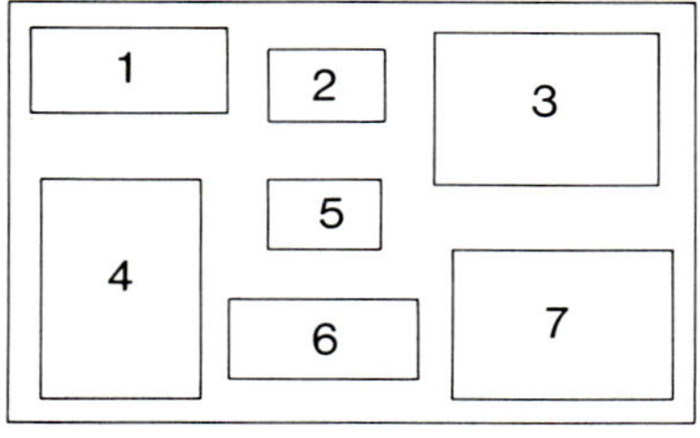

1	CONVAIR *F-106 Delta Dart*	**(Hasegawa)**
2	CURTISS *SBC-4 Helldiver*	**(Matchbox)**
3	CANT *Z 1007 Alcione Bideriva*	**(Supermodel)**
4*	CONVAIR *XP-81*	**(K.R.)**
5	CURTISS *P-6E*	**(Monogram)**
6	CHANCE VOUGHT *F4U-1D*	**(Hasegawa)**
7	CANT *Z.501*	**(Italaeri)**

CONVAIR *XP-81* — **K.R.**

Kenneth Rymal has sworn to make up a 1/72 scale collection of all USAF fighters . . .
From the **Curtiss** *P-1B* to the very latest, not forgetting prototypes, even those that didn't even fly. Some would have balked at the fact that many aircraft do not exist in kit form, but Ken took the challenge and produced the missing links himself.
This **Convair** *XP-81* is one of his astonishing products. Ken's vacuforms are characterised by an extreme accuracy in shape and dimensions and bear only light engravings on their surface, exactly as the connoisseurs of vacuforms like them to be.

CANT *Z.501* **Gabbiano** — Jacques **Niot**

This Italian *Seagull* belongs to the 148th Squadriglia Recognizione Maritima. About 200 of the type were operational when **Italy** started the hostilities in 1940. The **Italaeri** model is excellent and hardly needs any modifications at all.

▲

CANADAIR *CL-215* — Jean-Frédéric **Boullier**

As the photograph shows, these two flying boats sport different finishes.
That is because the colour schemes of Protection Civile **Canadair** are not quite the same when the aircraft is new as when it has been overhauled.

CONSOLIDATED *Privateer* — Didier **Palix**

Matchbox seldom come up with very fine kits but they offer very interesting models from time to time, as is the case with this *Privateer.*

▲
CONVAIR *F-102* — Claude **Boileau**

This snow-covered scene shows a **Convair** *F-102 Delta Dagger* sporting the colours of the 573rd FIS "Black Knights" based at Keflavik, **Iceland.**
The **Hasegawa** model is excellent in spite of its age and only a few improvements were made:
— the windscreen and canopy were vacuformed with a **Mattel** machine and the cockpit was completed with the help of drawings published in *Replica in Scale* Volume 1, No. 2, November 1972,
— the doors and missile wells (containing 6 *Falcon AIM-4G)* were reworked according to the pictures published in *Koku Fan* No. 51 and *Interavia* (March 1961),
— the main landing gear was modified and landing lights made from fake diamonds were added,
— the Pitot boom was made from an aluminium tube and copper wire and a thin stripe of black decal was wrapped around to save a troublesome paint job.
Paint was then sprayed on the model with a **Badger** 200 or 100 XF airbrush and the decals came from **Microscale** sheet No. 72-108 and **Modeldecal** sheet No. 11.
The diorama was built on a 300 x 270 x 22mm plywood base. The snow is made of plaster whitened with gouache. The Jeep is from **Hasegawa** with its steering wheel replaced by a finer one and its headlights vacuformed on a pin-head. The ground power unit was scratch-built, using the wheels of an **Airfix** *Sea King.*
The ground team came from modified **Preiser** figures.
This diorama has already been described in more detail in Volume 1, No. 5, 1977 *of La Vitrine du Maquettiste* (*VDM* is the magazine of **IMPS France**).

CURTISS *C-46 Commando* — Didier **Palix**

This **Curtiss** *C-46 Commando* — the least successful offering of the small **Williams Brothers** Company — is shown here in the version that was used for "flying the hump", ie, the Himalayas, hence its well worn and weathered aspect. The technique used for this effect is the following:
— dull the paint with the application of mud that can be brushed off when it is dry,
— overspray the structure lines with a thin dark film of paint,
— pick out the same panel lines with dark pastel drawing pencil,
— spray exhaust stains behind the engines,
— sparingly apply paint chips along the leading edges and the panel joint lines,
— paint mud stains behind the wheels.
Weathering paints available from model shops can also be used. Whatever technique will be used, one should strive for a realistic aspect and not overdo the weathering effects — an operational aircraft hardly looks like a wreck ready for the scrapyard.

CURTISS C-46 *Commando*

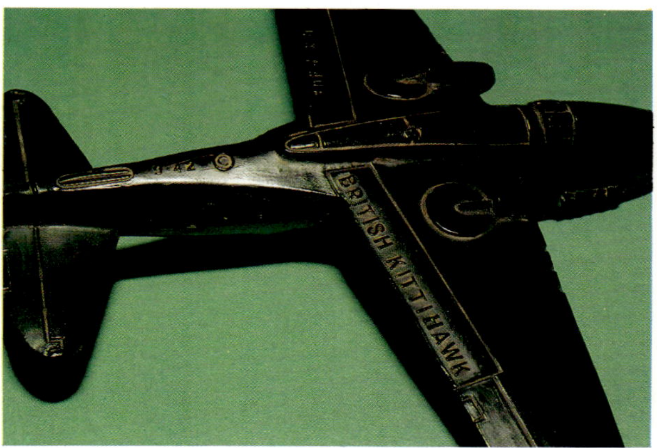

CURTISS *P-40E Kittyhawk* — Bernard **Macaire's** collection

DORNIER Do. 24 **(Italaeri)**
Jacques Niot.

This **Cruver Curtiss** *Kittyhawk* was a recognition model made of hard rubber and delivered already assembled. The date of origin of the first models was shown by figures, while later models bore letters to indicate the month when they were produced. The *Kittyhawk* on this photograph was produced in September 1942.

DASSAULT *Mirage F.1* — Philippe **Legrand**

This *Mirage F.1* was made by Philippe **Legrand** from the **Heller** model, which is more accurate than the **Airfix** *F.1.* However, the nose gear and the main wheels were cannibalised from the **Airfix** model. The airbrakes and spoilers were drilled out and the exhaust nozzle improved. All the navigation and anti-collision lights were made from tinted transparent plastic. Philippe also improved the section of the air intakes which are rounded on the fuselage side and do not have the sharp angles as on the **Heller** model. Those who want to add armament are advised by Philippe to use the *Matra 530* missile from the **Heller** *F.8 Crusader* and to borrow the *Magic 550* missiles as well as the pylons from the **Airfix** kit.
However, **Hasegawa's** *F.1* is finer and easier to assemble than **Heller's**; moreover, it captures the outline of the real *F.1* far better.

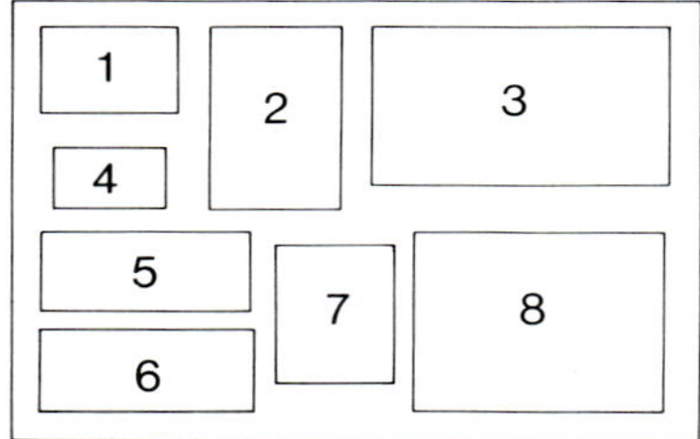

1*	DASSAULT *Super mystère B2*	**(M.A.F.)**
2	DE HAVILLAND *DH.1 1910*	**(Entex)**
3	CURTISS *C-46 Commando*	**(Williams Brothers)**
4	DE HAVILLAND *Comet Racer*	**(Triang)**
5	CURTISS *SB2C Helldiver*	**(Lindberg)**
6*	COUZINET *Arc-en-ciel*	**(Heller)**
7	CURTISS *XP-55 Ascender*	**(Airmodel)**
8*	DASSAULT *Falcon 20H*	**(M.E.E)**

DASSAULT *Super Mystère B2* — **M.A.F.**

This extremely rare **M.A.F.**-made *SM-B2* kit consists of two main parts to be assembled along a fuselage frame, thus leaving no horizontal gap **(M.A.F.** stands for **Maquettes Aériennes Françaises**, yet another company founded by Pierre **Brifaut**). The construction technique described above saves some puttying and sanding operations and makes for extra-quick assembly. Unfortunately, the technique requires the use of very expensive multiple-drawer moulds, so very few mass-produced models are designed along these lines. Indeed, before being distributed on a commercial basis, this *Super Mystère* was made to order for Marcel **Dassault.** These models were delivered all-assembled and chromium-plated, with the plane fixed on a sheet of green felt and presented in a clear box.

COUZINET *Arc-en-ciel* — **Heller**

Heller's *Arc-en-ciel* is no match for **Brifaut's** on the score of quality.
Unfortunately only a few test shots of the **Brifaut** model exist and only a dozen or so were distributed. What if **Heller** recovers the **Brifaut** moulds and put out again a good *Arc-en-ciel?*

DASSAULT *Falcon 20* — **M.E.E.**

M.E.E. or "La Maquette d'Etude et d'Exposition" formerly known as **Etex** chiefly makes desk-models. Yet, ever since Jean-Claude **Hasquenoph** convinced Jean **Kerjouan** to sell his models to a wider public, the company has made a substantial effort and now offers 5 models to 1/72 scale, most of them original subjects. The models are made of polystyrene, rigid polyurethane foam, metacrylate (for the transparencies) and are sold "straight from the mould" without any landing gear or stand-base,

in a polyethylene bag. The prices of **M.E.E.** 1/72 models are so attractive that the decal sheets, printed in small series, are actually more expensive than the unfinished models.

DE HAVILLAND *Vampire FB.5.* — Claude **Boileau**

This model was assembled from the **Frog** kit long before the far superior **Heller** model was available. The **Heller** far outstripped its predecessor for its ease of assembly and fine detail. The model photographed here depicts the *Vampire FB.5.* flown by the Commanding Officer of No. 112 Squadron based at Fassburg, **Germany**, in 1951. According to Richard L. **Ward** — the manufacturer of those excellent **Modeldecal** transfers — that colour-scheme, which is offered on sheet No. 14 (initially released in 1971) was used on the aircraft for about a month (in October 1951).

Later, when No. 112 Squadron was sent back to **Britain,** the red shark's-mouth emblem was replaced by a smaller black one, with the teeth remaining white, but with a red outline. The newer No. 14 **Modeldecal** sheet now offers the black shark's-mouth, probably so as not to duplicate the red one adopted by **Heller**.

This *Vampire* model had been made for a meeting of the 'late' **Camouflage Air Club** whose proposed subject for that day was aircraft sporting shark's-mouths!

DEWOITINE *510* — Didier **Palix**

Heller's Dewoitine *510* is a highly satisfactory model for various reasons. The subject is interesting in itself, the surface detailing is fine and the proportions are correct. All this makes the kit particularly attractive, even for the most demanding modeller.

DORNIER *217 N-1* **(Italaeri)**
Jacques Niot.

DEWOITINE *510*

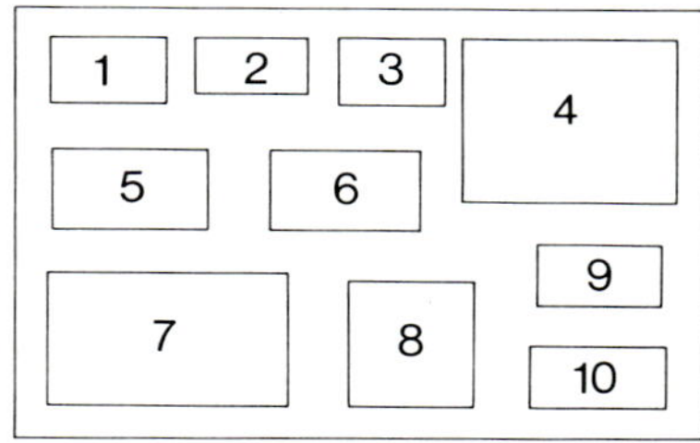

1	DE HAVILLAND *DH.2*	**(Revell)**
2*	CESSNA *310*	**(Aurora)**
3*	DASSAULT BREGUET *Alpha Jet*	**(Starfix)**
4	DOUGLAS *B-66 Destroyer*	**(Airmodel)**
5	DASSAULT *Ouragan*	**(Heller)**
6*	DASSAULT Super Mystère B2	**(Starlux)**
7*	DOUGLAS R4D-5 Skytrain	**(Esci)**
8*	DE HAVILLAND *Mosquito Mk.6*	**(Airfix)**
9	DE HAVILLAND *Gipsy Moth*	**(Frog)**
10	DOUGLAS *SBD Dauntless*	**(Airfix)**

CESSNA *310* — **Aurora**

Many authors, who plagiarise each other will state that this **Aurora Cessna** *310* is to 1/62 scale. In fact. its scale is 1/69.

DASSAULT-BREGUET-DORNIER *Alpha Jet* — **Starfix**

All **Starfix** models come from moulds borrowed from other manufacturers, except this *Alpha Jet* which looks like the **Matchbox** kit without being a copy of it.

DASSAULT *Super Mystère B2* — **Starlux**

In the sixties, a French kit producer released a few aircraft models, all of them presented with the same box-art and packaged without any lettering in identical cardboard boxes. The box photographed contains a **Dassault** *SM-B2.*

DOUGLAS *R4D-5 Skytrain* — **Esci**

Says Jean-Luc **Fouquet**, the modelling editor of the *Fanatique de l'Aviation* about this box-art:

"As the plane was taking off the two rear cables that held the left ski of *R4D-5* No. 17 239 gave way and the ski tilted downwards. A photographer took a snapshot of the incident that was later published in *Profile* No. 249. The **Esci** commissioned artist used the photograph for his painting of "Que Sera Sera" No. 12 418 but made a mistake: "Que Sera Sera" never suffered that mishap.

DE HAVILLAND *Mosquito Mk6* — **Airfix**

Everybody knows that **Airfix** aeroplane kits can be found under such trade marks as **MPC** or **Craft Masters**, but who could have guessed that some **Airfix** models (e.g. their 1/147 scale Concorde made by **Plastique Cle**) are of French origin? This **De Havilland** *Mosquito* is also moulded in **France**.

▲
DOUGLAS *A-4 Skyhawk* **(Esci)**
Gérard Cabot.

DOUGLAS *C-47 Dakota*

DOUGLAS *C-47 Dakota* —
Jean-Frédéric **Boullier**

On December 17th, 1935, exactly 32 years after the famous flight of the **Wright** brothers, the *Dakota* took off for the first time. The "Dak" is one of the most renowned aircraft in aviation history. According to the remarkable reference book *McDonnell Douglas Aircraft since 1920* written by René **Francillon**, 10,654 *DC-3* were built between 1935 and 1947. This French Navy *C-47* wears the same livery as those displayed on the cover of the book entitled *Le Dakota* by Jacques **Borge** and Nicolas **Viasnoff**. Aluminium plating technique was the same as of the *Constellation* and the *Boeing 737* built by the same author. The "dayglo" paint airbrushed on the model came from a real aircraft maintenance shop.

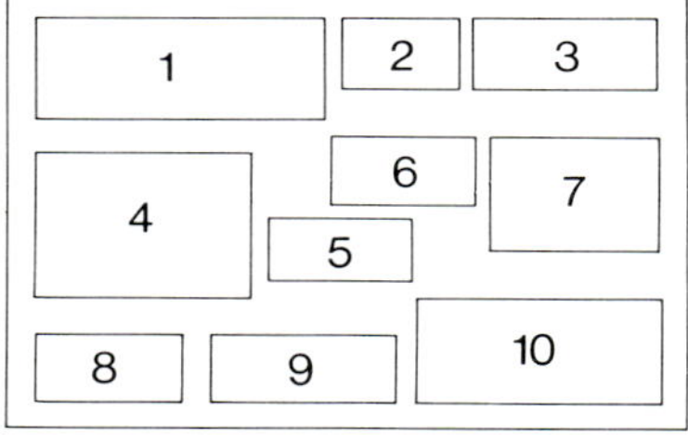

1* DOUGLAS *DC-9* **(Aurora)**
2 CURTISS *P-40E* **(Polistil)**
3 DE HAVILLAND *DH-110* **(Frog)**
4 DORNIER *Do.24* **(Italaeri)**
5 DE HAVILLAND *Sea Venom* **(Frog)**
6 DE HAVILLAND *CANADA Beaver* **(Airfix)**
7* DASSAULT *Mystère IV* **(New-Maquettes)**
8 DE HAVILLAND *Heron* **(Airfix)**
9 DORNIER *DO.335* **(Lindberg)**
10 DASSAULT *Mirage IVA* **(Heller)**

DOUGLAS *DC-9* — **Aurora**

Aurora's *DC-9* must surely rank among one of the much sought-after kits of that company, in spite of the crude moulding. Many modellers who have become used to the excellent Italian and Japanese models, wrongly blame kits that include few parts and details. In fact, a good kit is above all one whose dimensions are proportional in every point to the real plane. This basic requirement fulfilled, the model can be made of any rigid material and will serve as a working-base for the modeller who may be able to correct the possible errors, improve the trailing edges, mould new transparencies, scratchbuild landing gears, scribe in panels and, more generally, add surface details . . .
Connoisseurs do appreciate the quality of modern kits obtained from electrically-milled moulds, but they also show interest in such models as the *DC-9* they hope to find again one day. Airliner buffs have always been highly enthusiastic and attached to the *DC-9*, and often buy several models for possible conversion, as so many different versions and liveries of that aircraft exist.

DASSAULT *Mystère IV* — **New-Maquettes**

The first modelling materials were wood and metal. Then came cardboard, hard rubber, bakelite and finally polystyrene. The latter material was originally cheap and was easy to manufacture. It was therefore widely adopted and has made it possible for models to appear in every home. Nowadays however, the rising costs of tooling, the oil crisis and the lack of originality shown by manufacturers throughout the world, have raised questions about the future of polystyrene.

Those are the main reasons why Aficionados "blow" their own kits from ABS plastic card or use polyester resins, rigid polyurethane foam or epoxy-coated glass fibres. New methods for cutting costs and speeding up production are now being tested. Tomorrow's models will probably look the same as present ones but they will not be made from the same materials and will certainly cause no end of surprise to modellers.
French forerunners such as **New-Maquettes** offered the very first decals with their metal and wooden parts, some of which had been made with a lathe. Oddly enough, the canopy was represented by a mere metal wire, when older French models already offered rhodoïd canopies. All this sounds terribly obsolete but, in those days, when everything was so crude, these kits were quite popular.

DOUGLAS *F3D Skyknight* — Bernard **Macaire's** collection

The recognition models (or identification models) are officially provided by governments to military schools in charge of courses on aircraft identification. As an example, the first recognition models of the **US Navy** were produced by the workshops of the Bureau of Aeronautics, Special Devices Division. These models are well-suited to their function as they are correct in shape but lack details. These details are usually unknown on enemy aircraft, and anyway are useless for their training purpose. The designers of recognition models often work from pictures of aircraft in flight, and sometimes refer to the head of pilots for scaling the dimensions of the enemy planes. When manufactured, recognition models are identified by a serial number and sometimes an index containing updated information obtained on the type of aircraft. Any army of importance has its recognition models, but the largest range is deemed to be manufactured by the specialised concerns of the K.G.B. The model shown on the right was made by **Setco**.

ETRICH *Taube* — François **Portier**

Famous Professor **Etrich's** dove-like *Taube* is one of the first aircraft used for military purposes.
An Italian *Taube* dropped a few light bombs on a Turkish camp in 1911, causing little or no damage but raising very strong protests from the Turkish government.
It has to be said that the *Taube* was the most common German and Austrian aircraft before WWI.
In August 1914, a *Taube* dropped a few bombs on Paris and another aircraft of the same type helped the Germans to win a resounding victory against the Russians at Tannenberg.
When it became obsolete as a fighting machine, the *Taube* was used as a trainer until about 1916.
Indeed several manufacturers produced different types of that plane (e.g. **Rumpler, Jeannin, Gotha** and others), but **Airframe** chose to represent the original **Etrich** *Taube*. François **Portier** built this vacuformed kit and added a scratch-built engine and undercarriage assembly, as well as all the kingposts and numerous rigging wires. Pins and other metal parts were used to strengthen the structure, and **Krazy Glue** proved necessary to join those different materials together. The model was finished to represent a *Taube* of the Imperial German Military Aviation in 1914.

▲
ETRICH *Taube* **(Airframe)**
François Portier

DOUGLAS F3D Skyknight ▶

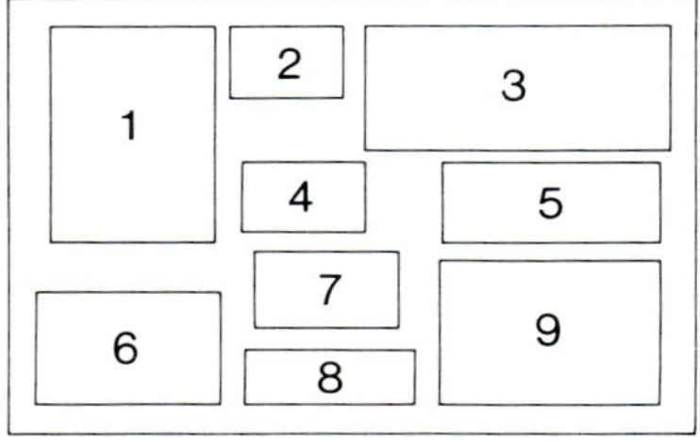

1*	DOUGLAS *A2D-1 Skyshark*	**(Rareplane)**
2	FIAT AERITALIA *G.91Y*	**(Matchbox)**
3	FAIRCHILD *C-119G Flying Boxcar*	**(Aurora)**
4*	FAIREY *FD.2 Delta*	**(Novo)**
5	DE HAVILLAND *DH.89*	**(Heller)**
6*	DOUGLAS *A-1H Skyraider*	**(Fujimi)**
7	FIAT *C.R.32*	**(Supermodel)**
8*	FIAT *G.91R1*	**(Airmec)**
9	DOUGLAS *C-47 Skytrain*	**(Italaeri)**

DOUGLAS *XA2D-1 Skyshark* — **Rareplanes**

Most frequent criticisms against vacuforms concern the delicate and tedious cutting of components from the moulded sheets and often their difficult assembly as well as the lack of accuracy of small parts such as landing gears. This latter drawback has been overcome by a few manufacturers by adding a tree of injection-moulded parts, as it can be seen from **Rareplane's** *Skyshark.*

FAIREY *FD.2 Delta* — **Frog**

The **Fairey** *Delta 2* was the first jet with a drooping nose. It is best known for the part it played in the development of *Concorde* and for the fact that it broke the world absolute speed record in March 1956 at 1132 mph thus exceeding the former record by 38%. No other aircraft since has been able to improve the record of its predecessor by such an extent.

This **Fairey** *Delta,* made in **USSR** by **Novo** from a former **Frog** mould, is quite a bargain and can introduce a modeller to the techniques of metallic finishes such as:
— the application of silver paint in aerosol spray-can similar to **Testor** (silver paint brushing should be avoided, except in the case of very small parts),
— the spraying of an extra fine metal finish (e.g. **Liqu'a Plate**),
— the use of metal foil panels stuck on with **Microscale's** "Micro Metal Foil Adhesive" (as a rule, self-adhesive foils may unstick themselves and so, are not recommended),
— the application of a metallised paste (e.g. **Rub'n Buff**),
— the polishing of light painted bases with an **ABT** metal powder called "Argental",
— or finally, the application of silver

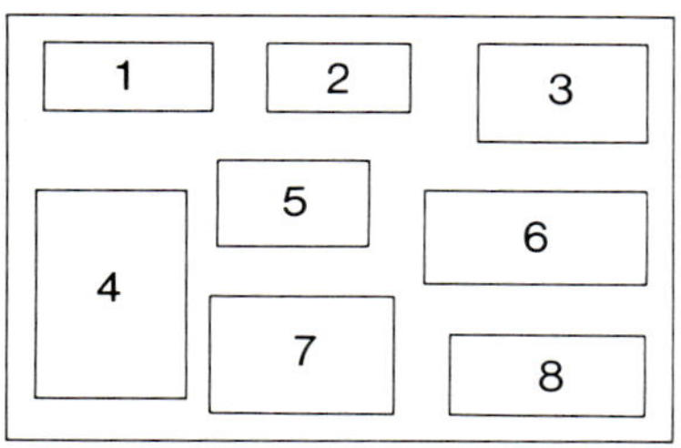

1	DE HAVILLAND *DH.110*	**(Frog)**
2	DOUGLAS *F4D-1 Skyray*	**(Hawk)**
3*	DOUGLAS *A-4E Skyhawk*	**(Esci)**
4	DOUGLAS *XB-42 Mixmaster*	**(Boleslav)**
5	DEWOITINE *D.520*	**(Heller)**
6	DOUGLAS *A-26 Invader*	**(Airfix)**
7	DORNIER *Do.217 K1*	**(Italaeri)**
8	DORNIER *Do.335 A*	**(Revell)**

coloured or metallised panels.
Each one of these techniques has its advantages and disadvantages but the final choice rests on the way a modeller sees the various shades of metal on the actual aircraft, which are very difficult to guess from the study of mere photographs.

DOUGLAS *A-1H Skyraider* — **Fujimi**

This is a very attractive box art but the kit inside is not to 1/72 scale although it is mentioned by the manufacturer.

FIAT *G.91R* — **Coma-Aermec**

In spite of its old moulding, this **Coma-Aermec Fiat** *G.91* is the only model which makes the reproduction of the *G.91R* as flown by the "Frecce Tricolori" aerobatic team possible.

DOUGLAS *A-4E Skyhawk* — **Esci**

This *A-4* from **Esci** is surely among the best 1/72 scale model available of this aircraft.

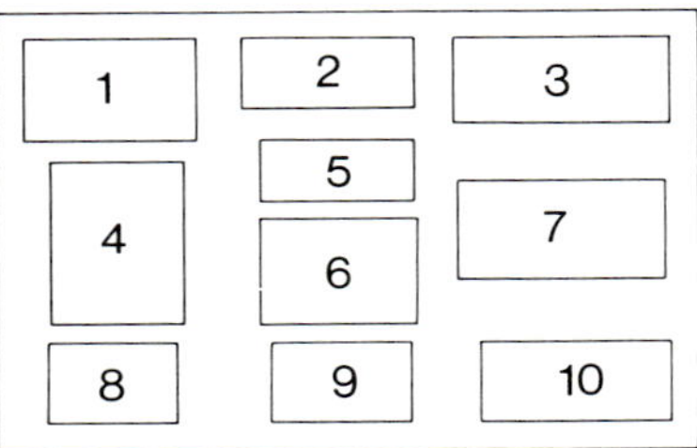

1*	FOKKER *Dr. l*	**(Gunze Sangyo)**
2	ENGLISH ELECTRIC *P. 1A*	**(Triang)**
3	DOUGLAS *A-IE Skyraider*	**(Monogram)**
4	FAIREY *Fox VII*	**(Rudel)**
5	DORNIER *217E-2*	**(Airfix)**
6	FAIREY *Barracuda II*	**(Frog)**
7	FAIREY *Gannet AS-4*	**(UPC)**
8	FOKKER *D. VII*	**(Renwal)**
9	FOCKE WULF *190D9*	**(Italaeri)**
10	FAIREY *Rotodyne*	**(Airfix)**

FOKKER *D. VIII* — Didier **Palix**

Vagn **Espensen**, a London-based photographer, got jaded with his job. He left the capital and settled at Wiveliscombe, a pleasant village near Taunton, Somerset, along with his wife Pam and his daughter Samantha. He then started producing **Veeday Models**, short-run injection-moulded aircraft kits. Production was limited to 500 or 1000 of each type.

This **Fokker** *D. VIII* produced in 1979 was Vagn's third kit, and remains a worthwhile collector's item.

FOKKER *Dr. I* — **Gunze Sangyo**

Japan, the country from which the best plastic models originate, was the unlikely birthplace of metal kits in 1981. The return to an obsolete technique hardly seems justified and the stamped duraluminium parts of **Gunze Sangyo** models cannot match plastic for the faithful reproduction of the third dimension. The only possible advantage of metal is its brightness, so **Gunze's** birds, once assembled, can be left unpainted, rather like kitsch trinkets parodying flying machines, and may be used for decorative purposes.

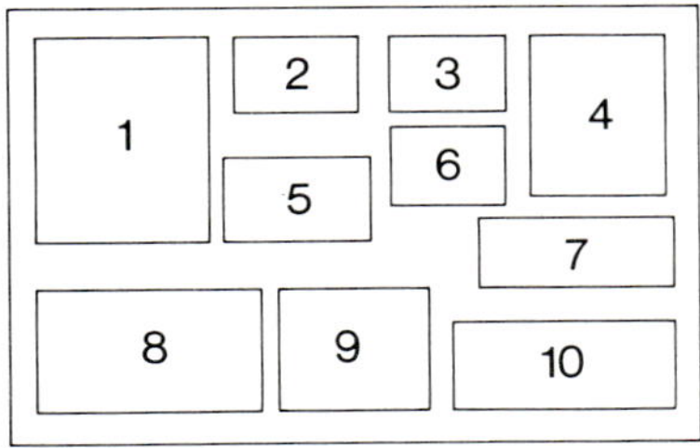

1*	FISHER *P-75A Eagle*	**(Rareplanes)**
2	FUJI *FA-200 Aero Subaru*	**(Eidai)**
3	FOCKE WULF *Ta.152H*	**(Revell)**
4	FOKKER *CV-E*	**(Trucker's Mate)**
5	FOCKE WULF *190A8 / F3*	**(Heller)**
6	FIAT *G-91R1*	**(Airfix)**
7	FUJI *T-1A*	**(Hasegawa)**
8	FOCKE-WULF *FW.200*	**(Revell)**
9	FAIREY *Firefly Mk.1*	**(Frog)**
10	FOKKER *F.27 Friendship*	**(Airfix)**

FISHER *P-75 Eagle* — **Rareplanes**

Once upon a time there was a young English boy called Gordon **Stevens.** He liked to cut out small aeroplanes from cardboard sheets when he was at school and he used to sell them for sixpence during the breaks. When he was 15 — during the war — he cut out aeroplanes, but this time from sheets of balsa. He traded them for preserves, chocolate bars and cigarettes with American Officers from the Bomber Command based at Wycombe.
As he tells us in an interview published in *Scale Aircraft Modelling* — December 1978 issue — he found out in 1969, as he was looking at a chocolate box and its divider tray, that he could produce kits from vacuformed sheets of plastic. He gave up his job in advertising and devoted himself to his new business.

Now Gordon **Stevens** has been at the head of **Rareplanes** for 15 years and also of **Rarejets, Rarebits, Raretanks** and **Warbirds**. He does everything on his own, aided only by his immediate family for administrative tasks. He works about 15 hours a day.
Like almost every model of the **Rareplanes** line, this **Fisher** *P-75A Eagle* sets new standards of quality that many manufacturers would be at pain to emulate.
Thanks to his proficiency, his dynamism and his professional consciousness, Gordon **Stevens** will surely be remembered as the greatest vacu-artist of all time.

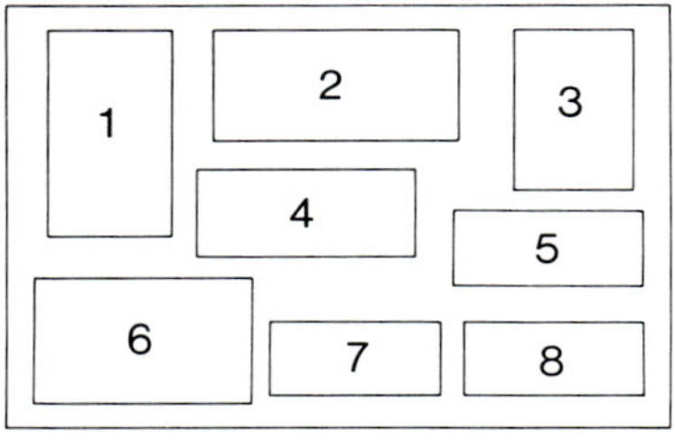

1 GRANVILLE *Gee Bee* **(Airframe)**
2 GRUMMAN *E-2A Hawkeye* **(Fujimi)**
3* GOTHA *Go.229V3 Horten* **(Boleslav)**
4 GRUMMAN *HU-16B* **(Monogram)**
5 GRUMMAN *F9F-8 Cougar* **(Hasegawa)**
6* GENERAL DYNAMICS *F-111* **(Revell)**
7 GRUMMAN *OV-IB Mohawk* **(Frog)**
8 GLOSTER *FAW.9 Javelin* **(Frog)**

GOTHA *Go.229V3 Horten* — **Boleslav**

A. Matejka from Mlada Boleslav produces exotic vacuforms in exciting colours such as red, blue or green. This flying wing is perhaps the best model of the **Gotha** *229* money can buy — though the expression "the best" is an exaggeration in a way, for there are no very precise references concerning this aircraft, so far as we know.

GENERAL DYNAMICS *F-111* — **Revell**

Revell is currently the only manufacturer to offer the short-nosed, long-span *F-111B* version of the Aardvark. It is possible to build the A version by combining parts from the **Revell** and **Airfix** kits, following the advice given by Jim **Rotramel** in Bert **Kinsey's** *F-111* in *detail* and *scale*.
Revell is unquestionably the biggest model manufacturer in the world, with five-hundred million kits sold over the years, a collection of 1000 moulds valued at over $50 million and an annual turnover estimated to be double that of **Monogram** or **Airfix**.
The founder of the company, Lewis G. **Glaser** had started off in 1951 with a series of car models, the first of which were the 1913 **Maxwell** and the **Ford T**. The success of the series encouraged **Revell** to develop new lines — aeroplanes, ships, missiles and spacecraft, military vehicles and guns, model soldiers, animals, cars and aero engines. They even tried tapestry craft (a technique that could dispense with needles) for ladies . . .
Lewis **Glaser** died in 1971 and his wife Royle G. **Lasky** took over the management of the group. She completely re-organised the firm. **Revell** offered an extensive range of models, but unfortunately, most of them were in

differing scales adapted, of all things, to the standard size of the boxes.
Royle G. **Lasky** then evinced the ideal of re-issuing old moulds with attractive new features, for example, electric motors or even electronic devices to produce light or sound effects. Some aeroplane models were thus modified to represent machines that starred in some TV serials such as *Baa Baa Black Sheep.* These would-be "new kits" proved quite successful, unlike such "gadgets" as the *Whip and Fly* series. The latter kits were supplied with putty ballast, a piece of string and a handle, for the owner of the models to fly them aerobatically around his head.
If it had not been for that basic error of adapting the scäle of the models to the size of the boxes, **Revell** would have probably been unassailable. The firm really had valuable assets, among which were an excellent and appropriate choice of subjects, good quality and good value for money. Moreover, the distribution network was outstanding.
Nowadays, **Revell** boasts no less than six factories and five branches abroad, namely in **West Germany, Great Britain, Canada, Australia, Hong-Kong,** the **United States, Japan, Mexico, Brasil, New Zealand** and **Spain. Revell** moulds have been produced in Venice and California since 1971 and they are conveyed to the various factories in accordance with their industrial capacity and the commercial strategy of the group.
An interesting anecdote will round off this account. Although **Revell** does remain one of the "Big Box" specialists with its 1/32 scale series and its 1/48 *B-1 Bomber,* the firm has also printed its tradename on the smallest aircraft models in the world. The boxes are about an inch long and contain two plastic parts to be assembled by the **Ken** and **Barbie** dolls!

GENERAL DYNAMICS *F-16* — Gérard **Cabot**

General Dynamics had been unfortunate in its early attempts at combining various state-of-the-art features on a single aircraft, for the outcome was often a complex, costly and unreliable aeroplane that was already obsolescent even before it was tuned up.
G.D. learned from past experience and introduced advanced technology in their *F-16,* but avoided excessive sophistication. Their choice turned out to be a winner. The *YF-16* which had been designed as a flying testbed has become an outstanding combat aircraft whose performance outstrips all those of its competitors or potential adversaries. The *F-16* was dubbed "Fighting Falcon" following its impact on the European market and has been continuously updated ever since. Various versions have already appeared of this highly successful fighter whose career is unlikely to end until the early 21st century.
This *F-16* model is marketed by **Hasegawa.** It is among the best on the market along with the **Italaeri, Esci** and **Fujimi** offerings.

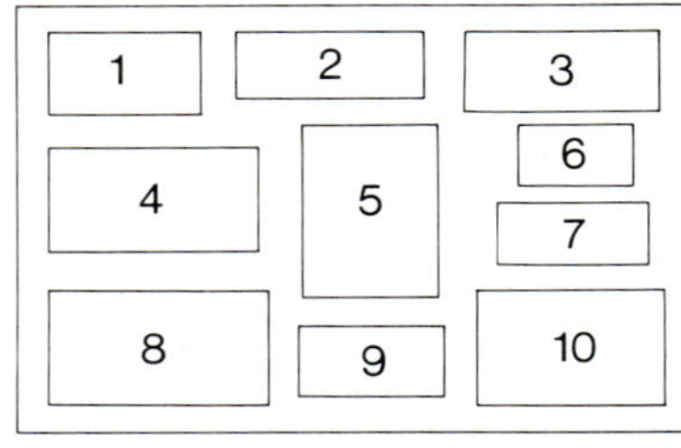

1 FOUGA *CM 170 Magister* **(Heller)**
2 GRUMMAN *F6F-5 Hellcat* **(Lindberg)**
3 GRUMMAN *F11F-1 Tiger* **(Hasegawa)**
4 GRUMMAN *E-2C Hawkeye* **(Fujimi)**
5 GRUMMAN *G.21 Goose* **(Arne Andersson)**
6* GLOSTER *G.40 Whittle* **(Frog)**
7* GRUMMAN *F8F-1B Bearcat* **(Frog)**
8 GRUMMAN *F-14A Tomcat* **(Hasegawa)**
9 GRUMMAN *TBF Avenger* **(Airfix)**
10 GENERAL DYNAMICS *F-16A/B* **(Italaeri)**

GLOSTER *G.40 (E.28/39)* — **Frog**

HEINKEL *He 178* August 24th, 1939 **Germany**
GLOSTER *G.40 Whittle E.28/39* May 15th, 1941 **UK**
BELL *XP-59 Airacomet* October 1st, 1942 **USA**
NAKAJIMA *J8N1 Kikka* August 7th, 1945 **Japan**
SUD-OUEST *S.O.6000 Triton* November 11th, 1946 **France**
SAAB-*21R* March 10th, 1947 **Sweden**
I.Ae. *27 Pulqúi* August 9th, 1947 **Argentina**

This is, to our knowledge, the chronological registration of the first flights of jet-propelled aircraft.
Designed by George **Carter's** team and fitted with a **Whittle** *W.1* engine, the **Gloster** *E.28/39* "Pioneer" was the first British jet to take off. This was done almost two years after the *He 178* flight.
Two aircraft were built of which only one survived: the first one, serial number *W4041/G* (the "G" suffix to the serial denoting that the prototype had to be guarded). This aircraft is still in perfect condition today and you can admire it, hanging from the roof of the **London Science Museum**, located in the heart of the City.
The second one, serial number *W4046/G*, crashed on July 30th, 1943 when its ailerons jammed.
Let us remark that the **Caproni-Campini** *N.1* which flew for the first time on August 27th, 1940 is not mentioned here. In fact, its engine cannot be considered as a turbojet.

GOTHA *Go 244 Bl* **(Italaeri)** ▲
Jacques Niot.

▼ GRUMMAN *F9F-2 Panther* **(Hasegawa)**
Gérard Cabot

GRUMMAN *F8F-1B Bearcat* — **Frog**

Frog's *Bearcat* is less crisp than **Monogram's**, but it is much sought-after in **France** for the decals of the *GC1/21* "Artois" a unit that fought in Indo-China in 1952.

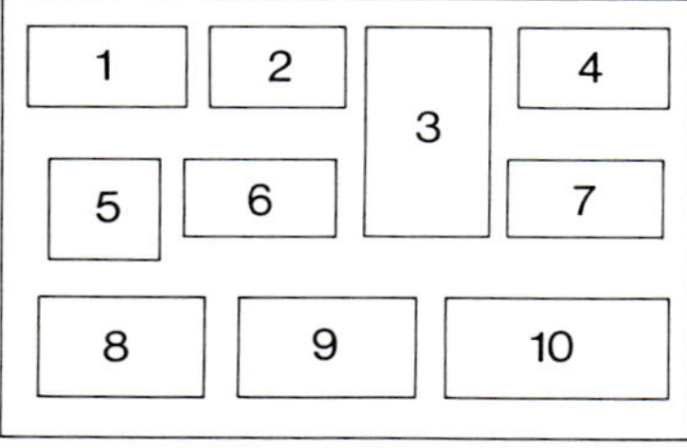

1 GRUMMAN *F7F-3 Tigercat* **(Monogram)**
2 KYUSHU *J7W1 Shinden* **(Tamiya)**
3* HEINKEL *He-178* **(Wings 72)**
4 JUNKERS *Ju 87B/R Stuka* **(Airfix)**
5* IKARUS *Ik.2* **(Guano)**
6 KAWANISHI *N1K2-J George* **(Hasegawa)**
7 HEINKEL *He.112B-0/1* **(Heller)**
8 HENSCHEL *Hs.126A-1/B-1* **(Italaeri)**
9 HANDLEY PAGE *Hampden* **(Airfix)**
10 HEINKEL *He.177A-5 Greif* **(Airfix)**

HEINKEL *He 178* — **Wings 72**

Wings 72 produces vacuforms with very good surface detailing. The models which have been released by this company are always off the beaten track, as Donald H. **Bratt**, the founder of **Wings,** is one of the most prominent model collectors and experts round the world. Don is also the Vice-President of **Stevens Inc.** (a film production and advertising agency), and all this enables him to reach markets commonly considered as unapproachable. The idea is to sell top-quality vacuforms depicting models specially designed to capture high-demanding markets. For instance, in order to consolidate quickly his position in **Japan, Wings** has had the masters of Japanese planes produced by Czechoslovakians. The Czech modellers' teams are already used to resin hand-moulding techniques and can produce models in a short time at attractive prices. Instead of using the regular commercial outlets of wholesalers or retailers, **Wings** markets its vacuforms mainly through non-profit making organisations. Of course, club members do appreciate the possibility of ordering models which are otherwise difficult to obtain through other channels, but only on the condition that these models can be bought at reasonable prices. On the other hand, people who are not affiliated to any such societies may be sorry not to find **Wings** products from their usual dealer. And last, let us remember that the **Heinkel** *178* was the world's first aircraft which took off powered solely by a turbojet.

IKARUS *IK-2* — **Guano**

When **Yugoslavia** entered the war in 1941, it could only muster a few warplanes among which there were eight locally built *IK-2s*. In spite of this, the **Ikarus** fighters put up a brave fight. Wesley F. **Moore** was so impressed by this episode of the war that he decided to make the *IK-2* better known by producing a replica in 1/72 scale. He gathered Greg **Reynolds**, Terry **Elmore**, Matt **Hargreaves**, Bill **Hawkins**, et al, all from **IPMS**-Seattle (Washington, USA) around the scheme and together they built the first *IK-2* in 1972. These models were made from resin and could only be produced at the rate of one a day, because the stuff took such a long time to harden.

Wesley decided to resort to injection techniques in 1976 and to this end, bought a **Quick Shooter** sold by *The Haygeman Machine Company* for $250. The **Quick Shooter** consisted of a 9 inch-long cylinder surrounded by a resistor whose temperature could be set by a rheostat. The end of the cylinder had a drilled 4 mm injection hole. The capacity of the machine was limited to 20 g of polystyrene. Wesley had his **Quick Shooter** fitted to the bench of his drilling-machine and used the lever of the mounting to drive the piston by hand. The mould was held into place by a vice and the injection runner was simply aligned with the end of the cylinder. Contrary to ordinary moulds which are bored out from special steel alloys, Wesley's moulds were cast in Furane 8067 around a copper alloy master (Furane 8067 is an epoxy resin compounded with aluminium powder and is able to withstand heavy pressures and high temperatures).

The first trials resulted in small, ill-smelling molten dungs, hence the name given by Wesley to his budding company — **Guano Aeroplane and Zeppelin Works.** Production was then increased to a rate of one model an hour, but snags still had to be ironed out, e.g. the cooling of the mould, which had to be improved if production was to be stepped up, and the mechanical resistance of the mounting-bench and the vice. Wesley also found it extremely difficult to obtain polystyrene pellets in small quantities and sometimes had to break up small plastic spoons of different colours in order to be able to feed his machine. One should not therefore be surprised to find strangely iridescent parts as one opens the **Ikarus** kit.

The first **Projekts Model** and **299 Models** kits were also built thanks to Wesley's machine. Since that time, and thanks to Ron **Downey's** help, Wesley has extensively modified his tools and his new machine can take up to 85 g of plastic. He will have several other machines and, so as to follow up his new productions, he has also obtained a decal printing press for an investment of $3000. Having started from his first idea — the **Ikarus** project — Wesley has been able to establish one of the first home-built injection workshops producing 1/72 scale models. His disciples and himself have brilliantly succeeded in transforming what was originally a hobby into a small business, whose efforts are widely appreciated.

JUNKERS *Ju. 86D-1* **(Italaeri)**
Jacques Niot.

HAWKER *Tempest II* — Bernard **Macaire** collection

HAWKER *Tempest II*

The *Tempest Mk II* was powered by an air-cooled 18-cylinder radial engine — a Centaurus V or VI — while the only version of the *Tempest* to be flown before the end of the hostilities, the *Mk V*, was equipped with a liquid-cooled Napier Sabre II which was a 24 cylinder H-type engine. The *Mk II* version had been designed for use against the Japanese but it was phased-in in November 1945, just too late.

This recognition model was produced by **Cruver**.

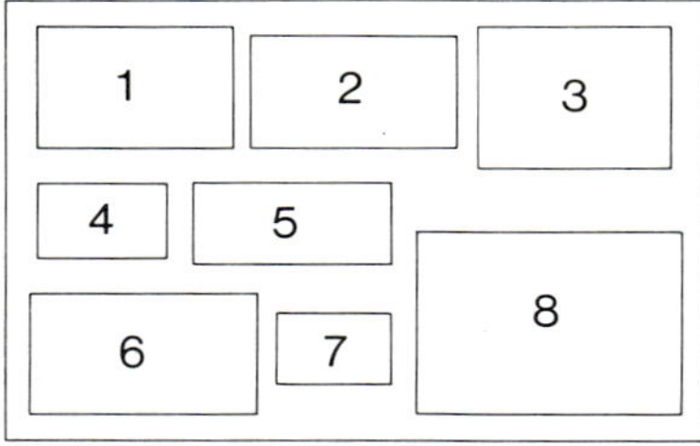

1* Mc DONNELL *AV-8B Harrier II* **(Italaeri)**
2 FOCKE-WULF *FW.189 A Uhu collection D. Palix* **(Aoshima)**
3 HAWKER-SIDDELEY *Harrier T.4* **(Heller Bobcat)**
4 GRUMMAN *F6F-5 Hellcat* **(Airflash)**
5 HAWKER-SIDDELEY *AV.8A* **(Fujimi)**
6 FAIRCHILD *A-10A* **(Hasegawa)**
7 GLOSTER *Gauntlet* **(Pegasus)**
8* HANDLEY PAGE *Victor K.2* **(Matchbox)**

HANDLEY-PAGE *Victor K.2* — **Matchbox**

The *Victor* was originally designed as a part of Britain's deterrent force and was to become a flying tanker in its *K.2* version. The crescent wing of the aircraft has a most unusual aspect which the box art fails to show as the *Victor* is not portrayed at its best angle. The moulded parts enables one to produce the *B.2* version although it has to be deplored that no thought was given to the *Blue Steel* missile and its cradle. In spite of these reservations, it has to be said that **Matchbox** gave a lot of satisfaction to modellers by offering this long-overdue model at the right time.

McDONNELL *AV-8B Harrier* — **Italaeri**

Most aircraft designers evinced interest in STOL (Short Take Off and Landing) and VTOL (Vertical Take Off and Landing) technology, particularly in the 50s and 60s (**Convair** engineer and test-pilot C. E. **Myers'** article in the No. 1, 1958, issue of *Interavia,* summarises all the research work of the period). Yet in spite of all the research effort, only the design developed in the **Hawker** *P-1127 Kestrel* project has survived. Thus its *Harrier* derivative is the only operational VTOL aircraft at present. It is used in **Great Britain** as well as in the **United States**, where the US Marine Corps has adopted the *AV-8B* version licensed-built by **McDonnell Douglas**.

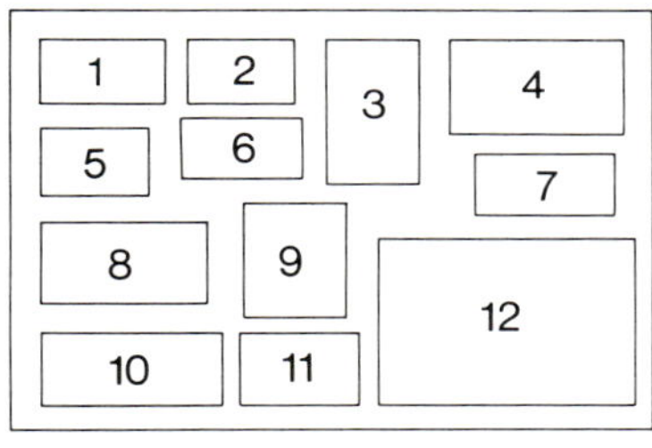

1	HAWKER *Sea Fury*	**(Air Lines)**
2	HEINKEL *He-100 D*	**(Lindberg)**
3	JUNKERS *D.I*	**(Warbirds)**
4	KAMAN *YSH-2E Lamps*	**(Fujimi)**
5*	HAWKER-SIDDELEY *Gnat T-1*	**(Matchbox)**
6	KAWANISHI *E15K2 Norm (Siun)*	**(Aoshima)**
7	HAWKER *Typhoon 1B*	**(Frog)**
8	ILYUSHIN *IL.28 Beagle*	**(Airfix)**
9	HAWKER-SIDDELEY *P.1127*	**(Airfix)**
10*	JUNKERS *Ju.88A-4*	*(voir p. 47)*
11	HAWKER *Hurricane IID*	**(Aoshima)**
12	KAWANISHI *H8K2 Emily*	**(Frog)**

HAWKER-SIDDELEY *Gnat T-1* — **Matchbox**

What happens when two kits of the same type of an aeroplane are on sale? How does the buyer make his choice? In fact, there is not a single category of purchaser but, at least two: those who are more attracted by the price and the box-art, and those who are more interested in the quality of the mouldings and what the box actually contains. Thanks to their policy of selling at lowest prices well-decorated boxes containing brightly-coloured kits, **Matchbox** captures the favour of the young modeller who is for instance more sensitive to the shades of his **Hawker-Siddeley** *Gnat T-1* than its crude moulding.
Conversely, by offering a better quality **Messerschmitt** *163B Komet* than their rival **Airfix** and adding a tractor and a cradle into the box, **Heller** has won the approval of all confirmed modellers, in spite of the higher price.
Congratulations for **Matchbox** and **Heller's** product managers who were both right. On the other hand, **Airfix** have proved unable to foresee the reactions of the market in the face of competition for these two particular planes. At last the design of a hobby kit depends on the targeted market: as the motivations of each category of purchaser are quite different, any compromise will inevitably lead to poor sales.

JUNKERS *Ju.88A-4*
Who produced this model whose box top bears no trademark or other indication?

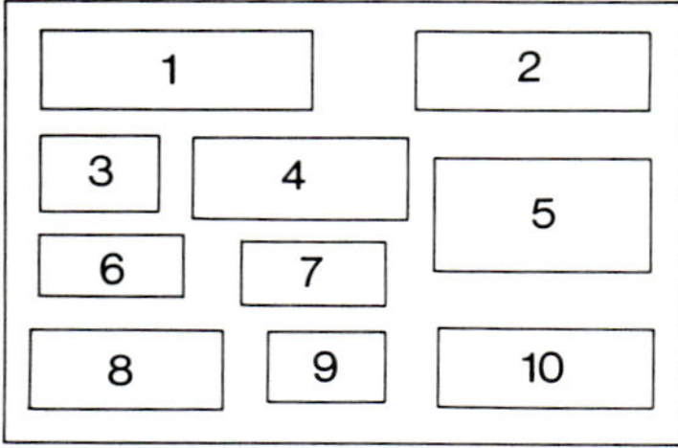

1	HANSA *320 Hansajet*	**(Airmodel)**
2	HANDLEY PAGE *Dart Herald*	**(Triang)**
3	HEINKEL *He 162A Salamander*	**(Revell)**
4*	HILLER *X-18*	**(Comet)**
5	GRUMMAN *S2F-1 Tracker*	**(Hasegawa)**
6	HAWKER-SIDDELEY *H.S.125*	**(Airfix)**
7	HANDLEY-PAGE *Jetstream*	**(Airfix)**
8	HAWKER *Hunter F6*	**(Central)**
9	GRUMMAN *F6F-3 Hellcat*	**(Matchbox)**
10	HEINKEL *He.219A Uhu*	**(Lindberg)**

HILLER *X-18* — **Comet**

Helicopters are unrivalled when it comes to vertical take-off and landing but their performances are strictly limited: reduced speed, high fuel consumption along with a low ceiling and payload. Conventional aircraft are of a simpler construction and offer much better performances but they lack manoeuvrability at low speed. In the fifties it was thought that a combination of the aeroplane and the helicopter basic concepts would allow better in-flight characteristics and performances. To achieve this, two types of research and experimental aircraft were built : compoundplanes and convertiplanes. Compoundplanes use rotary wings for take off and landing and one or several engines for propulsion in horizontal flight. A typical example is that of the **Fairey** Rotodyne, the **Airfix** model previously shown in this book.

Comet's Hiller *X-18,* displayed above, is a convertiplane: the engines supply the power both for lift and propulsion as the wings can be tilted. In theory, convertiplanes are far more efficient and promising than compoundplanes, but advanced technology and higher piloting skills are required, particularly for the transitional phases of flight.

The *X-18* was built as a test-bed. According to Jay **Miller,** the author of the very comprehensive book about the *X*-series of American aircraft prototypes, *The X-Planes,* it was made up of parts cannibalised from other aircraft in order to avoid undue expenses. The engines and propellers were those of the **Lockheed** *XFV-1* and the **Convair** *XFY-1,* the tail assembly and the nose came from a **Fairchild** *C-123,* the fuselage was that of the **Chase** *YC-122* and

many other parts came from existing types, among which was the **Convair** *R3Y-2 Tradewind* flying boat. The **Hiller** "patchwork aircraft" took off for the first time on November 24th, 1959 as a conventional aircraft and transitions between horizontal and vertical flight were tested until 1961. The programme was terminated before the entire series of VTOL flights could be tested.
It is more than 20 years since **Comet** was bold enough to offer this little-known aircraft. The unique kit is finely moulded and is eagerly sought-after nowadays. When **Comet** was written off, their moulds were bought up by **Aurora** who also went bankrupt in 1977. Former **Comet** productions then re-appeared under the **Monogram** and **Addar** tradenames, but the *X-18* moulds disappeared unaccountably.

GRUMMAN *F11F-1 Tiger* — Ousmane **Diagne**

This **Hasegawa** model was eagerly awaited by US Navy jet enthusiasts. The *Tiger* suffered from teething troubles, its armament proving particularly troublesome. During a flight test, the engine ingested a shell case fired by one of the four cannons which made up the armament of the aircraft. The pilot, Tom **Attridge**, crash-landed the aircraft and

JUNKERS *Ju. 52/3m* **(Italaeri)**
Jacques Niot.

managed to make his getaway before it caught fire. A splendid *F11F-1 Tiger* bearing the colours of the Blue Angels aerobatic team is exhibited in the **Pima Air Museum,** Arizona. The model shown here was awarded the **IPMS** 1st prize in the first French national championships, in 1982. The decals originate from **Microscale** sheet No. 255.

GRUMMAN *F11F-1 Tiger*

1	2	3
4	5	6
7	8	9

1*	HAWKER *Hart*	**(Skybirds)**
2	JUNKERS *Ju.52*	**(Airfix)**
3	GENERAL AIRCRAFT *Hotspur II*	**(Frog)**
4	HAWKER *Hunter*	**(Triang)**
5	HAWKER *Hurricane Mk.IIC*	**(Keil Kraft)**
6*	JUNKERS *Ju.88*	**(Air Lines)**
7	HEINKEL *He.111H-6*	**(Italaeri)**
8*	HUGHES *OH-6A Cayuse*	**(UDC)**
9	JUNKERS *Ju.86-D1*	**(Italaeri)**

HAWKER *Hart* — **Skybirds**

Among the men who played an important part in the history of modelling, James Hay **Stevens** deserves our particular attention as the creator of **Skybirds** models.
Skybirds are universally acknowledged as the first genuine models in the world. That is so because no one knows any older models sold in kit form and designed to a constant scale. At least 120 different 1/72 scale kits were available and the **Hawker** *Hart* shown here is the 20th of the line. It dates back to August 23rd, 1935. Inside the box wings and a fuselage made of finely carved wood can be found, along with vulcanised rubber tail and fin assembly, small parts made of moulded or stamped metal, a piece of sandpaper and a small bag containing brass wires and wheels moulded in lead. **Skybirds** were sold in paper envelopes during the war. The first model of theirs was a **Cierva** *C-24 Autogyro* and the last a *Mig 3* produced at the end of the war.
James Hay **Stevens** was not only the forerunner of all other kit manufacturers, he also founded the **"Skybirds League"** to associate enthusiasts. Four were enough to get assistance from the London-based **Skybirds League Headquarters** to create a **Skybirds** club. Club members would then receive badges, pamphlets giving advice and tips for better modelling and magazines with articles dealing with aviation subjects. Obviously **Skybirds** products were advertised as well as hangars and dioramas accessories, **Durofix** cement, paint or filler. All these activities have contributed to the creation of numerous clubs and enabled modellers to establish the **International**

JUNKERS *Ju. 188E-1*
Jacques Niot

Plastic Modellers Society in 1963. But contrary to the **Skybirds League**, the **IPMS** is ruled by its members, for its members, and owes nothing whatsoever to any manufacturer. This independence has no doubt encouraged its expansion and its perenniality.

JUNKERS *Ju.88A-4* — **Air Lines**

As was the case with the "unknown" kit — in fact from **AMT** — which has already been mentioned, this **Junkers** *Ju.88A-4* from **Air Lines** originates from a modified **Frog** mould. Manufacturers often market the same product — with or without modifications — under various tradenames and can confuse even experts.
The *Ju.88* model had been designed as a toy with moving parts and a retractable undercarriage. That aircraft was quite common during World War II when it was used as a light bomber, day and night fighter and reconnaissance aircraft. It was even used as a flying bomb at the end of the war. This version was known as *Mistel* and consisted of a combination of a *Ju.88A-4* and a **Messerschmitt** *Bf.109F*. The pilot of the *Bf.109F*, whose aircraft was fixed to the back of the *Ju.88*, controlled the compound machine which was thus propelled by three engines and could carry up to four tons of explosives.

HUGHES *500 Cayuse* — **UDC**

The **Hughes** *H-500D Cayuse* is a well-known type of helicopter that was built in many different versions and is to be found practically everywhere. However, anyone wishing to model this rotorcraft to 1/72 scale will have to resort to several kits of different origins as none of the kits on offer is quite accurate.
UDC, a **Hong-Kong** based company that specialises in metal toys certainly captured the broad outlines of the airframe successfully but paid no proper attention at all to the rotor. On the contrary, **Games** from **Italy** faithfully reproduced the rotor blades and the tail but their fuselage is inaccurate. Their *H-500D* is a snap-together kit wrongly advertised as a 1/144 scale model.
So long as no serious manufacturer offers a proper *Cayuse*, modellers will have to content themselves with combining vacuformed parts from **Italy** and **China**. Those who are really in a hurry to include that model in their collection and do not care too much for absolute faithfulness to 1/72 scale will be able to buy **Pilen's** *Cayuse* in **Spain**. The model is sold already assembled. It is rather crude but costs very little.

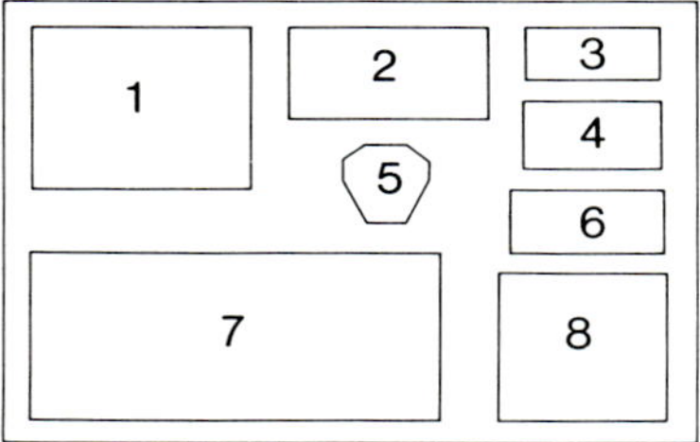

1 HANDLEY PAGE *Halifax* **(Matchbox)**
2 KAWASAKI *KI.48 Lily* **(Hasegawa)**
3* LOCKHEED *F-104 Starfighter* **(Compass Models)**
4 LETOV *S.328* **(Kovozavody)**
5* HANSA-BRANDENBURG *D.I* **(Edison)**
6 MARTIN *A-30 Baltimore* **(Frog)**
7* HAWKER-SIDDELEY *Nimrod* **(Formaplane)**
8 LOCKHEED *U-2A /B/C* **(Rareplanes)**

LOCKHEED *F-104 Starfighter* — **Compass Models**

Most desk models are sold ready assembled and painted. The opposite extreme can be found in the case of the **Compass Models Lockheed** *F-104 Starfighter* where all the parts have to be carved, for the box contains a piece of wood, a few sheets of balsa, a vacuformed canopy and a plan. The British manufacturer obviously did not burden himself with many difficulties.

HANSA-BRANDENBURG *D.I* **Edison**

Manufacturers sometimes try to boost their sales with small gifts and sales incentives. For example, the Spanish-based **Commando Jemsa** Company offers a chewing-gum with its *F-7U1 Cutlass* (a model derived from the original **Aurora** mould). **ATO** offers an ashtray as a stand for the model. Meanwhile **Edison** tries to win customers with two fine stamps, one in colour and the other in black and white. The idea is for modellers to keep the coloured stamp and return the other one to **Edison** to become members of the **Edison** Air Club. Club members not only receive a colour brochure on the models they bought, but are also allowed to take part in raffles every four months and win many prizes. **Edison's** plastic and die-cast models are sold assembled, painted and displayed in a transparent box. Decals are replaced by stickers. The **Hansa-Brandenburg** *D.I,* designed by **Heinkel**, was also produced by **Phönix** in **Austria.** This aircraft suffered from very weak lateral stability but in spite of this drawback, Austro-Hungarian Air Ace Julius **Arigi** scored 5 victories when he flew it over the northern Italian front, all during April and May, 1917.

HAWKER-SIDDELEY *Nimrod* — **Formaplane**

The *Nimrod* vacuforms were not among the best-sellers, but since the Falklands conflict, they have sold like hot cakes.

LEDUC *022* — Didier **Palix**

The **Fabulon Leduc** (release-1) is a resin model of high quality; nevertheless it requires significant work specially for the cockpit and for the internal part of the ramjet nozzle. The plane is very heavy, and a cavity should be carved in the nose area in order to locate some ballast. The resin can be filed easily, and sealing of joints is obtained with epoxy filling.

LEDUC *022*

1	2	3
4		8
5	6 / 7	

1	LTV *A-7A Corsair II*	**(Hasegawa)**
2*	LEDUC *022*	**(Fabulon)**
3	I.A.I. *Kfir-C2*	**(Hasegawa)**
4	HENSCHEL *Hs.129B-3/R2*	**(Lindberg)**
5	LOCKHEED *L-749 Constellation*	**(Heller)**
6	KAWASAKI *Ki.61 Tony (Hien)*	**(Revell)**
7	HAWKER-SIDDELEY *Sea Harrier*	**(Matchbox)**
8	MARTIN *404 Mainliner*	**(Airtec)**

LEDUC *022* — **Fabulon**

Resin models mainly evoke individual ventures, but they also challenge the lack of imagination of traditional manufacturers. This **Fabulon Leduc** *022* is the first model released as a file, which contains 29 accurately carved resin parts. Also included in the file (release-2) are a monography of 1/72 plans, a cutaway view of the aircraft, a stereophoto in colour of the cockpit and detail B & W and about 20 detail colour pictures as well as the copies of the original drawings of the **Leduc** at 1/5 scale. The design of this model required hundreds of working hours. A few "pirated" copies of **Fabulon Leduc** have been spotted in **Czechoslovakia**, in the **USA** and in **France**. The copies can be recognised from the genuine ones by their significantly poorer quality and accuracy and they have no documentation nor packaging.

The **Leduc** *022* appeared too early in a world which was not prepared to welcome it. It was designed at a time when prop-driven fighters were still in activity, but this interstellar-shaped prototype of an interceptor embodied a lot of advanced technical solutions: its wings were milled in a block of metal (first in the world); the air intake was encircled by boundary layer bleed holes; it was the first time titanium was used on an aircraft in **France**. The pilot was lying as on a lounge-chair in an all transparent escapable cockpit module; he could see ahead through a periscopic prism. The *022* took off with an **Atar** *101D-3* turbojet, then accelerated while climbing and cruising powered by the ramjet, designed — like the frame — by René **Leduc**.
Contrary to the turbojet, the ramjet does not include any moving parts. The air sucked in by the air-intake of the ramjet is compressed

only under the effect of the aircraft's speed; then it is brought to high temperature as the fuel burns in the combustion chamber; then it expands producing the necessary thrust. The faster the aircraft, the higher the pressure rate is and the stronger the ramjet thrust. The only limit for this type of aircraft seemed to be its fuel cells capacity and the heat barrier. But the fate of the **Leduc** *022* was to be different: it died from bureaucratic incompetence and shortsightedness. The **Fabulon Leduc** *022* resin models are produced in two short series. The second **Fabulon** releases include a cockpit moulded out of clear polyester resin — the aircraft has more parts and is made-up of a hollowed vacuum-moulded body in resin.

▲
LOCKHEED *Constellation* —
Jean-Frédéric **Boullier**

This *Constellation* was flown by **Conifair Aviation Inc.** of **Canada**, specialists in crop-spraying. Two of the type were still being used in 1984 along with three **Douglas** *DC-6* and four **Douglas** *DC-4*.
This model has been built from the **Heller** kit. All lovers of civilian propliners should buy Stephen **Piercy's** book, *Sky Truck*, which contains magnificent colour photographs, five of which depict **"Conifair** Connies".

▲
LOCKHEED *Constellation* — Jean-Frédéric **Boullier**

The *Constellation* shows that not all **Heller** products are of equal standards. To be fair, this model had been expected for such a long time that airliner buffs rushed to scrutinise every little bit. Their criticism can be summed up as follows:
— the model is a blend of the *L.049* and *L.749* versions, as is Francis **Bergese's** box art which represents *L.049 F-BAZB* and not *L.749 F-BAZT,*
— the number of portholes is not suitable for the *L.749* and their diameter is about 25% too large,*
— the engine nacelles should be shaped again with plastic card,
— finally, the decals for the fuselage stripes are not correct.
The shade of light blue is too pale and the stripe in the middle that runs across the portholes should be white instead of blue.
All that goes to show that photographs of the original aircraft are indispensable. That is true of every model but even more so in the case of **Heller's** *Constellation.* Among the reference material that should be obtained by all "Connie" lovers are:
— *The Lockheed Constellation* by Terry **Morgan**
— *Air Enthusiast* Volume 14
— *Lockheed C-121 Constellation* by Steve **Ginter**
— *L'Encyclopédie Illustrée de l'Aviation* No. 113

*For the purists, we checked the porthole's diameter on the *L.749* displayed in the Musée de l'Air at Le Bourget (this *L.749* flew as the **Air France** *F-BAZR,* then as the *F-ZVMV* of the French Flight Test Center). As a matter of fact, we found 365 mm corresponding to 5.1 mm, whereas 6.3 mm were measured on the **Heller** model.

LOCKHEED *C-60 Lodestar* — Bernard **Macaire's** collection

Recognition models were sometimes decorated with decals, but they never bore any inscriptions.
The "Grandpappy" lettering on the nose of this **CRUVER LOCKHEED** *Lodestar* is therefore apocryphal.

▲
LTV *Corsair II* — Gérard **Cabot**

This aggressive sting belongs to the bee of US Navy VA-113 Squadron. The *A-7E* version of this *Corsair II*, based on the aircraft carrier *USS Ranger* has been assembled from the **Hasegawa** model, with **Microscale** decals from sheet No. 82.

LOCKHEED *A-29 Hudson* — Bernard **Macaire's** collection

This **Lockheed** *Hudson* was made in **England** by **E.B.B.** as a recognition model for spotters. Wood and bakelite were used for its construction. The figure 52 written on the wing is the number of the military order for the model and 306 is its stocklist reference number.

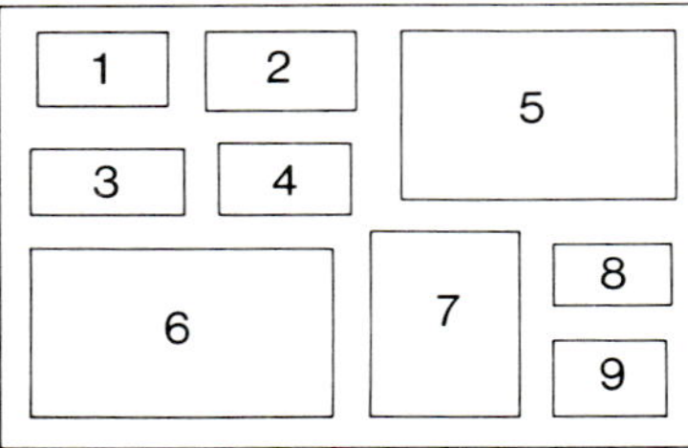

1 KAWASAKI *Ki. 100-II Goshikisen* **(Aoshima)**
2 MACCHI *C.202 Folgore* **(Supermodel)**
3 LOCKHEED *P-38 J/L Lightning* **(Frog)**
4 MITSUBISHI *A5M4 Claude* **(Nichimo)**
5 LOCKHEED *P-2V7 Neptune* **(Hasegawa)**
6 LOCKHEED *P-3A/B/C* **(Hasegawa)**
7 LOCKHEED *T2V-1 Seastar* **(Griffin)**
8 MILES *Magister* **(Frog)**
9* MESSERSCHMITT *Bf. 109G* **(Airfix)**

MESSERSCHMITT *Bf. 109G* — **Airfix Snap**

Packi-packi, clica-clac, snap-tite, snap-together, snap-fit, snap'n glue, . . . all those names from all over the world refer to the same thing, i.e., rather crude models designed for snap-together assembly. This **Airfix** *Bf. 109G* is an example of this mercantile trend to persuade young beginners to botch up sub-standard or shoddy articles, when it would be better to accustom them to fine workmanship gradually, thanks to helpful advice, clear assembly instructions and a good model, even though such learning process will induce difficulties at the beginning. It is obviously in the manufacturer's interest to make assembly easier so as not to put off beginners, but this should not be done at the expense of quality, the true "raison d'être" of a model. What is true of models is true of any hobby: one cannot improve one's standards by working with poor products. The only way is to learn with the best tools and techniques, by trial and error if necessary. The art of fine modelling lies in choosing the best available kit and using good methods of assembly and finishing, that have nothing in common with "snapping together".

LTV *Crusader* **(Hasegawa)** ▶
Gérard Cabot.

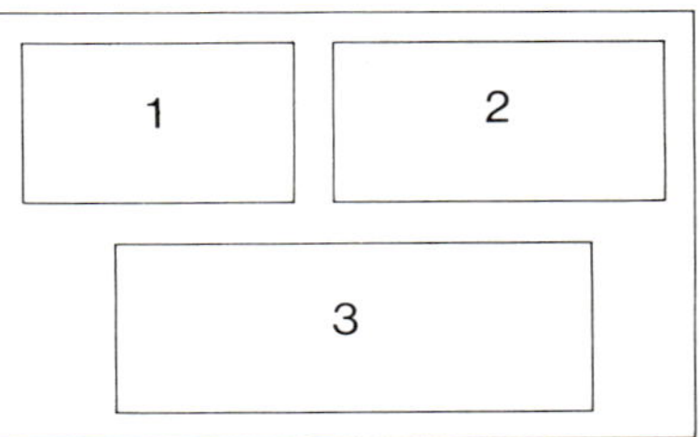

1 LOCKHEED *SR-71A Blackbird* **(Hasegawa)**
2 LOCKHEED *C-130E Hercules* **(Airfix)**
3* LOCKHEED *C-141A Starlifter* **(Nova)**

LOCKHEED *C-141 Starlifter* — **Nova**

Nova specialises in large-size vacuforms, but this *Starlifter* is not the largest of this make. The main parts of the landing gear are made of metal, while the beautiful decal sheet is from **Microscale**.

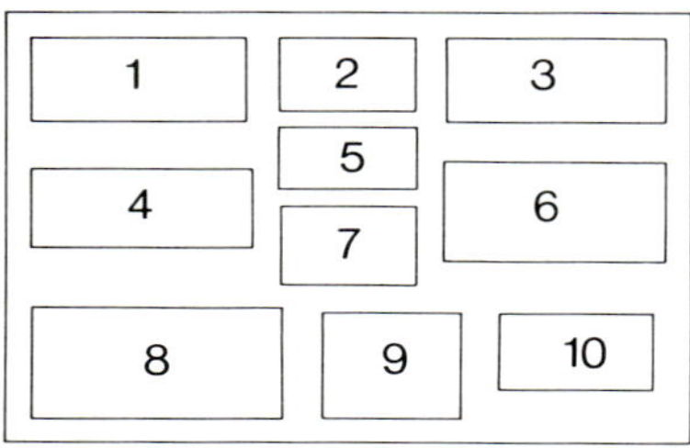

1	LOCKHEED *AH-56A Cheyenne* *collection P. Legrand*	**(Aurora)**
2	LAVOCHKIN *LA-5*	**(Italaeri)**
3	LIORE ET OLIVIER *Léo 451*	**(Heller)**
4*	MAX HOLSTE *Super-Broussard*	**(Heller)**
5	LOCKHEED *F-80 Shooting Star*	**(Airfix)**
6	Mc Donnell *F2H Banshee*	**(Airfix)**
7	MITSUBISHI *MU-2*	**(Otaki)**
8	LOCKHEED *YF-12 A*	**(AHM)**
9	LATECOERE *298*	**(Rudel)**
10	MITSUBISHI *A7M2 Sam (Reppu)*	**(Aoshima)**

HOLSTE *Super-Broussard* — **Heller**

This box top reads: "1/50 scale".
Did we make a mistake in presenting this Max **Holste** *Super-Broussard* on that picture? Not so, in fact this is an error of the manufacturer since this model is to 1/75 scale.
The 1/48 (or 1/50) buffs who rely on the scale mentioned on the box will be fairly disappointed when discovering the parts' size which is inconsistent with this assertion, at first sight . . .
However let us notice that the 1977 **Heller's** catalogue mentions the right scale.

McDONNELL *F3H-2 Demon* — Jean-Pierre **Balas**

The nose and the air intakes of this aircraft are particularly tormented in shape and have necessitated a complete modification of **Airmodel's** crude basis. Few reliable documents on the *Demon* are available, but an excellent article by Stephane **Nicolaou** with many colour and black and white photographs plus a three-view plan deserves notice. It was published in the January and February 1983 issues of *Air Fan* No. 51 and 52.

▶
Mc DONNELL F3H-2 *Demon*

▲ LOCKHEED *S-3A Viking* **(Hasegawa)** *Gérard Cabot*

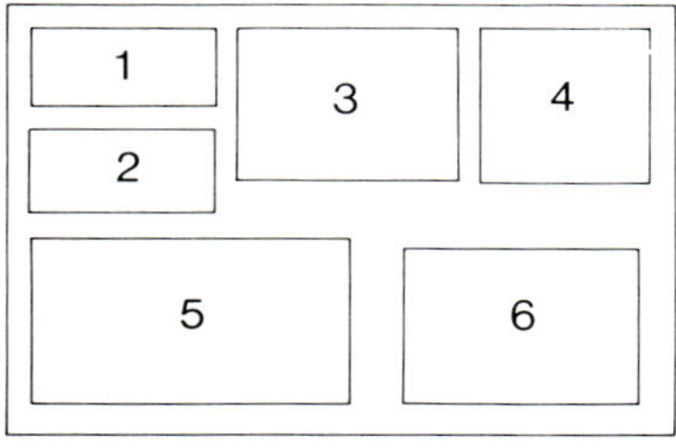

1	MITSUBISHI *MU-2S*	**(Hasegawa)**
2	LOCKHEED *P-38F/J/L Lightning*	**(Hasegawa)**
3*	NAMC *YS-11*	**(Bandai)**
4	NORD *262 Frégate*	**(Réducta)**
5	MARTIN *SP-5B*	**(Hasegawa)**
6	NORD *2501 Noratlas*	**(Heller)**

NAMC *YS-11* — **Imai**

This **Bandai** box of the *YS-11* also contains an aircraft tractor and splendid decals of top quality.

NORD *262 Frégate* — **Reducta**

Behind the railings of an old suburban house called "La Broussaille" (The Brushwood) at Vaucresson, west of Paris, a narrow alley leads to the former **Etablissements Lenoël,** now a dusty workshop. The rain that seeps in from the roof in some places makes large stains on the big crates piled up haphazardly on top of rusty machinery. A mouldy smell prevails but the place is fraught with magic as the very first French models were born there soon after the war. **Reducta** models produced by Henri **Lenoël** came out in numerous varieties. The models in kit form were sold in navy blue boxes. The aircraft (to 1/60 scale) was made up with about 15 wooden parts, all of which were carved and painted. The smaller parts were made of copper, aluminium, clear plastic and celluloïd. The roundels were made of coloured paper with glue on the back. A small bag full of putty and a three-view drawing were also supplied.
Other models, used for wind tunnel tests by **Breguet, Nord-Aviation, Bloch**, . . . were made of hard wood, often hornbeam. Like models dating back from the period that immediately preceded — or followed — the war, these models bear crossed stripes on their surface. This is due to the use of layers of different species of wood assembled cross-wise so as to prevent possible distortion and to facilitate repairs.
Finally, exhibition models should be

mentioned. They are sold fully assembled on their stand in brown wrapping cardboard. The scales vary between 1/10 and 1/250. Contrary to most exhibition models, **Reducta** models are quite accurate because they are built from original manufacturers' plans. Polystyrene, wood, ebonite, brass, aluminium and steel are used (aluminium is moulded in sand moulds). More than 200 different models have been produced by **Reducta** but only one is made of plastic and to 1/75 scale. This, the **Nord** *262 Frégate,* is particularly interesting as it is the only model of the aircraft available and is quite accurate and compatible with **Heller's** Max **Holste** *Super-Broussard.* Moreover, it is easy to convert the **Reducta** model into the *Mohawk 298,* an improved version of the **Nord** *262* used by several American airlines on domestic flights.

▲
NORD *262 Frégate* **(Réducta)**
Jean-Frédéric Boullier.

NORD *2501 Noratlas* **(Heller)**
Jean-Frédéric Boullier

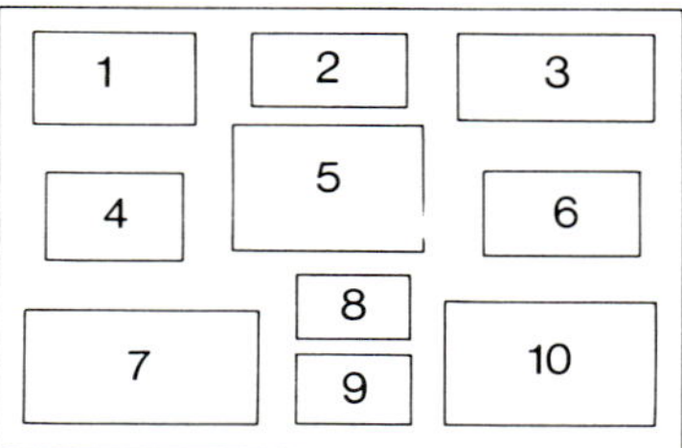

1 MACCHI *MC.205* **(Supermodel)**
2 MESSERSCHMITT *Me.163 Komet* **(Heller)**
3 MITSUBISHI *F-1* **(Hasegawa)**
4 MITSUBISHI *A6M3 Hamp* **(Tamiya)**
5 MC DONNELL *F3H-2 Demon* **(Intermodell)**
6 MESSERSCHMITT *Bf.109K-4* **(Heller)**
7* Mc DONNELL *F-15A/B Eagle* **(Airfix)**
8 MILES *Master III* **(Frog)**
9 MORANE-SAULNIER *N* **(Revell)**
10 PANAVIA *Tornado* **(Esci)**

McDONNELL *F-15 Eagle* — **Airfix**

Although **Airfix** has an unfortunate propensity to foist the "new" label on re-issued models, this **McDonnell Douglas** *F-15 Eagle* is really new. The great advantage of **Airfix** over their rivals is their efficient distribution and their ability to offer a wide range of reasonably good kits with a graded price range. This made it possible to distribute **Airfix** kits to all children of the world and many top modellers now acknowledge that they owe their proficiency to their first attempts with one of the *Series 1* models from that famous tradename.

NORTH AMERICAIN *FJ-2 Fury* **(Rareplane)**
Michel Martray. ▶

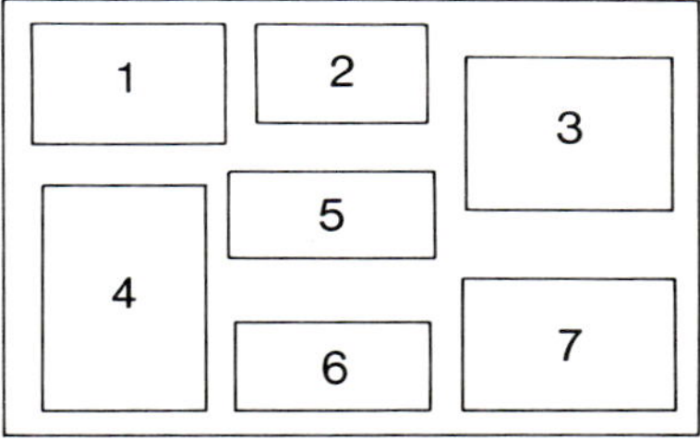

1	Mc DONNELL *F-4G/E/F*	**(Italaeri)**
2	MACCHI *MC.72 Castoldi*	**(Delta)**
3*	Mc DONNELL *XP-67 Bat*	**(Private venture)**
4	MARTIN *XB-51 Panther*	**(Execuform)**
5	MITSUBISHI *Ki.46-III Dinah*	**(L.S.)**
6	NORTH AMERICAN *B-25C Mitchell*	**(Frog)**
7	Mc DONNELL *F-18 Hornet*	**(Esci)**

McDONNELL *XP-67 Bat* — **Private Venture**

Silicon moulds make it possible for one person only to produce models in limited series (a few dozen kits) using basic tooling. Now small groups of enthusiasts can at last give vent to their talent and creativity. This model of the **McDonnell** *XP-67 Bat* has been produced by the Klub Plastikovych Modelaru of Prague in **Czechoslovakia**. About twenty people the world over have issued more than 150 different resin-moulded kits to 1/72 scale. They are mostly to be found in Eastern bloc countries, but the organisation of this production, from plan drawing to final product marketing, is rather relevant to the West — or even the Far-West. The pioneering make which appeared in **France** is **Fabulon.**

McDONNELL DOUGLAS *F-15 Eagle* — Gérard **Cabot**

The **McDonnell Douglas** *F-15 Eagle* is currently one of the world's best interceptors. It has been chosen for the air defence of the North American continent. On top of its many qualities, the *Eagle* is powered by engines able to provide it with a formidable acceleration. That would have enabled it to outclimb the famous *Saturn V* booster up to the altitude of 15,000 m if it had been available then (the *Saturn V* made it possible for Neil **Armstrong** and Buzz **Aldrin** to land on the moon in July 1969). However, the *F-15* is not merely an air superiority fighter. It also happens to be the first satellite-killing aircraft. In order to fulfil that mission, the *Eagle* receives during its flight, data provided by **United States Space Defense Operation Command** computers, that enable it to follow a flight path vector in synchronisation with the satellite trajectory. The on-board computer then gives the best interception profile to the pilot and when the *F-15* has reached an altitude of 70,000 feet, the computer warns the pilot to fire the **Vought** *Asat,* a two-stage compact missile carried under the belly of the aircraft. The *Asat* missile, which is guided by a gyro-laser system, then homes in on the satellite, tracks it down with opto-electronic sensors and manoeuvres with its 56 small rocket-engines to collide with its target. The speed at the moment of the impact is 12 m/s, which releases enough energy to blast the satellite. That method of interception, i.e., the *F-15* plus the *Asat* missile, even makes it possible to shoot down satellites during their climbing phase and is much more efficient and flexible a method than the former technique which consisted of launching a heavy booster from the ground. This former technique sometimes made it necessary to wait for 24 hours until the earth's rotation could place the intercepting missile on the course of the satellite. The booster was then fired which placed an intercepting craft on an orbit crossing that of the target. Several revolutions were necessary before it could home in on the hostile satellite. When it was within range, the intercepting craft exploded and riddled the satellite with shrapnel.

The *F-15* in the photograph comes from a **Hasegawa** kit. No *Eagle* is sold with the *Asat* missile yet.

1	Mc DONNELL *RF-101 C Voodoo*	**(Frog)**
2	MITSUBISHI *G4M2 Betty*	**(Lindberg)**
3	MESSERSCHMITT *Me.262 A/B1A*	**(Jo-Han)**
4	MITSUBISHI *Ki.109B*	**(L.S.)**
5*	MARTIN *P6M2 Seamaster*	**(Airmodel)**

MARTIN P6M2 Seamaster — **Airmodel**

Franz **Schädler**, the founder of **Airmodel**, unfortunately died in 1980. He left an abundant and original production, part of which is still sold by Richard **Frank (Frank-Modellbau)**. The questionable accuracy of **Airmodel** vacuformed kits has often come in for criticism and it has to be said that for **Airmodel**, quantity mattered more than quality. However, it should also be pointed out that the quality of these models was unequal because they were not the brainchild of a single progenitor. About 40 Czech models were used as "masters" for the production of **Airmodel** kits. This **Martin** *P6M2 Seamaster* is nevertheless an original creation and represents one of the best achievements of the make. That aeroplane was the only jet-powered flying boat bomber to have flown in the West.

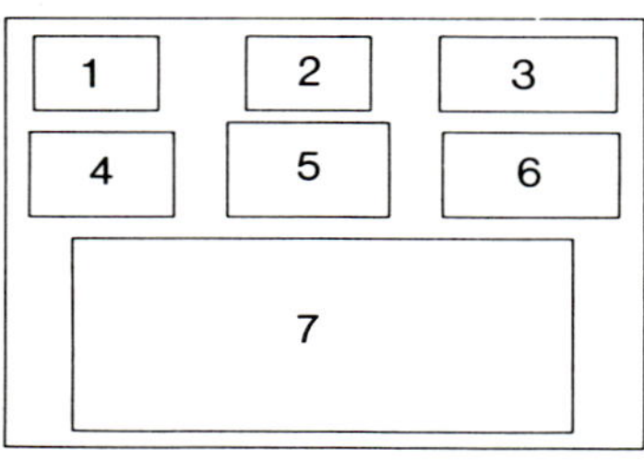

1 NAKAJIMA *C6N1 Myrt* **(Aoshima)**
2 NAKAJIMA *Ki.43-II Oscar* **(Fujimi)**
3 MITSUBISHI *A6M5 Zero* **(Jo-Han)**
4* MITSUBISHI *Ki.15 Kamikaze* **(Mania)**
5 KAWASAKI *Type 93* **(Gunze Sangyo)**
6 MARTIN *B-26B Marauder* **(Airfix)**
7 MYASISHCHEV *Mya.4 Bison* **(Contrail)**

MITSUBISHI *Ki-15 Kamikaze* — **Mania**

Mania models are unbelievably fine and all the minutest details are faithfully reproduced. This Japanese manufacturer pays particular attention to cockpit interiors and actually reproduces, for instance, oxygen bottles. It should be noted that **Mania** moulds are now at **Hasegawa's** plant.

MARTIN *404* — Jean-Frédéric **Boullier**

This short and medium haul airliner was almost exclusively produced for **Eastern** and **TWA** airlines which operated a total of about a hundred in all. A few **Martin** *404s* were still flying in 1984 although they were first introduced in the fifties. This photograph shows that it is not always necessary to resort to complicated techniques to represent the transparencies of civilian aircraft. The cockpit and cabin windows on this solid-resin **Airtec** model have just been painted on and the result seems quite satisfactory.

MIKOYAN-GUREVICH *MIG 21* — Serge P. **Lunazzi**

Serge P. **Lunazzi** who, as a French Army Reserve Captain, is in charge of recognition courses for Officers of the Reserve in the 3rd Military Region, has tried to portray all the known versions of the *MIG 21,* showing the different schemes actually adopted by the various countries that fly that aircraft as much as possible.
Will modellers-spotters be able to identify at a glance the version, the nationality and the make of the models shown here?

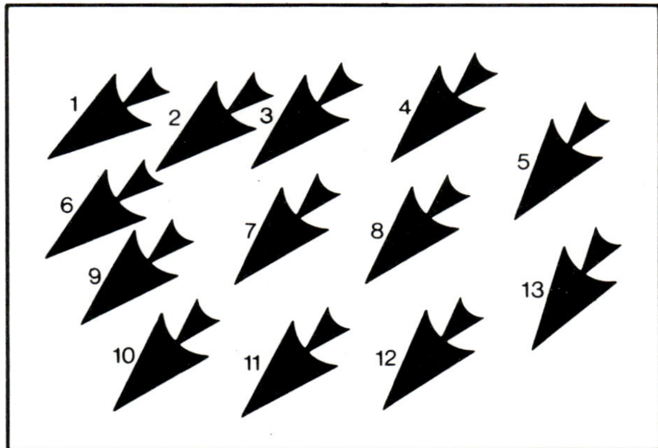

1 MIG 21 PF *Fishbed D*
Nord Vietnam
(*Fuselage* **Matchbox** + *Tail* **Airfix**)

2 MIG 21 F *Fishbed C*
Egypt
(**Airfix**)

3 MIG 21 PF *Fishbed E*
Syria
(**Matchbox**)

4 MIG 21 PFS *Fishbed E*
Egypt
(**Matchbox**)

5 MIG 21 F *Fishbed C*
Indonesia
(**Airfix**)

6 MIG 21 PFM *Fishbed F*
Egypt
(**Matchbox**)

7 MIG 21 PFM *Fishbed F*
USSR Aerobatic Team
(**Matchbox**)

8 MIG 21 FL *Fishbed E*
India
(**Matchbox**)

9 SHEN YANG F *7 Fishbed C*
China
(**Airfix**)

10 MIG 21 UM *Mongol B*
Egypt
(*Fuselage* **Airfix** + *Tail* **Matchbox** + *conversion* ***Airmodel***)

11 S-107 *Fishbed C*
Czechoslovakia
(**Airfix**)

12 MIG 21 PF *Fishbed D*
Egypt
(**Matchbox**) *modified*

13 MIG 21 PF (SPS) *Fishbed D*
(**Matchbox**) *modified*

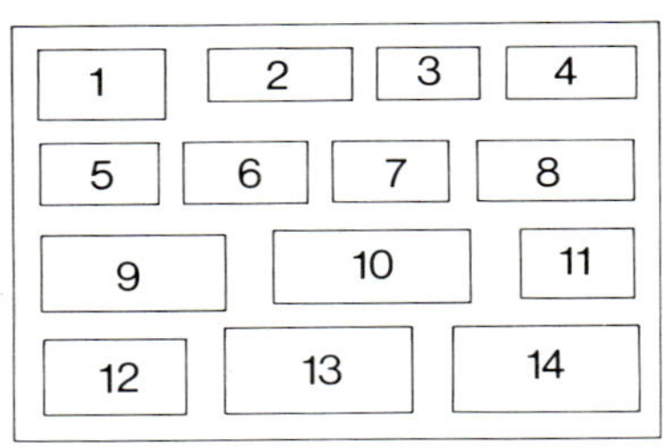

1	MIKOYAN *MIG3*	**(Cap Croix du Sud)**
2	MIKOYAN *MIG15 BIS Fagot*	**(Aermec)**
3	MIKOYAN *MIG15 BIS Fagot*	**(Novo Export)**
4	MIKOYAN *MIG15 BIS Fagot*	**(Kovozavody)**
5	MIKOYAN *MIG15 UTI Midget*	**(Kovozavody)**
6	MIKOYAN *MIG17 PF Fresco D*	**(Kovozavody)**
7	MIKOYAN *MIG19 SF Farmer C*	**(Kovozavody)**
8	MIKOYAN *MIG19 PM Farmer E*	**(LFI)**
9	MIKOYAN *MIG19 PM Farmer E*	**(Central)**
10	MIKOYAN *MIG21 PF Fishbed D*	**(IMC)**
11	MIKOYAN *MIG21 PF Fishbed D*	**(Matchbox)**
12	MIKOYAN *MIG23 Flogger B*	**(Airfix)**
13*	MIKOYAN *MIG25 Foxbat A*	**(Hasegawa)**
14	MIKOYAN *MIG27*	**(Hasegawa)**

MIKOYAN-GUREVICH *MiG 25* — **Hasegawa**

For the layman, Soviet aeroplanes mean *MIGs*. This is due to the fact that the aeroplanes designed by **Mikoyan** and **Gurevich** have often hit the headlines and proved their worth when pitted against the best fighters of the West, whenever there was a war on. Model manufacturers have naturally evinced interest in *MIGs* since 1953. Unfortunately little precise information about Eastern bloc aeroplanes was available, so the first *MIG* models were entirely inaccurate as they had been designed according to so-called "disclosures", in fact, fakes and photo-montages, released by the *Associated Press Agency* in 1951.

The *MIG-19* produced by **Aurora** (1/48), **Bachman** (1/200) and **Lindberg** (1/48) are patently absurd because they portray *the MIG 19* that only existed in the minds of journalists. Surely the most stunning of all is a great Soviet modelling company called **MCCNE**, the Moscow-based National Consortium for the production and distribution of metal and plastic toys. They faithfully copied the **Lindberg** mould of the faked *MIG 19* (however leaving out the American HVAR rocket armament) thus producing a faked *MIG 19* in the **USSR** itself. And the story does not end here, for that *MIG 19* is kitted in a box whose top represents a *MIG 15* . . . and not a *MIG 17* as some so-called specialists have claimed it to be.

Fortunately, 1/72 scale models of *MIGs* are somewhat more realistic and, in this field, the case of **Hasegawa** is indeed admirable. This company was still somewhat obscure as long as its main activity consisted of sub-contracting **Frog** moulds. But since 1970, the company has become distinguished in three fields, i.e., modern US aircraft (many of which had never been produced in kit form before), original Japanese aircraft and appealing types like the *MIG 25 Foxbat.*

The *MIG 25* was one of the best kept secret aeroplanes in the Soviet Union. It had chiefly been used for "reconnaissance" flights and had on various occasions shown a clean pair of heels to the best interceptors of the period (*Phantom* and *Mirage*) sent to intercept over **Israel** and **Europe.** On September 6th, 1976, Lieutenant Viktor **Belenko** defected to the West and landed his *Foxbat* at Hakodate, **Japan**, thus giving **Hasegawa** the opportunity for a resounding scoop. Before the officials of the base had had enough time to cover up the aircraft, **Hasegawa** had it already inspected by its 'informers' that took video films of all the details of the *MIG.* Five months later — quite a feat since it normally takes 18 months to produce a new model — millions of 1/72 scale models of this top secret aircraft were selling like hot cakes. **Hasegawa** is nowadays one of the most credible and promising manufacturers in the world. They boast high-grade moulding technicians, an admirable design department and a management with a flair for commercial opportunities and a policy of making long-lasting products. The only flaw is that **Hasegawa** models, however affordable they may be in **Japan**, are so expensive in **the West**.

MITSUBISHI *Ki 109* — Didier **Palix**

This photograph shows an example of spray painted camouflage colours. It is worth noting that the surface detailing is etched in spite of the age of this **L.S.** kit. Transparent parts such as one of the fuselage halves and the cowling panels are offered in the box so as to enable the modeller to show off the interior which is unfortunately too sparsely furnished.

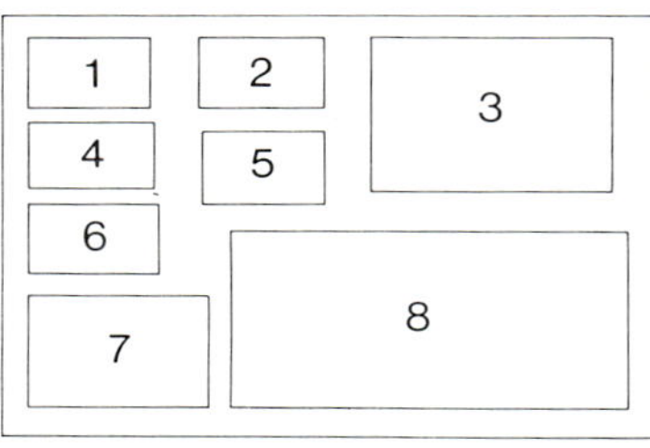

1 NAKAJIMA *Ki.44-II Tojo* **(Fujimi)**
2 NAKAJIMA *Ki.43-II Oscar* **(L.S.)**
3 NAKAJIMA *G8N1 Rita* **(Hasegawa)**
4 PIPER *Cherokee 180 C* **(Aurora)**
5* NIEUPORT *N.17* **(Plastiques Dermatt)**
6 MITSUBISHI *Ki.15-II Babs* **(L.S.)**
7 NORTHROP *F-5E Tiger II* **(Italaeri)**
8 NORTH AMERICAN *XB-70* **(Contrail)**

NIEUPORT *N.17* — **Plastiques Dermatt**

Sometimes models are sold as gifts or sales incentives with other products. The Italian publisher **Fratelli Fabri** thus offered **Revell** and **Airfix** remoulded kits along with their magazines — *Storia Dell Aviazione.* Another example could be found in the **USA** where **RCA** once gave **Park Plastics** models of the **Boeing** *707* to whoever bought a "His Master's Voice" TV set (oddly enough, the same model was sold in **France** in the sixties under the **Pegapan** label).
Many other models were given away to boost the sales of powdered chocolate, toothpaste, mopeds, Camembert cheese, petrol and detergent, etc . . . Perhaps the most comical example was that of "Father **Grap**".
On this **Nieuport** *17* kit Father **Grap's** partly toothless arch smile invites you to taste his wine. The caption overleaf reads:
"Start a collection of Father **Grap's** old crates — twelve models for you to assemble. Cut out the tab on each bottle of wine and paste it on the card. When your card has been completed your vintner will give you a kit of a trail-blazing old crate".
144 litres of wine had to be drunk if one wanted to have the entire collection of twelve models! Some amateurs took to swigging plonk, but the stuff was so diabolical that they soon had to give it up, so that few people have actually seen any of Father **Grap's** models. Yet there were some foolhardy *aficionados* who plucked up the courage to buy 144 litres — and sometimes even more — in their effort to obtain those twelve old crates. But however much they drank, the same six models always turned up.
In fact, **Grap** had ordered four moulds for

POTEZ *540* **(Heller)**
Jacques Niot.

four aeroplanes each, only four of which were to 1/72 scale. Only one of the four was apparently distributed by **Grap.** The three others (along with the one that was distributed by **Grap**) were finally sold under the **Joy** label.

Collectors generally say that a model is rare when it has been produced in a small series. That is often true but not always. Millions of models produced and offered as sales incentives can become unobtainable in a short time because their life expectancy is so short. Children play with them and a few hours later they end up in the dustbin. One can say that the rarity of a model depends on many factors such as its age, the number of kits produced, the type of distribution, the customers aimed at, the pricing, etc . . . Individual talents are necessary for the acquisition of a rare model, e.g., the knowledge of the channels of transactions or the ability to make light of linguistic or geographic barriers. When a model accumulates those difficulties (or when the collector's abilities are limited), the hope of finding it wanes proportionately. That is the reason why the image of an armchair collector is completely mistaken. In fact, a collector's life has a smell of adventure the homebirds will never know.

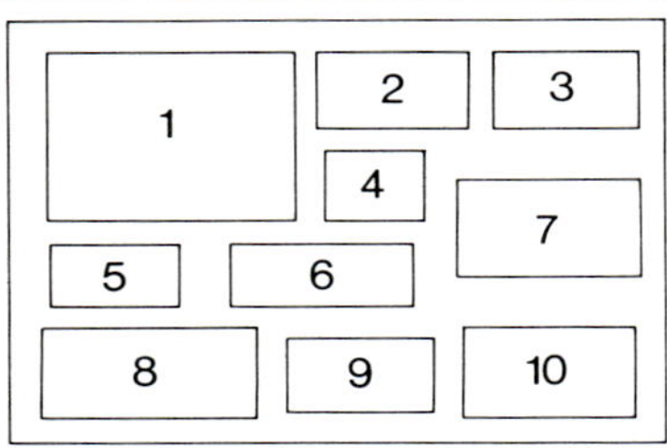

1 NORTH AMERICAN *F-108 A* **(K.R.)**
2* NORTH AMERICAN *X-15* **(Miyauchi)**
3 NORTH AMERICAN *T-28* **(Heller)**
4 NORTH AMERICAN *F-86 E* **(PMS)**
5 NORTH AMERICAN *F-86 D* **(Airfix)**
6 NORTH AMERICAN *P-51 B* **(Lindberg)**
7 NORTH AMERICAN *F-82* **(Monogram)**
8 NORTH AMERICAN *P-51 B* **(Monogram)**
9 NORTH AMERICAN *P-51 D* **(Hasegawa)**
10 NORTH AMERICAN *RA-5C* **(Airfix)**

NORTH AMERICAN *X-15* — **Miyauchi**

This kit is so rare and little known that most journalists who write for modelling magazines are unaware of its existence.
The **North American** *X-15* has been offered by several makers to different scales, but the **Miyauchi** kit is unquestionably the finest and most accurate portrayal of the aircraft. It is finer than the **Revell** *X-15* and better insofar as it is very close to 1/72 scale. Its compatibility with the **Monogram** *B-52* and the vacuformed cradle supplied by **Frank-Modellbau**, make it all the more interesting. Predictably though, the **Miyauchi** model is eagerly-sought after by the keenest collectors in the world.
The *X-15* was the outcome of a joint programme funded by **NASA**, the **US Air Force** and the **US Navy**. It was designed to explore the range of speeds in excess of Mach 5.

The *X-15* made use of many advanced techniques:
— The airframe was designed to withstand the high temperatures generated by the friction of air and embodied elements that were made from a new, highly resistant alloy called *Inconel X,* chiefly nickel and chromium.
— The main undercarriage consisted of two skids that retracted into the rear of the fuselage. They were lowered by gravity and aerodynamic effect.
— The flight controls comprised three sticks:

- a conventional one for low speed flight (for approach and landing). This later proved unnecessary and was removed,
- a mini-stick on the right console for high-acceleration phases of flight,
- a second mini-stick, placed on the left console, was designed to ensure

controllability when the aircraft was performing a ballistic flight in a rarefied atmosphere. This was achieved thanks to several jet controls.

— The nose boom equipped with angle of attack and side slip sensors was ultimately replaced by the so-called "hot nose", shaped like the tip of a ball-point pen. The sphere was pierced with holes for pressure measurement and was servoed to the airflow direction. It played the same role as traditional aerodynamic sensors, the latter being unusable during hypersonic flight.

— In spite of the reluctance of the **Air Force** that favoured an escape module concept, **North American** developed a rocket propelled ejection seat which could operate at speeds stretching from 90 kts to Mach 4.

— The engine of the *X-15*, the *XLR-99*, was the first to allow for a thrust adjustment from 40% to 100% of the maximum thrust. Re-starting of this engine was also possible in flight.

— The *X-15* generated many new technological developments that cannot be listed here but the reader will find further information on this aircraft in the following books and magazines:

● *L'Enthousiaste* No. 27 and 28 : a very thorough article by Jay **Miller** (translated in French by J. **Cuny)**

● *Air Enthusiast* No. 6 and *Flight* (23rd December 1978) : the history of the *X-15*.

● *X-15* : an account of Scott **Crossfield's** involvement with the *X-15* programme. Scott is a former **North American** test pilot.

● *The X-Planes* : Jay **Miller's** description of the *X-15* and its developed version, the *X-15A-2*, in chapters 20 and 21. A complete and chronological list of all the flights is also included. The same author's article in *Aerophile* Volume 1 No. 2 is also noteworthy.

North American built three *X-15s*.

No. 1 was the first to fly. On June 8th 1959, Scott **Crossfield** performed a gliding flight at Mach .79. Nine years later, on October 24th, 1968, No. 1 flew for the last time and was then exhibited in the National Air and Space Museum in Washington.

No. 2 was rebuilt after an accident and stretched by .74 m. It was then called *X-15A-2*. It was on this aircraft that the first, partially successful tests of a new ablative coating designed to protect the airframe from the heat, were performed. On October 3rd, 1967, the *A-2* broke all the speed records of the period, reaching the 6.72 Mach number (7270 km/h). It had been fitted with impressive jettisonable propellant tanks (supplied with the **Frank-Modellbau** kit). That proved to be the last flight of the *X-15A-2*. Once it was stripped of its half-burnt ablative coating, it was sent to the **US Air Force Museum** at Dayton, Ohio.

A few weeks after the last flight of the *A-2*, *X-15* No. 3 crashed when its airframe broke up as the aircraft was re-entering the atmosphere. Control had been lost. Major **Adams** was killed on that occasion, on November 15th, 1967. The report of the accident has been published in *Aviation Week* (August 12th and 26th, 1968).

The *X-15* programme, one of the most outstanding in the history of aeronautics, had lasted for over ten years.

NORTH AMERICAN *F-82* **(Monogram)**
Didier Palix.

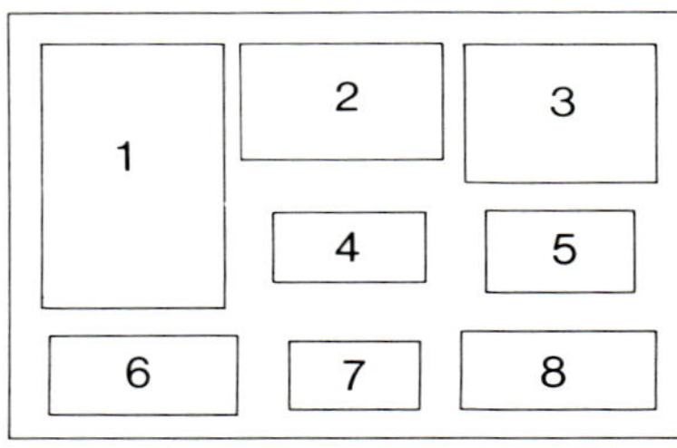

1 NORTH AMERICAN *B-45 C* **(Aeroform)**
2* NORTH AMERICAN *F-100 D* **(Esci)**
3 NORTH AMERICAN *T-39* **(Airtec)**
4 NORTH AMERICAN *T-6G* **(Heller)**
5 NORTH AMERICAN *F-86F* **(Heller)**
6 NORTH AMERICAN *OV-10A* **(Revell)**
7 NORTH AMERICAN *P-51B* **(Airfix)**
8 NORTH AMERICAN *F-100C* **(IMC)**

NORTH AMERICAN *F-100D Super Sabre* — **Esci**

Esci, a newcomer on the market place, are highly appreciated for their beautiful mouldings sold at very attractive prices. Their fine decals come from **Cartograf**. Collectors who are interested in the box shown on the picture are urged to get it, as the mention "with the French Air Force roundels" is no longer affixed.

NORTH AMERICAN *F-100 Super Sabre* — Didier **Palix**

Assembling the **Esci** *F-100* is a treat but the same can hardly be said for painting it. The main source of trouble is the weathering of the panels covering the afterburner section. The following painting technique was used on the *Super Sabre:*

— a first coat of aluminium finish was applied,
— then a second coat of gold paint,
— a third coat of thinned down ochre followed,
— seven dark brown streaks were painted,
— a shade of metallised blue was added to the last three streaks,
— a final coat of thinned yellow ochre was sprayed on at the end.

All these operations were performed with an airbrush.

Alfred E. **Harke** suggests, in *Scale Aircraft Modelling* Volume 4, No. 8, to use the "egg shell" technique:

— boil water in a pan and add three egg shells,
— let the water simmer and add the number of aluminium panels you need, then leave the whole to bubble away.

The greater the number of egg shells, the shorter the boiling time but, as a rule, three shells will give the aluminium shades similar to those on the rear of an *F-100*, after about 20 minutes. Then the foil should be applied down on the aircraft model's surface with Micro Metal Foil Adhesive from **Microscale**.

REPUBLIC *F-84* **(Airfix)**
Jean-Pierre Balas.

NORTH AMERICAN *F-100 Super Sabre*

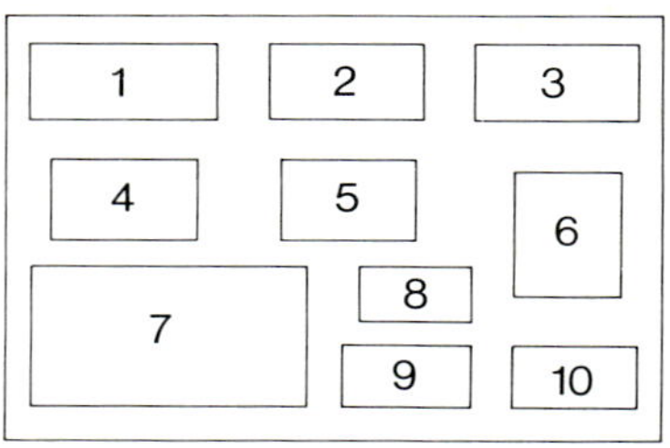

1 NORTHROP *P-61 Black Widow* **(Frog)**
2 NORTHROP *T-38 Talon* **(Hasegawa)**
3 NORTHROP *Gamma* **(Williams Brothers)**
4 NOORDUYN *UC-64A Norseman* **(Matchbox)**
5 NAKAJIMA *Ki-44 Tojo Shoki* **(Tamiya)**
6 NORTHROP *N-9M* **(Private Venture)**
7* NORTHROP *YB-49* **(Airmodel)**
8 PIPER *Aztec* **(Aurora)**
9 PZL *P-23 A Karas* **(Ruch)**
10 PFALZ *D.XII* **(Veeday)**

NORTHROP *YB-49* — **Airmodel**

Flying wings have always fascinated people. Already in 1914 the **Dunne,** a flying wing with a swept back biplane planform, caused wonder and astonishment wherever it appeared. Between 1930 and 1950 J. K. **Northrop** introduced new developments. The sleek, streamlined shape of his flying wings was so impressive and futuristic-looking that a film producer included shots of the *YB-49* in flight in his Science Fiction film *War of the Worlds*. The *YB-49* was the largest jet powered flying wing ever to have flown. Flying wings probably represent the most rational and advanced technique in the field of aeronautics as they offer the best compromise as far as structure and performances are concerned. Compared to its contemporaries of the same dimensions, the *YB-49* was the aircraft with the smallest turning radius; the highest speed, the longest range and the heaviest payload.
Unfortunately, flying wings proved to be highly unstable under certain conditions and this probably caused the accident that occurred to the second aircraft, killing Captain Glen **Edwards** and his crew on June 5th, 1948. The flying wing has been abandoned since, but the name of **Edwards** was given to the famous **Muroc** experimental base in California, USA.
The introduction of the "Control Configured Vehicle" concept (CCV) has given rise to new hopes for the flying wings. The small main cross section and aerodynamic cleanness of flying wings will prove to be valuable assets for designing new supersonic intruders that will be almost invisible to radars.

Will flying wings find their true place in the world of aeronautics 70 years after its inception?
If, in any case, you are interested in the *YB-49* there is no point in going around the museums for a chance to admire it, as all the aircraft of the type were scrapped in 1958 to the grief of museum curators.
The documentation describing those remarkable machines is very sparse but, however, let us mention the following:
— *The Flying Wings of Northrop* by Leo J. **Kohn**,
— *Northrop Flying Wings* by Edward T. **Maloney**,
— *Winged Wonders* by E. T. **Wooldridge**,
— *Air Classics* Volume 3, No. 5, May 1967,
— *Aeroplane Monthly* Volume 2, No. 2, February 1974,
— *Le Fanatique de l'Aviation* No. 29, 30 31 (January, February, March 1972).

SUD AVIATION *SE 117 Voltigeur* — Bernard **Macaire** collection

The *Voltigeur* came out on top in a competition that pitted it against the **Dassault** *D-450 Spirale* — the military version of the *D-415 Communauté* — towards the end of 1958. The second prototype broke up in flight during a high speed test in January 1959. The accident proved fatal to the crew and sounded the death-knell for the project shortly afterwards.
This **Reducta** model is built from very fine wooden parts. The transparencies are solid resin but look quite realistic.

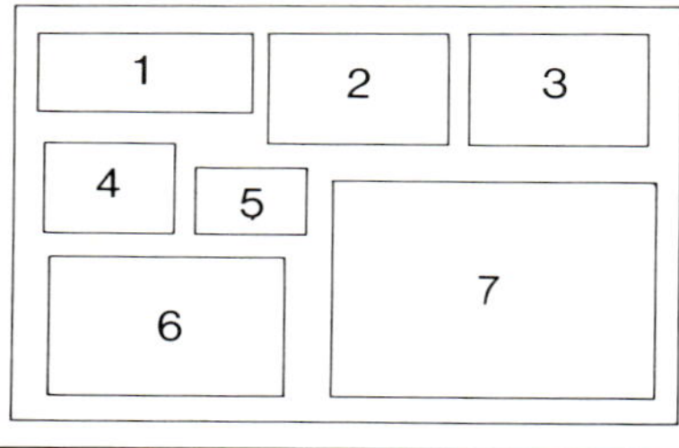

1	REPUBLIC *F-105A Thunderchief*	**(Heller / Revell)**
2	LOCKHEED *F-104G/S Starfighter*	**(Esci)**
3	PZL *P.37 Los* *collection F. Portier*	**(Mikro)**
4	MESSERSCHMITT *M35B*	**(Huma)**
5	SZD *IS-1 SEP BIS* *collection D. Palix*	**(PZD Siedlce)**
6	Mc DONNELL *F-4E/F Phantom II*	**(Esci)**
7*	ROCKWELL *B-1B*	**(Monogram)**

ROCKWELL *B-1B* — **Monogram**

A building without any windows, lost in a northern suburb of Chicago sports the name of **Monogram** on its blank façade, followed by . . . three dots. Three silos full of polystyrene grains stand nearby. The place is 8601, Waukegan Road, Morton Grove, Illinois, USA, and once you are inside, it becomes obvious that this is the home of one of the best manufacturers in the world. About 40 models are proudly displayed in the showroom, each one having been produced to more than one million copies, — e.g., the *Mustang (P-51 B* and *D)*, the *F4U Corsair*, the *P-40 Warhawk*, the *F-86 Sabre*, the *MIG 15*, . . .

Monogram came into being in 1945 with Bob **Reder**, producing the balsa flying models, then wooden kits to which plastic parts were gradually added for better details. Plastic definitely took over from March 1954 onwards for static models. The first plastic kit was the *PC-1 Midget Racer*, produced to be offered as a gift to purchasers of **Kellog's** breakfast cereals. Flying models also included more and more plastic parts until expanded polystyrene entirely took over from balsa in 1977.

Monogram owes it longevity to a choice of kits appearing on the market at the right time and also to higher standards of engineering and moulding than its American competitors. Moreover, the firm does not lack humour as some of their products show, — e.g., the **US Air "Farce"** *Flap Jack*, those mad *Funny Cars* and the *Shogun Warriors*, rather *Goldorak*-like, half-way between monstrous robots and spacecraft. Other examples include the *Head Lite*, a phosphorescent skull with flashing eyes and snapping jaws, and the *Missile Mobile*

(clouds and missiles to be fixed to the ceiling) . . . Since 1983 **Monogram** has become more serious, and they now concentrate on large 1/72 (and sometimes 1/48) scale, a field in which it has gained a good reputation.

SHORT *Empire* — Bernard **Macaire's** collection

This model of the **Short** *Empire* is extremely rare. It is one of a set of 1000 delivered ready assembled to **Imperial Airways Ltd.** by **Frog Penguin** in 1939. That airline used 33 flying boats of the type. The model was also available with a complete interior arrangement and a small battery powered lighting. One of the fuselage halves could be removed to display the passenger seats, the galleys and the carpeting as well as other equipment. **Frog Penguin** models were extremely accurate, thanks to careful design and the use of **Reed-Prentice** machine tools for the injection of ebonite, bakelite and acetate, and celluloid for transparencies. Those materials were not exempt from faults — the parts cracked too easily and the transparencies yellowed with time — however, they were a substantial improvement on wood. **Frog Penguin** models were pricy and cost the equivalent of ten of today's models. The **Short** *Empire* with the inside fitted out, cost the equivalent of three weeks' average pay, when it was ready assembled. That accounts for the fact that collectors who had to stint themselves to buy those models treasure them as they treasure their **Rolls**.

Frog Penguin also produced hangars, searchlights for AA defences, cannons, sound detectors, ambulances, wheeled or tracked vehicles, all to 1/72 scale. Flying models made from aluminium foil were available in a larger scale from 1930 onwards. They were the origin of the **Frog** tradename which stands for "**F**ly **R**ight **O**ff the **G**round".

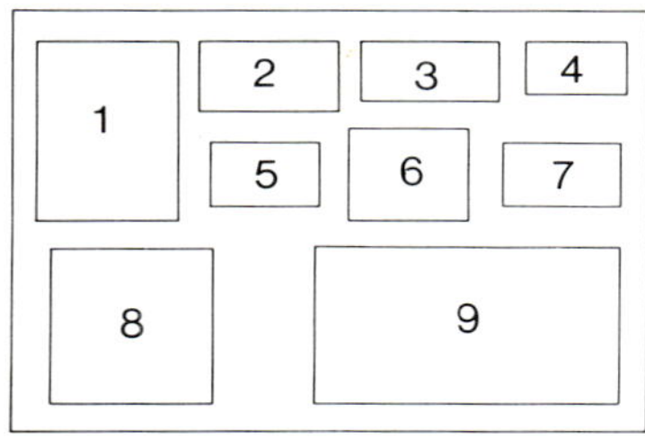

1	S.N.C.A.S.O. *6000/6001 Triton*	**(Rudel)**
2	REGGIANE *RE-2001 Falco I*	**(Supermodel)**
3*	SUPERMARINE *Swift F-4*	**(Hawk)**
4	SEVERSKY *P-35*	**(Veeday)**
5	SZD *41 Jantar Standard* *collection J.C. Hasquenoph*	**(PZW)**
6*	RYAN *M-1 Mailplane*	**(Greenbank Castle)**
7	RYAN *Spirit of St-Louis*	**(Novo)**
8	SIKORSKY *CH-54A Skycrane*	**(Aurora)**
9	SHINMEIWA *PS-1/SS-2*	**(Hasegawa)**

SUPERMARINE *Swift F.4* — **Hawk**

Hawk is one of the earliest kit manufacturers, since its origin goes back to 1928. At that time, the company produced recognition models for the US Government and these models were carved in plain wood. In 1959 **Hawk** released this *Swift* which has been the only injection moulding of this aircraft so far.

RYAN *M.1 Mailplane* — **Greenbank Castle**

This model of the well-known **Ryan** *M-1 Mailplane* can be built in two versions, either with a radial or with an in-line engine. Less than 3000 copies of it were produced in 1972 by a group of modellers from Coupeville, Washington, **USA**. Unfortunately odds were against the designers, since shortly after the model was marked by **Scalecraft Model Imports**, the **Greenbank Castle** vanished. To-day, this kit has become extremely rare and difficult to find.

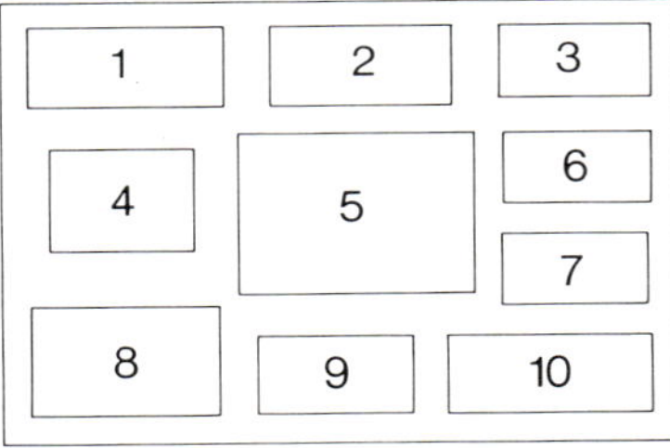

1 REPUBLIC *F-105D Thunderchief* **(Hasegawa)**
2 REPUBLIC *P-47 D Thunderbolt* **(Jo-Han)**
3 REPUBLIC *F-84G Thunderjet* **(Heller)**
4 REPUBLIC *XF-91 Thunderceptor* **(Private Venture)**
5* REPUBLIC *XF-103* **(K.R.)**
6 REPUBLIC *F.84F Thunderstreak* **(Airfix)**
7* REPUBLIC *F-84F Thunderstreak* **(Hawk)**
8 REPUBLIC *RF-84F Thunderflash* **(Italaeri)**
9 REPUBLIC *P-47D Thunderbolt* **(Hasegawa)**
10 REPUBLIC *F-105D Thunderchief* **(IMC)**

REPUBLIC *YF-96 Thunderstreak* — **Hawk**

Hawk's *F-84F* has been superseded by newer and better offerings, but has aroused new interest since the release of **Monogram's** *B-36*. This is due to the fact that the **Hawk** model does not really portray the *F-84F*, but its *YF-96* prototype. It is thus possible to represent the **Ficon** (Fighter-Conveyor) parasite fighter by cannibalising **Hawk's** *F-84F* with **K.R.'s** vacuformed *YF-96* and mate it with the **Monogram's** *B-36*.

REPUBLIC *XF-103* — **K.R.**

The *XF-103*, which the *Dayton Daily News* dubbed "the 100 Million Dollar Mystery Jet", is one of those extraordinary projects which never came to fruition owing to a shortage of funds. Yet this interceptor was optimised for speeds exceeding Mach 3 and featured new techniques such as a titanium structure and a mixed propulsion system combining a turbojet and a ramjet.
Maybe some day a 1/72 replica will be available of the French **Nord** *1500 Griffon II* which was powered by a similar powerplant system and which flew, thanks to André **Turcat**, at a speed close to Mach 2.2 in October 1959.

1*	SAAB *J.35*	**(Heller)**
2	SAUNDERS-ROE *S.R. 53*	**(Airfix)**
3	SAAB *J.21A*	**(Heller)**
4	SAAB *J.37 Viggen*	**(Heller)**
5	SAAB *J.29 Tunnan*	**(Heller)**
6	SAAB *91 Safir*	**(Heller)**
7	SAAB *J.32 Lansen*	**(Heller)**
8	SAAB *105*	**(Arne Andersson)**
9	SAVOIA MARCHETTI *S.M.81*	**(Supermodel)**

SAAB *J.35 Draken* — **Heller**

The **Republic** Corporation alone has inspired at least 25 kit manufacturers in many countries (a few makes of **Republic** aircraft are shown on the preceding page). Conversely, **Heller** moulded no less than six models from the same Swedish aircraft manufacturer **SAAB** in a short period. Was it mandatory for **Heller** to do so?

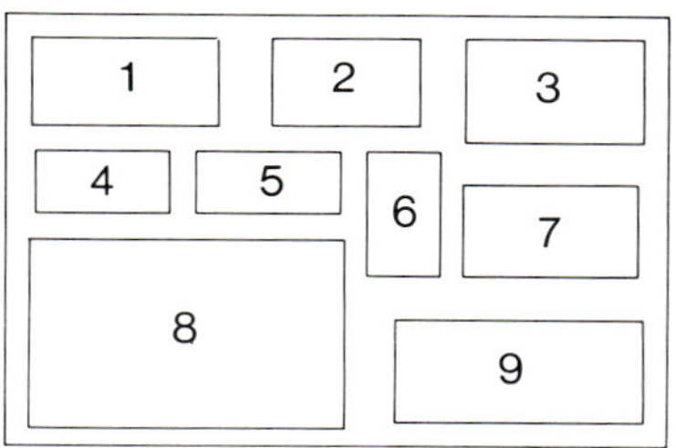

1	SIEBEL *Si.204D*	**(Kovozavody)**
2	SUPERMARINE *Spitfire*	**(Heller)**
3*	SIKORSKY *S.58 Wessex Mk.3*	**(Scalecraft)**
4	SIKORSKY *S.55 Whirlwind*	**(Airfix)**
5	WESTLAND *S.58 Wessex*	**(Frog)**
6*	SUPERMARINE *Spitfire II*	**(Frog)**
7	SHORT *Skyvan*	**(Airfix)**
8	SAVOIA MARCHETTI *S.55X*	**(Delta)**
9	SHORT *Sunderland III*	**(Airfix)**

SIKORSKY *S.58 Wessex Mk 3* — **Scalecraft**

Some specialised writers seem to think that this **Scalecraft** model was built to 1/48 scale which shows that they never bothered to open the box. It is in fact a 1/72 scale model.

SUPERMARINE *Spitfire II* — **Frog**

Some manufacturers contend that they have discovered a new policy for the sale of model kits, offering in the same box an easy to assemble model along with paints and a brush. In fact, **Frog** already made the same experiment 18 years back, with its **Inside Story** kits. This **Frog Inside Story** model of the *Spitfire II* was sold as a book and contained a rather crude model in twenty parts along with a fine colour brochure on the *Spit,* a historical account, a plan and a cutaway drawing. To this, **Frog** had added cement, paints, a paint brush, assembly instructions with a painting guide and a set of decals. Moreover, **Inside Story** kits offered a sales incentive in the guise of 10 "Gold Tokens" that could be exchanged for other kits, flying models or **Frog** books. These efforts to find new customers for their production have unfortunately not saved **Frog** from its fate, and the tradename disappeared.

Now **Bobcat's** venture seems questionable, as their only innovations consist of water-soluble paints and cement. One may wonder whether the real motivation of young modellers from 10 to 14 really consists of assembling models and taking them to pieces again several times. Will these young modellers still opt for **Bobcat** when the same model is available in other makes elsewhere, but better engineered, better boxed and sold at half price?

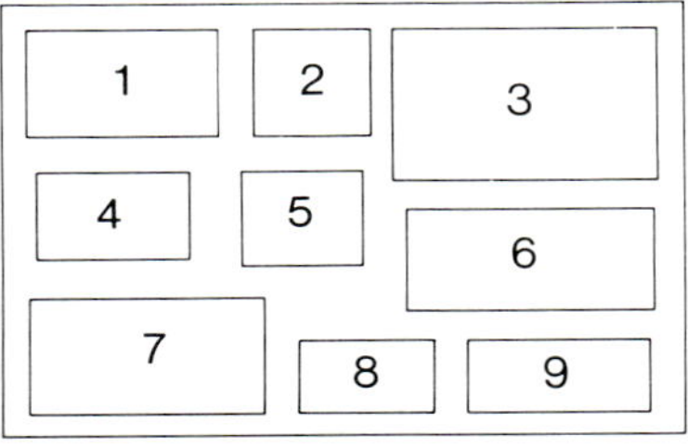

1	SIKORSKY *HH-3 Jolly Green Giant*	**(Lindberg)**
2	R.E. *8*	**(Airfix)**
3*	SOPWITH *Camel F-1*	**(Joy)**
4	SUD-AVIATION *Alouette III*	**(Heller)**
5	SUKHOI *SU.5*	**(Boleslav)**
6	SUKHOI *SU.7B Fitter A*	**(V.E.B.)**
7	SIKORSKY *HH-53C Super J.G.G.*	**(Airfix)**
8	SUPERMARINE *Spitfire VB*	**(Airfix)**
9*	SUPERMARINE *Scimitar*	**(Frog)**

SOPWITH *Camel F-1* — **Joy**

Manufacturers of yogurt often sell their products in packs of three or six. This technique has been adopted by model manufacturers in the guise of "gift sets". Their idea is to try and find a plausible reason for offering as many models as possible in the same box.
For instance, **Hasegawa** strives to sell old kits in a series devoted to the *Thunderbirds* aerobatic team. **Airfix** bundles together a tank, two aircraft and a ship model in the same box to initiate youngsters to the art of modelling, a praiseworthy intention. **Joy** for their own part make use of an historical argument to sell off their "Old Crates" in sets of 12. Children are always happy to be presented with so many aircraft in the same box. That is the way a collection of models sometimes gets started. Modellers will always remember the day when they took their first steps, but they never can tell when they will take the last. This **Joy** set is extremely rare and little-known, even among the specialists and will surely keep gift sets lovers or collectors of "Old Crates" very busy.

SUPERMARINE *Scimitar* — **Frog**

The *Scimitar* was the last fighter produced by **Supermarine** and came into service in 1958 as the first supersonic shipboard fighter of the British Royal Navy. The **Frog** model is still acceptable by today's standards. Only the cockpit area betrays the age of the model. The *Scimitar* is one of the most sought-after **Frog** kits and will remain an inaccessible dream to most English modellers for a long time to come. It is to be noted that the kits moulded in vivid red plastic by **Triang** are the most highly prized.

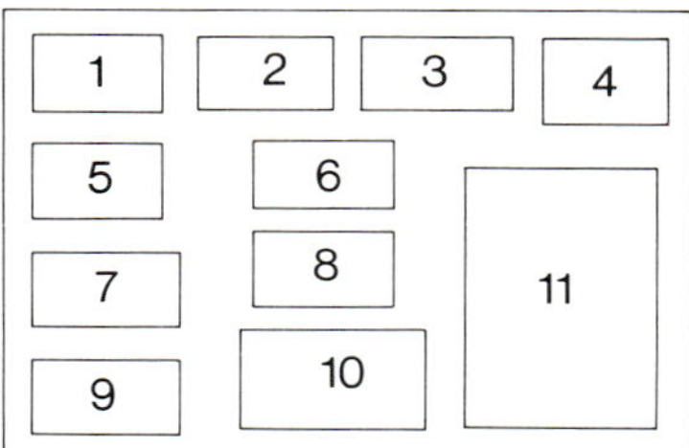

1*	YOKOSUKA *D4Y2 Judy*	**(L.S.)**
2	VOUGHT *F7U-1 Cutlass*	**(Aurora)**
3	VOUGHT *OS2U-3 Kingfisher*	**(Lindberg)**
4	YAKOVLEV *Yak.1 / 1M*	**(Mikro)**
5*	YOKOSUKA *D4Y2 Judy*	**(L.S.)**
6	WESTLAND *Wyvern*	**(Frog)**
7	WESTLAND *Lynx AH.1*	**(Airfix)**
8	YOKOSUKA *K5Y Willow*	**(L.S.)**
9	WESTLAND *Lynx*	**(Airfix)**
10	WRIGHT *Flyer 1903*	**(Renwal)**
11*	VICKERS *Viscount 700*	**(Airtec)**

YOKOSUKA *D4Y2 Judy* — **L.S.**

Some models die and are born again, only uglier. Others are improved for their second lease of life. This **L.S.** model of the *Judy* started as a 1/75 model, but was later lengthened and re-issued in 1/72 scale. **L.S.** is to be congratulated for this rejuvenation.

VICKERS *Viscount 700* — **Airtec**

New materials can offer new answers to old problems. Fibre-glass coated with epoxy resin is cheap and rigid enough to make the production of 1/72 scale airliners possible without expensive tooling. Models of the **Viscount** *700* have thus been produced in Miami, Florida, **USA** for **Airtec**.

YAKOVLEV *Yak.3* **(Cruver)**
Collection Bernard Macaire.

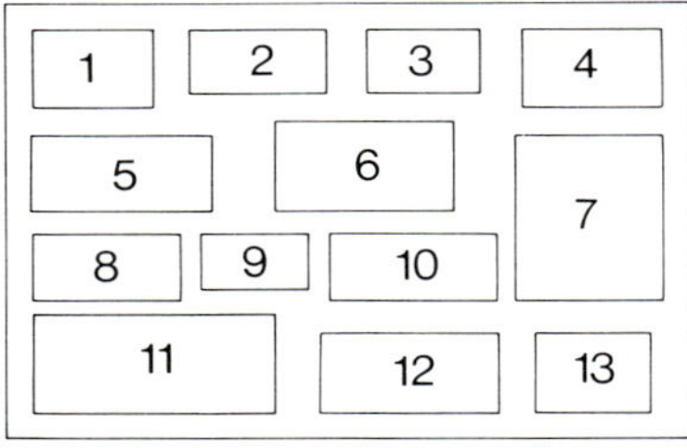

1	SPAD *XIII*	**(Renwal)**
2	WESTLAND *Lysander*	**(Frog)**
3	WSK MIELEC *TS-11 Iskra*	**(Ruch)**
4	VICKERS *Wellesley*	**(Matchbox)**
5	VICKERS *Vimy*	**(Triang)**
6*	VOISIN-FARMAN *1908*	**(Renwal)**
7	STINSON *Trimotor T*	**(J & L)**
8	TUPOLEV *Tu.2 Bat*	**(Frog)**
9	R.A.F. *B.E.2C*	**(Veeday)**
10	SUPERMARINE *Attacker FB.2*	**(Triang)**
11	TUPOLEV *Tu.2 Bat*	**(V.E.B.)**
12	VICKERS *Wellington*	**(Airfix)**
13	SCOTTISH AVIATION *Bulldog*	**(Airfix)**

VOISIN-FARMAN *1908* — **Renwal**

Following up on the trail blazed by **Brifaut** models, **Renwal** released a line of "Old Crates", now with a paper representation of the aircraft's fabric skin. Their process, known as Aero-Skin, later inspired many decal manufacturers, including France's famed and late Max **Abt**. The moulding of **Renwal** models is just as crisp as the earlier **Brifaut** ones but the pros and cons of paper or fabric skins have yet to be reconciled. Some other material and method will have to be found anyway, since a perfect reproduction of fabric skins is not to be discovered but still to be invented.

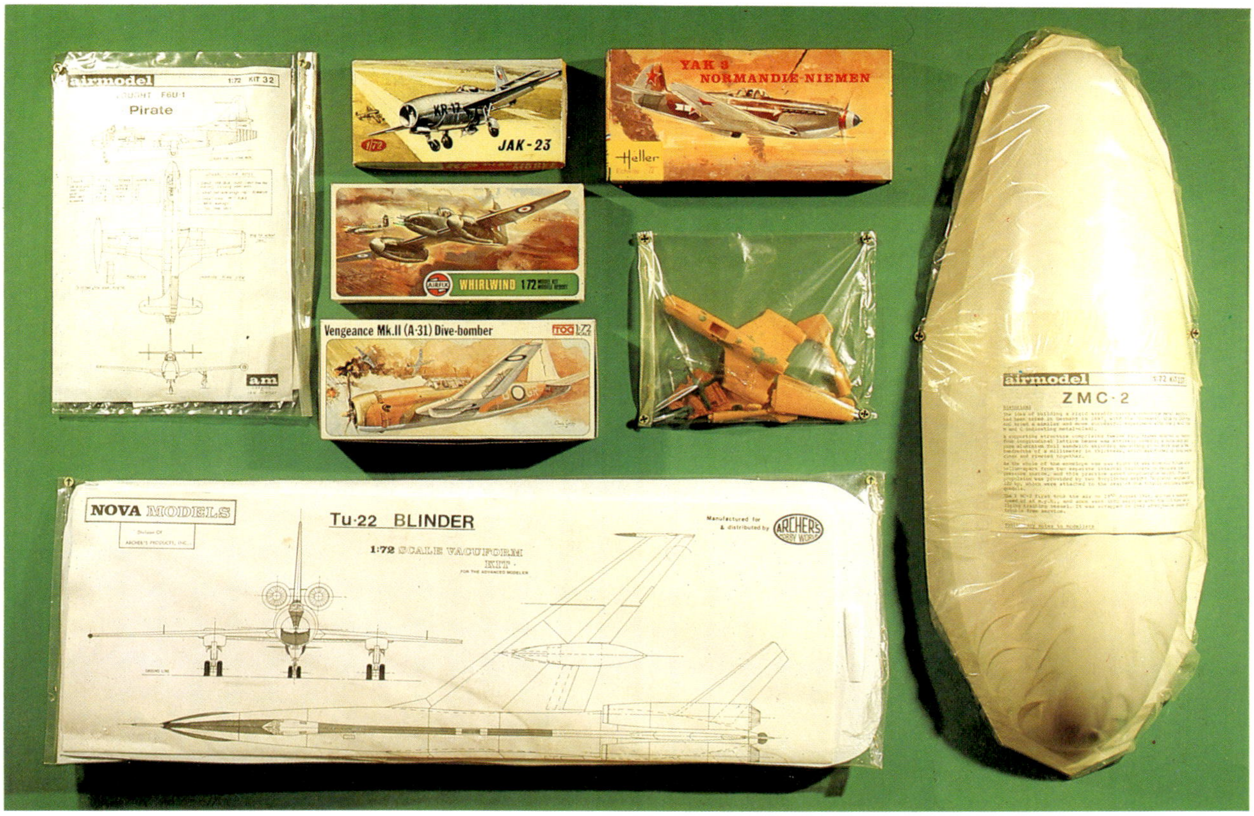

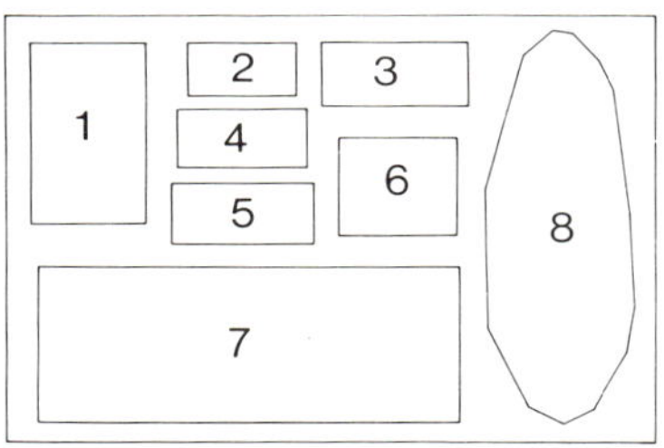

1	VOUGHT *F6U-1 Pirate*	**(Airmodel)**
2	YAKOVLEV *Yak.23 Flora*	**(Kovozavody)**
3	YAKOVLEV *Yak.3*	**(Heller)**
4	WESTLAND *Whirlwind I*	**(Airfix)**
5	VULTEE *Vengeance Mk.2*	**(Frog)**
6*	VULTEE *XP-54 Swoose Goose*	**(Private Venture)**
7	TUPOLEV *Tu.22 Blinder*	**(Nova)**
8	*ZMC-2*	**(Airmodel)**

VULTEE *XP-54 Swoose Goose* — **Private Venture**

Kits made of polymethane resin can have unexpected colours such as yellow, pink, black or pearl. This is due to the mineral and colouring additives they contain. Resin is heavier, harder and more brittle than polystyrene and more difficult to work with. However it can easily be softened by heating. If a fault is detected it can be rectified with the help of a hair drier. Cementing is carried out with epoxy glue (e.g., Araldite) or cyanoacrylates (e.g., Cyanolit). Unorthodox and rare models like this *XP-54 Swoose Goose* make resin kits attractive and should encourage everybody to learn the construction techniques.

▲
WACO *CG-4A Hadrian* **(Italaeri)**
Jacques Niot.

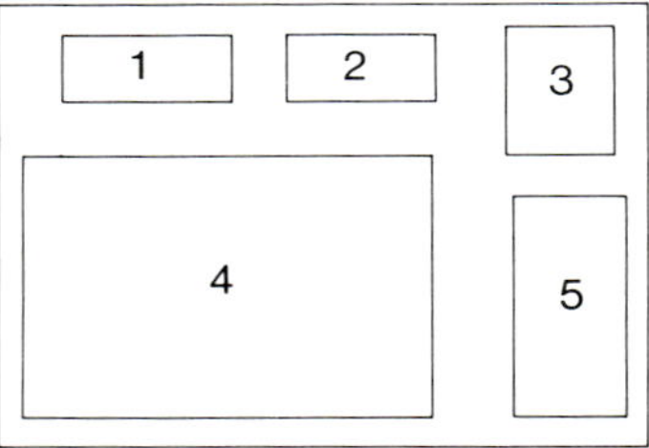

1* VOUGHT *Regulus II* **(Revell)**
2 SOVIET *Guideline SA-2* **(Airfix)**
3 RYAN *Firebee II BQM-34E* **(Private Venture)**
4 ROCKWELL *Space Shuttle* **(Revell)**
5 DOUGLAS *Thor-Able* **(Aurora)**

VOUGHT *Regulus II* — **Revell**
The **Vought** *SSM-N-9 Regulus II* was a submarine-launched cruise missile but it could only be launched on the surface of the sea with **Aerojet** or **Rocketdyne** J.A.T.O. rockets of respectively 115,000 and 135,000 pounds thrust. On account of this, the **Lockheed** *UGM-27A Polaris A-1* was chosen instead as it was a much faster ballistic missile and could be launched from a submerged submarine.
The *Regulus II* was designed to replace the subsonic *Regulus I* cruise missile and could reach more than twice the speed of its predecessor, thanks to its advanced aerodynamic design and the use of the best jet engine available then. The missile came out in two versions.
The **Revell** model displayed here in its original packaging, represented the prototype version of the *KD2U* drone propelled by a **Wright** *J-65* engine and remotely controlled by radio. The ordnance was replaced by a landing gear and a drag chute so that the missile could take off and land like a conventional unmanned aircraft. The **Revell** box art shows a *Regulus II* taking off from **Edwards AFB** in May 1956.
The **Monogram** model portrays the *RGM-15A* version on its **Fruehauf** trailer that allowed for the launching of the craft from a naval base, an aircraft carrier or a cruiser. The *RGM-15A* missile was controlled by an inertial guidance system and carried a nuclear warhead. It was powered by a **General Electric** *J-79-3A* engine of 15,000

pounds thrust that enabled it to exceed Mach 2. A total of 54 operational *Regulus IIs* were produced over a period of three months. They carried out 132 flights, suffering only two losses that were not due to missile malfunction.
It was probably wrong to replace *Regulus II* with *Polaris* missiles in 1959, for even though *Polaris*-type weapons have kept or improved their qualities nowadays, they will become more and more vulnerable because the trajectory of a ballistic missile can be predicted after launch. The enemy will thus try to intercept them with anti-missile missiles, laser-armed satellites, particle-beam cannons or hyper velocity projectiles thrown by electromagnetic pulses.
On the other hand cruise missiles offer significant advantages as long as technology progresses. They are as flexible and agile as manned aircraft and are protected by the atmosphere from space-based beam weapons. Airframes and engines have become so compact that it is now possible to fire missiles from submerged submarines. The so-called "mosaic" terminal guidance system, which merges optical and electronic sensors, has given cruise missiles a homing accuracy improved in a magnitude of 100 compared to ballistic missiles. These already considerable breakthroughs will be furthered with the introduction of "stealth" technology, damage-resistant airframes, hypersonic integrated scramjet engines as well as guidance activated by "expert systems" able to automatically reprogramme the missile in order to take new situations or threats into account. Fault-tolerant flight controls will enable the missile to complete its mission even if half a wing is torn off while fail-safe and auto-adaptative electronic counter-measures and defences will generate surgical responses to attacks . . .
In spite of all this, the 1985 version of the cruise missile is still slower than the *Regulus II* and if one feels the urge to build a model of that missile, one should know that **Revell** offers it again in its **History Makers II** series.

BOEING *AGM-86B Cruise Missile* — Claude **Boileau**

This model was built from the **Projekts Model Company** bagged kit. It does represent the first production missile as displayed in November, 1981, at the rollout ceremony which took place at the new manufacturing plant of the **Boeing Aerospace Company** installed in Kent (south of Seattle), Washington.
AGM-86B is typically a *B-52* and *B-1* weapon. The **Monogram Rockwell** *B-1* is provided with 17 cruise missiles but they are moulded in a stored configuration, i.e., with their wings, fins and vertical stabiliser folded along the fuselage.
The **Airfix** *B-1* is also provided with cruise missiles in a stored configuration.

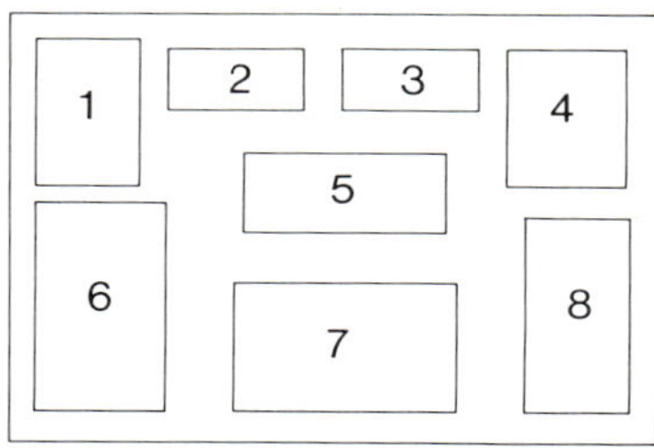

1 FRITZ *X* **(Guano)**
2 BRISTOL *Bloodhound* **(Airfix)**
3 FIESELER *Fi-103 (VI)* **(Frog)**
4* PHILCO-FORD *Sidewinder* **(SMDC)**
5 VOUGHT *Regulus II* **(Monogram)**
6 GERMAN *V2* **(Revell)**
7 GERMAN *V2* **(Grip)**
8 DOUGLAS *Thor SM-75* **(Aurora)**

PHILCO/FORD *Sidewinder* — **SMDC**

Ron **Downey,** an engineer working for **McDonnell Douglas,** had noticed that missiles sold with 1/72 scale model aircraft were often inaccurate. Then it occurred to him that it might be a good idea to offer a set of air-to-air missiles under the **SMDC** (Scale Model Development Company) tradename. Unfortunately, Ron only had a home-built injection press and the final product looked somewhat disappointing, all the more so as the parts were so small. However, it has to be said that the original idea, when it was taken up by **Hasegawa** with industrial means, gave off far better results.

Yet **SMDC** deserves to be better known and appreciated. Apart from his air-to-air and air-to-ground missiles, Ron has produced an excellent *JB-2 Loon* (a forerunner of cruise missiles and one of the first to be fired from a submarine) and a **Fieseler** *Fi.103A-1.* The latter was the unmanned version, without any ailerons whereas **Heller's** *Fi.103* is the *Reichenberg IV* version, a manned aircraft with a cockpit, ailerons and a different nose assembly. **SMDC** *V1* is sold with its trailer and, contrary to what has formerly been written about it in **France**, its price is quite competitive when matched against comparable products. **Frog's** *V1* (in fact **Frog** produced two slightly different moulds) is so hard to come by these days that **SMDC's** choice has to be congratulated.

It can only be hoped that Ron will have the success he deserves. Those who are interested in small series injected models will be interested to know that Ron is the first basement producer to number the parts of his models and to use so-called "pins" to extract his mouldings.

MARTIN *SM-68 Titan I* — Philippe **Legrand**

The second US **ICBM** — Intercontinental Ballistic Missile — to enter service into the **Strategic Air Command** was the **Martin** *SM-68 (HGM-25A) Titan I.* It was developed as a guarantee against any failure of the **Convair** *SM-65 Atlas* programme and widely benefited from its experience. Both of the missiles have the same diameter, but in spite of its superior length, the *Titan I* is lighter. Its two stages are not ignited simultaneously as on the *Atlas,* but in sequence, giving the missile a higher speed (about 17,000 mph) and a better range (about 8,000 miles). First stage propulsion was carried out by two **Aerojet General** *LR87* with twin gimballed chambers each rated at 150,000 lb, and the second stage motor was a *LR91* developing an 80,000 lb thrust. All those rocket motors were fed with **LOX** (liquid oxygen) and **RP-1** (kerosene). The operational missiles used a radio-inertial guidance system.

The *Titan I* programme, which started in 1955, reached operational status in April 1962 with the installation of missiles in underground silos capable of withstanding an over-pressure of 300 psi. One year later, there were six **SAC** squadrons, each with nine missiles. Launching the *Titan I* required a 20 mn count-down during which propellant tanks were filled up and the missile was hoisted to the surface, standing upright on its launching pad. In-silo launching was possible, but caused the destruction of the silo. Height from the rocket chambers to the nose cone was 90 to 95 ft, depending on payload installed. The **Topping** desk model is made up of hollowed moulded plastic parts and depicts a *Titan I* with an ablative **Avco** *Mk.4* nose cone containing a thermonuclear warhead of 4 megatons. At the end of its flight, the warhead was supposed to impact the target at about 5.5 km/s with a 1.5 mile CPE (circular probable error).

Every *Titan I* equipped base was de-activated in 1966, but one of those missiles is now displayed at the **Air Force Space Museum**, Cape Canaveral Air Force Station.

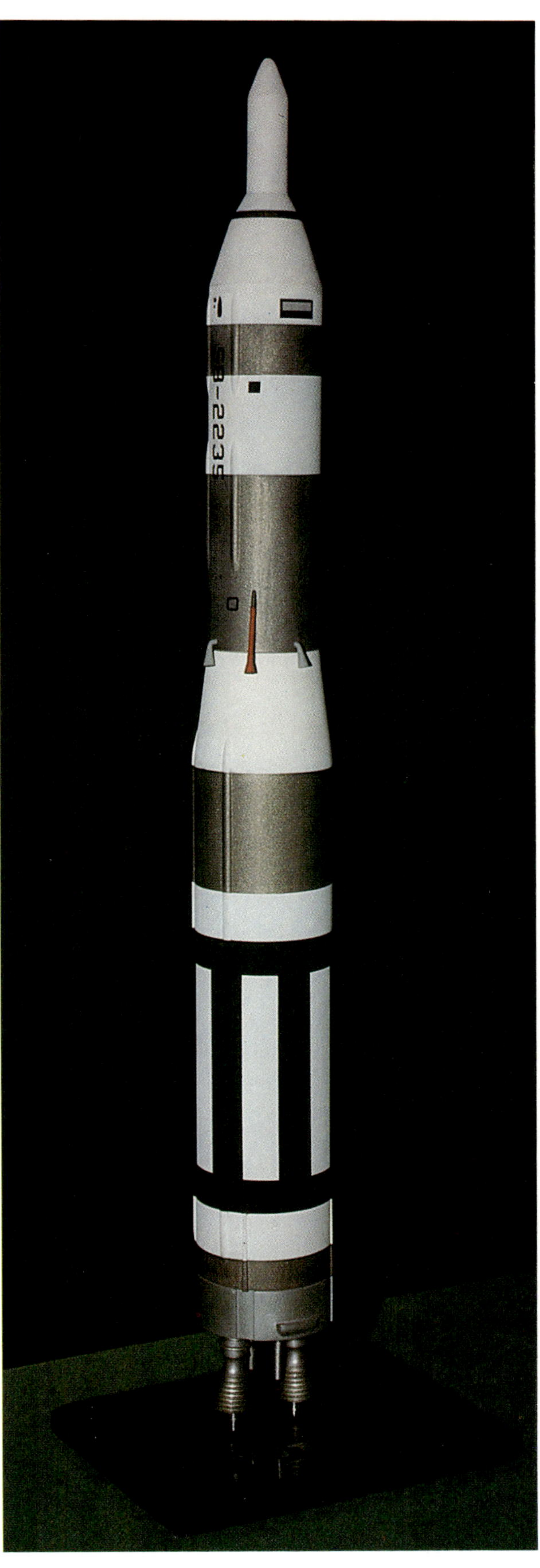

1*	UFO *The Invaders*	**(Aurora)**
2	HAWK *Spaceship* *Collection P. Lejoyeux*	**(Airfix)**
3	EAGLE 1 *Transporter* *Collection P. Lejoyeux*	**(Airfix)**
4	MILLENNIUM *Falcon* *Collection P. Lejoyeux*	**(MPC)**
5	PETER PAN *Pirate Ship*	**(Revell)**
6	MAGNETIC *Space Coupe*	**(Aurora)**

UFO *The Invaders* — **Aurora**

In the field of science-fiction, we are facing models of models, i.e., 1/72 scale representations of craft designed for fictional films. It may seem odd to be interested in spacecraft that do not even exist. Indeed the "to be or not to be" debate is misplaced. Models, whatever they may be, are sometimes the unconscious projections of a society for a short period of its history. Models of Zorro, the Three Musketeers, the Hunchback of Notre-Dame, Dracula or the Beatles' Yellow Submarine, or again James Bond, as well as the films from which they were issued, are mirrors in which the spectator recognises himself or recognises what he loves, what he would like to be or what he fears.
The **Aurora** *UFO* model (re-issued without any untinted clear parts by **Monogram**) depicts creatures from outer space as invaders: the world was then in the grips of the Cold War. But to-day, who could really consider **E.T.** an invader?

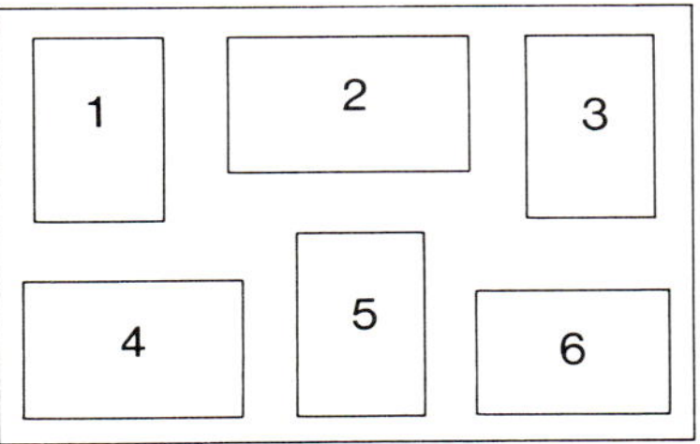

1	MACROSS *Battroïd Valkyrie*	(Imai)
2	THE EMPIRE STRIKES BACK	(Airfix)
3	MACROSS *Tactical Pod Regult*	(Imai)
4	THE INVADERS *Ufo*	(Monogram)
5	MACROSS *Destroid Spartan*	(Imai)
6	MACROSS *Gerwalk Valkyrie*	(Imai)

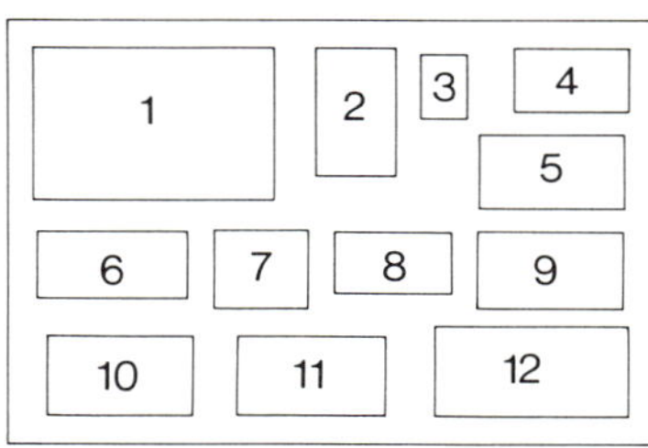

1	GERMAN LEOPOLD *Railway gun*	**(Hasegawa)**
2	GERMAN *Air/Ground Crew (35-45)*	**(Preiser)**
3	US AIRCRAFT *Seat Belt & Harness Buckles*	**(Waldron)**
4	PZ. Kw. VI *Tiger tank*	**(Polistil)**
5	TOYOTA GB *Starter Truck*	**(Hasegawa)**
6	WILLYS *Light Truck with 37 m/m gun*	**(Hasegawa)**
7	GERMAN *Oil Drums and Accessories*	**(Preiser)**
8	T.34 *Tank*	**(Polistil)**
9	RED GUARDS *Figures*	**(Esci)**
10	MATILDA *Mk.II Tank*	**(Polistil)**
11	FIAT-ANSALDO *M.13/40 Tank*	**(Polistil)**
12*	RESCUE AT DUNKIRK *Diorama*	**(MPC)**

RESCUE AT DUNKIRK Diorama — **MPC**

Arrangement of various models, figures and equipment in a scene of action, make up a diorama. Creating dioramas is an art which combines freedom with conventions. Modellers are free to use their own sensitivity to invent scenes or situations but must be careful to avoid any error that might dispel the illusion. They try to involve the spectator in the action presented by the diorama. The spectator should accept a "suspension of disbelief". He should try to understand what the modeller wanted to show and why he chose to capture the most pathetic, the most moving or simply, the most outstanding moment, just like a painter.

FIAT ANSALDO *75 MM* **(Polistil/Esci)**
Montage Didier Palix

JEEP **(Hasegawa)** Figures **(Preiser)** ▲
Claude Boileau

PANHARD *AMD 178* — Jean-Louis **Couston**

This light armoured-car was built from a polyurethane resin kit produced by Alain **Laffargue**.
The process — used for the first time in **France** — implements a technique of vacuum-moulding in silicon rubber moulds. However, in spite of its limited basement-production capabilities, the quality is very close to the result obtained by better manufacturers of injection moulded kits.
Alain **Laffargue** offers now some 50 vehicles (or conversions) and plans to issue his first aircraft, an improved version of the **Fokker** *D.XXI* **Frog** model.
In 1980, kits other than injection moulded were virtually unknown. Nowadays, they set up a new category sometimes dealing with odd subjects.
Among them we find the biggest 1/72 scale kit ever produced (an almost 5 m long model of the nuclear powered aircraft-carrier USS *Nimitz*) and the smallest flying object ever reproduced, that is the **Canadair** *CL-227* "Flying Peanut", a battlefield surveillance RPV (Remotely Piloted Vehicle).

PANHARD *AMD 178*

1	*PT 109* *Collection Philippe Legrand*	**(Revell)**
2	GERMAN *E-BOAT* *Collection Philippe Legrand*	**(Airfix)**
3	VOSPER *M.T.B.* *Collection Philippe Legrand*	**(Revell)**
4	VOSPER *M.T.B.* *Collection Didier Palix*	**(Revell)**
5	JAPAN TORPEDO BOAT *PT 15* *Collection Didier Palix*	**(Tamiya)**

PT-109/PT-167 — **Revell**

John Fitzgerald **Kennedy** was brought up to revere success and devotion. From his youngest age his parents instilled into him their desire to win, by constantly telling him that winning was not just an aim among others but the only aim one should have. He won his spurs when he was a Lieutenant in charge of an *E-Boat*. On the night of August 1st, 1943, his craft *PT-109* left Rendova Harbour in the Salomon Islands along with 15 other ships to intercept the so-called "Tokyo Express" (i.e., the Japanese convoy supplying the garrison at Guadalcanal). The craft, *PT-109*, was then attacked and cut into halves by one of the destroyers that escorted the convoy. John was injured but managed to extricate himself from the wreckage and rescue his crew-members. According to the account given by **Revell** on the assembly instructions, **Kennedy** dragged one of his men, who was worse-off than himself, with his own teeth. Maybe these facts will be confirmed one day. One thing is sure however, and that is, that the two men swam in the Straights of Blackett for four hours until they reached the small island of Plum-Pudding where they were met by other crew members. The survivors owe their lives to the help given by the natives of Kolombangara.

JFK always strived hard for success, throughout his career. He won the allegiance of his supporters thanks to his intelligence, his aristocratic and charismatic behaviour, and that charm of his, which was compounded with warmth but also aloofness. He even disarmed his opponents by declaring himself to be the "President for all opportunities". His speech on the new frontiers enthralled **America**. In fact, **JFK**

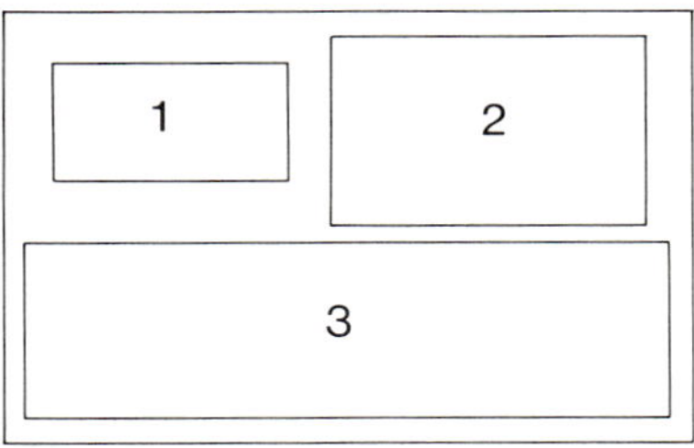

1 *RAF Rescue Launch* **(Airfix)**
Collection Philippe Legrand
2 VOSPER *Fast Patrol* **(Tamiya)**
Collection Didier Palix
3* *Corvette Classe « Flower »* **(Matchbox)**
Collection Didier Palix

simply brought back self-confidence to a nation frustated by Soviet technical successes, thanks to his sense of humour and his pugnacity, as well as his spirit of renovation and liberalism.
On November 8th, 1960, he was voted into the White House as the youngest President in the history of the USA. The **Revell** model gives one more than the mere pleasure of assembling a kit: it provides one with the opportunity of recalling the life of that exceptional man who embodied all the hopes of **America**. John Fitzgerald **Kennedy** met with glory and success but also drama and tragedy . . .

"Flower" Class Corvette — **Matchbox**

Men have always fought each other. In order to wage war, wherever it may break out, not only warriors but also weapons are necessary, and some nations have shown a remarkable capacity to use every means to achieve their ends. Thus, in the early stages of World War II, **Great Britain**, anticipating U-boat attacks on convoys, initiated the design of special ships to ward them off. As it was vital to work fast, a whaler called *Southern Pride* was chosen as a basis for the development of the new *Corvettes*. The whaler was strongly built, seaworthy and her speed was adequate. Moreover she could be launched from medium-sized, privately owned shipyards. Reservists did not find her too difficult to operate, and maintenance could be carried out by Merchant Navy staff. Those new "watchdogs" were all given the names of flowers in the Royal Navy, hence the "Flower Class" label. Over 300 of the type were launched from British or Canadian shipyards and they served in many navies all

over the world. Some reverted to the Merchant Navy after the war.
The **Matchbox** offering includes 1003 parts. The assembled model is 865 mm long and, according to the assembly instructions, can be made up to represent HMS *Bluebell* (Royal Navy), *HMCS* Snowberry (Canadian Navy) or *USS Saucy* (US Navy).
Matchbox have forgotten about the French Flower Class Corvettes. Yet nine of them served with the Free French Navy and flew the flag for **France** for over three years of conflict, thus ensuring the presence of that country alongside the Allies on all the oceans. One of them, the *Aconit,* achieved fame for the rescue of the castaways from the destroyer *Harvester* and the destruction of two types *VIIC* U-boats of the German Kriegsmarine on the same day, March 11th, 1943. That warship was the only one, along with the submarine *Rubis* to be awarded the cross of the Ordre de la Libération by Général **De Gaulle** himself. Her Captain L. V. **Levasseur** received the same medal. Other flower-type *Corvettes* sporting the Croix de Lorraine bear witness to the courage and determination of French sailors after the fall of their country. Modellers who evince interest in their stories, or who wish to convert the **Matchbox** to one of these *Corvettes,* should find interesting information in the first three issues of *Marines Internationales.*

HISTORY AND ACKNOWLEDGEMENTS

No book comparable to this one has been published and it is hard to imagine the amount of effort and research that was needed to make its publication possible. If that work had not been a labour of love, it would never have been brought to fruition. No one could possibly have carried out the task alone. That is the reason why an organisation had to be worked out from the outset to harness the talents of the best modelling specialists in the world. But it is by no means easy to collaborate on an encyclopedia about a little-known subject studied from its inception onwards. In the present case, difficulties were heightened by geographical distance between the participants, that made coordination work extremely complex. Fortunately, we did not start our study from scratch, as many people preceded us in our research. That is the reason why we wish to acknowledge their endeavours in the following lines.

The first listing of constant-scale models was published by *Aeromodeller* magazine in the December 1958 issue under the *Aeromodeller Plastic Kit Survey* heading. **IPMS Great Britain** published a 23-page brochure in the mid-sixties at the behest of W. R. **Matthews**. The latest edition dates back to 1973.

The first really comprehensive study originated from the USA. The *Collector's Guide to Model Aircraft & Rocket/Missiles and Space Kits* came out in two volumes in 1972. That great achievement was to the credit of Carlton **Shank** and an international team of 30 specialists. Ever since that time, some people have teamed up to further their knowledge in very specific fields, and have often published their works. Worthy of note are:

— John **Burns (USA)**, who pioneered the detection and pricing of rare models. He founded **SPESMKC** (Society for the Preservation and Encouragement of Scale Model Kit Collecting) in 1974 with the help of a score of friends. Their "institution" now includes over 1000 members, makes use of a bulletin (KCC or Kit Collector's Clearinghouse) and publishes its CVG (Collector's Value Guide) every year. The free ads of the KCC make it possible to buy or swap all the wanted kits,
— Bob **Keller (USA)**, the founder of KCI (Kit Collectors International), followed the lead of SPESMKC in 1980. However, thanks to face-to-face interviews, KCI has succeeded in establishing truth where only hearsay or rumour was available. VP (Vintage Plastic) is not only a news sheet, but also a medium for free expression, while the quotation of rare kits traded in the US swap-meetings is published in KCPG (Kit Collector's Pricing Guide),
— Brad **Hansen (USA)**, who specialises in early aeroplanes. His remarkable book *WWI in Plastic* is a masterpiece,
— John **Carlson (USA)**, who has carried out research on over 500 makes of plastic models,
— Gunther **Rubsam (West Germany)**, who specialises in civilian aircraft,
— Roger **Braatz (USA)**, who specialises in display models and founded **Roger's Jet Aviation Museum**,
— Leif **Hellstrom (Sweden)**, who is a FROG expert,
— Denis **Bowman (USA)**, who has been delving into **Revell's** *1 800 Series*,
— Andy **Yanchus (USA)**, a pundit in the field of **Aurora** kits and fictional models . . .

But it has to be said that no team has shown as much thoroughness as **Model-Aire International** in its research about 1/72 scale. Among the contributors to that organisation, some particularly deserve our attention:

— Libby **Young (USA)**, who is in charge of the reference department and helps to scrutinise books and magazines for scraps of information on aeroplanes and model kits,
— Jerry **Brewton (USA)**, a notable collector of models and catalogues, who carried out impressive research on military identification models,

— Tom **Willey (USA)**, who worked out the list of vehicles and guns,
— John **Sommerville (Australia)**, for his work on German aeroplanes,
— Armando **Gil (Venezuela)**, for his comments and extra information,
— Michael **Van Meerwiijk (Holland)**, for his contributions on Eastern Bloc model kits.

Several people have taken part in the completion of this book in **France** as well, among who are:

— Philippe **Legrand**, who worked out the list of missiles and ships. Philippe is one of the world's experts on missile models and 1/72 scale in general,
— Bernard **Macaire**, for his priceless advice and comments. Bernard is quite possibly the most outstanding collector we know. His expert knowledge encompasses every aspect of modelling, from toys to the most sophisticated kits. His vast experience, based on concrete facts and personal involvement, enables him to offer sound advice.

However, the remarkable amount of knowledge accumulated for over 20 years would probably have remained untapped if it had not been for:

— The translators. Our thanks to Douglas **Bromley (GB)**, Emmanuel **Zaks (France)**and François **Portier (France)** who bore the brunt of the work. François is a lecturer and also a modeller (he is the Secretary of one of the leading modelling clubs of the Paris area, the MKSB).
— Those who kindly showed their collection of unassembled and assembled kits and whose names have already been quoted.
— Those who helped us track down the rarest and most obscure models for us to take photos of. Our special thanks go to Jean-Claude **Goeury (Belgium)**, Norman **Tomkies (GB)**, John **Kuehnert (West Germany)**, Peter **Bengtson (Sweden)**, Jim **Lyzun (Canada)**, Masayuki **Hiratsuka (Japan)**, James **Jones (USA)** and all those that cannot be listed here due to lack of space.
— Hughes **Leblanc,** Chairman of the Board, **La Commande Electronique,** who gave the Authors the possibility to use two famous **Ashton Tate** software products for personal computers: **DBase III** Plus **Framework II.**

HOW TO OBTAIN RARE MODEL KITS

A model can be said to be rare when it cannot be obtained through the usual channels. Those who want off-beat models therefore have to find new channels.

Looking for models is a strenuous affair that calls for good organisation, diplomacy and assertiveness. It becomes necessary to concentrate on three steps:

A. **Knowing what one actually has.**
One only has to put down all one's models on the list of EM. When one buys a new kit, one should jot down the price for a possible sale or barter. One should not forget to mention models leaving one's collection.

B. **Setting out a target.**
Each one of us knows his particular field of interest precisely — a variety of flying machines, a particular period in history, etc. It is easy — with the help of the list included in this book — to define one's field of interest and to assess the quantity of models remaining to be acquired, or even to establish priorities. A bit of quick reckoning may reveal that one's ambitions are not matched by one's available cash. In that case, it becomes necessary to space out one's future acquisitions or to split up one's collection under three headings:

— The models one absolutely wants to keep,
— Those that can be used as bargaining counters. Many journals will accept classified ads for the sale of kits, but other solutions would be to dispose of them in club meetings, flying displays or local marts.
— Models that are not relevant to one's collection but may nevertheless prove of some value for barter. Those models can be used as a last resort, when money simply has no appeal for the person who owns the coveted object. Some **Solido, ITC, Geobra** or **Gladen** kits are remote from 1/72 scale but they are useful counterparts for rare 1/72 kits. If you do own many "golden oldies", you will find that KCPG or CVG valuation guides offer great help in sorting out the really tantalising baits.

C. **The hunt proper.**
A sportsman will study the habits of his quarry before he sets out on his chase. For the same reasons it is desirable to know why a kit is rare before starting out on a quest. The rarity of a moulding depends on the following factors:

— The number of kits produced from the mould. Models produced in successive series of 10,000 each are obviously more common than short runs (e.g., 1,000) kits.
— The delivery channel. Models distributed everywhere in toy shops, grocer's shops, department stores, booksellers and stationers, etc., are better known than those which are available by mail order only.
— The age of the model. A kit whose last examples came out in 1960 is obviously more difficult to find than another kit dating back to 1980. However, the continued existence of the mould sometimes makes it possible to re-issue old models that thereby become less rare. Certain makes, e.g.,**Revell, Monogram, Airfix**, etc., re-issue old models from time to time, and on account of that, the search for older kits from those makes should not take precedence over the others.
— The geographical areas affected by distribution. A Japanese kit that has never been marketed in **Italy** is rare for an Italian but not for a Belgian if it has been imported into **Belgium. Belgium** will therefore be a happier hunting ground for such models.
— The pricing at the time of the appearance of the kit on the market. Some models have become extremely rare only because they were far more expensive than contemporary kits.

For example, people who paid 2,980 francs (so-called "old francs" on account of currency change) for a 1/100 **Breguet 763** from **Etex** 28 years ago, are not likely to let it go for a fistful of sovereigns, even though the model was re-issued by M.E.E. in 1984 and offered at the so-called "reasonable" sum of 285 FF.
— Its average life-span. Some models hardly ever get assembled and if they originally were, they tend to last for a very long time. That is the case with sailing ship models or very large aeroplane kits. Others however only last for a few hours or days following their purchase. That is the case with "soft" models or snap-fit kits designed for young children. Those are the trickiest to find again, many people have seen them or actually owned them for a short while but scarcely anybody has kept them.
— Anticipated demand. A model which is merely "off-beat" may suddenly become extremely rare when everybody anticipates heavy demand and resorts to panic buying. An example is **Cunarmodel's Aermacchi M.B. 326** — a typical case. When the worldwide modelling community learned that **Cunarmodel** was to give up kit production in favour of industrial models, there was a rush on the M.B. 326 — and not the M.B. 339 from the same manufacturer — simply because rumour had it that **Esci** was about to release that 339.
Anticipated demand stems from speculation: prices soar and for a limited period it is impossible to find a supplier. That situation remains until the model becomes available again thanks to a re-issue or the appearance of a new mould on the market.
— Your own proficiency in foreign languages, your know-how and "gumption" to find the person who has the coveted model and to negotiate with him or her. Never forget that he or she will not necessarily show signs of life after reading your advertisement. Why? Because most people only bother to answer if they think they can deal with someone who can bring them what they want. They are not interested in what *you* are looking for. Your aim must therefore be to generate interest in your ads or letters. If your knowledge of foreign languages is scanty and you have to look for very rare kits in distant countries, you should not try to contact collectors directly but find, in the countries concerned, reliable correspondents who will help you with your research. It will be up to you to find common ground with them. The following organisations — among others — will publish advertisements for kits and this enables you to find correspondents:

- Kit Collector's Clearinghouse (KCC) — 3213 Hardy Drive, Edmond, Oklahoma 73034 — USA.
- Kit Collectors International (KCI) — P.O. Box 38, Stanton, California 90680 — USA.
- The International Kit Exchange (IKE) — 11 Moss Close, Caversham, Reading, Berks, RG4 0HH — England.
- International Plastic Modellers Society whose world office is at 20 Yerdley Close, Woodloes Park, Warwick, CV34 5EX — England.

IPMS has branches in some 25 different countries. Each country has local branches. The head office will supply the addresses of the various national branches.
In the USA, IPMS is housed at P.O. Box 480, Denver, Colorado 80201.
In France, IPMS is housed at 73 rue Alexandre Dumas, 75020 Paris.
The following publications also allow one to publish ads. They are obtainable from newsagents, hobby shops or aviation bookshops:
— USA: *Scale Modeler, Aviation Week and Space Technology, Space Frontiers, Fine Scale Modeler*
— France: *Air Fan, Aviation Magazine, Planeurs et Avions Magazine*
— England: *Scale Models, Airfix Magazine, Aeroplane Monthly, Flight International, Aviation News, Aircraft Modelworld*
— Germany: *Modell Magazin, Modell-Fan*
— Italy: *JP 4 Mensile Di Aeronautica, Aeri*
Tracking down models thanks to advertisements means abiding by a certain number of rules. One should always:
— answer letters at reasonable short notice,
— be precise: give one's full name and address, state the origin of the ad one is answering, or the name of the person on whose behalf one is writing and why, and, most important, what one can do or offer in exchange. Finally, one's letters should always remain polite, even when they bring no concrete results.
— Put the right postage on one's letter,
— when an answer is expected, it is desirable to include a SAE with IRC for foreign correspondents.

Ads can be complemented with model-hunting in the following haunts:
— Toy shops. If you get to know the shop well enough, you can ask to see the stocks, take a better look behind the first rows of boxes. Quite often you will find interesting models hidden away in some corner of the shop or some warehouse. Take advantage of your holidays and travels to bring back rare kits. Organise your hunting expeditions with the help of telephone directories. Use the phone to weed out the less interesting shops so as to avoid useless trips. When you arrive at a small village, have a chat with the local retailers, they will often help you to find the small shops where there is a fair chance of finding interesting things.

— Clubs and other associations. Attend their meetings regularly and chat about old kits, showing that you are interested in them and listen to all the tips that could put you on the right track. Get together and call on toy and model distributors, ask to buy up their stocks in bulk, you will then have a chance to get to their reserves and sweep up all the goodies. Another possibility is to write to model manufacturers using the addresses provided in this book. Most manufacturers will not bother to answer back if you are asking for out of production kits, but some will if you wish to order kits which are still in production. In that case, never hesitate to buy them, as smaller manufacturers may go out of business any time. Attend fairs and exhibitions, airshows such as the one which is organised at La Ferté Alais (near Paris, **France**) by Jean **Salis**, in which old models are put up for sale. US **IPMS** conventions organise exchange marts — a single day spent there will enable one to reap the same harvest as in a year of letter-writing. Other worthwhile haunts include antique dealers selling toys, "flea-markets" and junk-shops.

When, at last, you have all the models you have been looking for, try to find "the gold nugget" that will be your pride and joy and will perhaps enable us to add yet one more model to our list. There remains one category of rare models — the rarest of them all, the ones that require research to discover long bygone and forgotten manufacturers. Old modelling magazines can be helpful but the most efficient method is to peruse the professional publications of toy manufacturers and producers of plastic objects. In **France** alone, research carried out with a computer on **INSEE** files (Institut National de la Statistique et des Etudes Economiques) has made it possible to discover about 40 manufacturers, when only a dozen were known before. Once a few shreds of information on a manufacturer become available, Sherlock Holmes' methods are required to discover the history of the firm, its former managers, then to arrange for interviews and finally track down interesting moulds. As is the case with any type of research work, one can waste years on dead-ends but also discover genuine gold mines. What a thrill when you find the prize at long last! But the greatest discovery will surely be the one that will confront you with a model that is unknown to the world experts — somewhere in a basement, a loft or the dusty shelf of an old shop. There are surely other ways of tracking down rare models. The ones listed above have proved their worth — in eight years the **Huynh-Dinh Khuong** collection was made up thus — and all the box tops illustrated in this book (apart from the ones mentioned in the credits) come from that collection.

1/72 SCALE MODEL MANUFACTURERS

1/72 scale has been with us for fifty years. As is the case with so many recent developments, that all started during the Second World War, when spotters had to identify any aircraft that flew in the allied airspace, and give advance warning to the AA defences. They were helped in this by the Army, who supplied them with wooden recognition models.

Why was the 1/72 scale retained? Because, after a period of trial and error, it was discovered that the 1/6 inch scale, in which an inch represents a foot, was the best compromise. The smallest types were still recognisable when reduced to that scale, while even the largest aircraft remained handy. Thus it was accepted that 1/72 scale would make it possible to represent with sufficient realism any type of aircraft in existence, or indeed to come.

With hindsight, it has also been found out that the 1/72 scale meets two of the fundamental requirements of modellers, i.e., handiness and ease of assembly. Most modellers are short of space and free time. While it is extremely tempting to build a large model, the need for detailing soon becomes apparent, if only to achieve realism, and detailing takes time. Some 1/72 modellers will go to great lengths to improve cockpit interiors, undercarriage or engines, but even those who are in a hurry are able to produce fine-looking models, since omissions are far less conspicuous in this scale . . .

Economic factors should not be left out either, and most 1/6 inch scale models remain affordable. While some models cost a small fortune, particularly for the young modeller, many models are really quite cheap.

Those facts have led manufacturers to go for that scale. More than 4,500 different moulds for aircraft models were produced, as against about 1,200 to 1/48 scale. The gap gets wider and wider as the years go by even when some manufacturers wish to leave the beaten track and try a 1/8 engine or 1/12 cockpit interior . . .

1/72 has prevailed over other scales, ever since the inception of modelling not because manufacturers imposed it, but because 70% of all modellers have chosen it deliberately.

The history of modelling boils down to a few figures — several billion kits produced by some 250 manufacturers listed in the following list -.

These manufacturers have produced original moulds. The name of manufacturers or the tradenames of companies that only produce kits from a mould that they did not make themselves are not mentioned here. For example, **Buzco (USA)** is not quoted in the list because that company only produces kits from **Heller** moulds. The same applies to **Airflash** from **Canada**, that produces kits from **Fujimi** moulds.

A manufacturer that copies an original mould but alters it, however little, is mentioned in the list. The technique that has been adopted makes it possible for the reader to have a list that includes only authentic and differing moulds.

The addresses listed in the EM are up-to-date to the best of our knowledge. The addresses of the manufacturers that have gone out of business are those of the premises they occupied at the time when they were still active. When the address of a manufacturer is not known, the country of origin is indicated all the same. In that case, and so as to help readers in their quest for kits, we provide the address of a distributor, whenever possible (example: **Air Vac** c/o **Archer's Hobby World**).

LIST OF MANUFACTURERS

299 MODELS
(USA)
299 MODELS
14515 6th Avenue N.E.
Seattle, Washington 98155
USA

3DFV

AAA MODELS
(USA)
c/o R.V.F. HOBBY IMPORTS
P.O. Box 107
Burbank, CA 91503
USA

ABORN
(USA)
ABORN c/o IMPS Lawrence
80 Manchester Street
Lawrence, Massachusetts 01841
USA

ACADEMY MINICRAFT
(USA)
c/o MINICRAFT Models Inc.
P.O. Box 3577
Torrance, California 90510
USA

AERO KIT
(FRANCE)
TROCHAIN-PYRACAR
19 Avenue du Général Leclerc
95390 Saint-Prix
FRANCE

AEROCLUB MODELS
(ENGLAND)
AEROCLUB MODELS
5 Silverwood Avenue
Ravenshead, Nottingham
NG15 9BU
ENGLAND

AEROFORM
(USA)
AEROFORM c/o MAIL CALL MODELS
1525 W. Mac ARTHUR Blvd. 20
Costa Mesa, California 92626
USA

AEROMODELL
(WEST GERMANY)
c/o WK MODELS Werner KILLERSREITER
Dorfstrasse 29
D-8050 Freising-Attaching
WEST GERMANY

AEROSPACE CASTING
(USA)
AERO-SPACE and CASTING Co.
P.O. Box 307
Visalia, California 93277
USA

AGL MODELCRAFTS
(ENGLAND)
AGL MODELCRAFTS
7 Chapel Hill
Newquay, Cornwall
ENGLAND

AIR CONVERSIONS
(ENGLAND)
AIR CONVERSIONS
P.O. Box 31
Sutton Coldfield, Warwickshire
ENGLAND

AIR JET ADVANCE
(USA)
AIR JET ADVANCE Models Inc.
2100 N.W. 96 Ave
Miami, Florida 33172
USA

AIRFIX
(ENGLAND)
HUMBROL Ltd.
Marfleet, Hull
North Humberside HU9 5NE
ENGLAND

AIRFORM
(ITALY)
AIRFORM
ITALY

AIRFRAME
(CANADA)
AIRFRAME
5209 Rumble Street
Barnaby,
British Columbia
V5J 2B7
CANADA

AIRMODEL
(WEST GERMANY)
AIRMODEL/ FRANK-MODELLBAU
Obere Vorstadt 21
D7470 Albstadt
WEST GERMANY

AIRTEC
(USA)
AIRTEC/CRAFTEC Inc.
128 South Road
Engfield, Connecticut 06082
USA

AIRVAC
(USA)
AIRVAC
P.O. Box 17501
Irvine, California 92714
USA

AIRWAVES
(ENGLAND)
PREMIER PRODUCTIONS Ltd.
123 Wolverhampton Street
Walsall, West Midlands
ENGLAND

ALBY
(FRANCE)
LAFFARGUE
31 Rue de Blois,
La Ferté Villeneuil
28220 Cloyes-sur-le-Loir
FRANCE

ALIPLAST
(ITALY)
ALIPLAST
Via Moline 11
Bologna
ITALY

ALLYN
(USA)
ALLYN SALES Co.
Los Angeles 1
California
USA

ALPHA
(BELGIUM)
ALPHA
Rue du Pot d'Or, 24
Liège
BELGIUM

AMERANG
(ENGLAND)
AMERANG BILLING BOATS
440 Chiswick High Road
London W4 5TT
ENGLAND

AMT
(USA)
AMT CORPORATION
1225 E. Maple
Troy, Michigan 48084
USA

AOSHIMA (JAPAN)
AOSHIMA BUNKA KYOZAISHA CO.
8-1 2 Chome Ando
Shizuoka
JAPAN

ARCHER'S (USA)
ARCHER'S HOBBY WORLD
15432 Alsace
Irvine, California 92714
USA

ARII (JAPAN)
JAPAN

ARISTO CRAFT (USA)
ARISTO CRAFT
Newark 5, New Jersey
USA

ARMTEC (USA)
ARMTEC
5 Belinda Lane
Enfield, Connecticut
USA

ARNE ANDERSSON (SWEDEN)
ARNE ANDERSSON
Erikslundsvägen 4
61100 Nyköping
SWEDEN

ARTCRAFT AIRCRAFT (USA)
USA

ASTRA (CANADA)
ASTRA SCALE MODELS LTD.
P.O. Box 1541, St. Catharines
Ontario L2R 7J9
CANADA

ATLANTIC MODELS (USA)
ATLANTIC MODELS Inc.
7661 N.W. 68 St. 117
Miami, Florida 33166
USA

ATO (NORTHERN IRELAND)
ATO MODEL CRAFTS
36 Wellington Place
Belfast
NORTHERN IRELAND

AURORA (USA)
AURORA PLASTICS Corp.
44 Cherry Valley Road
West Hempstead,
New York 11552
USA

AVF (ENGLAND)
AIRWAYS VAC FORM (Dept. E)
3 Calton Road
New Barnet, Herts. EN5 1BY
ENGLAND

BANDAI (JAPAN)
BANDAI Co. Ltd.
1-4-14 Komagata Taitoko
Tokyo
JAPAN

BARE-METAL FOIL (USA)
BARE-METAL FOIL Co.
16419 Ingram
Livonia, Michigan 48152
USA

BARY WALBY

BELL (ENGLAND)
ENGLAND

BEUELITE (USA)
USA

BIG SKY (ENGLAND)
BIG SKY MODELS
Highfields
Brisley, Norfolk NR20 5LQ
ENGLAND

BILLING BOATS (DENMARK)
BILLING BOATS
Handelsselskab A/S
Gejsing, 6640 Lunderskov
DENMARK

BLUE RIDER (ENGLAND)
BLUE RIDER MODELS
(Dept SAM)
43A Glasford Street
Tooting, London SW17 9HL
ENGLAND

BOLESLAV (CZECHOSLOVAKIA)
CZECHOSLOVAKIA

BONUX (FRANCE)
PROCTER & GAMBLE FRANCE
96 Avenue Charles de Gaulle
92200 Neuilly-sur-Seine
FRANCE

BRIFAUT (WEST GERMANY)
c/o France BRIFAUT
Engertstrasse 2
8035 Gauting
WEST GERMANY

BRITAVIA MODELS (ENGLAND)
BRITAVIA MODELS
13 St Justin Close
St Mary Croy, Arpington,
Kent
ENGLAND

C. SCALE (ENGLAND)
c/o E.D. Models
64 Stratford Road, Shirley
Solihull, West Midlands
B90 3LP
ENGLAND

C.A. ATKINS (ENGLAND)
C.A. ATKINS
17 Ashbourne Avenue
Bridlington, N. Humberside
YO16 4PE
ENGLAND

CADET

CAN-VAC (CANADA)
CAN-VAC MODELS
2255 Cape Horn Avenue
Coquitlam, British Columbia
V3K 1J6
CANADA

CAP CROIX DU SUD (FRANCE)
CAP CROIX DU SUD Sarl
160 Rue de Bagnolet
75020 Paris
FRANCE

CENTRAL
(JAPAN)
CENTRAL MODEL TOYS
Co. Ltd.
50-11 5 Chome Nitsupori
Arakawa-Ku, Tokyo
JAPAN

CHALLENGE
(ITALY)
CHALLENGE Plastic-Models
Tosco Virginio,
Via Guido Rossa 27A
28048 Verbania
ITALY

CHARMORE
(USA)
CHARMORE
126 Market Street
Paterson, New Jersey
USA

CLARK
(ENGLAND)
ERICK CLARK MODELS
19 Lonsdale Road
Southport, Merseyside PR8 6NL
ENGLAND

CLARKE
(ENGLAND)
ENGLAND

CLASSIC PLANE
(WEST GERMANY)
CLASSIC PLANE
Möllney's Nocken 6a
D-4300 Essen 15
WEST GERMANY

COMA
(ITALY)
COMA-AERMEC Prodotti
Milano
ITALY

COMBAT MODEL
(USA)
COMBAT MODEL
400 3rd Street
West Easton, PA 18042
USA

COMET
(USA)
COMET MODEL HOBBYCRAFT
Inc.
501 West 35th Street
Chicago, Illinois 60616
USA

COMMAND

COMPASS
(ENGLAND)
COMPASS MODELS
Adastra Works
Southport
ENGLAND

CONSTRUCTO MODRISA
(BRAZIL)
BRAZIL

CONTRAIL
(ENGLAND)
SUTCLIFFE PRODUCTIONS
(CONTRAIL)
The Orchard, Westcombe
Shepton Mallet, Somerset
BA4 6ER
ENGLAND

CONTRAIL
(ENGLAND)
c/o MILSLIDES MODELS
106 Selsdon Road
South Croydon, Surrey CR2 6PF
ENGLAND

CONVERT A KITS
(USA)
CONVERT A KITS
P.O. Box 17733
Rochester, New York 17733
USA

CRAMER
(USA)
CRAMER CRAFT FAME
157 Imperial Drive
Gahanna, Ohio 43230
USA

CREST
(USA)
CREST
USA

CRUVER
(USA)
CRUVER Co.
a div. of WERNER Manf. Co.
Chicago
USA

CUNARMODEL
(ITALY)
CUNARMODEL
Via Leopardy 15
21035 Cunardo
ITALY

D & R
(USA)
D & R VACUFORM
P.O. Box 212
Anchorville, MI 48004
USA

DANBURY MINT
(ENGLAND)
DANBURY MINT
Cox Lane
Chessington, Surrey KT9 1SE
ENGLAND

DART CASTINGS

DAVRIC

DELTA
(ITALY)
DELTA
Bologna
ITALY

DENIZEN
(ENGLAND)
DENIZEN ROBENAU Ltd.
17/20 Sunbeam Road, Park Royal
London NW 10
ENGLAND

DESIGN CENTER
(USA)
DESIGN CENTER
New York, New York
USA

DM MODELS
(ENGLAND)
DM MODELS
45 Fife Street, Carr Hall
Barrowford, Lancs BB9 6DD
ENGLAND

DOYUSHA
(JAPAN)
JAPAN

DRAGON
(USA)
DRAGON MODELS WORKS
5721 Scotwood Road
Paradise, CA 95969
USA

DRAGON MPW
(USA)
DRAGON MODEL and
PATTERN WORKS
P.O. Box 55
Gray River, WA 98621
USA

E.B.B. (ENGLAND) — ENGLAND

E.D.H.

EAGLES TALON (USA)
The EAGLES TALON Inc.
P.O. Box 33875
Grenada Hills, California 91344
USA

EDISON (ITALY)
EDISON GIOCATTOLI S.p.A
50019 Sesto Fiorentino
ITALY

EIDAI (JAPAN)
EIDAI CORPORATION
1-37-7 Nishi-Onohisa
Arkawa-Ku, Tokyo
JAPAN

ELDON (USA)
ELDON INDUSTRIES Inc.
P.O. Box 1002
Hawtorne, California
USA

ENTEX (JAPAN)
ENTEX Corp.
15/19-20063 Cernusco sul Naviglio
Milano
ITALY

ESCI (ITALY)
ESCI MODELLISTICA s.n.c.
15/19-20063 Cernusco sul Naviglio
Milano
ITALY

ESOTERIC (ENGLAND)
ESOTERIC MODELS
Hangar 3a, Main Road,
East Hagbourne
Didcot, Oxon OX11 9LJ
ENGLAND

ESTES (USA)
ESTES INDUSTRIES
P.O. Box 227
Penrose, CO 81240
USA

EXECUFORM (USA)
EXECUFORM
721 N. Prospect Avenue
Redondo Beach,
California 90277
USA

EXECUTIVE (ENGLAND)
EXECUTIVE DISPLAY MODELS
Sheraton Skyline Hotel,
Bath Road
Hayes UB3 5BP
ENGLAND

FABULON (FRANCE)
FABULON,
Domaine des Grands Prés
6 rue des Nénuphars
78310 Elancourt
FRANCE

FAIRY (FRANCE)
FAIRY MODELS, c/o MOPICOM
104 Avenue Pierre Semard
95400 Villiers-le-Bel
FRANCE

FAIRY (USA)
FAIRY MODELS,
c/o DATESCAST
P.O. Box 691406
Houston, Texas 77269
USA

FALCON (NEW ZEALAND)
FALCON INDUSTRIES
P.O. Box 42-093
Wellington
NEW ZEALAND

FANAMODELE (FRANCE)
c/o LE FANA DE L'AVIATION
15-17 Quai de l'Oise
75019 Paris
FRANCE

FORMAPLANE (ENGLAND)
c/o MHW MODELS Ltd.
Concorde House,
46 Haworth Road
Crossroads, Keighley,
W. Y. BD22 9DL
ENGLAND

FOWLER (USA)
FOWLER AVIATION RESEARCH
P.O. Box 148, 21798 Bay Ave
Sunnymead, California 92388
USA

FRANK-MODELLBAU (WEST GERMANY)
FRANK-MODELLBAU
Obere Vorstadt 21
D-7470 Albstadt 1
WEST GERMANY

FRANKLIN (FRANCE)
LE MEDAILLER FRANKLIN
4 Avenue de l'Escouvrier
95200 Sarcelles
FRANCE

FROG (ENGLAND)
ROVEX Models and
HOBBIES Ltd.
Westwood
Margate, Kent CT9 4JX
ENGLAND

FROG PENGUIN (ENGLAND)
FROG PENGUIN Int.
Model Aircraft Ltd.
Morden Road, Merton
London S.W.19
ENGLAND

FUJIMI (JAPAN)
FUJIMI MOKEI Co. Ltd.
21-1 Toro 4-Chome
Shizuoka City
JAPAN

G.E.F. (ENGLAND)
G.E.F. MODELS
42 Belgrave Road, Newtake
Newton Abbott, Devon TQ12 4JP
ENGLAND

GAMES (ITALY)
GAMES
Viale Argonne N 54
20133 Milano
ITALY

GARRICK (ENGLAND)
GARRICK LEISURE
CONSULTANTS Ltd.
ENGLAND

GEE'S AERO WORKS (ENGLAND)
GEE'S AERO WORKS
2 Miller Street
Blackpool, S.S.
ENGLAND

GENERAL PRODUCTS
(JAPAN) JAPAN

GLASSLITE
(BRAZIL) BRAZIL

GORNIG

GRAMODEL
(ENGLAND)
GRAMODEL
116 Chaul End Road
Caddington, Beds LU1 4A5
ENGLAND

GRAPHY-AIR
(FRANCE)
GRAPHY-AIR
Route du Broustet
40190 Villeneuve de Marsan
FRANCE

GREENBANK CASTLE
(USA)
GREENBANK CASTLE Ltd.
P.O. Box 485
Coupeville, Washington 98239
USA

GRIFFIN
(USA)
c/o MAIL CALL MODELS
1525 W. Mac Arthur Blvd. 20
Costa Mesa, California 92626
USA

GRIP
(JAPAN) JAPAN

GRUMMAN
(USA)
GRUMMAN AEROSPACE CORP.
South Oyster Bay Road
Bethpage, New York 11714
USA

GUANO
(USA)
GUANO AEROPLANE AND
ZEPPELIN WORKS
5802 N.E. 59th Street
Seattle, Washington 98105
USA

GUILLOW
(USA)
Paul GUILLOW Inc.
Wakefield, Massachusetts 01880
USA

GUNZE SANGYO
(JAPAN)
GUNZE SANGYO Inc.
3-17 Kanda Nishiki-Cho
Chiyoda-Ku, Tokyo 101
JAPAN

H & S
(USA)
H & S MODELS
9546 Metro Street
Downey, California 90240
USA

H.D.H.
(USA) USA

HARRIER
(ENGLAND)
c/o CHOTA SAHIB
124 Springfield Road
Brighton BN1 6DE, Sussex
ENGLAND

HASEGAWA
(JAPAN)
HASEGAWA SEISAKUSHO
Co. Ltd.
1193-2 Yagusu, Yaizu
Shizuoka 425
JAPAN

HAUSSER
(WEST GERMANY) WEST GERMANY

HAWK
(USA)
HAWK MODEL Company
4600 North Olcott Avenue
Chicago, Illinois 60556
USA

HELLER
(FRANCE)
HUMBROL/BORDEN
Model Product Group
24 rue de Paradis
75010 Paris
FRANCE

HIGHWAY
(ENGLAND)
HIGHWAY MODELS
Astral House, Hutton Hill, Hutton
Weston-Super-Mare,
Avon BS24 95X
ENGLAND

HINCHLIFFE
(ENGLAND)
HINCHLIFFE MODELS Ltd.
Station Street, Meltham
Huddersfield HD7 3NX, Yorkshire
ENGLAND

HISPANO-AVIO-KIT
(SPAIN)
HISPANO-AVIO-KIT
Avda de Portugal
13 Móstoles, Madrid
SPAIN

HOBBY CRAFT
(CANADA)
c/o HOBBY HOUSE Ltd.
Dept. F89 Montreal Rd.
Vanier (Ottawa) Ontario, K1L 6EB
CANADA

HOBBY HEAVEN
(SWEDEN)
HOBBY HEAVEN
P.O. Box 19030
500 09 Borås
SWEDEN

HOBBYTIME
(USA)
Western Coil and Electric Co.
Toy Division
Racine, Wisconsin
USA

HOOKER

HUMA
(WEST GERMANY)
HUMA MODELL
Kilianstädter Strasse 9
D-645 Hanau 6
WEST GERMANY

I.D. MODELS
(ENGLAND)
c/o MHW MODELS Ltd.
Concorde House,
46 Haworth Road
Crossroads, Keighley,
W. Y. BD22 9DL
ENGLAND

I.M.C.
(THE NETHERLANDS)
c/o Amsterdam Airport Avia.
Mailorder
P.O. Box 7544
1118 ZG Schiphol-Centrum
THE NETHERLANDS

IKKO
(JAPAN)

IMAI (JAPAN)	IMAI KANKU Co. Ltd. Kuramae Building 1-1 3 Chome, Kuramae, Taito-Ku JAPAN
IMC (USA)	INDUSTRO-MOTIVE CORPORATION Troy, Michigan 48084 USA
IPMS FRANCE (FRANCE)	IPMS FRANCE 73 Rue Alexandre Dumas 78020 Paris FRANCE
IPMS UK (ENGLAND)	IPMS UK 3 Orchard, Close Lower Banbury, Brailles, Oxon OX1 55E ENGLAND
IPMS USA (USA)	IPMS USA P.O. Box 6369 Lincoln, NE 68506 USA
ISPA (ITALY)	ISPA MODELS Foglizzo, Torino ITALY
ITALERI (ITALY)	ITALERI S. p. A. Via Pradazzo 6 I-40012 Caldera di Reno, Bologna ITALY
ITALPLANES (ITALY)	c/o MODELMARKET Via Quintilio Varo N.15.19 00174 Roma ITALY
ITC (USA)	Ideal Toy Company 200 5th Avenue Hollis, New York USA
J & L (USA)	J & L MODELS P.O. Box 6004 Torrance, California 90504 USA
J.B. MODEL'S (ENGLAND)	J.B. MODEL'S 27 Hereward Way, Deeping St James Peterborough PE6 8OA ENGLAND
J.W. CLARKE (ENGLAND)	J.W. CLARKE 2 Burton Cross, Wool Wareham, Dorset ENGLAND
JACKLEX	
JO HAN (USA)	JO HAN MODELS Inc. 17255 Moran Avenue Detriot, Michigan 48212 USA
JOY (FRANCE)	JOY 21 Rue Roger Salengro 95470 Survilliers FRANCE
JOYSTICK (ENGLAND)	JOYSTICK MODELS 6 Cheltenham Road Blackburn, Lancs BB2 6HR ENGLAND
JRC (JAPAN)	Japan Resin Craft JAPAN
K. MODELS (JAPAN)	c/o SAITAMA HOBBY SHOP Kawamata Building, 5-10-1 Hachiôji Yono-Shi, Saitama-Ken JAPAN
KEIL KRAFT (ENGLAND)	KEIL KRAFT Ltd. Commerce Way Lancing, Sussex BN15 8TE ENGLAND
KOVOZAVODY (CZECHOSLOVAKIA)	KOVOZAVODY PROSTEJOV Volkerova 25 796 93 Prostejoy CZECHOSLOVAKIA
KPL MODELS (USA)	KPL MODELS 703 Cannon Road Silver Spring, Maryland 20904 USA
KPM (Boleslav) (CZECHOSLOVAKIA)	KLUB PLASTIKOVYCH MODELARU P.O. Box 77 29380 Mlada Boleslav CZECHOSLOVAKIA
KPM (Kodice) (CZECHOSLOVAKIA)	KLUB PLASTIKOVYCH MODELARU Prazska 19 04001 Kosice CZECHOSLOVAKIA
KPM (Praha) (CZECHOSLOVAKIA)	KLUB PLASTIKOVYCH MODELARU 12000 Praha CZECHOSLOVAKIA
KR (USA)	KR MODELS P.O. Box 5 Shelby, Ohio 44875 USA
L.S. (JAPAN)	L & S Ltd. 8-8 Nakano-Machi Honjyo, Gifu-City JAPAN
LAIRD (ENGLAND)	AEROPLAN 23 Logan Tower Cambuslang, Glasgow G72 8XA ENGLAND
LEAD SLED MODELS (ENGLAND)	LEAD SLED MODELS U.4, Tindle Centre, St Marychurch Rd Newton Abbot, Devon TQ12 4UQ ENGLAND

LEOMAN
(USA)
LEOMAN
P.O. Box 9840
Glendale, California 91206
USA

LFI
(USSR)

LIBRAMODELS
(ENGLAND)
LIBRAMODELS
P.O. Box 214
London SW17 8AP
ENGLAND

LILLIPUT
(ENGLAND)
ENGLAND

LINDBERG
(USA)
LINDBERG PRODUCTS Inc.
Skokie, Illinois 60075
USA

LONE STAR MODELS
(USA)
LONE STAR MODELS
1088 Comanche NE, #138
Albuquerque, NM 87111
USA

LVGD
(BELGIUM)
BELGIUM

M & E
(ENGLAND)
M & E MODELS
62 Periwinkle Close
Sittingbourne, Kent ME10 2JU
ENGLAND

M.A.F.
(FRANCE)
MAQUETTES AERIENNES FRANCAISES
7 Rue du Chemin de Fer
01100 Oyonnax
FRANCE

M.C.C.N.E.
(USSR)
Moskovskii Zavod Unyi Technik Moskva
4 Cyromjatnitheskii Per., 3/5
Moskva B-120
USSR

M.E.E.
(FRANCE)
La Maquette d'Etude et d'Exposition
9 Rue Quentin
93300 Aubervilliers
FRANCE

M.H.W.
(USA)
USA

MAC VAC CANOPY
(USA)
c/o MINIATURE AIRCRAFT
Box 26331
Indianapolis, Indiana 46226
USA

MACH
(FRANCE)
MACH
Rue des Girauds
Maillet 03190 Herisson
FRANCE

MAI
(USA)
MODEL-AIRE INTERNATIONAL
P.O. Box 159
Olema, California 94950
USA

MAINTRACK
(ENGLAND)
MAINTRACK MODELS
79 Queens Road
Hastings, East Sussex TN34 1RL
ENGLAND

MAIRCRAFT
(USA)
MAIRCRAFT
Chicago 18, Illinois
USA

MAJORETTE
(FRANCE)
MAJORETTE Administration Z.I.
69140 Rilleux
FRANCE

MALKA
(ISRAEL)
ISRAEL

MALVERN

MANIA
(JAPAN)
MIYANO & Co. Ltd.
2nd Floor, Asia Building
9-4 Kaminarimon, 1 Chome, Daito-ku
JAPAN

MARUSAN

MATCHBOX
(ENGLAND)
Lesney Products & Co. Ltd.
London E9 5PA
ENGLAND

MATH
(JAPAN)
MATH Modelling Project
#1108 3-49-1 Tanimachi
Higashi-Ku
Osaka 540
JAPAN

MAZ

MD
(FRANCE)
Maquettes DAUZIE
1 Rue des Martyrs de Chateaubriand
94490 Ormesson
FRANCE

MERIT
(ENGLAND)
J & L RANDALL Ltd.
Potters Bar
ENGLAND

MERLIN
(ENGLAND)
MERLIN MODELS
P.O. Box 5
Sturminster Newton,
Dorset DT10 1QW
ENGLAND

MHW
(ENGLAND)
MHW MODELS
Concorde House,
46 Haworth Road
Crossroads, Keighley,
W. Y. BD22 9DL
ENGLAND

MIAMI AIRPLANE
(USA)
MIAMI AIRPLANE MODELS
962 N.W. 106th Avenue Circle
Miami, Florida 33172
USA

MICRO SCALE
(USA)

MICRO SCALE MODEL KIT
KRASEL INDUSTRIES Inc.
Santa Ana, California 92705
USA

MICRO-WEST
(USA)

MICRO-WEST Inc.
955 N. Eckhoff Street
Orange, California 92667
USA

MIDORI
(USA)

MIDORI-KSN
USA

MIKRO
(POLAND)

MIKRO Zaklady Tworzyw
Sztucznych Pl.
Spoldzielnia Pracy-Pruskow
UL. Parkowa 1
POLAND

MILITMEN
(USA)

MINICRAFT/HASEGAWA
1510W 228th Street
Torrance, California 90501
USA

MINICRAFT
(USA)

MINICRAFT Models Inc.
P.O. Box 3577
Torrance, California 905010
USA

MINIPLAST
(POLAND)

MINIPLAST
67-100 Nowa S61
UL. Nowotki 19 B/2
POLAND

MIYAUCHI
(JAPAN)

JAPAN

MODAKIT
(ENGLAND)

MODAKIT
13 Larchfiels Way
Hordean, Hants PO8 9HE
ENGLAND

MODEL MASTER
(AUSTRALIA)

MODEL MASTER
18 William Street
Mount Waverley, Victoria, 3149
AUSTRALIA

MODEL TECHNOLOGIES
(USA)

MODEL TECHNOLOGIES
2761 Saturn, Unit E
Brea, CA 92621
USA

MODELAIR
(CANADA)

MODELAIR
Suite 204, 6205 Airport Road
Mississauga, Ontario L4V IE3
CANADA

MODELMARKET

MODELMASTERS
(ENGLAND)

MODELMASTERS
5 Winchester Street
Overton, Hampshire RG25 3HR
ENGLAND

MODELPOINT
(WEST GERMANY)

MODELPOINT
Meisenstrasse 4
8500 Nurenberg 70
WEST GERMANY

MONOGRAM
(USA)

MONOGRAM MODELS Inc.
8601 Waukegan Road
Morton Grove, Illinois 60053
USA

MPC
(USA)

MODEL PRODUCT
CORPORATION
126 Groesbeck Highway
Mount Clemens, Michigan 48043
USA

NAKAMURA
(JAPAN)

JAPAN

NEW HOPE DESIGN
(ENGLAND)

NEW HOPE DESIGN
Tynwald Mill
St John's, Isle of Man
ENGLAND

NEW-MAQUETTES
(FRANCE)

NEW-MAQUETTES
Paris
FRANCE

NEWARK
(ENGLAND)

NEWARK MODEL CLUB
Manor Farm Cottage,
Pinfold Lane
Averham, Newark,
Notts NG23 5RD
ENGLAND

NICHIMO
(JAPAN)

JAPAN

NITTO
(JAPAN)

NITTO
24-30 Chuo 3 Chome
Edogawaku
JAPAN

NORTH CENTRAL
(USA)

USA

NOVA MODELS
(USA)

NOVA MODELS
P.O. Box 9809
Fountain Valley, California 92728
USA

NOVO
(ENGLAND)

NOVO TOYS LTD.
Maxey, Nr. Peterborough
PE6 9HQ
ENGLAND

NOVOEXPORT
(USSR)

V/O NOVOEXPORT
Moscow 103287
Bashilovskaya 19
USSR

O'NEILL
(USA)

O'NEILL
1515 Sycamore Avenue
N. Merrick, New York 11566
USA

O.D.K.
(USA)

ODAKA MODELS Inc.
USA

OBR
(POLAND)

OSRODEK BADAWCZO-
ROZWOJOWY
UL. Wolczanska 27
90.607 Lodz
POLAND

OTAKI
(JAPAN)
OTAKI MODEL TOY
Mfg. Co. Ltd.
3-10 Senju, Midori-Cho
Adachi-Ku, Tokyo
JAPAN

P. WHELAN
(USA)
Paul WHELAN
Bloomfield, New Jersey
USA

P.M.S.
(TURKEY)
PLASTIK MODEL SANOYJ
133 Bakirköy
Istanbul
TURKEY

P.P. MODELS
(ENGLAND)
P.P. MODELS (HAMBROOK)
8 York Close, Stoke Gifford
Bristol BS12 6NU
ENGLAND

P.Z.W. SIEDLCE
(POLAND)
PODLASKIE ZAKLADY
WYTWORCZE
UL. Krasickiego 15
08-110 Siedlce
POLAND

PATHFINDERS
(IRELAND)
PATHFINDERS AEROCASTINGS
7 Park Avenue
Belfast
IRELAND

PEGASUS
(ENGLAND)
PEGASUS Models Dept SMI
Island Wall
Whitstable, Kent CT5 1EE
ENGLAND

PHOENIX
(ENGLAND)
PHOENIX
P.O. Box 214
London SW17 8AP
ENGLAND

PIAGGIO
(ITALY)
PIAGGIO
4 Via Cibriario
16154 Genoa
ITALY

PICCOLINO
(ENGLAND)
BELLINI MODELS Ltd.
Charwell House, Wilson Road
Alton, Hants. GU34 2TJ
ENGLAND

PILEN
(SPAIN)
PILEN sa.
SPAIN

PIONEER 2
(ENGLAND)
PIONEER 2
46 Haworth Road
Crossroads, Keighley BD22 9DL
ENGLAND

PIRATE
(ENGLAND)
PIRATE MODELS Ltd.
430 Hoe Street
London 417 9AA
ENGLAND

PLASTIQUES DERMATT
(FRANCE)
FRANCE

PLYCRAFT
(USA)
USA

POLISTIL
(ITALY)
POLISTIL S.p.A.
Via G. Chiostergi, 15
20153 Milano
ITALY

PREISER
(WEST GERMANY)
Paul M. PREISER KG
Kleinkunst-Werkstätter
Steinfeld bei Rothenburg O.T.
WEST GERMANY

PROJEKTS
(USA)
PROJEKTS MODEL Co.
17341 32nd Ave. S. D-118
Seattle, Washington 98188
USA

RACCOON
(JAPAN)
c/o HIKOSEN
68 Tamachi Taira Iwaki-shi
Fukushima-ken 970
JAPAN

RAISE-UP
(NETHERLAND)
RAISE-UP
Rotterdam
NETHERLAND

RAREPLANES
(ENGLAND)
RAREPLANES
69 Redstone Hill
Redhill, Surrey
ENGLAND

RED BARON
(USA)
c/o DATESCAST
P.O. Box 691406
Houston, Texas 77629
USA

RED STAR
(ENGLAND)
RED STAR Model Kits Ltd.
Beckenham, Kent
ENGLAND

REDUCTA
(FRANCE)
REDUCTA
46 Allée du Butard
92420 Vaucresson
FRANCE

REKNOWN
(ENGLAND)
PHOENIX MODEL
DEVELOPMENTS Ltd.
The Square, Earls Barton,
Northants
ENGLAND

RENWAL
(USA)
RENWAL PRODUCTS Inc.
1 Newbold Road
Fairless Hill, PA 19030
USA

REPLICA
(FRANCE)
REPLICA
3 Rue de l'Asile Popincourt
75011 Paris
FRANCE

REVELL (GB)
(ENGLAND)
REVELL Inc.
Cranborne Road, Potters Bar
Herts. EN6 3JX
ENGLAND

REVELL (GERMANY)
(WEST GERMANY)
REVELL Inc.
Postfach 2609
D-4980 Bünde I
WEST GERMANY

REVELL (USA)
(USA)
REVELL Inc.
4223 Glencoe Avenue
Venice, California 90291
USA

RICK'S
(USA)
RICK'S MODELS
8377 East State Route 571
New Carlisle, Ohio 45344-9633
USA

ROSEPLANE
(USA)
ROSEPLANE
P.O. Box 139, Trexler Mall
Trexlertown, PA 18087
USA

RUCH
(POLAND)
ZAKLADY PRZEMYSLOWE
"RUCH"
UL. Kobylka K. Warszawy,
Napoleona 7
Powiat Wolomin
POLAND

RUDEL
(FRANCE)
RUDEL
25 Rue Edgard Quinet
93120 La Courneuve
FRANCE

RVF
(USA)
RVF
P.O. Box 107
Burbank, CA 91503
USA

S.F.M.A.
(USA)
S.F.M.A.
P.O. Box 1838
Springfield, Massachusetts 01101
USA

SA
(JAPAN)
c/o HOBBY CENTER ENDO
1-59-8, Sasazuka
Shibuya-ku, Tokyo
JAPAN

SABRE
(ENGLAND)
ENGLAND

SANWA
(JAPAN)
JAPAN

SCALECRAFT
(ENGLAND)
Thames Toy Ltd.
Shad Thames
London, S.E. 1
ENGLAND

SCALEPLANES
(ENGLAND)
SCALEPLANES
P.O. Box 214
London SW17 8AP
ENGLAND

SCANKIT
(DENMARK)
SCANKIT
5270 Odense N.
DENMARK

SDELAND
(USSR)
SDELAND
USSR

SETCO
(USA)
c/o ALL NATION HOBBY SHOP
Chicago
USA

SKYBIRDS
(ENGLAND)
SKYBIRDS
3 Aldermanbury Avenue
London E.C.2
ENGLAND

SKYBIRDS 86
(ENGLAND)
SKYBIRDS 86
Orchard House, Chetnole
Sherborne, Dorset DT9 6PE
ENGLAND

SKYLAND MODELS
(THE NETHERLANDS)
c/o Amsterdam Airport Avia.
Mailorder
P.O. Box 7544
1118 ZG Schiphol-Centrum
THE NETHERLANDS

SMDC
(USA)
SCALE MODEL DEVELOPMENT
COMPANY
7708 Nightingale Dr.
Godfrey, Illinois 62035
USA

SPECIALTRYCK
(SWEDEN)
SPECIALTRYCK
CARTONGMODELL
Gustavsbergsgatan 8
S 431 37 Molndal
SWEDEN

STARFIX
(ISRAEL)
Starplast industries Ltd.
Industrial Area Migdal Haemek
P.O. Box 91
ISRAEL

STARLUX
(FRANCE)
STARLUX
24000 Périgueux
FRANCE

STEINGRAEBER
(WEST GERMANY)
STEINGRAEBER-Holz-
Modellbaukasten
WEST GERMANY

STROMBECKER
(USA)
STROMBECK-BECKER Mfg. Co.
51st and 4th Avenue
Moline, Illinois 61265
USA

SUPERMODEL
(ITALY)
ITALY

SUTCLIFFE
(ENGLAND)
Cf. CONTRAIL
ENGLAND

T.W.R.
(ENGLAND)
T.W.R. Models
8 The Acre
Windsor, Berks
ENGLAND

TAI
(FRANCE)
TAI
23 Rue de la Paix
Paris
FRANCE

TAIMEI
(JAPAN) JAPAN

TAKARA
(JAPAN) JAPAN

TAMIYA TAMIYA MOKEI
(JAPAN) Plastic Models Co.
915 Oshika, Shizuoka-Shi
JAPAN

TANDAIR TANDAIR MODELS
(ENGLAND) 6 Church Road
Spratton, Northampton NN6 8HR
ENGLAND

TAYLORCRAFT

TCHAIKA

TEE PEE TEE PEE MARKETING Dept ICA
(USA) 3941 Blackthorn Street
Irvine, California 92714
USA

TEE-JAY TEE-JAY MODELS
(ENGLAND) 46/48 Lavender Hill, Battersea
London SW11 5RH
ENGLAND

TESTOR (CANADA) The TESTOR Corporation
(CANADA) 206 Milvan Drive
Weston, Ontario M9L I29
CANADA

TESTOR (USA) The TESTOR Corporation
(USA) 620 Buckbee Street
Rockford, Illinois 61108
USA

TOHO TOHO MOKEI Co. Ltd.
(JAPAN) JAPAN

TOMIYAMA
(JAPAN) JAPAN

TOMY TOMY Corp.
(USA) 901 E. 233rd Street
Carson, California 90749
USA

TOPPING TOPPING Desk Top Models
(USA) 132 Mackinaw
Akron, Ohio 44313
USA

TRANSPORT REPLICAS TRANSPORT REPLICAS

TRUCKER'S MATE TRUCKER'S MATE
(SWEDEN) Mariebergsrägen 33
61100 Nyköping
SWEDEN

TSUKUDA TSUKUDA
(JAPAN) 3-1-3 Moto Asakusa
Daitô-Ku, Tokyo
JAPAN

TWELVE SQUARED TWELVE SQUARED
(USA) P.O. Box 21-567
Eagan, MN 55121
USA

UDC
(HONG-KONG) HONG-KONG

UNIKIT RES PLASTIC S.p.A.
(ITALY) Corsico, Milano
ITALY

UNIQUE FORM
(USA) USA

UNIQUE SCALE UNIQUE SCALE ACCESSORIES
(USA) Springfield, Massachusetts
USA

VACU-SPECIAL
(WEST GERMANY) WEST GERMANY

VAMI VAMI MODELS
(BELGIUM) 33 Ave du Manoir
1410 Waterloo
BELGIUM

VARNEY
(USA) USA

VEB PLASTICART VEB PLASTICART
(EAST GERMANY) August-Bebel Strasse 2
936 Zschopau
EAST GERMANY

VEEDAY VEEDAY MODELS
(IRELAND) P.O. Box 8
Birr, County Offaley
IRELAND

VERKUYL c/o Amsterdam Airport Avia.
(THE NETHERLANDS) Mailorder
P.O. Box 7544
1118 ZG Schiphol-Centrum
THE NETHERLANDS

VERLINDEN VERLINDEN PRODUCTIONS
(BELGIUM) Berlaarsestraat 36
2500 Lier
BELGIUM

VERNON
(ENGLAND) ENGLAND

VETROMEDELLI c/o Penzani Giuseppe
(ITALY) Via Brescia, 102
26100 Cremona
ITALY

VICTOR SIXTY-SIX VICTOR SIXTY-SIX
(USA) P.O. Box 66, 8541 De Vos Drive
Santee, California 92071
USA

VP CANADA (CANADA)	VICTORIA PRODUCTS 930 Foul Bay Road Victoria, British Columbia V8S 4H8 CANADA
W & T (ENGLAND)	ENGLAND
WAKU (POLAND)	WAKU Zabawkarskich w Kielcach 90-607 Lódz UL. Wólczanska 27 POLAND
WALDRON (USA)	WALDRON MODEL PRODUCTS 1358 Stephen Way San Jose, California 95129 USA
WAR EAGLE (USA)	WAR EAGLE P.O. Box 225 Dept. FSM New Baltimore, MI 48047 USA
WATERCRAFT (ENGLAND)	WATERCRAFT MODEL KITS 61 High Street Teddington, Middlesex ENGLAND
WESTERN (ENGLAND)	WESTERN MODELS Ltd. (METALKIT) Morris Road, South Nutfield Redhill, Surrey ENGLAND
WESTWAY (ENGLAND)	ENGLAND
WHITE EAGLE (USA)	WHITE EAGLE P.O. Box 1834 Dearborn, Michigan 48121 USA
WILLIAMS BROTHERS (USA)	WILLIAMS BROTHERS 181 Pawnee Street San Marcos, California 92069 USA
WINGS 72 (USA)	WINGS 72 Inc. 3349 Wildridge Dr. N.E. Grand Rapids, Michigan 49505 USA
WK (WEST GERMANY)	WK MODELS Werner KILLERSREITER Dorfstrasse 29 D-8050 Freising-Attaching WEST GERMANY
WOODCRAFT (ENGLAND)	WOODCRAFT Back Greenwell Street Darlington, Co. Durham DL1 5DJ ENGLAND
WOODLAND SCENICS (USA)	WOODLAND SCENICS P.O. Box 98 Linn Creek, Missouri 65052 USA
Y.M.C. (JAPAN)	JAPAN
YODEL (JAPAN)	JAPAN
ZA (JAPAN)	JAPAN
ZABAWKARSTWO (POLAND)	ZABAWKARSTWO Marek Praszcyk Wroclaw, UL. Rózana 17/2 POLAND

LIST OF MODELS

The list of models includes the following chapters:
— **Aircraft:** all the manned aircraft designed primarily to fly in the atmosphere. The mock-ups of projects that did not come to a head are also included.
— **Missiles** and **Spacecraft:** that includes rockets, guided or otherwise, ballistic missiles and winged missiles of all types and categories, as well as manned and unmanned spacecraft designed for missions in outer space.
— **Science-Fiction:** all imagined types that only exist in literature, the cinema, TV and models.
— **Vehicles:** civilian and military vehicles, motorised or not, and designed to move on the ground.
— **Artillery:** guns and large calibre cannons.
— **Accessories:** objects, accessories and equipment to complete a model or a diorama.
— **Model Figures:** all representations of human beings through the ages.
— **Dioramas:** sets supplied with stands, model figures, and the various craft and accessories necessary for the depiction of a scene.
— **Ships:** sailing craft, ships, submarines and hovercraft.
The models we listed are of all sorts: recognition models, display models, hobby kits, ready-assembled toy models and conversion kits.
Each one is described in the following order:
— NAME of the MANUFACTURER of the REAL SUBJECT: the manufacturers of the same type can take up various names, so we often settled for the name of the first manufacturer. In the case of certain items of military equipment, the name can be unknown or the type can be produced by several manufacturers, so the country of origin is quoted.
— NAME, TYPE and DESIGNATION of the SUBJECT: the various versions indicated correspond to what one can actually build, and not necessarily to what the manufacturer states on the boxtop.
— TRADEMARK of the MANUFACTURER of the ORIGINAL MOULD: when the production of the mould originates from a PRIVATE VENTURE, i.e., from an individual or group of persons, it is listed as such. PRIVATE VENTURES A, B, C, X, Y, Z refer to different sources in Eastern Bloc countries, mainly in Czechoslovakia. For personal reasons, these manufacturers want to stay anonymous. Many of the kits produced are available through the most famous hobby shops. They are also obtainable through IPMS channels or can be swapped with modellers having Eastern correspondents.

1 AIRCRAFT REFERENCE PUBLICATIONS

1.1 GENERAL
ENCYCLOPEDIE DE L'AVIATION (ORBIS in GB, ATLAS in FRANCE)
1.2 GERMAN AIRCRAFT
WARPLANES OF THE THIRD REICH (William GREEN)
1.3 JAPANESE AIRCRAFT
JAPANESE AIRCRAFT OF THE PACIFIC WAR (René FRANCILLON)
1.4 SOVIET AIRCRAFT
AIRCRAFT OF THE SOVIET UNION (Bill GUNSTON)
1.5 Complementary documentation
COMBAT AIRCRAFT OF THE WORLD (John W. R. TAYLOR) AIR INTERNATIONAL

2 ABBREVIATIONS and TERMS

"c." : canopy **"m."** : missile **"p."** : parts
"v." : version **"cf."** : confer (example : cf. SARO)
"ex-" : former identification (example : FOKKER D VIII, ex-E V)
"id." : identical (example : id. CIERVA)
"+" : with additional model (example : + Reichenberg)
"w." : with equipment (example : w. INJ parts)

C : CATEGORY

H HOBBY
D DISPLAY (or DESK)
R RECOGNITION
T TOY

MAT : MATERIAL

INJ Injected Plastic
VAC Vacuformed Plastic
RSN Resin

ML Metal
EB Photo Etched Brass
WD Wood
FG Fibre-Glass
FM Solid Foam
HR Hard Rubber
CB Cardboard

XT : EXTRA FEATURES

AS Assembled
CV Conversion kit, to modify an existing model
MT Motorised
RM Remoulded model, originating from a modified older mould
SN Snap-fit model
WK Working, mobile or transformable model.

SC : SCALE (between 1/66 and 1/78)

3 AIRCRAFT MANUFACTURER

AERITALIA : cf. also FIAT
AEROSPATIALE : cf. also WESTLAND
AGUSTA : cf. also BELL
ANTONOV : cf. also PETLYAKOV
AUSTER : cf. also BEAGLE
BAC : cf. also SEPECAT, HUNTING
BAe : cf. BRITISH AEROSPACE (HS)
BEAGLE : cf. also AUSTER
BELL : cf. also AGUSTA-BELL
BERG : cf. AVIATIK
BOEING-VERTOL : cf. also KAWASAKI
BOLKÖV : cf. also MBB
BRISTOL : cf. also WESTLAND
BRITISH : designation "Mk" may be replaced with "."
("Beaufighter TF Mk X" and "Beaufighter TF.X" are equivalent)
BRITISH AEROSPACE : cf. also HAWK, HAWKER-SIDDELEY
CHANCE VOUGHT : cf. also VOUGHT or LING-TEMCO-VOUGHT (LTV)
CIERVA : cf. also LIORE-ET-OLIVIER
CURTISS : cf. also CURTISS-WRIGHT
DOUGLAS : cf. also McDONNELL DOUGLAS
ENGLISH ELECTRIC : cf. also BAC
FIAT : cf. also AERITALIA
FOUGA : cf. also AEROSPATIALE
GENERAL AVIATION : cf. also FOKKER
GOTHA : cf. also HORTEN
HAWKER-SIDDELEY : cf. also AVRO, BRITISH AEROSPACE
I.Ae : cf. FMA
JAPANESE Example : MITSUBISHI A6M2 Reisen (Zero Fighter).
"Zero Fighter" is the translation of Reisen. Allied code name (Zeke) is mentioned as a comment.
KAWASAKI : cf. also BOEING-VERTOL
KLEMM : cf. also BOLKÖV
LE PERE : cf. PACKARD-LE PERE
LING-TEMCO-VOUGHT (LTV) : cf. also VOUGHT or CHANCE VOUGHT
MBB : MESSERSCHMITT-BÖLKOV-BLOHM
MERIDIONALI : cf. also IMAM
MESSERSCHMITT-BOLKÖV-BLOHM : cf. MBB
McDONNELL : cf. also McDONNELL DOUGLAS
PETLYAKOV : cf. also ANTONOV
REPUBLIC : cf. also SEVERSKY
ROLAND : cf. LFG ROLAND
SAUNDERS-ROE : cf. SARO
SCOTTISH AVIATION : cf. also BRITISH AEROSPACE
SIKORSKY : cf. also WESTLAND
SNCASE : cf. SUD-EST
SNCASO : cf. SUD-OUEST
SOVIET : NATO codes are mentioned between ()
VOUGHT : cf. also CHANCE VOUGHT, LING-TEMCO-VOUGHT (LTV)
WESTLAND : cf. also AEROSPATIALE, BRISTOL, SIKORSKY

At the time of publication, the list was as accurate as was possible, but a work of such scope inevitably contains errors. If you can supply concrete proof of an omission or an error, we should be grateful if you could write to one of the following addresses:

HUYNH-DINH Khuong
Domaine des Grands Prés
6 rue des Nénuphars
78310 Elancourt
FRANCE

Thomas A. YOUNG
MODEL-AIRE INTERNATIONAL
P.O. Box 159
Olema, California 94950
USA

Claude M. BOILEAU
c/o Editions Arthaud
20 rue Monsieur-le-Prince
75006 Paris
FRANCE

Our list is to be updated for a later edition.

LIST OF AIRCRAFT

ABRAMS	PC-4 Explorer	EXECUFORM	H VAC	72		1
ADER	Eole	BRIFAUT	H INJ	70		2
AEG	C.IV	FORMAPLANE	H VAC	72		3
AEG	G.IV	CLASSIC PLANE	H VAC	72		4
AEG	G.IV	CRAMER	H VAC	72		5
AERITALIA	G-91	SETCO	R HR·	72		6
AERITALIA	G-91R	ABORN	H VAC	72	canopy	7
AERITALIA	G-91PAN	COMA	H INJ	72		8
AERITALIA	G-91R-1	AIRFIX	H INJ	72		9
AERITALIA	G-91T	AIRMODEL	H VAC CV	72	canopy, + Mirage + Jaguar	10
AERITALIA	G-91Y	MATCHBOX	H INJ	72		11
AERITALIA	G-222	CHALLENGE	H VAC	72		12
AERITALIA/AERMACCHI/EMB	AMX	VETROMODELLI	H FG·	72		13
AERMACCHI	MB-326	CHALLENGE	H VAC	72		14
AERMACCHI	MB-326B/E/G/L	CUNARMODEL	H INJ	72	GB = AT-26 EMBRAER Xavante	15
AERMACCHI	MB-326K (ATLAS Impala Mk.2)	CUNARMODEL	H INJ	72		16
AERMACCHI	MB-339	CHALLENGE	H VAC	72		17
AERMACCHI	MB-339	VETROMODELLI	H FG·	72		18
AERMACCHI	MB-339K Veltro II	CUNARMODEL	H INJ	72		19
AERO	A.300	KPM	H VAC	72		20
AERO	A.300	VP CANADA	H VAC	72		21
AERO	L.29 Delfin	KOVOZAVODY	H INJ	72		22
AERO	L.39 Albatros	KOVOZAVODY	H INJ	72		23
AERO	L.39 Albatros	PRIVATE VENTURE A	H RSN	72		24
AERO	MB.200	KOVOZAVODY	H INJ	72		25
AERO COMMANDER	Jet Commander	AURORA	H INJ	72		26
AERO SPACELINES	Super Guppy 201	WHITE EAGLE	H VAC	72		27
AERONCA	100	SKYBIRDS	H ML·	72	JAP engine	28
AEROSPATIALE	AS 332 Super Puma	HELLER BOBKIT	H INJ	72	Army version	29
AEROSPATIALE	AS 332F Super Puma	HELLER BOBKIT	H INJ	72	w. Exocet missile	30
AEROSPATIALE	AS 332L Super Puma	HELLER BOBKIT	H INJ	72		31
AEROSPATIALE	SA 316B/319B Alouette III	HELLER	H INJ	72		32
AEROSPATIALE	SA 330B/E Puma	AIRFIX	H INJ	72		33
AEROSPATIALE	SA 341 Gazelle	AIRFIX	H INJ	72		34
AEROSPATIALE	SA 341 Gazelle	MAJORETTE	T ML·	72		35
AEROSPATIALE	SA 365N Dauphin 2	MATCHBOX	H INJ	72		36
AEROSPATIALE	SE 313B Alouette II	MD	H RSN	72	w. EB parts	37
AEROSPATIALE (FOUGA)	CM.170 Magister	AIRFIX	H INJ	72		38
AEROSPATIALE (FOUGA)	CM.170 Magister	AIRMODEL	H VAC	72		39
AEROSPATIALE (FOUGA)	CM.170 Magister	HELLER	H INJ	72		40
AEROSPATIALE (FOUGA)	CM.170 Magister	O'NEILL	H VAC	72		41
AEROSPATIALE (FOUGA)	CM.170 Magister	T.W.R.	H VAC	72		42
AEROSPATIALE (NORD)	N.262C/D Frégate	REDUCTA	D INJ	75		43
AEROSPATIALE-BAe	Concorde	EXECUTIVE	D —	72		44
AEROSPATIALE-BAe	Concorde	MODELMASTERS	D —	72		45
AEROSPATIALE-BAe	Concorde	SKYLAND MODELS	D FG·	72		46
AGUSTA	A.109	VETROMODELLI	H FG·	72		47
AGUSTA-BELL	AB.205	ESCI	H INJ	72		48
AGUSTA-BELL	AB.212ASW	FUJIMI	H INJ	72		49
AICHI	B7A1 Ryusei (Shooting Star)	FUJIMI	H INJ	72	Grace	50
AICHI	B7A1 Ryusei (prototype)	FUJIMI	H INJ	72	Grace	51
AICHI	B7A2 Ryusei (Shooting Star)	EAGLES TALON	H VAC	72	Grace	52
AICHI	B7A2 Ryusei-Kai	FUJIMI	H INJ	72	Grace	53
AICHI	B7A2 Ryusei (Shooting Star)	IKKO	H INJ	72	Grace	54
AICHI	B7A2 Ryusei (Shooting Star)	WINGS 72	H VAC	72	Grace	55
AICHI	D1A1/A2	O'NEILL	H VAC	72	Susie	56
AICHI	D3A1	AIRFIX	H INJ	72	Val	57
AICHI	D3A1	ARISTO CRAFT	H INJ	72	Val	58
AICHI	D3A1	COMET	H WD·	72	Val	59
AICHI	D3A1	CRUVER	R HR·	72	Val	60
AICHI	D3A1	FUJIMI	H INJ	72	Val	61
AICHI	D3A1	MAC VAC CANOPY	H VAC	72	Val	62
AICHI	D3A2	CRUVER	R HR·	72	Val	63
AICHI	D3A2	FUJIMI	H INJ	72	Val	64
AICHI	E11A	PRIVATE VENTURE	H RSN	72	Laura	65
AICHI	E11A1	O'NEILL	H VAC	72	Laura	66
AICHI	E13A1	CRUVER	R HR·	72	Jake	67

AICHI	E13A1	HASEGAWA	H INJ	72	Jake	68
AICHI	E13A1	HASEGAWA	H INJ	72	Jake, w. catapult	69
AICHI	H9A	O'NEILL	H VAC	72		70
AICHI	M6A1 Seiran (Mountain Haze)	AOSHIMA	H INJ	78		71
AICHI	M6A1 Seiran (Mountain Haze)	O'NEILL	H VAC	72		72
AICHI	M6A1 Seiran (Mountain Haze)	WINGS 72	H VAC	72	w. ML parts	73
AICHI	M6A1-K (South. Moutain)	WINGS 72	H VAC	72	w. ML parts, ex-Seiran Kai	74
AIRBUS INDUSTRIE	A300B Airbus	WESTWAY	D —	72		75
AIRBUS INDUSTRIE	A300B4 Airbus	MODELMASTERS	D —	72		76
AIRBUS INDUSTRIE	A310	SKYLAND MODELS	D FG·	72		77
AIRCO	DH.1 1910	TAIMEI	H INJ	72	DE HAVILLAND design	78
AIRCO	DH.2	REVELL	H INJ	72	DE HAVILLAND design	79
AIRCO	DH.4	AIRFIX	H INJ	72	DE HAVILLAND design	80
AIRCO	DH.4	CLASSIC PLANE	H VAC	72	DE HAVILLAND design	81
AIRCO	DH.4	SKYBIRDS	H WD·	72	DE HAVILLAND design	82
AIRCO	DH.5	CRAMER	H VAC	72	DE HAVILLAND design	83
AIRCO	DH.5	LIBRAMODELS	H VAC	72	DE design, w. ML parts	84
AIRCO	DH.5	MERLIN	H INJ	72	DH design, w. ML parts	85
AIRCO	DH.5	PRIVATE VENTURE	H RSN	72		86
AIRCO	DH.6	LAIRD	H VAC	72	DE HAVILLAND design	87
AIRCO	DH.9	CLASSIC PLANE	H VAC	72	DE HAVILLAND design	88
AIRCO	DH.9	REPLICA	H RSN	72	DE HAVILLAND design	89
AIRCO	DH.9A	CLASSIC PLANE	H VAC	72	DH design, w. INJ parts	90
AIRCO	DH.9A	MERLIN	H INJ	72	DH design, w. ML parts	91
AIRSPEED	AS.5 Courier	SKYBIRDS	H WD·	72		92
AIRSPEED	AS.6 Envoy	FROG PENGUIN	H INJ	72	military version	93
AIRSPEED	AS.6 Envoy	FROG PENGUIN	H INJ	72	civil version	94
AIRSPEED	AS.10 Oxford	PIONEER 2	H INJ	72		95
AIRSPEED	AS.10 Oxford	SKYBIRDS	H WD·	72		96
AIRSPEED	AS.10 Oxford Mk II	FROG	H INJ	72		97
AIRSPEED	AS.51/58 Horsa Mk I/II	CRUVER	R HR·	72		98
AIRSPEED	AS.51/58 Horsa Mk I/II	ITALERI	H INJ	72		99
AIRSPEED	AS.51/58 Horsa Mk I/II	SUTCLIFFE	H INJ	72		100
AIRSPEED	AS.57 Ambassador	EXECUTIVE	D —	72		101
AIRSPEED	AS.57 Ambassador	MODELMASTERS	D —	72		102
AIRSPEED	AS.57 Ambassador	SUTCLIFFE	H VAC	72		103
AIRSPEED	AS.65 Consul	PIONEER 2	H INJ	72		104
ALBATROS	B.II	FORMAPLANE	H VAC	72		105
ALBATROS	D.I/D.II	CLASSIC PLANE	H VAC	72		106
ALBATROS	D.II	CRAMER	H VAC CV	72		107
ALBATROS	D.III	ELDON	H INJ	72		108
ALBATROS	D.III	REVELL	H INJ	72		109
ALBATROS	D.III	SKYBIRDS	H WD·	72		110
ALBATROS	D.III (53.2 & 153 series)	BLUE RIDER	H VAC CV	72	w. ML parts	111
ALBATROS	D.III (253 series)	BLUE RIDER	H VAC CV	72	w. ML parts	112
ALBATROS	D.V	AIRFIX	H INJ	72		113
ALBATROS	D.V	RENWAL	H INJ	72		114
ALBATROS	D.XI	FORMAPLANE	H VAC	72		115
ALBATROS	D.XI	VEEDAY	H INJ	72	+ PFALZ D.III	116
ALBATROS	W.4	MERLIN	H INJ	72		117
AMES	AD.1	PRIVATE VENTURE B	H RSN	72		118
AMIOT	143	HELLER	H INJ	72		119
AMIOT	340	CHALLENGE	H VAC	72		120
AMIOT	351	CHALLENGE	H VAC	72		121
AMIOT	351	REPLICA	H RSN	72		122
AMIOT	351/354	O'NEILL	H VAC	72		123
AMIOT	351/354	RUDEL	H VAC	72		124
AMIOT	354	KPL MODELS	H VAC	72		125
AMIOT	354	REPLICA	H RSN	72		126
ANATRA	DS Anasal	FROG	H INJ	72		127
ANF LES MUREAUX	117	HELLER	H INJ	72		128
ANSALDO	A-1 Balilla	EDISON	H ML· AS	72	w. plastic parts	129
ANSALDO	SVA.5 Primo	AIRFRAME	H VAC	72		130
ANSALDO	SVA.5 Primo	J & L	H VAC	72		131
ANSALDO	Scout	FORMAPLANE	H VAC	72		132
ANTOINETTE	Monoplan 1908	BRIFAUT	H INJ	72		133
ANTOINETTE	Monoplan 1908	RENWAL	H INJ	72		134

ANTOINETTE	Monoplan 1908	TAIMEI	H INJ	72		135
ANTONOV	A-7 (RF-8)	AIRMODEL	H VAC	72	Red Front assault glider	136
ANTONOV	A-7 (RF-8)	PRIVATE VENTURE Y	H RSN	72	Red Front assault glider	137
ANTONOV	A-7 (RF-8)	WINGS 72	H VAC	72	Red Front assault glider	138
ANTONOV	An-2 (Colt)	AIRMODEL	H VAC	72	w. RSN parts	139
ANTONOV	An-2 (Colt)	O'NEILL	H VAC	72		140
ANTONOV	An-2 (Colt)	VEB PLASTICART	H INJ	75		141
ANTONOV	An-4 (Clod)	VEB PLASTICART	H INJ	72		142
ARADO	Ar 66c	PRIVATE VENTURE	H RSN	72		143
ARADO	Ar 68c (3rd prototype)	PRIVATE VENTURE A	H RSN	72		144
ARADO	Ar 68E	WINGS 72	H VAC	72		145
ARADO	Ar 68E/F	AIRMODEL	H VAC	72		146
ARADO	Ar 68E/F	PRIVATE VENTURE	H RSN	72		147
ARADO	Ar 76	AIRMODEL	H VAC	72	w. RSN parts	148
ARADO	Ar 76	PRIVATE VENTURE C	H RSN	72		149
ARADO	Ar 79	VACU-SPECIAL	H VAC	72		150
ARADO	Ar 95	VACU-SPECIAL	H VAC	72		151
ARADO	Ar 95L	PRIVATE VENTURE C	H RSN	72		152
ARADO	Ar 95W	PRIVATE VENTURE C	H RSN	72		153
ARADO	Ar 96B	AIRMODEL	H VAC	72	id. AVIA C.2B	154
ARADO	Ar 96B	KOVOZAVODY	H INJ	72	id. AVIA C.2B	155
ARADO	Ar 96B	PRIVATE VENTURE A	H RSN	72	id. AVIA C.2B	156
ARADO	Ar 96B-1/B-5	HELLER	H INJ	72	id. AVIA C.2B	157
ARADO	Ar 196	ARISTO CRAFT	H INJ	72		158
ARADO	Ar 196	CRUVER	R HR·	72		159
ARADO	Ar 196A	HELLER	H INJ	72		160
ARADO	Ar 196A-3	AIRFIX	H INJ	72		161
ARADO	Ar 197	AIRMODEL	H VAC	72	w. RSN parts	162
ARADO	Ar 197V3	PRIVATE VENTURE C	H RSN	72		163
ARADO	Ar 199	PRIVATE VENTURE C	H RSN	72		164
ARADO	Ar 199	VACU-SPECIAL	H VAC	72		165
ARADO	Ar 231	AIRFRAME	H VAC	72		166
ARADO	Ar 231	AIRMODEL	H VAC	72		167
ARADO	Ar 231	PRIVATE VENTURE B	H RSN	72		168
ARADO	Ar 232A/B	AIRMODEL	H VAC	72		169
ARADO	Ar 232B/C	AIRMODEL	H VAC	72		170
ARADO	Ar 234B Blitz	LINDBERG	H INJ	72		171
ARADO	Ar 234B Blitz	MAC VAC CANOPY	H VAC	72		172
ARADO	Ar 234B-2/C-2/C-3 Blitz	FROG	H INJ	72	w. Fi 103 (V-1)	173
ARADO	Ar 234C Blitz	AIRMODEL	H VAC CV	72	canopy, + Fi 103 + Fw 190	174
ARADO	Ar 240A	AIRMODEL	H VAC	72		175
ARADO	Ar 396A	AIRMODEL	H VAC	72		176
ARADO	Ar 396A	PRIVATE VENTURE B	H RSN	72		177
ARMSTRONG WHITWORTH	AW.15 Atalanta	SKYBIRDS	H WD·	72		178
ARMSTRONG WHITWORTH	AW.35 Scimitar	FROG PENGUIN	H INJ	72		179
ARMSTRONG WHITWORTH	AW.38 Whitley	ARISTO CRAFT	H INJ	72		180
ARMSTRONG WHITWORTH	AW.38 Whitley	CRUVER	R HR·	72		181
ARMSTRONG WHITWORTH	AW.38 Whitley	SUTCLIFFE	H VAC CV	72		182
ARMSTRONG WHITWORTH	AW.38 Whitley Mk II/III/IV/V	ELLIOTT	H VAC	72	w. ML parts	183
ARMSTRONG WHITWORTH	AW.38 Whitley Mk V/VII	FROG	H INJ	72		184
ARMSTRONG WHITWORTH	AW.41 Albemarle	CRUVER	R HR·	72		185
ARMSTRONG WHITWORTH	AW.41 Albemarle	SUTCLIFFE	H VAC	72		186
ARMSTRONG WHITWORTH	Argosy	EXECUTIVE	D FG·	72		187
ARMSTRONG WHITWORTH	Argosy 200	AVF	H VAC	72		188
ARMSTRONG WHITWORTH	Argosy 200	MODELMASTERS	D —	72		189
ARMSTRONG WHITWORTH	FK.8	ROSEPLANE	H VAC	72	Frederick KOOLHOVEN design	190
ARMSTRONG WHITWORTH	FK.10	FORMAPLANE	H VAC	72	Frederick KOOLHOVEN design	191
ARMSTRONG WHITWORTH	FK.10	PRIVATE VENTURE	H RSN	72	Frederick KOOLHOVEN design	192
ARMSTRONG WHITWORTH	FK.10	WINGS 72	H VAC	72	w. ML parts, F.K. design	193
ARMSTRONG WHITWORTH	Siskin IIIA	MATCHBOX	H INJ	72		194
ARMSTRONG WHITWORTH	Siskin	SKYBIRDS	H WD·	72		195
ARSENAL	10C.2	PRIVATE VENTURE B	H RSN	72		196
ARSENAL	VG-33	AIRMODEL	H VAC	72	w. RSN parts	197
ARSENAL	VG-33	KPL MODELS	H VAC	72		198
ARSENAL	VG-33	PRIVATE VENTURE	H RSN	72		199
ARSENAL	VG-33	RUDEL	H VAC	72		200
AUSTER	AOP.6	AIRFIX	H INJ	72	w. floats, skis	201

AUSTER	AOP.9	AEROCLUB MODELS	H VAC	72		202
AUSTER	AOP.9	HALLAM-VAC	H VAC	72	w. ML parts	203
AVIA	B.35	KOVOZAVODY	H INJ	72		204
AVIA	B.135	PRIVATE VENTURE Z	H RSN	72		205
AVIA	B.534	KOVOZAVODY	H INJ	72		206
AVIA	B.534	PRIVATE VENTURE C	H RSN CV	72		207
AVIA	B.634	KPM	H VAC	72		208
AVIA	B.634	VP CANADA	H VAC	72		209
AVIA	BH-3	KOVOZAVODY	H INJ	72		210
AVIA	BH-3	KPM	H VAC	72		211
AVIA	BH-9	KPM	H VAC	72		212
AVIA	BH-9	PRIVATE VENTURE	H RSN	72		213
AVIA	BH-9	VP CANADA	H VAC	72		214
AVIA	BH-21	BOLESLAV	H VAC	72		215
AVIA	BH-21	KOVOZAVODY	H INJ	72		216
AVIA	BH-21	KPM	H VAC	72		217
AVIA	BH-21	PRIVATE VENTURE A	H RSN	72		218
AVIA	BH-21	VP CANADA	H VAC	72		219
AVIA	CS.92	STAVEBRUCE	H INJ	72	Czechoslovak Me 262B	220
AVIA	CS.199	KOVOZAVODY	H INJ	72	Czechoslovak 2-seat Bf 109	221
AVIA	S.199	KOVOZAVODY	H INJ	72	Czechoslovak Bf 109	222
AVIATIK	B.II	FORMAPLANE	H VAC	72	w. ML parts	223
AVIATIK	B.II	JOYSTICK	H VAC	72		224
AVIATIK	C.I	CLASSIC PLANE	H VAC	72		225
AVIATIK (BERG)	D.I	AERO 72	H INJ	72		226
AVIATIK (BERG)	D.I	C.A. ATKINS	H ML·	72		227
AVIATIK (BERG)	D.I	CLASSIC PLANE	H VAC	72		228
AVIATIK (BERG)	D.I	EDISON	H ML· AS	72	w. plastic parts	229
AVIATIK (BERG)	D.I	PRIVATE VENTURE	H RSN	72		230
AVIATION TRADERS	ATL.98 Carvair	J & L	H VAC	72		231
AVIATION TRADERS	ATL.98 Carvair	MODELMASTERS	D —	72		232
AVRO	504	ATO	H WD·	72		233
AVRO	504K	AIRFIX	H INJ	72		234
AVRO	504K	FROG PENGUIN	H INJ	72		235
AVRO	707A/C	I.D. MODELS	H VAC	72		236
AVRO	Anson Mk II (652A)	AIRFIX	H INJ	72		237
AVRO	Anson C.19 (652A)	AIRMODEL	H VAC CV	72		238
AVRO	Lancaster (683)	ARISTO CRAFT	H INJ	72		239
AVRO	Lancaster (683)	CRUVER	R HR·	72		240
AVRO	Lancaster (683)	CRUVER	R HR·	72	post-War variant	241
AVRO	Lancaster (683)	SETCO	R HR·	72	post-War variant	242
AVRO	Lancaster I (683)	EXECUTIVE	D FG·	72	renamed B.I in 1942	243
AVRO	Lancaster B.I (683)	AIRFIX	H INJ	72		244
AVRO	Lancaster B.I (683)	FROG	H INJ	72		245
AVRO	Lancaster B.I (683)	REVELL	H INJ	72		246
AVRO	Lancaster B.I (683)	REVELL	H INJ RM	72	Dam Buster	247
AVRO	Lancaster B.I/III (683)	MATCHBOX	H INJ	72		248
AVRO	Lancaster B.II (683)	AEROCLUB MODELS	H VAC CV	72		249
AVRO	Lancaster B.II (683)	NEWARK	H RSN CV	72		250
AVRO	Lancaster B.III (683)	AIRFIX	H INJ RM	72		251
AVRO	Lancastrian (691)	DM MODELS	H RSN CV	72		252
AVRO	Lancastrian (691)	M & E	H INJ CV	72		253
AVRO	Lancastrian (691)	MODELMASTERS	D —	72		254
AVRO	Lancastrian (691)	SUTCLIFFE	H VAC CV	72	+ C-97	255
AVRO	Lincoln (694)	SUTCLIFFE	H VAC	72		256
AVRO	Manchester (679)	ARISTO CRAFT	H INJ	72		257
AVRO	Manchester (679)	CRUVER	R HR·	72		258
AVRO	Manchester (679)	SUTCLIFFE	H VAC CV	72		259
AVRO	Manchester (679)	SUTCLIFFE	H VAC	72		260
AVRO	Rota (671)	FROG PENGUIN	H INJ	72	CIERVA C.30A under licence	261
AVRO	Shackleton MR Mk 1 (696)	ELLIOTT	H VAC	72		262
AVRO	Shackleton MR Mk 2 (696)	ELLIOTT	H VAC	72		263
AVRO	Shackleton MR Mk 3 (696)	ELLIOTT	H VAC	72		264
AVRO	Shackleton MR Mk 3 (696)	FROG	H INJ	72		265
AVRO	Shackleton MR Mk 3 (696)	PIONEER 2	H —	72		266
AVRO	Shackleton AEW Mk 2 (696)	PIONEER 2	H —	72		267
AVRO	Triplane n°1	RENWAL	H INJ	72		268

AVRO	Tudor 1 (688)/ Tudor 4 (689)	SUTCLIFFE	H VAC	72		269
AVRO	Tutor (621)	ATO	H WD·	72		270
AVRO	Tutor (621)	PEGASUS	H INJ	72		271
AVRO	Tutor (621)	SKYBIRDS	H WD·	72		272
AVRO	Vulcan B Mk 1A (698)	NEWARK	H RSN CV	72		273
AVRO	Vulcan B Mk 2 (698)	AIRFIX	H INJ	72	w. Blue Steel missile	274
AVRO	Vulcan B Mk 2 (698)	FORMAPLANE	H VAC	72		275
AVRO	Vulcan B Mk 2 (698)	NOVA MODELS	H VAC	72	w. Skybolt, Blue Steel m.	276
AVRO	Vulcan B Mk 2 (698)	RAREPLANES	H VAC	72		277
AVRO	Vulcan K Mk 2 (698)	C. SCALE	H VAC CV	72		278
AVRO	Vulcan K Mk 2 (698)	HARRIER	H ML· CV	72		279
AVRO	York (685)	CRUVER	R HR·	72		280
AVRO	York (685)	EXECUTIVE	D FG·	72		281
AVRO	York (685)	MODELMASTERS	D —	72		282
AVRO	York (685)	SUTCLIFFE	H VAC CV	72		283
AVRO	York (685)	SUTCLIFFE	H VAC	72		284
AVRO CANADA	CF-100 Canuck	HOBBY CRAFT	H INJ	72		285
AVRO CANADA	CF-100 Mk 4 Canuck	AURORA	H INJ	70		286
AVRO CANADA	CF-100 Mk 4/5 Canuck	ALPHA	H VAC	72		287
AVRO CANADA	CF-100 Mk 4/5 Canuck	ASTRA	H VAC	72		288
AVRO CANADA	CF-105 Arrow	AURORA	H INJ	77		289
AVRO CANADA	CF-105 Arrow	HOBBY CRAFT	H INJ	71	some small parts ex-AURORA	290
AVRO CANADA	CF-105 Arrow	VICTOR SIXTY-SIX	H VAC	72		291
AVRO CANADA	CF-105 Arrow	VP CANADA	H VAC	72		292
AVRO CANADA	CF-105 Arrow Mk 1	ASTRA	H VAC	72		293
BAC	Canberra	CRUVER	R HR·	72		294
BAC	Canberra	I.D. MODELS	H VAC CV	72		295
BAC	Canberra B(I) Mk 6/B Mk 20	AIRFIX	H INJ	72		296
BAC	Canberra B(I) Mk 8/Mk 12	FROG	H INJ RM	72		297
BAC	Canberra B Mk 2	AIRFRAME	H VAC CV	72		298
BAC	Canberra B Mk 2/6	AEROCLUB MODELS	H VAC CV	72		299
BAC	Canberra PR Mk 7	FROG	H INJ	72		300
BAC	Canberra PR Mk 9	MATCHBOX	H INJ	72		301
BAC	Canberra T Mk 4/B Mk 6	AEROCLUB MODELS	H VAC CV	72		302
BAC	Canberra T Mk 17	C. SCALE	H ML· CV	72		303
BAC	Canberra TT Mk 18/T Mk 22	C. SCALE	H ML· CV	72		304
BAC	Jet Provost Mk 3	AIRFIX	H INJ	72	id. HUNTING (PERCIVAL)	305
BAC	Jet Provost T Mk 5	AIRMODEL	H VAC CV	72	canopy, + NF.14/T.7	306
BAC	One-Eleven	SKYLAND MODELS	D FG·	72		307
BAC	One-Eleven Series 200	EXECUTIVE	D FG·	72		308
BAC	One-Eleven Series 200	MODELMASTERS	D —	72		309
BAC	One-Eleven Series 400	EXECUTIVE	D —	72		310
BAC	One-Eleven Series 500	EXECUTIVE	D —	72		311
BAC	One-Eleven Series 500	MODELMASTERS	D —	72		312
BAC	TSR.2	SUTCLIFFE	H VAC	72		313
BAC	TSR.2	T.W.R.	H VAC	72		314
BAC	TSR.2	T.W.R.	H VAC RM	72		315
BAC (ENGLISH ELECTRIC)	Lightning F Mk 1A	AIRFIX	H INJ	72	w. Firestreak missile	316
BAC (ENGLISH ELECTRIC)	Lightning F Mk 1A	AIRFIX	H INJ SN	72		317
BAC (ENGLISH ELECTRIC)	Lightning F Mk 1/3	MAINTRACK	H RSN CV	72		318
BAC (ENGLISH ELECTRIC)	Lightning F Mk 2A/6	MATCHBOX	H INJ	72	w. Firestreak, Red Top m.	319
BAC (ENGLISH ELECTRIC)	Lightning F Mk 6	FROG	H INJ	72	w. Red Top missile	320
BAC (ENGLISH ELECTRIC)	Lightning F Mk 6	HASEGAWA	H INJ	72		321
BAC (ENGLISH ELECTRIC)	Lightning P.1A	FROG	H INJ	72		322
BAC (ENGLISH ELECTRIC)	Lightning P. 1B	SETCO	R HR·	72		323
BAC (ENGLISH ELECTRIC)	Lightning T Mk 4/5	AIRMODEL	H VAC CV	72	canopy, + Hunter T.7/T.8	324
BAC (ENGLISH ELECTRIC)	Lightning T Mk 4/54/5/55	TANDAIR MODELS	H VAC CV	72		325
BAC (ENGLISH ELECTRIC)	Lightning T Mk 55	MATCHBOX	H INJ RM	72	w. Firestreak, Red Top m.	326
BACHEM	Ba 349 Natter	AIRFRAME	H VAC	72		327
BACHEM	Ba 349 Natter	HELLER	H INJ	72	+ FIESELER Fi.103 Reich.IV	328
BACHEM	Ba 349 Natter	KPM	H VAC	72		329
BACHEM	Ba 349 Natter	PRIVATE VENTURE B	H RSN	72		330
BACHEM	Ba 349B Natter	AIRMODEL	H VAC	72		331
BACHEM	Ba 349B Natter	PRIVATE VENTURE C	H RSN RM	72		332
BAT	FK.23 Bantam	CRAMER	H VAC	72		333
BAT	FK.23 Bantam	LIBRAMODELS	H VAC	72	w. ML parts	334
BEAGLE	A.109 Airedale	AIRFRAME	H VAC	72	id. AUSTER Airedale	335

BEAGLE	B.206 Basset	AIRFIX	H INJ	72		336
BEDE	BD-5	299 MODELS	H INJ	72		337
BEDE	BD-5/BD-5J	299 MODELS	H INJ RM	72		338
BEDE	BD-5/BD-5J	L.S.	H INJ	72		339
BEECH	17 Staggerwing	PRIVATE VENTURE	H RSN	72		340
BEECH	D17 Staggerwing	RAREPLANES	H VAC	72		341
BEECH	D17 Staggerwing	RAREPLANES	H VAC RM	72		342
BEECH	18 (C-45) Expeditor	RAREPLANES	H VAC	72		343
BEECH	26 (AT-10) Wichita	O'NEILL	H VAC	72		344
BEECH	28 (XA-38) Grizzly	EXECUFORM	H VAC CV	72	id. Destroyer	345
BEECH	28 (XA-38) Grizzly	O'NEILL	H VAC	72	id. Destroyer	346
BEECH	S35 Bonanza	DINKY TOYS	T ML·AS	77		347
BEECH	36 Bonanza	EIDAI	H INJ	72		348
BEECH	45 (T-34A) Mentor	HASEGAWA	H INJ	72		349
BEECH	45 (T-34C) Turbo-Mentor	ASTRA	H VAC CV	72		350
BEECH	C55 Baron	DINKY TOYS	T ML· AS	72		351
BEECH	99 Airliner	EXECUTIVE	D FG·	72		352
BEECH	200 C-12A Huron (Super King Air)	RAREPLANES	H VAC	72	w. INJ parts	353
BELL	206 Jet Ranger	RAREPLANES	H VAC	72		354
BELL	476	PRIVATE VENTURE	H RSN	72		355
BELL	AH-1G Huey Cobra	COMMAND	H INJ	75		356
BELL	AH-1G Huey Cobra	MAC VAC CANOPY	H VAC	72		357
BELL	AH-1G Huey Cobra	MATCHBOX	H INJ	72		358
BELL	AH-1G Huey Cobra	MONOGRAM	H INJ	72		359
BELL	AH-1J Sea Cobra	FUJIMI	H INJ	72		360
BELL	AH-1S Huey Cobra	FUJIMI	H INJ	72	w. Tow missile	361
BELL	AH-1S Huey Cobra	FUJIMI	H INJ RM	72	w. Tow m., JGSDF version	362
BELL	AH-1W Super Cobra	ITALERI	H INJ	72		363
BELL	H-13J Sioux	AIRMODEL	H VAC	72	+ H-43B	364
BELL	L-39-2	PRIVATE VENTURE C	H RSN	72		365
BELL	OH-58D Kiowa	MATCHBOX	H INJ	72		366
BELL	P.39 Airacobra	ARISTO CRAFT	H INJ	72		367
BELL	P-39 Airacobra	CRUVER	R HR·	72		368
BELL	P-39D Airacobra	FROG	H INJ	72		369
BELL	P-39Q Airacobra	AIRFIX	H INJ	72		370
BELL	P-39Q Airacobra	MINIPLAST	H VAC	72		371
BELL	P-39Q Airacobra	REVELL	H INJ	72		372
BELL	P-39Q Airacobra	REVELL	H INJ RM	72	4-blade propeller version	373
BELL	P-39Q/N Airacobra	HELLER	H INJ	72		374
BELL	P-39A Airacomet	GEE'S AERO WORKS	H WD·	72		375
BELL	P-59A Airacomet	RAREPLANES	H VAC	72		376
BELL	P-63 Kingcobra	AOSHIMA	H INJ	72		377
BELL	P-63 Kingcobra	AOSHIMA	H INJ	70		378
BELL	P-63 Kingcobra	CRUVER	R HR·	72		379
BELL	P-63 Kingcobra	PRIVATE VENTURE	H RSN	72		380
BELL	P-63 Kingcobra	RUDEL	H VAC	72		381
BELL	P-63A/D Kingcobra	WINGS 72	H VAC	72	w. ML parts	382
BELL	UH-1B Iroquois	AIRMODEL	H VAC CV	72	+ HUP (UH-25)	383
BELL	UH-1B Iroquois	MONOGRAM	H INJ	73		384
BELL	UH-1B Iroquois	MONOGRAM	H INJ RM	73		385
BELL	UH-1D Iroquois	ESCI	H INJ	72		386
BELL	UH-1D Iroquois	HASEGAWA	H INJ	72		387
BELL	UH-1N Iroquois	FUJIMI	H INJ	72		388
BELL	XS-1	AIRVAC	H VAC	72		389
BELL	XS-1	RACCOON	H RSN	72		390
BELL	XS-1	SA	H RSN	72		391
BELL	X-1E	AIRVAC	H VAC	72		392
BELL	X-5	DRAGON	H VAC	72	+ NORTHROP X-4	393
BELL	XP-77	AIRFRAME	H VAC	72		394
BELL	XP-83	KR MODELS	H VAC	72		395
BELL	XF-109	KR MODELS	H VAC	72		396
BELL	XFL-Airabonita	ABORN	H VAC	72	canopy	397
BELL	XFM-1 Airacuda	RAREPLANES	H VAC	72		398
BELL	XV-3	EAGLES TALON	H VAC	72		399
BELL	XV-15	PRIVATE VENTURE	H RSN	72		400
BELLANCA	Cruisair	MAIRCRAFT	H WD·	72		401
BELLANCA	XC-27 Aircruiserr	EXECUFORM	H VAC	72		402

BEREZNYAK-ISAYEV	BI-1	AIRMODEL	H VAC	72		403
BEREZNYAK-ISAYEV	BI-1	KPM	H VAC	72		404
BEREZNYAK-ISAYEV	BI-1	PRIVATE VENTURE B	H RSN	72		405
BEREZNYAK-ISAYEV	BI-1	PRIVATE VENTURE B	H RSN RM	72		406
BERIEV	KOR-1 (Be-2)	AIRMODEL	H VAC	72		407
BERIEV	KOR-1 (Be-2)	KPM	H VAC	72		408
BERIEV	KOR-1 (Be-2)	VP CANADA	H VAC	72		409
BERIEV	KOR-2 (Be-4)	BOLESLAV	H VAC	72		410
BERIEV	KOR-2 (Be-4)	KPM	H VAC	72		411
BERIEV	KOR-2 (Be-4)	PRIVATE VENTURE C	H RSN	72		412
BERIEV	KOR-2 (Be-4)	WINGS 72	H VAC	72		413
BERIEV	Be-6 (Madge)	CRUVER	R HR·	72		414
BERIEV	Be-6 (Madge)	VEB PLASTICART	H INJ	72		415
BERIEV	MBR-2 (Mote)	FORMAPLANE	H VAC	72		416
BERIEV	MBR-2 (Mote)	O'NEILL	H VAC	72		417
BERLIN	B.9	PRIVATE VENTURE C	H RSN	72		418
BERLINER-JOYCE	OJ-2	ESOTERIC	H VAC	72	w. ML parts	419
BERLINER-JOYCE	OJ-2	O'NEILL	H VAC	72		420
BERLINER-JOYCE	PB-1	O'NEILL	H VAC	72		421
BERNARD	191 GR (Oiseau Canari)	MACH	H RSN	72		422
BLACKBURN	Airedale	AIRFRAME	H VAC	72		423
BLACKBURN	Baffin	SUTCLIFFE	H VAC	72		424
BLACKBURN	Beverley	SUTCLIFFE	H VAC	72		425
BLACKBURN	Blackburn	SUTCLIFFE	H VAC	72		426
BLACKBURN	Botha	CRUVER	R HR·	72		427
BLACKBURN	Botha	SUTCLIFFE	H VAC	72		428
BLACKBURN	Botha	SUTCLIFFE	H VAC RM	72		429
BLACKBURN	Buccaneer	AIRFIX	H INJ	72		430
BLACKBURN	Buccaneer	MAC VAC CANOPY	H VAC	72		431
BLACKBURN	Buccaneer	SETCO	R HR·	72		432
BLACKBURN	Buccaneer S Mk 1	MAINTRACK	H RSN CV	72		433
BLACKBURN	Buccaneer S Mk 2	IMPS UK	H VAC	72		434
BLACKBURN	Buccaneer S Mk 2B	FROG	H INJ	72	w. Martel missile	435
BLACKBURN	Buccaneer S Mk 2B	MATCHBOX	H INJ	72		436
BLACKBURN	Firebrand	AIRMODEL	H VAC	72		437
BLACKBURN	Firebrand	MAC VAC CANOPY	H VAC	72		438
BLACKBURN	Firebrand	PATHFINDERS	H ML·	72		439
BLACKBURN	Firebrand	RAREPLANES	H VAC	72		440
BLACKBURN	Firebrand	SUTCLIFFEE	H VAC	72		441
BLACKBURN	Iris	SUTCLIFFE	H VAC	72		442
BLACKBURN	Monoplane	SCALEPLANES	H VAC	72		443
BLACKBURN	Perth	SUTCLIFFE	H VAC	72		444
BLACKBURN	Ripon/Baffin	SUTCLIFFE	H VAC	72		445
BLACKBURN	Roc	CRUVER	R HR·	72		446
BLACKBURN	Seagrave	SKYBIRDS	H WD·	72		447
BLACKBURN	Shark	FROG PENGUIN	H INJ	72	w. floats	448
BLACKBURN	Shark	SKYBIRDS	H WD·	72		449
BLACKBURN	Shark Mk IV	FROG	H INJ	72	w. floats	450
BLACKBURN	Shark Mk IV	FROG PENGUIN	H INJ	72		451
BLACKBURN	Skua	ARISTO CRAFT	H INJ	72		452
BLACKBURN	Skua	CRUVER	R HR·	72		453
BLACKBURN	Skua	FROG	H INJ	72		454
BLACKBURN	Skua	FROG PENGUIN	H INJ	72		455
BLACKBURN	Skua	SKYBIRDS	H WD·	72		456
BLERIOT	XI	BRIFAUT	H INJ	72		457
BLERIOT	XI	FROG	H INJ	72		458
BLERIOT	XI	RENWAL	H INJ	72		459
BLOCH	MB.131	O'NEILL	H VAC	72		460
BLOCH	MB.152	HELLER	H INJ	72		461
BLOCH	MB.174	HELLER	H INJ	72		462
BLOCH	MB.200	O'NEILL	H VAC	72		463
BLOCH	MB.210	HELLER	H INJ	72		464
BLOCH	MB.220	O'NEILL	H VAC CV	72		465
BLOHM UND VOSS	BV 40	AIRMODEL	H VAC	72		466
BLOHM UND VOSS	BV 40	KPM	H VAC	72		467
BLOHM UND VOSS	BV 40 V2	PRIVATE VENTURE A	H RSN	72	w. RSN canopy	468
BLOHM UND VOSS	BV 40 V1	PRIVATE VENTURE B	H RSN	72		469

BLOHM UND VOSS	BV 138	ARISTO CRAFT	H INJ	72		470
BLOHM UND VOSS	BV 138	CRUVER	R HR·	72		471
BLOHM UND VOSS	BV 138B-1/C-1/MS	SUPERMODEL	H INJ	72		472
BLOHM UND VOSS	BV 141A	AIRFIX	H INJ	72		473
BLOHM UND VOSS	BV 151	AIRMODEL	H VAC	72		474
BLOHM UND VOSS	BV 155B	PRIVATE VENTURE B	H RSN	72		475
BLOHM UND VOSS	BV 155 V2	AIRMODEL	H VAC	72		476
BLOHM UND VOSS	BV 155 V2	WINGS 72	H VAC	72		477
BLOHM UND VOSS	BV 222 Viking	AIRMODEL	H VAC	72		478
BLOHM UND VOSS	BV 222 Viking	ARISTO CRAFT	H INJ	72		479
BLOHM UND VOSS	BV 222 Viking	CRUVER	R HR·	72		480
BLOHM UND VOSS	BV 238	AIRMODEL	H VAC	72		481
BLOHM UND VOSS	BV P212-03	AIRMODEL	H VAC	72		482
BLOHM UND VOSS	FGP 227	KPM	H VAC	72	¼ scale model of BV 238	483
BLOHM UND VOSS	FGP 227	PRIVATE VENTURE C	H RSN	72	¼ scale model of BV 238	484
BLOHM UND VOSS	FGP 227	WINGS 72	H VAC	72	¼ scale model of BV 238	485
BLOHM UND VOSS	Ha 137	WINGS 72	H VAC	72		486
BLOHM UND VOSS	Ha 137B	PRIVATE VENTURE C	H RSN	72		487
BLOHM UND VOSS	Ha 139	AIRFRAME	H VAC	72		488
BLOHM UND VOSS	Ha 139	ARISTO CRAFT	H INJ	72		489
BLOHM UND VOSS	Ha 139	CRUVER	R HR·	72		490
BLOHM UND VOSS	Ha 139 V3/U1	AIRMODEL	H VAC	72		491
BLOHM UND VOSS	Ha 142 V1/BV 142 V2	AIRMODEL	H VAC	72		492
BOEING	247	WILLIAMS BROTHERS	H INJ	72		493
BOEING	307 Stratoliner	AIRMODEL	H VAC CV	72		494
BOEING	307 Stratoliner	ATLANTIC MODELS	D INJ	72		495
BOEING	307 Stratoliner	O'NEILL	H VAC CV	72		496
BOEING	307 Stratoliner	SUTCLIFFE	H VAC	72		497
BOEING	314 Clipper	EXECUTIVE	D FG·	72		498
BOEING	314 Clipper	COMBAT MODEL	H VAC	72	w. ML parts	499
BOEING	314 Clipper	MODELMASTERS	D —	72		500
BOEING	314 Dixie Clipper	ATLANTIC MODELS	D FG·	72		501
BOEING	377 Stratocruiser	ATLANTIC MODELS	D FG·	72		502
BOEING	707	EXECUTIVE	D —	72		503
BOEING	707	SKYLAND MODELS	D FG·	72		504
BOEING	707	T.W.R.	H VAC	72		505
BOEING	707-320	AIRTEC	D FM·	72		506
BOEING	707-320	MODELMASTERS	D —	72		507
BOEING	707-320A	HELLER	H INJ	72		508
BOEING	707-320C	MODELMASTERS	D —	72		509
BOEING	720-720B	J & L	H VAC	72		510
BOEING	727-100	EXECUTIVE	D FG·	72		511
BOEING	727-100	MODELMASTERS	D —	72		512
BOEING	727-200	EXECUTIVE	D FG·	72		513
BOEING	727-200	MODELMASTERS	D —	72		514
BOEING	727-200	SKYLAND MODELS	D FG·	72		515
BOEING	727-200	WESTWAY	D —	72		516
BOEING	737-100	AURORA	H INJ	72		517
BOEING	737-200	EXECUTIVE	D FG·	72		518
BOEING	737-300	EXECUTIVE	D FG·	72		519
BOEING	747	EXECUTIVE	D —	72		520
BOEING	747	MODELMASTERS	D —	72		521
BOEING	747	T.W.R.	H VAC	72		522
BOEING	747-200	SKYLAND MODELS	D FG·	72		523
BOEING	757	EXECUTIVE	D FG·	72		524
BOEING	767	EXECUTIVE	D FG·	72		525
BOEING	767	SKYLAND MODELS	D FG·	72		526
BOEING	B-9	FORMAPLANE	H VAC	72		527
BOEING	B-9	O'NEILL	H VAC	72		528
BOEING	B-17 Flying Fortress	ARISTO CRAFT	H INJ	72		529
BOEING	B-17 Flying Fortress	COMPASS	H WD·	72		530
BOEING	B-17B Flying Fortress	STROMBECKER	H WD·	72		531
BOEING	B-17C/Flying Fortress	EXECUFORM	H VAC CV	72		532
BOEING	B-17C/D Flying Fortress	RAREPLANES	H VAC	72	+ Y1B-17	533
BOEING	B-17E Flying Fortress	CRUVER	R HR·	72		534
BOEING	B-17E Flying Fortress	FROG	H INJ	72		535
BOEING	B-17E Flying Fortress	REVELL	H INJ	72		536

BOEING	B-17E Flying Fortress	STROMBECKER	H WD·	72		537
BOEING	B-17E Flying Fortress	TESTOR	H WD·	72		538
BOEING	B-17F Flying Fortress	HASEGAWA	H INJ	72		539
BOEING	B-17F Flying Fortress	REVELL	H INJ	72		540
BOEING	B-17G Flying Fortress	AIRFIX	H INJ	72		541
BOEING	B-17G Flying Fortress	EXECUTIVE	D FG·	72		542
BOEING	B-17G Flying Fortress	HASEGAWA	H INJ	72		543
BOEING	B-17G Flying Fortress	MATCHBOX	H INJ	72		544
BOEING	B-17G Flying Fortress	STROMBECKER	H WD·	72		545
BOEING	SB-17/PB-1W Fortress	299 MODELS	H INJ CV	72		546
BOEING	Y1B-17 Flying Fortress	RAREPLANES	H VAC	72	+ B-17C/D	547
BOEING	B-29 Superfortress	ARISTO CRAFT	H INJ	72		548
BOEING	B-29 Superfortress	AURORA	H INJ	76		549
BOEING	B-29 Superfortress	CRUVER	R HR·	72		550
BOEING	B-29 Superfortress	STROMBECKER	H WD·	72		551
BOEING	B-29 Superfortress	TESTOR	H WD·	72		552
BOEING	B-29/40B Superfortress	AIRFIX	H INJ	72		553
BOEING	B-29A Superfortress	CRUVER	R HR·	72		554
BOEING	B-47E Stratojet	HASEGAWA	H INJ	72		555
BOEING	B-50D	AIRMODEL	H VAC CV	72		556
BOEING	B-50D	CRUVER	R HR·	72		557
BOEING	B-52D	MONOGRAM	H INJ	72		558
BOEING	NB-52B	MONOGRAM	H INJ RM	72	+ X-152A-2	559
BOEING	NB-52B	FRANK-MODELLBAU	H VAC CV	72	X-15 rack	560
BOEING	C-97 Stratocruiser	CRUVER	R HR·	72		561
BOEING	C-97 Stratocruiser	EXECUTIVE	D —	72		562
BOEING	C-97 Stratocruiser	MODELMASTERS	D —	72		563
BOEING	C-97 Stratofreighter	SUTCLIFFE	H VAC CV	72	+ Lancastrian	564
BOEING	C-97/KC-97 Stratofreighter	AIRMODEL	H VAC CV	72		565
BOEING	KC-97 Stratotanker	AIRTEC	D FM·	72		566
BOEING	KC-97 Stratotanker	MODELMASTERS	D —	72		567
BOEING	KC-97G Stratotanker	EXECUTIVE	D FG·	72		568
BOEING	KC-97G Stratotanker	RAREPLANES	H VAC	72	w. INJ parts	569
BOEING	KC-135 Stratotanker	AIRTEC	D FM·	72		570
BOEING	KC-135 Stratotanker	NOVA MODELS	H VAC	72		571
BOEING	E-3A Sentry (AWACS)	HELLER	H INJ	72		572
BOEING	E-3A Sentry (AWACS)	AIRTEC	D FM·	72		573
BOEING	F2B	O'NEILL	H VAC	72		574
BOEING	F3B	O'NEILL	H VAC	72		575
BOEING	F4B-1/2	RAREPLANES	H VAC CV	72		576
BOEING	F4B-4	MONOGRAM	H INJ	72		577
BOEING	P-12E (USAAC version of F4B)	MATCHBOX	H INJ	72		578
BOEING	P-12B (USAAC version of F4B)	RAREPLANES	H VAC CV	72	+ P-1 Hawk	579
BOEING	P-26A Peashooter	REVELL	H INJ	72		580
BOEING	PW-9	O'NEILL	H VAC	72		581
BOEING	X-20 Dyna Soar	RACCOON	H RSN	72		582
BOEING	X-20 Dyna Soar	KR MODELS	H VAC	72		583
BOEING	XF8B-1	MAC VAC CANOPY	H VAC	72		584
BOEING VERTOL	107/II	AIRFIX	H INJ	72		585
BOEING VERTOL	CH-46 Sea Knight	AIRFIX	H INJ	72		586
BOEING VERTOL	CH-46 Sea Knight	AIRFIX	H INJ SN	72		587
BOEING VERTOL	CH-46D Sea Knight	FUJIMI	H INJ	72		588
BOEING VERTOL	CH-46E/F Sea Knight	FUJIMI	H INJ	72		589
BOEING VERTOL	CH-47 Chinook	AIRMODEL	H VAC	72		590
BOEING VERTOL	Chinook HC Mk 1	MAINTRACK	H RSN	72	w. ML parts	591
BOEING VERTOL	Chinook HC Mk 1	MATCHBOX	H INJ	72		592
BOEING-STEARMAN	PT-17 Kaydet	REVELL	H INJ	72		593
BOEING-STEARMAN	PT-17 Super Stearman	REVELL	H INJ	72	+ P-51D Hoover in kit #666	594
BOEING-STEARMAN	XA-21	O'NEILL	H VAC	72		595
BOULTON PAUL	Balliol	ELLIOTT	H VAC	72		596
BOULTON PAUL	Defiant	ARISTO CRAFT	H INJ	72		597
BOULTON PAUL	Defiant	COMPASS	H WD·	72		598
BOULTON PAUL	Defiant	CRUVER	R HR·	72		599
BOULTON PAUL	Defiant F Mk 1	AIRFIX	H INJ	72		600
BOULTON PAUL	Defiant TT Mk 3	AIRMODEL	H VAC CV	72	+ Martinet + Battle	601
BOULTON PAUL	Overstrand	O'NEILL	H VAC	72		602
BOULTON PAUL	Overstrand/Sidestrand	SUTCLIFFE	H VAC	72		603

BOULTON PAUL	P.111A	MERLIN	H INJ	72		604
BOULTON PAUL	P.111A	PEGASUS	H INJ	72		605
BOULTON PAUL	P.111A	PRIVATE VENTURE	H RSN	72		606
BREDA	Ba.65	RAREPLANES	H VAC	72		607
BREDA	Ba.88 Lince	CHALLENGE	H VAC	72		608
BREDA	Ba.88 Lince	KPL MODELS	H VAC	72		609
BREDA	Ba.88 Lince	O'NEILL	H VAC	72		610
BREDA	Ba.88 Lince	PRIVATE VENTURE	H RSN	72		611
BREGUET	14	CRAMER	H VAC	72		612
BREGUET	14	RUDEL	H VAC	72		613
BREGUET	14	WINGS 72	H VAC	72	w. ML parts	614
BREGUET	14 A.2/B.2	CLASSIC PLANE	H VAC	72		615
BREGUET	14 B.2	MERLIN	H INJ	72		616
BREGUET	14 B.2	PRIVATE VENTURE	H RSN	72		617
BREGUET	19	AIRMODEL	H VAC	72	w. RSN parts	618
BREGUET	19	CLASSIC PLANE	H VAC	72		619
BREGUET	19	HISPANO-AVIO-KIT	H VAC	72		620
BREGUET	19	RUDEL	H VAC	72		621
BREGUET	19 (Elizalde Motor)	PRIVATE VENTURE	H RSN	72		622
BREGUET	19 (Elizalde Motor)	REPLICA	H RSN	72		623
BREGUET	19 (Lorraine-(Dietrich Motor)	REPLICA	H RSN	72		624
BREGUET	27	O'NEILL	H VAC	72		625
BREGUET	693	HELLER	H INJ	72		626
BREGUET	1050 Alizé	MACH	H INJ	72		627
BREGUET	1050 Alizé	O'NEILL	H VAC	72		628
BREGUET	1050 Alizé	REPLICA	H RSN	72		629
BREGUET	1050 Alizé	SETCO	R HR·	72		630
BREGUET (CASA)	19 Super Bidon	HISPANO-AVIO-KIT	H VAC	72	"Cuatro Vientos"	631
BREWSTER	F2A Buffalo	AOSHIMA	H INJ	72		632
BREWSTER	F2A Buffalo	CRUVER	R HR·	72		633
BREWSTER	F2A Buffalo	REVELL	H INJ	72		634
BREWSTER	F2A-1/2 Buffalo	AIRFIX	H INJ	72		635
BREWSTER	F2A-1/2 Buffalo	MAC VAC CANOPY	H VAC	72		636
BREWSTER	B-339 Mk I/B-339D Buffalo	MATCHBOX	H INJ	72		637
BREWSTER	SB2A Buccaneer	KPL MODELS	H VAC	72		638
BREWSTER	SB2A-1 Buccaneer	ARISTO CRAFT	H INJ	72		639
BREWSTER	SB2A-3 Buccaneer	RAREPLANES	H VAC	72		640
BREWSTER	XA-32	O'NEILL	H VAC	72		641
BREWSTER-N.A.F.	SBN-1	O'NEILL	H VAC	72		642
BRISTOL	Scout D	CRAMER	H VAC	72		643
BRISTOL	Scout D	LIBRAMODELS	H VAC	72	w. ML parts	644
BRISTOL	14 F.2B Fighter	AIRFIX	H INJ	72		645
BRISTOL	14 F.2B Fighter	ATO	H WD·	72		646
BRISTOL	14 F.2B Fighter	LIBRAMODELS	H-VAC	72	double kit, w. ML parts	647
BRISTOL	14 F.2B Fighter	RENWAL	H INJ	72		648
BRISTOL	14 F.2B Fighter	SKYBIRDS	H WD·	72		649
BRISTOL	20 M.1C Monoplane Scout	AIRFRAME	H VAC	72		650
BRISTOL	20 M.1C Monoplane Scout	PEGASUS	H INJ	72		651
BRISTOL	20 M.1C Monoplnae Scout	PRIVATE VENTURE	H RSN	72		652
BRISTOL	72 Racer	CLASSIC PLANE	H VAC	72		653
BRISTOL	130 Bombay	SUTCLIFFE	H VAC	72		654
BRISTOL	130 Bombay	SUTCLIFFE	H VAC RM	72		655
BRISTOL	138A	FROG	H INJ	72		656
BRISTOL	138A	SKYBIRDS	H WD·	72		657
BRISTOL	152 Beaufort	ARISTO CRAFT	H INJ	72		658
BRISTOL	152 Beaufort	CRUVER	R HR·	72		659
BRISTOL	152 Beaufort Mk II	FROG	H INJ	72		660
BRISTOL	156 Beaufighter Mk I	ARISTO CRAFT	H INJ	72		661
BRISTOL	156 Beaufighter Mk I	CRUVER	R HR·	72		662
BRISTOL	156 Beaufighter Mk I	PATHFINDERS	H ML·	72		663
BRISTOL	156 Beaufighter Mk IF/VIC/TC.X	FROG	H INJ	72		664
BRISTOL	156 Beaufighter Mk II	ARISTO CRAFT	H INJ	72		665
BRISTOL	156 Beaufighter Mk II	CRUVER	R HR·	72		666
BRISTOL	156 Beaufighter Mk VI	ARISTO CRAFT	H INJ	72		667
BRISTOL	156 Beaufighter Mk VI	CRUVER	R HR·	72		668
BRISTOL	156 Beaufighter Mk VIF	AIRFRAME	H VAC CV	72	+ Mosquito	669
BRISTOL	156 Beaufighter Mk 21	FROG	H INJ RM	72		670

BRISTOL	156 Beaufighter TF Mk X	AIRFIX	H INJ	72		671
BRISTOL	156 Beaufighter TF Mk X	AIRMODEL	H VAC CV	72	+ Sea F. + Typhoon + Spit.	672
BRISTOL	156 Beaufighter TF Mk X	FROG PENGUIN	H INJ	72		673
BRISTOL	156 Beaufighter TF Mk X	MAC VAC CANOPY	H VAC	72		674
BRISTOL	156 Beaufighter TF Mk X	MATCHBOX	H INJ	72		675
BRISTOL	156 Beaufighter TF Mk X	POLISTIL	H UNJ	72		676
BRISTOL	156 Beaufighter TF Mk X	SUTCLIFFE	H VAC CV	72		677
BRISTOL	160 Blenheim	COMPASS	H WD·	72		678
BRISTOL	160 Blenheim Mk I	FROG PENGUIN	H INJ	72		679
BRISTOL	160 Blenheim Mk I	SKYBIRDS	H WD·	72		680
BRISTOL	160 Blenheim Mk I/IF	FROG	H INJ	72		681
BRISTOL	160 Blenheim Mk IV	AIRFIX	H INJ	72		682
BRISTOL	160 Blenheim Mk IV	ARISTO CRAFT	H INJ	72		683
BRISTOL	160 Blenheim Mk IV	CRUVER	R HR·	72		684
BRISTOL	163 Buckingham	ELLIOTT	H VAC	72	w. ML parts	685
BRISTOL	164 Brigand	AIRMODEL	H VAC	72		686
BRISTOL	164 Brigand	ELLIOTT	H VAC	72	w. ML parts	687
BRISTOL	164 Brigand	HALLMA-VAC	H VAC	72	w. ML parts	688
BRISTOL	164 Brigand	O'NEILL	H VAC	72		689
BRISTOL	164 Brigand	SABRE	H VAC	72		690
BRISTOL	164 Brigand	SUTCLIFFE	H VAC	72		691
BRISTOL	166 Buckmaster	ELLIOTT	H VAC	72	w. ML parts	692
BRISTOL	170 Freighter Mk 31	AIRMODEL	H VAC CV	72		693
BRISTOL	170 Superfreighter Mk 31	AIRFIX	H INJ	72		694
BRISTOL	170 Superfreighter Mk 31	MODELMASTERS	D —	72		695
BRISTOL	171 Sycamore	RUDEL	H VAC	72		696
BRISTOL	171 Sycamore HR Mk 14	MAINTRACK	H RSN	72	w. ML parts	697
BRISTOL	175 Britannia 300	EXECUTIVE	D —	72		698
BRISTOL	175 Britannia 300	MODELMASTERS	D —	72		699
BRISTOL	175 Britannia 312	AVF	H VAC	72		700
BRISTOL	188	DRAGON	H VAC	72		701
BRISTOL	191	SETCO	R HR·	72		702
BRISTOL	192 Belvedere	AIRFIX	H INJ	72		703
BRITISH AEROSPACE	ATP	EXECUTIVE	D FG·	72		704
BRITISH AEROSPACE	EAP	PEGASUS	H INJ	72	w. ML parts	705
BRITISH AEROSPACE	Sea Harrier FRS Mk 1	ESCI	H INJ	72		706
BRITISH AEROSPACE	Sea Harrier FRS Mk 1	FUJIMI	H INJ	72	w. Martel, Sidewinder m.	707
BRITISH AEROSPACE	Sea Harrier FRS Mk 1	HASEGAWA	H INJ	72	w. Sea Eagle, Sw missile	708
BRITISH AEROSPACE	Sea Harrier FRS Mk 1	MATCHBOX	H INJ	72	w. Sidewinder missile	709
BRITISH AEROSPACE	Hawk 200	MATCHBOX	H INJ	72		710
BRITISH AEROSPACE	Jetstream 31 (C-10A USAF)	AIRFIX	H INJ	72		711
BRITISH AEROSPACE	Jetstream T Mk 1/2	M & E	H INJ CV	72		712
BRITISH AEROSPACE	Strikemaster Mk 80/86 (167)	MATCHBOX	H INJ	72		713
BRITISH AEROSPACE	Strikemaster Mk 82 (167)	AIRFIX	H INJ	72		714
BRITISH AEROSPACE (DH/HS)	HS 125	MICRO-WEST	H INJ	72		715
BRITISH AEROSPACE (DH/HS)	HS 125 Dominie T Mk 1	AIRFIX	H INJ	72		716
BRITISH AEROSPACE (DH/HS)	HS 125-600 Dominie	MATCHBOX	H INJ	72		717
BRITISH AEROSPACE (HS)	146 Series 100	PIONEER 2	H FG·	72		718
BRITISH AEROSPACE (HS)	146 Series 200	EXECUTIVE	D FG·	72		719
BRITISH AEROSPACE (HS)	AV-8A Harrier/Matador	ESCI	H INJ	72	w. Sidewinder missile	720
BRITISH AEROSPACE (HS)	AV-8A Harrier/Matador	FUJIMI	H INJ	72	w. Sidewinder missile	721
BRITISH AEROSPACE (HS)	Harrier FRS.1/GR.3/T.2/T.4	I.D. MODELS	H VAC CV	72		722
BRITISH AEROSPACE (HS)	Harrier GR Mk 1	AIRFIX	H INJ	72		723
BRITISH AEROSPACE (HS)	Harrier GR Mk 1	DINKY TOYS	T ML· AS	72		724
BRITISH AEROSPACE (HS)	Harrier GR Mk 1	HASEGAWA	H INJ	72		725
BRITISH AEROSPACE (HS)	Harrier GR Mk 1	LINDBERG	H INJ SN	72		726
BRITISH AEROSPACE (HS)	Harrier GR Mk 1/AV-8A	MATCHBOX	H INJ	72		727
BRITISH AEROSPACE (HS)	Harrier GR Mk 3	AIRFIX	H INJ RM	72		728
BRITISH AEROSPACE (HS)	Harrier GR Mk 3	ESCI	H INJ	72	w. Sidewinder missile	729
BRITISH AEROSPACE (HS)	Harrier GR Mk 3	FUJIMI	H INJ	72	w. Martel, Sidewinder m.	730
BRITISH AEROSPACE (HS)	Harrier GR Mk 3	HASEGAWA	H INJ	72		731
BRITISH AEROSPACE (HS)	Harrier GR Mk 3	MATCHBOX	H INJ	72		732
BRITISH AEROSPACE (HS)	Harrier T Mk 2	AIR CONVERSIONS	H INJ CV	72		733
BRITISH AEROSPACE (HS)	Harrier T Mk 2	PEGASUS	H INJ CV	72		734
BRITISH AEROSPACE (HS)	Harrier T Mk 2A/FRS Mk 1	VACU-SPECIAL	H VAC CV	72		735
BRITISH AEROSPACE (HS)	Harrier T Mk 4M	C. SCALE	H ML· CV	72		736
BRITISH AEROSPACE (HS)	Harrier T Mk 4	HELLER BOBCAT	H INJ SN	72		737

BRITISH AEROSPACE (HS)	Harrier T Mk 4/GR Mk 3	VACU-SPECIAL	H VAC CV	72		738
BRITISH AEROSPACE (HS)	Hawk	AIRFIX	H INJ	72		739
BRITISH AEROSPACE (HS)	Hawk	FUJIMI	H INJ	72		740
BRITISH AEROSPACE (HS)	Hawk	MATCHBOX	H INJ	72		741
BRITISH AEROSPACE (HS)	Nimrod MR Mk 1	FORMAPLANE	H VAC	72		742
BRITISH AIRCRAFT	BA.2 Eagle	SKYBIRDS	H WD·	72		743
BRITTEN-NORMAN	BN-2 Islander	AIRFIX	H INJ	72		744
BRITTEN-NORMAN	BN-2 Islander	T.W.R.	H VAC	72		745
BRITTEN-NORMAN	BN-2 Islander/Defender	AIRFIX	H INJ RM	72		746
BUCKER	Bü 40	AIRMODEL	H VAC	72		747
BUCKER	Bü 40	FRANK-MODELLBAU	H VAC	72		748
BUCKER	Bü 131 Jungmann	AIRMODEL	H VAC	72	id. AVIA C.104	749
BUCKER	Bü 131 Jungmann	HUMA	H INJ	72	w. skis	750
BUCKER	Bü 133 Jungmeister	HELLER	H INJ	72		751
BUCKER	Bü 133 Jungmeister	PRIVATE VENTURE A	H RSN	72		752
BUCKER	Bü 180 Student	VACU-SPECIAL	H VAC	72		753
BUCKER	Bü 181 Bestmann	AIRMODEL	H VAC	72		754
BUCKER	Bü 181 Bestmann	ARNE ANDERSSON	H VAC	72		755
BUCKER	Bu 181 Bestmann	PRIVATE VENTURE A	H RSN	72		756
BUCKER	Bü 181 Bestmann	VEEDAY	H INJ	72		757
BUGATTI	100 Racer	PROJEKTS	H INJ	72		758
BURGESS	Dunne	SCALEPLANES	H VAC	72		759
CANADAIR	C-4 North Star	EXECUTIVE	D FG·	72		760
CANADAIR	CL-41 (CT-114) Tutor	ASTRA	H VAC	72		761
CANADAIR	CL-41 (CT-114) Tutor	CAN-VAC	H VAC	72		762
CANADAIR	CL-41 Tutor	CRUVER	R HR·	72		763
CANADAIR	CL-44	EXECUTIVE	D FG·	72		764
CANADAIR	CL-44D	MODELMASTERS	D —	72		765
CANADAIR	CL-215	AIRMODEL	H VAC	72		766
CANADAIR	CL-215	HELLER	H INJ	72		767
CANADAIR	CL-601 Challenger	EXECUFORM	H VAC	72		768
CANT	Z.501 Gabbiano	ITALERI	H INJ	72		769
CANT	Z.506 Airone	CHALLENGE	H VAC	72		770
CANT	Z.506 Airone	CRUVER	R HR·	72		771
CANT	Z.506B Airone	ARISTO CRAFT	H INJ	72		772
CANT	Z.506B Airone	SUPERMODEL	H INJ	72		773
CANT	Z.1007 Alcione	ARISTO CRAFT	H INJ	72		774
CANT	Z.1007 Alcione	CRUVER	R HR·	72		775
CANT	Z.1007 Alcione Bideriva	SUPERMODEL	H INJ	72		776
CANT	Z.1007 Alcione Monoderiva	SUPERMODEL	H INJ	72		777
CANT	Z.1018 Leone	CHALLENGE	H VAC	72		778
CANT	Z.1018 Leone	KPL MODELS	H VAC	72		779
CANT	Z.1018 Leone	O'NEILL	H VAC	72		780
CAPRONI	Ca 97/101	CHALLENGE	H VAC	72		781
CAPRONI	Ca 101	O'NEILL	H VAC	72		782
CAPRONI	Ca 133	ARISTO CRAFT	H INJ	72		783
CAPRONI	Ca 133	CHALLENGE	H VAC	72		784
CAPRONI	Ca 133	O'NEILL	H VAC	72		785
CAPRONI	Ca 135	CHALLENGE	H VAC	72		786
CAPRONI	Ca 135 Bis	O'NEILL	H VAC	72		787
CAPRONI	Ca 311	ITALERI	H INJ	72		788
CAPRONI	Ca 311/314	ITALERI	H INJ	72		789
CAPRONI VIZZOLA	F.5	KPL MODELS	H VAC	72		790
CAPRONI VIZZOLA	F.6M	KPL MODELS	H VAC	72		791
CAPRONI-CAMPINI	N.1	DELTA	H INJ	72		792
CAPRONI-CAMPINI	N.1	KPL MODELS	H VAC	72		793
CASA	C-212 Aviocar	HISPANO-AVIO-KIT	H VAC	72		794
CASA	C-212 Aviocar	MIAMI AIRPLANE	D FM·	72		795
CAUDRON	C.445 Goéland	AIRMODEL	H VAC	72	w. RSN parts	796
CAUDRON	C.445 Goéland	O'NEILL	H VAC	72		797
CAUDRON	C.445 Goéland	RUDEL	H VAC	72		798
CAUDRON	C.445 Goéland	VACU-SPECIAL	H VAC	72		799
CAUDRON	C.450 (1934)	MACH	H RSN	72		800
CAUDRON	C.460	SKYBIRDS	H ML·	72		801
CAUDRON	C.635 Simoun	RUDEL	H VAC	72		802
CAUDRON	C.635/635M Simoun	HELLER	H INJ	72		803
CAUDRON	C.714 Cyclone	HELLER	H INJ	72		804

CAUDRON	G.3 Cau 3 A.2/E.2	ROSEPLANE	H VAC	72	w. ML parts	805
CAUDRON	R.11	CRAMER	H VAC	72		806
CAVALIER	Turbo Mustang	MAC VAC CANOPY	H VAC	72		807
CESSNA	152	WESTERN	H MTA	72		808
CESSNA	172 Skyhawk	EIDAI	H INJ	72		809
CESSNA	172 Skyhawk	EIDAI	H INJ	72	w. floats	810
CESSNA	305A (L-19A Bird Dog)	CRUVER	R HR·	72		811
CESSNA	305A (O-1E/F Bird Dog)	AIRFIX	H INJ	72		812
CESSNA	310	AURORA	H INJ	69		813
CESSNA	318 (A37-A/B Dragonfly)	HASEGAWA	H INJ	72		814
CESSNA	337 Skymaster (O-2)	AIRFIX	H INJ	72		815
CESSNA	337 Skymaster	AURORA	H INJ	72		816
CESSNA	337 Skymaster (O-2)	EIDAI	H INJ	72		817
CESSNA	337 Skymaster	EIDAI	H INJ	72		818
CESSNA	T-50 (AT-17)	DESIGN CENTER	H INJ	72		819
CESSNA	T-50 (AT-17)	EXECUFORM	H VAC	72		820
CESSNA	T-50 (UC-78 Bobcat)	ARISTO CRAFT	H INJ	72	UC-78 = ex-C-78	821
CESSNA	T-50 (UC-78 Bobcat)	CRUVER	R HR·	72	UC-78 = ex-C-78	822
CESSNA	T-50 (UC-78 Bobcat)	FORMAPLANE	H VAC	72	UC-78 = ex-C-78	823
CESSNA	T-50 (UC-78 Bobcat)	O'NEILL	H VAC	72	UC-78 = ex-C-78	824
CHANCE VOUGHT	F4U-1 Corsair	ARISTO CRAFT	H INJ	72		825
CHANCE VOUGHT	F4U-1 Corsair	CRUVER	R HR·	72		826
CHANCE VOUGHT	F4U-1 Corsair	HASEGAWA	H INJ	72	birdcage canopy	827
CHANCE VOUGHT	F4U-1 Corsair	MAC VAC CANOPY	H VAC	72	birdcage canopy	828
CHANCE VOUGHT	F4U-1A Corsair	HELLER	H INJ	72		829
CHANCE VOUGHT	F4U-1D Corsair	AIRFIX	H INJ	72		830
CHANCE VOUGHT	F4U-1D Corsair	DANBURY MINT	H ML·	72		831
CHANCE VOUGHT	F4U-1D Corsair	FROG	H INJ	72		832
CHANCE VOUGHT	F4U-1D Corsair	HASEGAWA	H INJ	72		833
CHANCE VOUGHT	F4U-1D Corsair	HAWK	H INJ	72		834
CHANCE VOUGHT	F4U-1D Corsair	HAWK	H HR·	72		835
CHANCE VOUGHT	F4U-1D Corsair	JO HAN	H INJ	72		836
CHANCE VOUGHT	F4U-1D Corsair	MAC VAC CANOPY	H VAC	69		837
CHANCE VOUGHT	F4U-1D Corsair	PATHFINDERS	H ML·	72		838
CHANCE VOUGHT	F4U-1D Corsair	REVELL	H INJ	72		839
CHANCE VOUGHT	F4U-4 Corsair	FUJIMI	H INJ	71		840
CHANCE VOUGHT	F4U-4 Corsair	MATCHBOX	H INJ	72		841
CHANCE VOUGHT	F4U-7/AU-1/F4U-5/F4U-5N Corsair	IPMS FRANCE	H VAC CV	72	w. EB, RSN parts	842
CHANCE VOUGHT	F4U-5 Corsair	CRUVER	R HR·	72		843
CHANCE VOUGHT	F4U-5N Corsair	FUJIMI	H INJ	70		844
CHANCE VOUGHT	F6U-1 Pirate	AIRMODEL	H VAC	72		845
CHANCE VOUGHT	F6U-1 Pirate	HAWK	H HR·	72		846
CHANCE VOUGHT	F6U-1 Pirate	MAC VAC CANOPY	H VAC	72		847
CHANCE VOUGHT	F6U-1 Pirate	O'NEILL	H VAC	72		848
CHANCE VOUGHT	F6U-1 Pirate	PRIVATE VENTURE B	H RSN	72		849
CHANCE VOUGHT	F7U-1 Cutlass	AURORA	H INJ	72		850
CHANCE VOUGHT	F7U-1 Cutlass	MAC VAC CANOPY	H VAC	72		851
CHANCE VOUGHT	F7U-1 Cutlass	O'NEILL	H VAC	72		852
CHANCE VOUGHT	F7U-1 Cutlass	STROMBECKER	H WD·	72		853
CHANCE VOUGHT	F7U-1 Cutlass	VERNON	H WD·	72		854
CHANCE VOUGHT	F7U-3 Cutlass	FUJIMI	H INJ	72		855
CHANCE VOUGHT	F7U-3 Cutlass	FALCON	H VAC	72		856
CHANCE VOUGHT	F7U-3/3P Cutlass	AIRMODEL	H VAC	72		857
CHANCE VOUGHT	F7U-3/3P Cutlass	RAREPLANES	H VAC	72		858
CHANCE VOUGHT	F7U-3M Cutlass	FUJIMI	H INJ	72		859
CHANCE VOUGHT	F7U-3P Cutlass	FUJIMI	H INJ	72		860
CHANCE VOUGHT	V-173 Flying Pancake	EAGLES TALON	H VAC	72		861
CHANCE VOUGHT	XF5U-1 Flying Flapjack	AIRMODEL	H VAC	72		862
CHANCE VOUGHT	XF5U-1 Flying Flapjack	KPM	H VAC	72		863
CHANCE VOUGHT	XF5U-1 Flying Flapjack	PRIVATE VENTURE C	H RSN	72		864
CHANCE VOUGHT	XFT-1	MAC VAC CANOPY	H VAC	72		865
CHASE	XC-123 Avitruk	CRUVER	R HR·	72		866
CIERVA	C.24 Autogyro	SKYBIRDS	H WD·	72		867
CIERVA	C.30	HISPANO-AVIO-KIT	H VAC	72		868
CIERVA	C.30	PRIVATE VENTURE	H RSN	72		869
CIERVA	C.30 Autogyro	VEEDAY	H INJ	72		870
COMMONWEALTH AIRCRAFT	CA-1 Wirraway	PRIVATE VENTURE	H RSN	72		871

COMMONWEALTH AIRCRAFT	CA-11 Woomera	KPL MODELS	H VAC	72		872
COMMONWEALTH AIRCRAFT	CA-13 Boomerang	AIRFIX	H INJ	72		873
COMMONWEALTH AIRCRAFT	CA-15 Kangaroo	EAGLES TALON	H VAC	72		874
COMMONWEALTH AIRCRAFT	CA-19 Boomerang	DESIGN CENTER	H INJ	72		875
COMMONWEALTH AIRCRAFT	CA-19 Boomerang	MAC VAC CANOPY	H VAC	72		876
COMMONWEALTH AIRCRAFT	CA-27 Sabre	AIRMODEL	H VAC	72	+ F-86H/K + TF-86F	877
COMPER	CLA.7 Swift	SKYBIRDS	H WD·	72		878
COMPER	CLA.7 Swift	AEROCLUB MODELS	H VAC	72	w. ML parts	879
CONSOLIDATED	C-87 Liberator	CRUVER	R HR·	72	transport version	880
CONSOLIDATED	C-87C/RY-3 Liberator	MATCHBOX	H INJ	72	+ PB4Y-2 Privateer	881
CONSOLIDATED	C-87 Liberator	SETCO	R HR·	72	transport version	882
CONSOLIDATED	LB-30A Liberator	SUTCLIFFE	H VAC CV	72	transport version	883
CONSOLIDATED	B-24 Liberator (PB4Y-3)	ARISTO CRAFT	H INJ	72		884
CONSOLIDATED	B-24A Liberator	CRUVER	R HR·	72		885
CONSOLIDATED	B-24D Liberator	REVELL	H INJ	72		886
CONSOLIDATED	B-24J Liberator	AIRFIX	H INJ	72		887
CONSOLIDATED	B-24J Liberator	STROMBECKER	H WD·	72		888
CONSOLIDATED	B-32 Dominator	CRUVER	R HR·	72		889
CONSOLIDATED	B-32 Dominator	O'NEILL	H VAC	72		890
CONSOLIDATED	B-32 Dominator	SUTCLIFFE	H VAC	72		891
CONSOLIDATED	P2Y Commodore	O'NEILL	H VAC	72		892
CONSOLIDATED	P2Y-2	SUTCLIFFE	H VAC	72		893
CONSOLIDATED	PB-2A/P-30A	EXECUFORM	H VAC	72		894
CONSOLIDATED	PB-2A/P-30A	O'NEILL	H VAC	72		895
CONSOLIDATED	PBY-1/2/3/4/6A/10A Catalina	AIRMODEL	H VAC CV	72	+ TA-7C + TA-4F	896
CONSOLIDATED	PBY-5 Catalina	ARISTO CRAFT	H INJ	72		897
CONSOLIDATED	PBY-5 Catalina	CRUVER	R HR·	72		898
CONSOLIDATED	PBY-5 Catalina	REVELL	H INJ	72		899
CONSOLIDATED	PBY-5A Catalina	AIRFIX	H INJ	72		900
CONSOLIDATED	PBY-5A Catalina	AURORA	H INJ	74		901
CONSOLIDATED	PBY-5A Catalina	GEE'S AERO WORKS	H WD·	74		902
CONSOLIDATED	PBY-5A Catalina	REVELL	H INJ	72		903
CONSOLIDATED	PBY-5A Catalina	TOHO	H INJ MT	70		904
CONSOLIDATED	PBY-5A Catalina	TOLMER	H INJ	70		905
CONSOLIDATED	PBY-6A Catalina	REVELL	H INJ	72	Cousteau version	906
CONSOLIDATED	PB2Y Coronado	EXECUFORM	H VAC	72		907
CONSOLIDATED	PB2Y Coronado	O'NEILL	H VAC	72		908
CONSOLIDATED	PB2Y-2/3 Coronado	SUTCLIFFE	H VAC	72		909
CONSOLIDATED	PB2Y-3 Coronado	ARISTO CRAFT	H INJ	72		910
CONSOLIDATED	PB2Y-3 Coronado	CRUVER	R HR·	72		911
CONSOLIDATED	PB4Y Privateer	J & L	H VAC CV	72		912
CONSOLIDATED	PB4Y Privateer	SUTCLIFFE	H VAC CV	72		913
CONSOLIDATED	PB4Y Privateer	UNIQUE FORM	H VAC CV	72		914
CONSOLIDATED	PB4Y-2 Privateer	MATCHBOX	H INJ	72	+ C-87C/RY-3	915
CONVAIR	B-36 Peacemaker	CRUVER	R HR·	72		916
CONVAIR	B-36D/RB-36D/GRB-36D Peacemaker	SUTCLIFFE	H VAC	72		917
CONVAIR	B-36H/RB-36H Peacemaker	MONOGRAM	H INJ	72		918
CONVAIR	B-58 Hustler	AIRMODEL	H VAC	72		919
CONVAIR	B-58 Hustler	AURORA	H INJ	76		920
CONVAIR	B-58 Hustler	SETCO	R HR·	72		921
CONVAIR	B-58A Hustler	ITALERI	H INJ	72		922
CONVAIR	TB-58A Boomerang	ITALERI	H INJ	72		923
CONVAIR	C-131A Samaritan	SETCO	R HR·	72		924
CONVAIR	CV-240 Convairliner	AIRTEC	H FM·	72		925
CONVAIR	CV-240	EXECUFORM	H VAC	72		926
CONVAIR	CV-240 Convairliner	EXECUTIVE	D —	72		927
CONVAIR	CV-340	EXECUTIVE	D —	72		928
CONVAIR	CV-340/440/540/580	EXECUFORM	H VAC	72	CV-440 Metropolitan	929
CONVAIR	CV-440 Metropolitan	RAISE-UP	H INJ	72		930
CONVAIR	CV-580	AIR JET ADVANCE	D FG·	72		931
CONVAIR	CV-580	AIRTEC	H FM·	72		932
CONVAIR	CV-580	MIAMI AIRPLANE	D FM·	72		933
CONVAIR	CV-580	NORTH CENTRAL	H RSN	72		934
CONVAIR	CV-880	ATLANTIC MODELS	D RSN	72		935
CONVAIR	Challenger	MAC VAC CANOPY	H VAC	72		936
CONVAIR	F-102 Delta Dagger	CRUVER	R HR·	72		937
CONVAIR	F-102 Delta Dagger	HASEGAWA	H INJ	72	w. Falcon missile	938

CONVAIR	F-102 Delta Dagger	REVELL	H INJ	77		939
CONVAIR	TF-102 Delta Dagger	AIRMODEL	H VAC CV	72		940
CONVAIR	F-106B Delta Dart	FALCON	H VAC CV	72	+ F9F-8T + Mirage IIID	941
CONVAIR	F-106 Delta Dart	HASEGAWA	H INJ	72	w. Falcon missile	942
CONVAIR	F-106 Delta Dart	REVELL	H INJ	67		943
CONVAIR	F-106 Delta Dart	SETCO	R HR·	72		944
CONVAIR	F-106A Delta Dart	BARE-METAL FOIL	H VAC CV	72	canopy	945
CONVAIR	F-106B Delta Dart	AIRMODEL	H VAC CV	72	canopy, + HC-130H + F-80C	946
CONVAIR	F-106B Delta Dart	BARE-METAL FOIL	H VAC CV	72		947
CONVAIR	R3Y Tradewind	O'NEILL	H VAC	72		948
CONVAIR	TBY-1/2 Sea Wolf	WINGS 72	H VAC	72	w. ML parts	949
CONVAIR	XP-81 Duplex	KR MODELS	H VAC	72		950
CONVAIR	XP-81 Duplex	MAC VAC CANOY	H VAC	72		951
CONVAIR	XF-92A	HAWK	H INJ	72	w. Sparrow missile	952
CONVAIR	XC-99	RICK'S	H FM· CV	72	for B-36 MONOGRAM	953
CONVAIR	XF2Y-1 Sea Dart	AIRMODEL	H VAC	72		954
CONVAIR	XF2Y-1 Sea Dart	EXECUFORM	H VAC	72		955
CONVAIR	XF2Y-1 Sea Dart	PRIVATE VENTURE B	H RSN	72		956
CONVAIR	XFY-1 Pogo	AIRMODEL	H VAC	72		957
CORNELIUS	XFG-1	AIRMODEL	H VAC	72		958
CORNELIUS	XFG-1	PRIVATE VENTURE C	H RSN	72		959
COUZINET	Arc-en-Ciel	BRIFAUT	H INJ	72		960
COUZINET	Arc-en-Ciel	HELLER	H INJ	75		961
CURTISS	Y1A-8 Shrike	RAREPLANES	H VAC	72		962
CURTISS	Y1A-8 Shrike	RAREPLANES	H VAC RM	72		963
CURTISS	A-12 Shrike	RAREPLANES	H VAC	72		964
CURTISS	A-18 Shrike II	EXECUFORM	H VAC	72		965
CURTISS	BF2C Goshawk	O'NEILL	H VAC CV	72		966
CURTISS	BF2C-1 Goshawk	GUNZE SANGYO	H ML·	72		967
CURTISS	F11C-2 Goshawk	MONOGRAM	H INJ	72		968
CURTISS	CR-1/CR-2/CR-3	PRIVATE VENTURE	H RSN	72		969
CURTISS	F6C Hawk	RAREPLANES	H VAC CV	72		970
CURTISS	F6C-1/3 Hawk	ESOTERIC	H VAC	72	w. ML parts	971
CURTISS	F6C-4 Hawk	O'NEILL	H VAC CV	72		972
CURTISS	F7C Seahawk	O'NEILL	H VAC	72		973
CURTISS	F7C-1 Seahawk	ESOTERIC	H VAC	72	w. ML parts	974
CURTISS	F8C Helldiver	O'NEILL	H VAC	72		975
CURTISS	F8C-4/02C-1 Helldiver	ESOTERIC	H VAC	72	w. ML parts	976
CURTISS	F9C Sparrowhawk	EAGLES TALON	H VAC	72		977
CURTISS	F9C Sparrowhawk	O'NEILL	H VAC	72		978
CURTISS	F9C-2 Sparrowhawk	BOLESLAV	H VAC	72		979
CURTISS	F9C-2 Sparrowhawk	PEGASUS	H INJ	72		980
CURTISS	F9C-2 Sparrowhawk	PRIVATE VENTURE	H RSN	72		981
CURTISS	Golden Flyer	RENWAL	H INJ	72		982
CURTISS	JN-4C/D Jenny	CLASSIC PLANE	H VAC	72		983
CURTISS	JN-4D Jenny	CRAMER	H VAC	72		984
CURTISS	JN-4D Jenny	VEEDAY	H INJ	72		985
CURTISS	O-1/A-3	O'NEILL	H VAC	72		986
CURTISS	O-52 Owl	EXECUFORM	H VAC	72		987
CURTISS	O-52 Owl	O'NEILL	H VAC	72		988
CURTISS	P-1 Hawk	RAREPLANES	H VAC CV	72	+ BOEING P-12B	989
CURTISS	P-6E Hawk	MONOGRAM	H INJ	72		990
CURTISS	P-36 Mohawk	MAC VAC CANOPY	H VAC	72		991
CURTISS	P-36 Mohawk	SKYBIRDS	H WD·	72		992
CURTISS	P-36A Mohawk	AOSHIMA	H INJ	72		993
CURTISS	P-36A Mohawk	HELLER	H INJ	72		994
CURTISS	P-36A Mohawk	MONOGRAM	H INJ	72		995
CURTISS	P-36C Mohawk	REVELL	H INJ	72		996
CURTISS	P-40B Tomahawk	ACADEMY MINICRAFT	H INJ	72		997
CURTISS	P-40B Tomahawk	FROG	H INJ	72		998
CURTISS	P-40B Tomahawk	MAC VAC CANOPY	H VAC	72		999
CURTISS	P-40B Tomahawk	RAREPLANES	H VAC CV	72	+ YO-37	1000
CURTISS	P-40B Tomahawk	SKYBIRDS	H WD·	72		1001
CURTISS	P-40 Kittyhawk	ARISTO CRAFT	H INJ	72		1002
CURTISS	P-40D Kittyhawk	FROG	H INJ	72		1003
CURTISS	P-40D Kittyhawk	MAC VAC CANOPY	H VAC	72		1004
CURTISS	P-40E Kittyhawk	ABORN	H VAC	72	canopy	1005

CURTISS	P-40E Kittyhawk	AIRFIX	H INJ	72		1006
CURTISS	P-40E Kittyhawk	CRUVER	R HR·	72		1007
CURTISS	P-40E Kittyhawk	DANBURY MINT	H ML·	72		1008
CURTISS	P-40E Kittyhawk	HASEGAWA	H INJ	72		1009
CURTISS	P-40E Kittyhawk	HELLER	H INJ	72		1010
CURTISS	P-40E Kittyhawk	NICHIMO	H INJ	70		1011
CURTISS	P-40E Kittyhawk	POLISTIL	H INJ	72		1012
CURTISS	P-40E Kittyhawk	REVELL	H INJ	72		1013
CURTISS	P-40E Kittyhawk	STROMBECKER	H WD·	72		1014
CURTISS	P-40F/K/M	ALPHA	H VAC	72		1015
CURTISS	P-40N Warhawk	AIRMODEL	H VAC CV	72	+ FG-1A + P-51D	1016
CURTISS	P-40N Warhawk	CRUVER	R HR·	72		1017
CURTISS	P-40N Warhawk	FUJIMI	H INJ	70		1018
CURTISS	P-40N Warhawk	HASEGAWA	H INJ	70		1019
CURTISS	P-40N Warhawk	MATCHBOX	H INJ	70		1020
CURTISS	P-40N Warhawk	NITTO	H INJ	75		1021
CURTISS	R3C-1/2	PRIVATE VENTURE	H RSN	72		1022
CURTISS	R3C-2	MERLIN	H ML·	72		1023
CURTISS	SBC-3/4 Helldiver	RAREPLANES	H VAC	72		1024
CURTISS	SBC-4 Helldiver	AIRMODEL	H VAC	72		1025
CURTISS	SBC-4 Helldiver	HELLER	H INJ	72		1026
CURTISS	SBC-4 Helldiver	MATCHBOX	H INJ	72		1027
CURTISS	SBC-4 Helldiver	STROMBECKER	H WD·	72		1028
CURTISS	SB2C-1 Helldiver	ARISTO CRAFT	H INJ	72		1029
CURTISS	SB2C-1 Helldiver	CRUVER	R HR·	72		1030
CURTISS	SB2C-1 Helldiver	DESIGN CENTER	R INJ	72		1031
CURTISS	SB2C-1 Helldiver	MATCHBOX	H INJ	72		1032
CURTISS	SB2C-1C Helldiver	CRUVER	R HR·	72		1033
CURTISS	SB2C-3 Helldiver	LINDBERG	H INJ	72		1034
CURTISS	SB2C-3/5 Helldiver	AIRFIX	H INJ	72		1035
CURTISS	SB2C-5 Helldiver	NITTO	H INJ	72		1036
CURTISS	XSB2C-2 Helldiver	DESIGN CENTER	H INJ	72	float version	1037
CURTISS	SC-1 Seahawk	CRUVER	R HR·	72		1038
CURTISS	SC-1 Seahawk	FORMAPLANE	H VAC	72		1039
CURTISS	SC-1 Seahawk	MAC VAC CANOPY	H VAC	72		1040
CURTISS	SOC-2/3 Seagull	HASEGAWA	H INJ	72	w. wheels, floats (SOC-3)	1041
CURTISS	SO3C-1 Seagull	ARISTO CRAFT	H INJ	72		1042
CURTISS	SO3C-1 Seagull	CRUVER	R HR·	72	land version	1043
CURTISS	SO3C-1 Seagull	CRUVER	R HR·	72	float version	1044
CURTISS	SO3C-2C Seamew	ARISTO CRAFT	H INJ	72		1045
CURTISS	SO3C-2C Seamew	GRIFFIN	H VAC	72		1046
CURTISS	SO3C-2C Seamew	PLYCRAFT	H CB·	72		1047
CURTISS	SO3C-2C Seamew	PLYCRAFT	H CB.	72		1048
CURTISS	T-32 Condor II	J & L	H VAC	72		1049
CURTISS	T-32 Condor II	O'NEILL	H VAC	72		1050
CURTISS	XF15C-1	AIRMODEL	H VAC	72		1051
CURTISS	XF15C-1	MAC VAC CANOPY	H VAC	72		1052
CURTISS	XF15C-1	O'NEILL	H VAC	72		1053
CURTISS	XP-31 Swift	EXECUFORM	H VAC	72		1054
CURTISS	XP-46	MAC VAC CANOPY	H VAC	72		1055
CURTISS	XP-87 Blackhawk	EXECUFORM	H VAC	72		1056
CURTISS	YP-37	MAC VAC CANOPY	H VAC	72	+ P-40B	1057
CURTISS	YP-37	RAREPLANES	H VAC CV	72	+ P-40B	1058
CURTISS	YP-37	RAREPLANES	H VAC CV	72	+ P-40B (Remoulded CV)	1059
CURTISS-WRIGHT	CW-25 (AT-9) Jeep	EXECUFORM	H VAC	72		1060
CURTISS-WRIGHT	CW-25 (AT-9) Jeep	O'NEILL	H VAC	72		1061
CURTISS-WRIGHT	C-46 Commando (CW-20)	ARISTO CRAFT	H INJ	72		1062
CURTISS-WRIGHT	C-46 Commando (CW-20)	CRUVER	R HR·	72		1063
CURTISS-WRIGHT	C-46 Commando (CW-20)	E.D.H.	H FM·	72		1064
CURTISS-WRIGHT	C-46 Commando (CW-20)	EXECUTIVE	D FG·	72		1065
CURTISS-WRIGHT	C-46 Commando (CW-20)	MODELMASTERS	D —	72		1066
CURTISS-WRIGHT	C-46 Commando (CW-20)	SUTCLIFFE	H VAC	72		1067
CURTISS-WRIGHT	C-46 Commando (CW-20)	WILLIAMS BROTHERS	H INJ	72		1068
CURTISS-WRIGHT	CW-21 Demon	MAC VAC CANOPY	H VAC	72		1069
CURTISS-WRIGHT	CW-21 Demon	MERLIN	H ML·	72		1070
CURTISS-WRIGHT	CW-21 Demon	RAREPLANES	H VAC	72		1071
CURTISS-WRIGHT	CW-24 (XP-55) Ascender	AIRMODEL	H VAC	72		1072

CURTISS-WRIGHT	CW-24 (XP-55) Ascender	MAC VAC CANOPY	H VAC	72		1073
CURTISS-WRIGHT	CW-24 (XP-55) Ascender	O'NEILL	H VAC	72		1074
CURTISS-WRIGHT	CW-24 (XP-55) Ascender	PRIVATE VENTURE	H RSN	72		1075
CURTISS-WRIGHT	CW-24 (XP-55) Ascender	WINGS 72	H VAC	72	w. ML parts	1076
DASSAULT	Etendard IV	SETCO	R HR·	72		1077
DASSAULT	Etendard IVM	HELLER	H INJ	72		1078
DASSAULT	Etendard IVM	O'NEILL	H VAC	72		1079
DASSAULT	Etendard IVM	PRIVATE VENTURE A	H RSN	72		1080
DASSAULT	Etendard IVM/P	AIRMODEL	H VAC	72		1081
DASSAULT	Etendard IVP	GRAPHY-AIR	H RSN CV	72	w. refuelling pod	1082
DASSAULT	Falcon 10	M.E.E.	D FM·	70		1083
DASSAULT	Falcon 20	M.E.E.	D FM·	70		1084
DASSAULT	Falcon 20	T.W.R.	H VAC	72		1085
DASSAULT	Falcon 20H	M.E.E.	D FM·	70		1086
DASSAULT	Falcon 50	M.E.E.	D FM·	70		1087
DASSAULT	Falcon 900	M.E.E.	D FM·	72		1088
DASSAULT	MD.312 Flamant	AERO KIT	H RSN	72	w. ML parts	1089
DASSAULT	MD.311/312/315/315R Flamant	REPLICA	H RSN	72		1090
DASSAULT	Mirage III	SETCO	R HR·	72		1091
DASSAULT	Mirage IIIB	AIRMODEL	H VAC CV	72	canopy, + G-91T + Jaguar E	1092
DASSAULT	Mirage IIIB	MATCHBOX	H INJ	72		1093
DASSAULT	Mirage IIIBE/5BD/IIIOD	GRAPHY-AIR	H RSN	72	w. HELLER, EB parts	1094
DASSAULT	Mirage IIIC	AIRFIX	H INJ	72	w. R.511 missile	1095
DASSAULT	Mirage IIIC	CENTRAL	H INJ	72	w. R.530 missile	1096
DASSAULT	Mirage IIIC	MATCHBOX	H INJ	72		1097
DASSAULT	Mirage IIID	FALCON	H VAC CV	72	+ F-106B + F9F-8T	1098
DASSAULT	Mirage IIIE	P.M.S.	H INJ	72		1099
DASSAULT	Mirage IIIE/O	FROG	H INJ	72	w. Sidewinder missile	1100
DASSAULT	Mirage IIIE/R/5BA	HELLER	H INJ	72		1101
DASSAULT	Mirage IIIE/R/S/RS	REVELL	H INJ	72	w. Sidewinder missile	1102
DASSAULT	Mirage IIIR	AIRMODEL	H VAC CV	72		1103
DASSAULT	Mirage IIIS/O	LINDBERG	H INJ SN	72		1104
DASSAULT	Mirage IVA	HELLER	H INJ	72		1105
DASSAULT	Mirage 2000	HELLER	H INJ	72	w. Super 530, Magic m.	1106
DASSAULT	Mirage 2000B	MD	H RSN CV	72		1107
DASSAULT	Mirage F.1B/C	HELLER	H INJ	72	w. R.530 missile	1108
DASSAULT	Mirage F.1C	AIRFIX	H INJ	72	w. R.530, Magic missile	1109
DASSAULT	Mirage F.1C	HASEGAWA	H INJ	72	w. R.530, Magic, Sidewinder. m.	1110
DASSAULT	Mirage F.1C	UNIKIT	H INJ SN	72	w. R.530, Magic missile	1111
DASSAULT	Mirage F.1CR	HELLER	H INJ RM	72	remoulded, F.1B/C	1112
DASSAULT	Mystère II	SETCO	R HR·	72		1113
DASSAULT	Mystère IV	NEW-MAQUETTES	H WD·	72		1114
DASSAULT	Mystère IV	O'NEILL	H VAC	72		1115
DASSAULT	Mystère IV	RUDEL	H VAC	72		1116
DASSAULT	Mystère IVA	GRAPHY-AIR	H RSN	72	w. EB parts	1117
DASSAULT	Mystère IVA	MATCHBOX	H INJ	72		1118
DASSAULT	Ouragan	CRUVER	R HR·	72		1119
DASSAULT	Ouragan	HELLER	H INJ	72		1120
DASSAULT	Ouragan	O'NEILL	H VAC	72		1121
DASSAULT	Super Etendard	HELLER	H INJ	72	w. Exocet missile	1122
DASSAULT	Super Etendard	PRIVATE VENTURE	H RSN	72	w. Exocet missile	1123
DASSAULT	Super Etendard	SUNNY	H INJ	72	w. Exocet missile	1124
DASSAULT	Super Mystère B.2	AIRFIX	H INJ	72		1125
DASSAULT	Super Mystère B.2	M.A.F.	H INJ	69		1126
DASSAULT	Super Mystère B.2	STARLUX	H INJ	75		1127
DASSAULT-BREGUET/DORNIER	Alpha Jet (Mock-up)	MATCHBOX	H INJ	72		1128
DASSAULT-BREGUET/DORNIER	Alpha Jet (Mock-up)	STARFIX	H INJ	72		1129
DASSAULT-BREGUET/DORNIER	Alpha Jet A (prototype)	HELLER	H INJ	72		1130
DASSAULT-BREGUET/DORNIER	Alpha Jet A	FUJIMI	H INJ	72		1131
DASSAULT-BREGUET/DORNIER	Alpha Jet A	REVELL	H INJ	72		1132
DASSAULT-BREGUET/DORNIER	Alpha Jet A/B	AIRFIX	H INJ	72		1133
DASSAULT-BREGUET/DORNIER	Alpha Jet A/E	MATCHBOX	H INJ RM	72		1134
DASSAULT-BREGUET/DORNIER	Alpha Jet E	FUJIMI	H INJ	72		1135
DE HAVILLAND	DH.34	AIRFRAME	H VAC	72		1136
DE HAVILLAND	DH.60 Moth Major	SKYBIRDS	H WD·	72		1137
DE HAVILLAND	DH.60G Gipsy Moth	FROG	H INJ	72		1138
DE HAVILLAND	DH.80 Puss Moth	SKYBIRDS	H WD·	72		1139

DE HAVILLAND	DH.82A/C Tiger Moth	AERO 72	H INJ	72	w. ML parts	1140
DE HAVILLAND	DH.82A Tiger Moth	AIRFIX	H INJ	72		1141
DE HAVILLAND	DH.82A Tiger Moth	ATO	H WD·	72		1142
DE HAVILLAND	DH.83 Fox Moth	AEROCLUB MODELS	H VAC	72		1143
DE HAVILLAND	DH.85 Leopard Moth	SKYBIRDS	H WD·	72		1144
DE HAVILLAND	DH.86A	FROG PENGUIN	H INJ	72		1145
DE HAVILLAND	DH.88 Comet	AIRFIX	H INJ	72		1146
DE HAVILLAND	DH.88 Comet	C.A. ATKINS	H ML·	72		1147
DE HAVILLAND	DH.88 Comet	FROG	H INJ	72		1148
DE HAVILLAND	DH.88 Comet	SKYBIRDS	H WD·	72		1149
DE HAVILLAND	DH.89 Dragon Rapide	VEEDAY	H INJ	72		1150
DE HAVILLAND	DH.89A Dragon Rapide	FROG	H INJ	72		1151
DE HAVILLAND	DH.89A Dragon Rapide	HELLER	H INJ	72		1152
DE HAVILLAND	DH.89A/M Dragon Rapide	RAREPLANES	H INJ	72		1153
DE HAVILLAND	DH.90 Dragonfly	AIRFRAME	H VAC	72		1154
DE HAVILLAND	DH.91 Albatross	AEROSPACE CASTING	H RSN	72		1155
DE HAVILLAND	DH.94 Moth Minor	SKYBIRDS	H WD·	72		1156
DE HAVILLAND	DH.98 Mosquito (canopies)	AEROCLUB MODELS	H VAC CV	72	B.IV/XVI/PR.IX/XVI/34/35	1157
DE HAVILLAND	DH.98 Mosquito	ARISTO CRAFT	H INJ	72		1158
DE HAVILLAND	DH.98 Mosquito	CRUVER	R HR·	72		1159
DE HAVILLAND	DH.98 Mosquito	DANBURY MINT	H ML·	72		1160
DE HAVILLAND	DH.98 Mosquito	FROG PENGUIN	H INJ	72		1161
DE HAVILLAND	DH.98 Mosquito	GEE'S AERO WORKS	H WD·	72		1162
DE HAVILLAND	DH.98 Mosquito	PATHFINDERS	H ML·	72		1163
DE HAVILLAND	DH.98 Mosquito B Mk IV	MD	H RSN CV	72		1164
DE HAVILLAND	DH.98 Mosquito B Mk IV/FB Mk VI	FROG	H INJ	72		1165
DE HAVILLAND	DH.98 Mosquito FB Mk VI	AIRFIX	H INJ	72		1166
DE HAVILLAND	DH.98 Mosquito FB Mk VI	MAC VAC CANOPY	H VAC	72		1167
DE HAVILLAND	DH.98 Mosquito FB.VI/XVIII/NF.III	AIRFIX	H INJ RM	72		1168
DE HAVILLAND	DH.98 Mosquito NF Mk X/NF Mk 30	MATCHBOX	H INJ	72		1169
DE HAVILLAND	DH.98 Mosquito NF Mk XIII	AIRFRAME	H VAC CV	72	+ Beaufighter	1170
DE HAVILLAND	DH.98 Mosquito PR Mk 34/35	AEROCLUB MODELS	H VAC CV	72	Belley	1171
DE HAVILLAND	DH.98 Sea Mosquito TR Mk 33	C. SCALE	H ML· CV	72	+ DH.103	1172
DE HAVILLAND	DH.103 Hornet	MAC VAC CANOPY	H VAC	72		1173
DE HAVILLAND	DH.103 Hornet F Mk 3	FROG	H INJ	72		1174
DE HAVILLAND	DH.103 Sea Hornet F Mk 20	SKYBIRDS 86	H INJ	72	w. ML parts	1175
DE HAVILLAND	DH.103 Sea Hornet NF Mk 21	C. SCALE	H ML· CV	72	+ DH.98	1176
DE HAVILLAND	DH.104 Dove	BRITAVIA MODELS	H VAC	72		1177
DE HAVILLAND	DH.104 Dove	EXECUTIVE	D —	72		1178
DE HAVILLAND	DH.104 Dove	T.W.R.	H VAC	72		1179
DE HAVILLAND	DH.104 Devon/Dove	AIRMODEL	H VAC	72		1180
DE HAVILLAND	DH.104 Devon/Dove	RAREPLANES	H VAC	72	w. INJ parts	1181
DE HAVILLAND	DH.106 Comet	SKYLAND MODELS	D FG·	72		1182
DE HAVILLAND	DH.106 Comet 4	EXECUTIVE	D FG·	72		1183
DE HAVILLAND	DH.106 Comet 4	MODELMASTERS	D —	72		1184
DE HAVILLAND	DH.106 Comet 4B	EXECUTIVE	D FG·	72		1185
DE HAVILLAND	DH.108 Swallow	AIRFRAME	H VAC	72		1186
DE HAVILLAND	DH.108 Swallow	DE HAVILLAND	H ML·	72		1187
DE HAVILLAND	DH.108 Swallow	PRIVATE VENTURE	H RSN	72		1188
DE HAVILLAND	DH.110 Sea Vixen (prototype)	FROG	H INJ	72		1189
DE HAVILLAND	DH.110 Sea Vixen	CRUVER	R HR·	72		1190
DE HAVILLAND	DH.110 Sea Vixen	UNIQUE SCALE	H RSN	72		1191
DE HAVILLAND	DH.110 Sea Vixen	VERNON	H WD·	72		1192
DE HAVILLAND	DH.110 Sea Vixen FAW Mk 1/2	FROG	H INJ RM	72	w. Red Top missile	1193
DE HAVILLAND	DH.112 Venom	CRUVER	R HR·	72		1194
DE HAVILLAND	DH.112 Venom FB Mk 4	CRUVER	R HR·	72		1195
DE HAVILLAND	DH.112 Venom FB Mk 4	FROG	H INJ	72		1196
DE HAVILLAND	DH.112 Venom FB Mk 4	RAREPLANES	H VAC	72	w. INJ parts	1197
DE HAVILLAND	DH.112 Sea Venom Mk 21/FAW Mk 53	FROG	H INJ	72		1198
DE HAVILLAND	DH.113/115 Vampire NF.10/T.11	AIRMODEL	H VAC CV	72		1199
DE HAVILLAND	DH.114 Heron Mk 2	AIRFIX	H INJ	72		1200
DE HAVILLAND	DH.115 Vampire F Mk 3	CRUVER	R HR·	72		1201
DE HAVILLAND	DH.115 Vampire FB Mk 5	CRUVER	R HR·	72		1202
DE HAVILLAND	DH.115 Vampire FB Mk 5	GEE'S AERO WORKS	H WD·	72		1203
DE HAVILLAND	DH.115 Vampire FB Mk 5	HELLER	H INJ	72		1204
DE HAVILLAND	DH.115 Vampire FB Mk 5	PATHFINDERS	H ML·	72		1205
DE HAVILLAND	DH.115 Vampire FB Mk 5/50	FROG	H INJ	72		1206

DE HAVILLAND	DH.115 Vampire FB Mk 5/50	FROG PENGUIN	H INJ	72		1207
DE HAVILLAND	DH.115 Vampire T Mk 11	AERO 72	H INJ	72		1208
DE HAVILLAND	DH.115 Vampire T Mk 11	MERLIN	H INJ	72	w. ML parts	1209
DE HAVILLAND	DH.115 Vampire T Mk 11/55	I.D. MODELS	H VAC CV	72		1210
DE HAVILLAND CANADA	DHC-1 Chipmunk T Mk 1/10	AIRFIX	H INJ	72		1211
DE HAVILLAND CANADA	DHC-2/L-20A Beaver	AIRFIX	H INJ	72	w. floats, skis	1212
DE HAVILLAND CANADA	DHC-2/L-20A Beaver	CRUVER	R HR·	72		1213
DE HAVILLAND CANADA	DHC-3 Otter	VP CANADA	H VAC	72	w. RSN p., w. floats, skis	1214
DE HAVILLAND CANADA	DHC-3 Otter	ASTRA	H VAC	72	w. floats	1215
DE HAVILLAND CANADA	DHC-4 Caribou	ASTRA	H VAC	72		1216
DE HAVILLAND CANADA	DHC-4 Caribou	COMBAT MODEL	H VAC	72	w. ML parts	1217
DE HAVILLAND CANADA	DHC-6 Twin Otter	AIRTEC	H FM·	72		1218
DE HAVILLAND CANADA	DHC-6 Twin Otter	ASTRA	H VAC	72		1219
DE HAVILLAND CANADA	DHC-6 Twin Otter	EXECUTIVE	D —	72		1220
DE HAVILLAND CANADA	DHC-6 Twin Otter	MATCHBOX	H INJ	72		1221
DE HAVILLAND CANADA	DHC-7 Dash 7/100	MIAMI AIRPLANE	D FM·	72		1222
DEPERDUSSIN	Monocoque (Modèle 1913)	CLASSIC PLANE	H VAC	72		1223
DEPERDUSSIN	Monocoque (Modèle 1913)	MACH	H INJ	72		1224
DEWOITINE	D.27	O'NEILL	H VAC	72		1225
DEWOITINE	D.371	O'NEILL	H VAC	72		1226
DEWOITINE	D.371	REPLICA	H RSN	72		1227
DEWOITINE	D.500	SKYBIRDS	H WD·	72		1228
DEWOITINE	D.500/501	HELLER	H INJ	72		1229
DEWOITINE	D.510	HELLER	H INJ	72		1230
DEWOITINE	D.510	RAREPLANES	H VAC	72		1231
DEWOITINE	D.520	HELLER	H INJ	72		1232
DEWOITINE	D.520	SKYBIRDS	H WD·	72		1233
DEWOITINE	D.520C	FROG	H INJ	72		1234
DFS	194	AIRMODEL	H VAC	72		1235
DFS	194	PRIVATE VENTURE	H RSN	72		1236
DFS	194	VP CANADA	H VAC	72		1237
DFS	228 V1	FRANK-MODELLBAU	H VAC	72		1238
DFS	230	AIRFRAME	H VAC	72		1239
DFS	230	AIRMODEL	H VAC	72		1240
DFS	230	ARISTO CRAFT	H INJ	72		1241
DFS	230	CRUVER	R HR·	72		1242
DFS	230	HUMA	H INJ	72		1243
DFS	A 20 Habicht	WK	H RSN	72		1244
DFS	Kranich	ARNE ANDERSSON	H VAC	72		1245
DFS	Kranich	WK	H RSN	72		1246
DFS	Olympia Meise (NORD 2000)	ARNE ANDERSSON	H VAC	72		1247
DFS	Weihe (VMA 200)	ARNE ANDERSSON	H VAC	72	cf. FOCKE-WULF	1248
DFW	B I	FORMAPLANE	H VAC	72		1249
DFW	B I	LIBRAMODELS	H VAC	72	w. ML parts	1250
DFW	C V	CLASSIC PLANE	H VAC	72		1251
DFW	T 28 Floh	CLASSIC PLANE	H VAC	72		1252
DFW	T 28 Floh	PRIVATE VENTURE	H RSN	72		1253
DFW	T 28 Floh	TWELVE SQUARED	H INJ	72		1254
DFW	T 28 Floh	WINGS 72	H VAC	72	w. ML parts	1255
DORAND	AR.1	FORMAPLANE	H VAC	72		1256
DORNIER	D.I	CRAMER	H VAC	72		1257
DORNIER	Do 15 Wal	AIRMODEL	H VAC	72		1258
DORNIER	Do 17E-1/F-1	AIRFIX	H INJ	72		1259
DORNIER	Do 17E/F	SKYBIRDS	H WD·	72		1260
DORNIER	Do 17E/F/K	AIRMODEL	H VAC CV	72	+ Do 215B	1261
DORNIER	Do 17P-1	AIRMODEL	H INJ CV	72		1262
DORNIER	Do 17Z	ARISTO CRAFT	H INJ	72		1263
DORNIER	Do 17Z	CRUVER	R HR·	72		1264
DORNIER	Do 17Z	LINDBERG	H INJ	72		1265
DORNIER	Do 17Z	MONOGRAM	H INJ	72		1266
DORNIER	Do 17Z-2	FROG	H INJ	72		1267
DORNIER	Do 18D/F/G/L	AIRMODEL	H VAC	72		1268
DORNIER	Do 18V-2/D-2/G-1	MATCHBOX	H INJ	72		1269
DORNIER	Do 22	ALPHA	H VAC	72		1270
DORNIER	Do 23G	AIRMODEL	H VAC	72		1271
DORNIER	Do 23G	REPLICA	H RSN	72		1272
DORNIER	Do 24	ARNE ANDERSSON	H VAC	72		1273

DORNIER	Do 24T	ITALERI	H INJ	72		1274
DORNIER	Do 26	AIRMODEL	H VAC	72		1275
DORNIER	Do 27	AIRMODEL	H VAC	72		1276
DORNIER	Do 27	AIRMODEL	H RSN	72		1277
DORNIER	Do 27	HISPANO-AVIO-KIT	H VAC	72		1278
DORNIER	Do 28D Skyservant	MATCHBOX	H INJ	72		1279
DORNIER	Do 215	ARISTO CRAFT	H INJ	72		1280
DORNIER	Do 215	CRUVER	R HR·	72		1281
DORNIER	Do 215	FROG PENGUIN	H INJ	72		1282
DORNIER	Do 215B	AIRMODEL	H VAC CV	72	+ Do 17E/F/K	1283
DORNIER	Do 217	ARISTO CRAFT	H INJ	72		1284
DORNIER	Do 217E	AIRMODEL	H VAC CV	72	+ Ju 188A/E	1285
DORNIER	Do 217E	CRUVER	R HR·	72		1286
DORNIER	Do 217E-2	AIRFIX	H INJ	72		1287
DORNIER	Do 217E-2/J-1	AIRFIX	H INJ RM	72		1288
DORNIER	Do 217J-1	AIRMODEL	H INJ CV	72		1289
DORNIER	Do 217K-1	AIRMODEL	H INJ CV	72		1290
DORNIER	Do 217K-1	GUANO	H INJ CV	72		1291
DORNIER	Do 217K-1	ITALERI	H INJ	72		1292
DORNIER	Do 217K-2	GUANO	H INJ CV	72	w. Fritz X guided bomb	1293
DORNIER	Do 217M/N	AIRMODEL	H VAC CV	72	+ Ju 88A-15/P/G	1294
DORNIER	Do 217N-1	ITALERI	H INJ	72		1295
DORNIER	Do 228	I.M.C.	D INJ	72		1296
DORNIER	Do 228	REVELL	H INJ SN	72		1297
DORNIER	Do 228-100 Polar 2	REVELL	H INJ	72		1298
DORNIER	Do 228-100	REVELL	H INJ	72		1299
DORNIER	Do 335 Pfeil	LINDBERG	H INJ	72		1300
DORNIER	Do 335 Pfeil	MAC VAC CANOPY	H VAC	72		1301
DORNIER	Do 335 Pfeil	VOLKS	H RSN	72		1302
DORNIER	Do 335A-6/12 Pfeil	FROG	H INJ	72		1303
DORNIER	Do 335A-10/11 Pfeil	AIRMODEL	H VAC CV	72	+ Fw 200C-1	1304
DORNIER	Do 335A-10/12 Pfeil	MAC VAC CANOPY	H VAC CV	72	rear canopy	1305
DOUGLAS	A-20 Havoc	ARISTO CRAFT	H INJ	72		1306
DOUGLAS	A-20 Havoc	COMET	H WD·	72		1307
DOUGLAS	A-20 Havoc	CRUVER	R HR·	72		1308
DOUGLAS	A-20 Havoc	GEE'S AERO WORKS	H WD·	72		1309
DOUGLAS	A-20 Havoc	STROMBECKER	H WD·	72		1310
DOUGLAS	A-20C Havoc	REVELL	H INJ	72		1311
DOUGLAS	A-20G Havoc/Boston Mk IV	72	H INJ	72		1312
DOUGLAS	Boston Mk III	FROG	H INJ	72		1313
DOUGLAS	Boston Mk III	FROG	H INJ RM	72		1314
DOUGLAS	Boston Mk IIIA	AIRFIX	H INJ	72		1315
DOUGLAS	A-24 Dauntless	ARISTO CRAFT	H INJ	72		1316
DOUGLAS	A-24 Dauntless	CRUVER	R HR·	72		1317
DOUGLAS	A-26 Invader	CRUVER	R HR·	72		1318
DOUGLAS	B-26B Invader	MONOGRAM	H INJ	67		1319
DOUGLAS	A-26B/C Invader	AIRFIX	H INJ	72		1320
DOUGLAS	B-26B/JD-1 Invader	CRUVER	R HR·	72		1321
DOUGLAS	A-3 (A3D) Skywarrior	ALLYN	H INJ	66		1322
DOUGLAS	A-3 (A3D) Skywarrior	O'NEILL	H VAC	72		1323
DOUGLAS	A-3 (A3D) Skywarrior	SETCO	R HR·	72		1324
DOUGLAS	KA-3B Skywarrior	RAREPLANES	H VAC	72	w. INJ parts	1325
DOUGLAS	AD-1 Skyraider	CRUVER	R HR·	72		1326
DOUGLAS	AD-3 Skyraider	CRUVER	R HR·	72		1327
DOUGLAS	AD-4W Skyraider	AIRMODEL	H VAC CV	72	+ TBF/TBM-3U/3W	1328
DOUGLAS	AD-4W Skyraider	AIRMODEL	H VAC CV	72	+ TBF/TBM/3U/3S/3W	1329
DOUGLAS	AD-5 (A-1E) Skyraider	MONOGRAM	H INJ	72		1330
DOUGLAS	AD-5W Skyraider	FALCON	H VAC CV	72	+ FJ-3 + C-2A	1331
DOUGLAS	AD-6 (A-1H) Skyraider	FUJIMI	H INJ	70		1332
DOUGLAS	AD-6 (A-1H) Skyraider	IMC	H INJ	72		1333
DOUGLAS	AD-6 (A-1H) Skyraider	TOMIYAMA	H INJ	70		1334
DOUGLAS	AD-6 (A-1H) Skyraider	TSUKUDA	H INJ	72		1335
DOUGLAS	AD-7 (A-1J) Skyraider	AIRFIX	H INJ	72		1336
DOUGLAS	AD-7 (A-1J) Skyraider	MAC VAC CANOPY	H VAC	72		1337
DOUGLAS	AEW 1 Skyraider	C. SCALE	H ML· CV	72		1338
DOUGLAS	B-18 Bolo	AIRMODEL	H VAC	72		1339
DOUGLAS	B-18 Bolo	O'NEILL	H VAC	72		1340

DOUGLAS	B-23 Dragon	O'NEILL	H VAC	72		1341
DOUGLAS	B-66 Destroyer	AIRMODEL	H VAC	72		1342
DOUGLAS	B-66B Destroyer	ITALERI	H INJ	72		1343
DOUGLAS	BTD Destroyer	MAC VAC CANOPY	H VAC	72		1344
DOUGLAS	C-124 Globemaster II	AIRMODEL	H VAC	72		1345
DOUGLAS	C-124 Globemaster II	COMBAT MODEL	H VAC	72	w. ML parts	1346
DOUGLAS	C-124A Globemaster II	CRUVER	R HR·	72		1347
DOUGLAS	C-133A/B Cargomaster	RICK'S	H VAC	72		1348
DOUGLAS	D-558-1 Skystreak	KR MODELS	H VAC	72		1349
DOUGLAS	D-558-2 Skyrocket	AEROMODELL	H RSN	72		1350
DOUGLAS	D-558-2 Skyrocket	KR MODELS	H VAC	72	2-canopy version	1351
DOUGLAS	D-558-2 Skyrocket	STROMBECKER	H WD·	72		1352
DOUGLAS	D-558-3 Model 671/684	KR MODELS	H VAC	72		1353
DOUGLAS	DC-1	EXECUFORM	H VAC	72	+ DC-2	1354
DOUGLAS	DC-2	EXECUFORM	H VAC	72	+ DC-1	1355
DOUGLAS	DC-2	J & L	H VAC	72		1356
DOUGLAS	DC-2	PIONEER 2	H FG·	72		1357
DOUGLAS	DC-2/R2D/C-33	O'NEILL	H VAC	72		1358
DOUGLAS	DC-3	ESCI	H INJ	72		1359
DOUGLAS	DC-3	GEE'S AERO WORKS	H WD·	72		1360
DOUGLAS	DC-3	ITALERI	H INJ	72		1361
DOUGLAS	DC-3/C-47 Skytrain	AIRFIX	H INJ	72		1362
DOUGLAS	DC-3/C-47 Skytrain	EXECUTIVE	D FG·	72		1363
DOUGLAS	DC-3/C-47 Skytrain	RICK'S	D FM·	72		1364
DOUGLAS	C-47 Skytrain	ARISTO CRAFT	H INJ	72		1365
DOUGLAS	C-47 Skytrain	CRUVER	R HR·	72		1366
DOUGLAS	C-47 Skytrain	ESCI	H INJ	72		1367
DOUGLAS	C-47 Skytrain	ITALERI	H INJ	72		1368
DOUGLAS	C-47D Skytrain	CRUVER	R HR·	72		1369
DOUGLAS	AC-47 Gunship	AIRFIX	H INJ RM	72		1370
DOUGLAS	AC-47 Gunship	ESCI	H INJ	72		1371
DOUGLAS	R4D-5 Skytrain	ESCI	H INJ	72	w. skis & RATO version	1372
DOUGLAS	R4D-8/C-117 Super DC-3	AIRMODEL	H VAC CV	72		1373
DOUGLAS	R4D-8 Super DC-3	SETCO	R HR·	72		1374
DOUGLAS	DC-4	J & L	H VAC	72		1375
DOUGLAS	DC-4	RAISE-UP	H ML·	72		1376
DOUGLAS	DC-4/4M Skymaster/Argonaut	RAREPLANES	H VAC	72		1377
DOUGLAS	DC-4/C-54 Skymaster	EXECUTIVE	D FG·	72		1378
DOUGLAS	C-54 Skymaster	ARISTO CRAFT	H INJ	72		1379
DOUGLAS	C-54 Skymaster	CRUVER	R HR·	72		1380
DOUGLAS	C-54G Skymaster	CRUVER	R HR·	72		1381
DOUGLAS	DC-5	EXECUFORM	H VAC	72		1382
DOUGLAS	DC-6	EXECUTIVE	D FG·	72		1383
DOUGLAS	DC-6	MODELMASTERS	D —	72		1384
DOUGLAS	DC-6	RAISE-UP	D —	72		1385
DOUGLAS	DC-6	VERKUYL	H FG·	72		1386
DOUGLAS	DC-6B	HELLER	H INJ	72		1387
DOUGLAS	DC-6B "Sécurité Civile"	HELLER	H INJ	72		1388
DOUGLAS	C-118 Liftmaster	HELLER	H INJ RM	72	remoulded DC-6B	1389
DOUGLAS	DC-7	EXECUTIVE	D FG·	72		1390
DOUGLAS	DC-7	J & L	H VAC	72		1391
DOUGLAS	DC-8	MARKETING AIDS	D —	72		1392
DOUGLAS	DC-8-52	SKYLAND MODELS	D FG·	72		1393
DOUGLAS	DC-8-53	TAI	D ML·	72		1394
DOUGLAS	DC-8-55	EXECUTIVE	D FG·	72		1395
DOUGLAS	DC-8-62	EXECUTIVE	D FG·	72		1396
DOUGLAS	DC-8-63	EXECUTIVE	D FG·	72		1397
DOUGLAS	DC-8-63	SKYLAND MODELS	D FG·	72		1398
DOUGLAS	DWC World Cruiser	WILLIAMS BROTHERS	H INJ	72		1399
DOUGLAS	F3D Skynight	O'NEILL	H VAC	72		1400
DOUGLAS	F3D-1 Skynight	RAREPLANES	H VAC	72		1401
DOUGLAS	F3D-1 Skynight	SETCO	R HR·	72		1402
DOUGLAS	F3D-2 Skynight	AIRMODEL	H VAC	72		1403
DOUGLAS	F3D-2 Skynight	FALCON	H VAC	72		1404
DOUGLAS	F4D-1 Skyray	AIRFIX	H INJ	72	w. Sidewinder missile	1405
DOUGLAS	F4D-1 Skyray	HAWK	H INJ	72		1406
DOUGLAS	F4D-1 Skyray	HAWK	R HR·	72		1407

DOUGLAS	F4D-1 Skyray	HOBBYTIME	H INJ	75		1408
DOUGLAS	O-35/B-7	SUTCLIFFE	H VAC	72		1409
DOUGLAS	Y1B/XO-35	O'NEILL	H VAC	72		1410
DOUGLAS	O-38	O'NEILL	H VAC	72		1411
DOUGLAS	O-43	O'NEILL	H VAC	72		1412
DOUGLAS	O-43	RAREPLANES	H VAC	72	+ YO-31C parts	1413
DOUGLAS	O-46	O'NEILL	H VAC	72		1414
DOUGLAS	OA-4 Dolphin	EXECUFORM	H VAC	72		1415
DOUGLAS	OA-4/RD-4/C-26 Dolphin	O'NEILL	H VAC	72		1416
DOUGLAS	P-70	REVELL	H INJ	72		1417
DOUGLAS	SBD-3 Dauntless	COMET	H WD·	72		1418
DOUGLAS	SBD-3 Dauntless	CRUVER	R HR·	72		1419
DOUGLAS	SBD-3 Dauntless	PLYCRAFT	H CB·	72		1420
DOUGLAS	SBD-3/5 Dauntless	AIRFIX	H INJ	72		1421
DOUGLAS	SBD-5 Dauntless	AOSHIMA	H INJ	72		1422
DOUGLAS	SBD-5 Dauntless	HAWK	H INJ	72		1423
DOUGLAS	SBD-5 Dauntless	MAC VAC CANOPY	H VAC	72		1424
DOUGLAS	T2D/P2D	O'NEILL	H VAC	72		1425
DOUGLAS	TBD Devastator	MAC VAC CANOPY	H VAC	72		1426
DOUGLAS	TBD-1 Devastator	ARISTO CRAFT	H INJ	72		1427
DOUGLAS	TBD-1 Devastator	COMET	H WD·	72		1428
DOUGLAS	TBD-1 Devastator	CRUVER	R HR·	72		1429
DOUGLAS	TBD-1 Devastator	AIRFIX	H INJ	72		1430
DOUGLAS	XA2D-1 Skyshark	AIRMODEL	H VAC	72		1431
DOUGLAS	XA2D-1 Skyshark	CRUVER	R HR·	72		1432
DOUGLAS	XA2D-1 Skyshark	O'NEILL	H VAC	72		1433
DOUGLAS	XA2D-1 Skyshark	RAREPLANES	H VAC	72	w. INJ parts	1434
DOUGLAS	XB-42 Mixmaster	BOLESLAV	H VAC	72		1435
DOUGLAS	XB-42 Mixmaster	EXECUFORM	H VAC	72		1436
DOUGLAS	XB-42 Mixmaster	O'NEILL	H VAC	72		1437
DOUGLAS	XB-42 Mixmaster	WINGS 72	H VAC	72		1438
DOUGLAS	XB-42/42A Mixmaster	EAGLES TALON	H VAC	72		1439
DOUGLAS	XB-43 Versatile II	EAGLES TALON	H VAC	72		1440
DOUGLAS	XB-43 Versatile II	EXECUFORM	H VAC	72		1441
DOUGLAS	YO-31C	RAREPLANES	H VAC	72	+ O-43	1442
DUFAUX	5	LIBRAMODELS	H VAC	72		1443
DUFAUX	Fighter	SCALEPLANES	H VAC	72		1444
EDGLEY	EA7 Optica	PRIVATE VENTURE	H RSN	72		1445
EDO	XOSE-1	AIRMODEL	H VAC	72		1446
EDO	XOSE-1	PRIVATE VENTURE	H RSN	72		1447
ERCO	Ercoupe	MAIRCRAFT	H WD·	72		1448
ERCO	Ercoupe	SETCO	R HR·	72		1449
ETRICH	Taube	AIRFRAME	H VAC	72		1450
FAIRCHILD	91	EXECUFORM	H VAC	72		1451
FAIRCHILD	A-10A Thunderbolt II	ACADEMY MINICRAFT	H INJ	72		1452
FAIRCHILD	A-10A Thunderbolt II	AIRFIX	H INJ	72		1453
FAIRCHILD	A-10A Thunderbolt II	HASEGAWA	H INJ RM	72		1454
FAIRCHILD	A-10A Thunderbolt II	HASEGAWA	H INJ	72	w. Maverick, Paveway m.	1455
FAIRCHILD	A-10A Thunderbolt II	MATCHBOX	H INJ	72		1456
FAIRCHILD	A-10A Thunderbolt II	MONOGRAM	H INJ	72	w. Paveway	1457
FAIRCHILD	A-10A Thunderbolt II	MONOGRAM	H INJ RM	72	w. Paveway	1458
FAIRCHILD	A-10B Thunderbolt II	FALCON	H VAC CV	72	+ HC-130P + F4H-1	1459
FAIRCHILD	AT-21 Gunner	O'NEILL	H VAC	72		1460
FAIRCHILD	Argus/UC-61K Forwarder	FORMAPLANE	H VAC	72		1461
FAIRCHILD	Argus/UC-61K Forwarder/UC-86	O'NEILL	H VAC	72		1462
FAIRCHILD	C-82 Packet	AIRMODEL	H VAC	72		1463
FAIRCHILD	C-82A Packet	CRUVER	R HR·	72		1464
FAIRCHILD	C-119 Flying Boxcar	ABORN	H VAC CV	72		1465
FAIRCHILD	C-119 Flying Boxcar	AIRMODEL	H VAC	72		1466
FAIRCHILD	C-119 Flying Boxcar	CHALLENGE	H VAC	72		1467
FAIRCHILD	C-119 Flying Boxcar	MAC VAC CANOPY	H VAC CV	72		1468
FAIRCHILD	C-119A Flying Boxcar	AURORA	H INJ	77		1469
FAIRCHILD	C-119C Flying Boxcar	CRUVER	R HR·	72		1470
FAIRCHILD	C-119G Flying Boxcar	ITALERI	H INJ	72		1471
FAIRCHILD	AC-119K Gunship	ITALERI	H INJ	72		1472
FAIRCHILD	C-123 Provider	AIRMODEL	H VAC	72		1473
FAIRCHILD	FH-227	AIRTEC	D —	72		1474

FAIRCHILD	PT-19	MAI	H RSN	72		1475
FAIRCHILD	PT-19/23/26 Cornell	EXECUFORM	H VAC	72		1476
FAIRCHILD SWEARINGEN	Metro II	AIR JET ADVANCE	D FG·	72		1477
FAIRCHILD SWEARINGEN	Metro III	AIR JET ADVANCE	D FG·	72		1478
FAIREY	Albacore	AIRMODEL	H VAC	72		1479
FAIREY	Albacore	ARISTO CRAFT	H INJ	72		1480
FAIREY	Albacore	CRUVER	R HR·	72		1481
FAIREY	Albacore	FORMAPLANE	H VAC	72		1482
FAIREY	Albacore	MAC VAC CANOPY	H VAC	72		1483
FAIREY	Albacore	O'NEILL	H VAC	72		1484
FAIREY	Albacore	PRIVATE VENTURE	H RSN	72		1485
FAIREY	Albacore TB Mk I	PEGASUS	H INJ	72		1486
FAIREY	Barracuda	ARISTO CRAFT	H INJ	72		1487
FAIREY	Barracuda	CRUVER	D HR·	72		1488
FAIREY	Barracuda	FROG PENGUIN	H INJ	72		1489
FAIREY	Barracuda	MAC VAC CANOPY	H VAC	72		1490
FAIREY	Barracuda Mk II	FROG	H INJ	72		1491
FAIREY	Battle	AIRFIX	H INJ	72		1492
FAIREY	Battle	FROG PENGUIN	H INJ	72		1493
FAIREY	Battle	SKYBIRDS	H WD·	72		1494
FAIREY	Battle Trainer	AIRMODEL	H VAC CV	72	c., + Defiant + Martinet	1495
FAIREY	FD.2	FROG	H INJ	72		1496
FAIREY	Fantôme	PRIVATE VENTURE C	H RSN	72		1497
FAIREY	Firefly T Mk 1/T Mk 2/FR Mk I	C. SCALE	H ML· CV	72	+ Sea Fury	1498
FAIREY	Firefly Mk 1	FROG	H INJ	72		1499
FAIREY	Firefly Mk I	GEE'S AERO WORKS	H WD·	72		1500
FAIREY	Firefly Mk IV	CRUVER	R HR·	72		1501
FAIREY	Firefly Mk IV	PATHFINDERS	H ML·	72		1502
FAIREY	Firefly Mk 5	AIRFIX	H INJ	72		1503
FAIREY	Firefly Mk 5	MAC VAC CANOPY	H VAC	72		1504
FAIREY	Firefly (Biplane)	RUDEL	H VAC	72		1505
FAIREY	Flycatcher	VEEDAY	H INJ	72	+ Gamecock	1506
FAIREY	Fox Mk I	PEGASUS	H INJ	72		1507
FAIREY	Fox Mk II/III	RUDEL	H VAC	72		1508
FAIREY	Fox Mk VI/VIII	RUDEL	H VAC	72		1509
FAIREY	Fox Mk VII	RUDEL	H VAC	72		1510
FAIREY	Fulmar	AIRMODEL	H VAC	72		1511
FAIREY	Fulmar	ARISTO CRAFT	H INJ	72		1512
FAIREY	Fulmar	CRUVER	R HR·	72		1513
FAIREY	Fulmar Mk I/II	RAREPLANES	H VAC	72		1514
FAIREY	Gannet	HAWK	H HR	72		1515
FAIREY	Gannet	THEATRE SPECIALITY	H INJ	72		1516
FAIREY	Gannet AS Mk 1/4	FROG	H INJ	72		1517
FAIREY	Gannet AEW Mk 3	AIRMODEL	H VAC CV	72		1518
FAIREY	Gannet AEW Mk 3	I.D. MODELS	H VAC CV	72		1519
FAIREY	Gannet AS Mk 4	LINCOLN	H INJ	72		1520
FAIREY	Gordon	SKYBIRDS	H WD·	72		1521
FAIREY	Gordon	SUTCLIFFE	H VAC CV	72	+ Seal	1522
FAIREY	Hendon	SKYBIRDS	H WD·	72		1523
FAIREY	Hendon	SUTCLIFFE	H VAC	72		1524
FAIREY	IIIF	AIRMODEL	H VAC	72		1525
FAIREY	IIIF	SUTCLIFFE	H VAC	72		1526
FAIREY	Long-Range Monoplane	AIRFRAME	H VAC	72		1527
FAIREY	Rotodyne	AIRFIX	H INJ	72		1528
FAIREY	Rotodyne	FROG	H INJ	72		1529
FAIREY	Rotodyne	REVELL	H VAC	78		1530
FAIREY	Seafox	FORMAPLANE	H VAC	72		1531
FAIREY	Seafox	MATCHBOX	H INJ	72		1532
FAIREY	Seafox	O'NEILL	H VAC	72		1533
FAIREY	Seafox	SKYBIRDS	H WD·	72		1534
FAIREY	Seal	SKYBIRDS	H WD·	72		1535
FAIREY	Seal	SUTCLIFFE	H VAC	72	+ Gordon	1536
FAIREY	Spearfish	SUTCLIFFE	H VAC	72		1537
FAIREY	Swordfish Mk I	ARISTO CRAFT	H INJ	72		1538
FAIREY	Swordfish Mk I	FROG	H INJ	72	w. floats	1539
FAIREY	Swordfish Mk I/III	MATCHBOX	H INJ	72		1540
FAIREY	Swordfish Mk III	AIRFIX	H INJ	72		1541

FAIREY	Swordfish Mk III	AIRFIX	H INJ RM	72		1542
FARMAN	F.221	REPLICA	H RSN	72		1543
FARMAN	F.222.1	REPLICA	H RSN	72		1544
FARMAN	F.222.2	O'NEILL	H VAC	72		1545
FARMAN	F.222.2	REPLICA	H RSN	72		1546
FARMAN	NC.223.3	O'NEILL	H VAC	72		1547
FBA-Lévêque		FORMAPLANE	H VAC	72	w. ML parts	1548
FBA-Lévêque		LIBRAMODELS	H VAC	72	w. ML parts	1549
FFVS	J.22	ARNE ANDERSSON	H VAC	72		1550
FFVS	J.22	KPL MODELS	H VAC	72		1551
FFVS	J.22	PRIVATE VENTURE	H RSN	72		1552
FIAT	BR.20 Cigogna	ARISTO CRAFT	H INJ	72		1553
FIAT	BR.20 Cigogna	CRUVER	R HR·	72		1554
FIAT	BR.20 Cigogna	ITALERI	H INJ	72		1555
FIAT	CR.20	O'NEILL	H VAC	72		1556
FIAT	CR.25	CHALLENGE	H VAC	72		1557
FIAT	CR.25	O'NEILL	H VAC	72		1558
FIAT	CR.25 bis	KPL MODELS	H VAC	72		1559
FIAT	CR.32	GUNZE SANGYO	H ML·	72		1560
FIAT	CR.32/32 bis/32 quater	SUPERMODEL	H INJ	72		1561
FIAT	CR.42 Falco	AIRFORM	H INJ CV	72	+ G.50	1562
FIAT	CR.42 Falco	ARISTO CRAFT	H INJ	72		1563
FIAT	CR.42 Falco	REVELL	H INJ	72		1564
FIAT	CR.42/J.11 Falco	ARNE ANDERSSON	H VAC	72		1565
FIAT	FC.20 Cansa	KPL MODELS	H VAC	72		1566
FIAT	G.12	O'NEILL	H VAC	72		1567
FIAT	G.50 Freccia	AIRFORM	H INJ CV	72	in kit #003	1568
FIAT	G.50 Freccia	ARISTO CRAFT	H INJ	72		1569
FIAT	G.50 Freccia	CRUVER	R HR·	72		1570
FIAT	G.50 Freccia	MAC VAC CANOPY	H VA	72		1571
FIAT	G.50 bis	AIRFIX	H INJ	72		1572
FIAT	G.55 Centauro	ALIPAST	H INJ	72		1573
FIAT	G.55 Centauro	FROG	H INJ	72		1574
FIAT	G.55 Centauro	ITALPLANES	H VAC CV	72		1575
FIAT	G.55 Centauro	POLISTIL	H INJ	72		1576
FIAT	G.55 Centauro	SUPERMODEL	H INJ	72		1577
FIAT	G.55S Silurante	SUPERMODEL	H INJ	72		1578
FIAT	G.59	ITALPLANES	H VAC CV	72		1579
FIAT	G.59	VETROMODELLI	H FG·	72		1580
FIAT	G.82	ARTIPLAST	H INJ	75		1581
FIAT	G.95	ABORN	H VAC	72	canopy	1582
FIAT	RS.14	O'NEILL	H VAC	72		1583
FIESELER	Fi 103R-IV Reichenberg	AIRMODEL	H VAC CV	72	canopy, + Fw 190 + Ar 234	1584
FIESELER	Fi 103R-IV Reichenberg	HELLER	H INJ	72	+ Natter	1585
FIESELER	Fi 156 Storch	ARISTO CRAFT	H INJ	72		1586
FIESELER	Fi 156A/C-3 Storch	AIRFIX	H INJ	72		1587
FIESELER	Fi 156C-3/MS.500 Storch	HELLER	H INJ	72		1588
FIESELER	Fi 167	PRIVATE VENTURE	H RSN	72		1589
FIESELER	Fi 167A-0	FORMAPLANE	H VAC	72		1590
FIESELER	Fi 256	PRIVATE VENTURE C	H RSN	72		1591
FISHER	P-75 Eagle	MAC VAC CANOPY	H VAC	72		1592
FISHER	P-75 Eagle	RAREPLANES	H VAC	72		1593
FLEET	60 Fort	AIRFRAME	H VAC	72		1594
FLETTNER	Fl 265	AIRMODEL	H VAC	72		1595
FLETTNER	Fl 265	PRIVATE VENTURE A	H RSN	72		1596
FLETTNER	Fl 282B-0/B-2 Kolibri	HUMA	H INJ	72		1597
FMA	I.Ae. 24 Calquin	O'NEILL	H VAC	72		1598
FMA	IA-58 Pucara	PRIVATE VENTURE	H RSN	72		1599
FMA	IA-58 Pucara	RAREPLANES	H VA	72		1600
FOCKE-ACHGELIS	Fa 223 Drache	AIRMODEL	H VAC	72	w. RSN parts	1601
FOCKE-WULF	F-19 Ente	AIRMODEL	H VAC	72		1602
FOCKE-WULF	Fw 44 Stieglitz	AIRMODEL	H VAC	72		1603
FOCKE-WULF	Fw 44 Stieglitz	HUMA	H INJ	72		1604
FOCKE-WULF	Fw 44 Stieglitz	PRIVATE VENTURE A	H RSN	72		1605
FOCKE-WULF	Fw 44J Stieglitz	PEGASUS	H INJ	72		1606
FOCKE-WULF	Fw 56 Stösser	AIRMODEL	H VAC	72		1607
FOCKE-WULF	Fw 56 Stösser	HELLER	H INJ	72		1608

FOCKE-WULF	Fw 58B/C Weihe	AIRMODEL	H VAC	72		1609
FOCKE-WULF	Fw 187 Falke	AIRMODEL	H VAC	72		1610
FOCKE-WULF	Fw 187 Falke	ARISTO CRAFT	H INJ	72		1611
FOCKE-WULF	Fw 187 Falke	CRUVER	R HR·	72		1612
FOCKE-WULF	Fw 187 Falke	O'NEILL	H VAC	72		1613
FOCKE-WULF	Fw 187 Falke	PRIVATE VENTURE A	H RSN	72		1614
FOCKE-WULF	Fw 189 Uhu	AIRFIX	H INJ	72		1615
FOCKE-WULF	Fw 189 Uhu	ARISTO CRAFT	H INJ	72		1616
FOCKE-WULF	Fw 189 Uhu	CRUVER	R HR·	72		1617
FOCKE-WULF	Fw 189A-1 Uhu	AOSHIMA	H INJ	72		1618
FOCKE-WULF	Fw 190A-8/U1 (S5/S8)	MD	H RSN CV	72		1619
FOCKE-WULF	Fw 190A Wurger	ARISTO CRAFT	H INJ	72		1620
FOCKE-WULF	Fw 190A Wurger	CADET	H WD·	72		1621
FOCKE-WULF	Fw 190A Wurger	CRUVER	R HR·	72		1622
FOCKE-WULF	Fw 190A Wurger	GEE'S AERO WORKS	H WD·	72		1623
FOCKE-WULF	Fw 190A Wurger	MAC VAC CANOPY	H VAC	72		1624
FOCKE-WULF	Fw 190A Wurger	MAC VAC CANOPY	H VAC	72	blown canopy	1625
FOCKE-WULF	Fw 190A/G/K/V-1 Wurger	AIRMODEL	H VAC CV	72	canopy	1626
FOCKE-WULF	Fw 190A-3/4 Wurger	MATCHBOX	H INJ	72		1627
FOCKE-WULF	Fw 190A-4 Wurger	REVELL	H INJ	72		1628
FOCKE-WULF	Fw 190A-4 Wurger	SANWA	H INJ	72		1629
FOCKE-WULF	Fw 190A-5 Wurger	DANBURY MINT	H ML·	72		1630
FOCKE-WULF	Fw 190A-5 Wurger	FROG	H INJ	72		1631
FOCKE-WULF	Fw 190A-5 Wurger	HASEGAWA	H INJ	72		1632
FOCKE-WULF	Fw 190A-5 Wurger	NICHIMO	H INJ	72		1633
FOCKE-WULF	Fw 190A-8/F-8 Wurger	AIRFIX	H INJ	72		1634
FOCKE-WULF	Fw 190A-8/F-3 Wurger	HELLER	H INJ	72		1635
FOCKE-WULF	Fw 190C	MAC VAC CANOPY	H VAC	72		1636
FOCKE-WULF	Fw 190C	PRIVATE VENTURE B	H RSN	72		1637
FOCKE-WULF	Fw 190C/V-18	PRIVATE VENTURE C	H RSN	72		1638
FOCKE-WULF	Fw 190D-9	AIRMODEL	H VAC CV	72	canopy, + Fi 103, + Ar 234	1639
FOCKE-WULF	Fw 190D	FROG PENGUIN	H INJ	72		1640
FOCKE-WULF	Fw 190D	MAC VAC CANOPY	H VAC	72		1641
FOCKE-WULF	Fw 190D	MAC VAC CANOPY	H VAC	72	blown canopy	1642
FOCKE-WULF	Fw 190D	SANWA	H INJ	72		1643
FOCKE-WULF	Fw 190D-9	AIRFIX	H INJ RM	72		1644
FOCKE-WULF	Fw 190D-9	HASEGAWA	H INJ	72		1645
FOCKE-WULF	Fw 190D-9	ITALERI	H INJ	72		1646
FOCKE-WULF	Fw 190D-9	LINDBERG	H INJ	72		1647
FOCKE-WULF	Fw 190D-13	AIRFIX	H INJ	72		1648
FOCKE-WULF	Fw 200C Condor	CRUVER	R HR·	72		1649
FOCKE-WULF	Fw 200C-1 Condor	AIRMODEL	H VAC CV	72	+ Do 335	1650
FOCKE-WULF	Fw 200C-3/U1 Condor	REVELL	H INJ	72		1651
FOCKE-WULF	Fw 200K Condor	ARISTO CRAFT	H INJ	72		1652
FOCKE-WULF	Fw 200K Condor	CRUVER	R HR·	72		1653
FOCKE-WULF	Ta 152	MAC VAC CANOPY	H VAC	72		1654
FOCKE-WULF	Ta 152H	FROG	H INJ	72		1655
FOCKE-WULF	Ta 154 Moskito	AIRMODEL	H VAC	72	w. INJ parts	1656
FOCKE-WULF	Ta 154 Moskito	BOLESLAV	H VAC	72		1657
FOCKE-WULF	Ta 154 Moskito	KPL MODELS	H VAC	72		1658
FOCKE-WULF	Ta 154 Moskito	PIONEER 2	H INJ	72		1659
FOCKE-WULF	Ta 154 Moskito	PRIVATE VENTURE C	H RSN	72		1660
FOCKE-WULF	Ta 154 V15 Moskito	WINGS 72	H VAC	72		1661
FOCKE-WULF	Ta 183 Entwurf	FRANK-MODELLBAU	H VAC	72		1662
FOCKE-WULF	Triebflugel	PROJEKTS	H INJ	72		1663
FOCKE-WULF	Weihe 50	WK	H RSN	72	cf. DFS (sailplane)	1664
FOKKER	C-2	O'NEILL	H VAC CV	72		1665
FOKKER	C V-D	ALPHA	H VAC	72		1666
FOKKER	C V-D/E	ALPHA	H VAC	72		1667
FOKKER	C V-E	TRUCKER'S MATE	H VAC	72		1668
FOKKER	C X	ALPHA	H VAC	72		1669
FOKKER	C XIV/XV	O'NEILL	H VAC	72		1670
FOKKER	D I	CLASSIC PLANE	H VAC	72		1671
FOKKER	D I	CRAMER	H VAC	72		1672
FOKKER	D II	CLASSIC PLANE	H VAC	72		1673
FOKKER	D II	CRAMER	H VAC	72		1674
FOKKER	D II	GUNZE SANGYO	H ML·	72		1675

FOKKER	D III	CRAMER	H VAC	72		1676
FOKKER	D IV	CRAMER	H VAC	72		1677
FOKKER	D V	CRAMER	H VAC	72		1678
FOKKER	D VI	CLASSIC PLANE	H VAC	72		1679
FOKKER	D VI	CRAMER	H VAC CV	72		1680
FOKKER	D VII	ATO	H WD·	72		1681
FOKKER	D VII	ELDON	H INJ	72		1682
FOKKER	D VII	GUNZE SANGYO	H ML·	72		1683
FOKKER	D VII	RENWAL	H INJ	72		1684
FOKKER	D VII	REVELL	H INJ	72		1685
FOKKER	D VII	SKYBIRDS	H WD·	72		1686
FOKKER	D VIII	AIRFRAME	H VAC	72	ex-E V	1687
FOKKER	D VIII	C.A. ATKINS	H ML·	72	ex-E V	1688
FOKKER	D VIII	CLASSIC PLANE	H VAC	72	ex- E V	1689
FOKKER	D VIII	MERLIN	H INJ	72	ex-E V, w. ML parts	1690
FOKKER	D VIII	VEEDAY	H INJ	72	ex-E V	1691
FOKKER	D XVII	CLASSIC PLANE	H VAC	72		1692
FOKKER	D XVII	PRIVATE VENTURE	H RSN	72		1693
FOKKER	D XXI	ALPHA	H VC	72		1694
FOKKER	D XXI	FROG	H INJ	72		1695
FOKKER	D XXI	PIONEER 2	H INJ	72		1696
FOKKER	D XXIII	AIRFRAME	H VAC	72		1697
FOKKER	D XXIII	KPL MODELS	H VAC	72		1698
FOKKER	D XXIII	PRIVATE VENTURE	H RSN	72		1699
FOKKER	Dr I	AIRFIX	H INJ	72		1700
FOKKER	Dr I	GUNZE SANGYO	H ML·	72		1701
FOKKER	Dr I	RENWAL	H INJ	72		1702
FOKKER	Dr I	REVELL	H INJ	72		1703
FOKKER	Dr I	SKYBIRDS	H WD·	72		1704
FOKKER	Dr I	EDISON	H ML· AS	72	w. plastic parts	1705
FOKKER	E III	REVELL	H INJ	72		1706
FOKKER	F 27 Friendship	AIRFIX	H INJ	72		1707
FOKKER	F 27 Friendship	EXECUTIVE	D ML·	72		1708
FOKKER	F 27 Friendship	MODELMASTERS	D —	72		1709
FOKKER	50	I.M.C.	D FG·	72		1710
FOKKER	F 28 Fellowship	EXECUTIVE	D FG·	72		1711
FOKKER	F 28 Fellowship	MODELMASTERS	D —	72		1712
FOKKER	100	I.M.C.	D FG·	72		1713
FOKKER	F II	CLASSIC PLANE	H VAC	72		1714
FOKKER	F III	CLASSIC PLANE	H VAC	72		1715
FOKKER	F VIIB/3M Southern Cross	FROG	H INJ	72		1716
FOKKER	F VIII	HOBBY HEAVEN	H VAC	72		1717
FOKKER	G I Grim Reaper	AIRMODEL	H VAC	72		1718
FOKKER	G I Grim Reaper	PRIVATE VENTURE A	H RSN	72		1719
FOKKER	G I Grim Reaper	RAREPLANES	H VAC	72		1720
FOKKER	M VII	CLASSIC PLANE	H VAC	72		1721
FOKKER	S 14 Mach-Trainer	ALPHA	H VAC	72		1722
FOKKER	Super Universal	O'NEILL	H VAC	72		1723
FOKKER	T IV	O'NEILL	H VAC	72		1724
FOKKER	T V	KPL MODELS	H VAC	72		1725
FOKKER	T V	O'NEILL	H VAC	72		1726
FOKKER	T V	RUDEL	H VAC	72		1727
FOKKER	T VIII	PRIVATE VENTURE	H RSN	72		1728
FOKKER	T VIII-W	WINGS 72	H VAC	72	w. ML parts	1729
FOKKER	T VIII-W	ARISTO CRAFT	H INJ	72		1730
FOKKER	T VIII-W	CRUVER	R HR·	72		1731
FOKKER	T VIII-W	O'NEILL	H VAC	72		1732
FOKKER	T VIII-WG/M	RUDEL	H VAC	72		1733
FOKKER	T IX	KPL MODELS	H VAC	72		1734
FOKKER	YO-27	O'NEILL	H VAC	72	id. GENERAL AVIATION	1735
FOLLAND	Gnat	SETCO	R HR·	72		1736
FOLLAND	Gnat F Mk 1	AERO 72	H INJ	72	w. ML parts	1737
FOLLAND	Gnat GR Mk 3	AIRFIX	H INJ	72		1738
FOLLAND	Gnat T Mk 1	AIRFIX	H INJ	72		1739
FOLLAND	Gnat T Mk 1	MATCHBOX	H INJ	72		1740
FORD	4-AT Tri-Motor	MONOGRAM	H INJ	77		1741
FORD	4-AT Tri-Motor	MONOGRAM	H INJ RM	77		1742

FORD	5-AT Tri-Motor	AIRFIX	H INJ	72		1743
FOURNIER	RF4	LAIRD	H VAC	72		1744
FRIEDRICHSHAFEN	FF 331	FORMAPLANE	H VAC	72		1745
FRIEDRICHSHAFEN	FF 43	AIRFRAME	H VAC	72		1746
FRIEDRICHSHAFEN	G III	FORMAPLANE	H VAC	72		1747
FUJI	FA-200 Aero Subaru	EIDAI	H INJ	72		1748
FUJI	T1A	HASEGAWA	H INJ	72		1749
FUJI	T1A	NITTO	H INJ	75		1750
FUJI	T1F-2	T.W.R.	H VAC	72		1751
GATES	Learjet 24	MICRO-WEST	H INJ	72		1752
GATES	Learjet 25	MICRO-WEST	H INJ	72		1753
GATES	Learjet 35	MICRO-WEST	H INJ	72		1754
GATES	Learjet 35A/C-21A	RAREPLANES	H VAC	72		1755
GENERAL AIRCRAFT	GAL.48 Hotspur	ARISTO CRAFT	H INJ	72		1756
GENERAL AIRCRAFT	GAL.48 Hotspur	CRUVER	R HR·	72		1757
GENERAL AIRCRAFT	GAL.48 Hotspur II	FROG	H INJ	72		1758
GENERAL AIRCRAFT	GAL.49/58 Halmilcar	SUTCLIFFE	H VAC	72		1759
GENERAL AVIATION	FLP (PJ-1)	O'NEILL	H VAC	72		1760
GENERAL DYNAMICS	F-16 AFTI	IPMS USA	H RSN CV	72	IMPS USA DAYTON CHAPTER	1761
GENERAL DYNAMICS	YF-16	MODELAIR	H INJ	72		1762
GENERAL DYNAMICS	YF-16 CCV	HASEGAWA	H INJ RM	72	w. Sidewinder missile	1763
GENERAL DYNAMICS	F-16A Fighting Falcon	ESCI	H INJ	72	w. Sidewinder missile	1764
GENERAL DYNAMICS	F-16A Fighting Falcon	EXECUTIVE	D —	72		1765
GENERAL DYNAMICS	F-16A Fighting Falcon	HELLER BOBKIT	H INJ	72		1766
GENERAL DYNAMICS	F-16A Fighting Falcon	MONOGRAM	H INJ	72	w. Sidewinder, Paveway, m.	1767
GENERAL DYNAMICS	F-16A Fighting Falcon	REVELL	H INJ	72	w. Sidewinder missile	1768
GENERAL DYNAMICS	F-16A Plus Fighting Falcon	FUJIMI	H INJ	72	w. Penguin, Sidewinder m.	1769
GENERAL DYNAMICS	F-16A Plus Fighting Falcon	HASEGAWA	H INJ	72	w. Sidewinder, Paveway m.	1770
GENERAL DYNAMICS	F-16A/YF-16A Fighting Falcon	HASEGAWA	H INJ	72	w. Sidewinder missile	1771
GENERAL DYNAMICS	F-16A/B Fighting Falcon	AIRFIX	H INJ	72	w. Maverick, Sidewinder m.	1772
GENERAL DYNAMICS	F-16A/B Fighting Falcon	ITALERI	H INJ	72	w. Paveway, Sparrow, Sw m.	1773
GENERAL DYNAMICS	F-16A/B Fighting Falcon	MATCHBOX	H INJ	72	w. Sidewinder missile	1774
GENERAL DYNAMICS	F-16B Fighting Falcon	ESCI	H INJ	72	w. Sidewinder missile	1775
GENERAL DYNAMICS	F-16B Plus Fighting Falcon	FUJIMI	H INJ	72		1776
GENERAL DYNAMICS	F-16B Plus Fighting Falcon	HASEGAWA	H INJ	72		1777
GENERAL DYNAMICS	F-16C Fighting Falcon	HASEGAWA	H INJ RM	72	remoulded F-16A	1778
GENERAL DYNAMICS	F-16D Fighting Falcon	HASEGAWA	H INJ RM	72	remoulded F-16b	1779
GENERAL DYNAMICS	F-16N/TF-16N Fighting Falcon	FUJIMI	H VAC	72		1780
GENERAL DYNAMICS	F-16XL	MONOGRAM	H INJ	72	w. AMRAAM, Sidewinder m.	1781
GENERAL DYNAMICS	F-111 Aardvark	AMERICAN AIRCRAFT	H INJ	72		1782
GENERAL DYNAMICS	F-111A Aardvark	AIRFIX	H INJ	72		1783
GENERAL DYNAMICS	F-111A Aardvark	NITTO	H INJ	72		1784
GENERAL DYNAMICS	F-111A/B Aardvark	REVELL	H INJ	72		1785
GENERAL DYNAMICS	F-111C Aardvark	REVELL	H INJ	72		1786
GENERAL DYNAMICS	F-111E Aardvark	AIRFIX	H INJ RM	72		1787
GENERAL DYNAMICS	FB-111 Aardvark	EXECUTIVE	D —	72		1788
GENERAL DYNAMICS	EF-111A Raven	EXECUTIVE	D —	72		1789
GENERAL DYNAMICS	EF-111A Raven	MONOGRAM	H INJ	72		1790
GLOBE	Swift	MAIRCRAFT	H WD·	72		1791
GLOSTER	E.28/39 Whittle	FROG	H INJ	72		1792
GLOSTER	Gamecock	PEGASUS	H INJ	72		1793
GLOSTER	Gamecock	PRIVATE VENTURE C	H RSN	72		1794
GLOSTER	Gamecock	VEEDAY	H INJ	72	+ Flycatcher	1795
GLOSTER	Gauntlet	PRIVATE VENTURE C	H RSN	72		1796
GLOSTER	Gauntlet	PRIVATE VENTURE	H RSM RM	72	w. skis	1797
GLOSTER	Gauntlet	SKYBIRDS	H WD·	72		1798
GLOSTER	Gauntlet Mk II	PEGASUS	H INJ	72		1799
GLOSTER	Gladiator	ATO	H WD·	72		1800
GLOSTER	Gladiator	FROG PENGUIN	H INJ	72		1801
GLOSTER	Gladiator	SKYBIRDS	H WD·	72		1802
GLOSTER	Gladiator Mk I	AIRFIX	H INJ	72		1803
GLOSTER	Gladiator Mk I	MATCHBOX	H INJ	72		1804
GLOSTER	Gladiator Mk I/II	FROG	H INJ	72		1805
GLOSTER	Gladiator Mk I/II	HELLER	H INJ	72		1806
GLOSTER	Gladiator Mk II	AIRFIX	H INJ	72	3-blade propeller	1807
GLOSTER	Grebe	MERLIN	H INJ	72	+ 2-seat CV, w. ML parts	1808
GLOSTER	Javelin	HAWK	R HR·	72		1809

GLOSTER	Javelin F(AW) Mk 1	FROG	H INJ	72		1810
GLOSTER	Javelin F(AW) Mk 1	HAWK	H INJ	72	w. Sparrow missile	1811
GLOSTER	Javelin F(AW) Mk 1	VERNON	H WD·	72		1812
GLOSTER	Javelin F(AW) Mk 9/9R	FROG	H INJ RM	72	w. Firestreak missile	1813
GLOSTER	Javelin T Mk 3	HELLER	R INJ	72		1814
GLOSTER	Meteor F Mk III	AIRFIX	H INJ	72		1815
GLOSTER	Meteor F Mk III	FROG PENGUIN	H INJ	72		1816
GLOSTER	Meteor F Mk III	PATHFINDERS	H ML·	72		1817
GLOSTER	Meteor F Mk III	SKYBIRDS	H WD·	72		1818
GLOSTER	Meteor F Mk 4	FROG	H INJ	72		1819
GLOSTER	Meteor F Mk 8	AEROCLUB MODELS	H INJ CV	72		1820
GLOSTER	Meteor F Mk 8	AIRMODEL	H VAC CV	72		1821
GLOSTER	Meteor F Mk 8	CRUVER	R HR·	72		1822
GLOSTER	Meteor F Mk 8	FROG	H INJ	72		1823
GLOSTER	Meteor F Mk 8	MERLIN	H INJ	72	w. ML parts	1824
GLOSTER	Meteor F Mk 8/PR Mk 10	RAREPLANES	H VAC	72		1825
GLOSTER	Meteor FR Mk 9	AEROCLUB MODELS	H INJ CV	72		1826
GLOSTER	Meteor NF Mk 11/12/14	MATCHBOX	H INJ	72		1827
GLOSTER	Meteor NF Mk 11/12/14	PRIVATE VENTURE C	H RSN	72		1828
GLOSTER	Meteor NF Mk 14/T Mk 7	AIRMODEL	H VAC CV	72	canopy, + Jet Provost	1829
GLOSTER	Meteor NF Mk 14	RAREPLANES	H VAC	72		1830
GLOSTER	Meteor PR Mk 10	AEROCLUB MODELS	H INJ CV	72		1831
GLOSTER	Meteor T Mk 7	AEROCLUB MODELS	H INJ CV	72		1832
GOODYEAR	466 Inflatoplane	AIRMODEL	H RSN	72		1833
GOODYEAR	F2G	LONE STAR MODELS	H RSN CV	72		1834
GOODYEAR	FG-1A Corsair	AIRMODEL	H VAC CV	72	canopy, + P-40N + P-51D	1835
GOODYEAR	FG-1A Corsair	MAC VAC CANOPY	H VAC	72		1836
GOPPINGEN	Go 4	PRIVATE VENTURE	H RSN	72		1837
GOPPINGEN	Go 9	PRIVATE VENTURE C	H RSN	72		1838
GOTHA	G IV	RAREPLANES	H VAC	72		1839
GOTHA	Go 145	KPM	H VAC	72		1840
GOTHA	Go 145	PRIVATE VENTURE C	H RSN	72		1841
GOTHA	Go 145	VACU-SPECIAL	H VAC	72		1842
GOTHA	Go 145	WINGS 72	H VAC	72		1843
GOTHA	Go 242	ARISTO CRAFT	H INJ	72		1844
GOTHA	Go 242/244	AIRMODEL	H VAC	72		1845
GOTHA	Go 242/244	FROG	H WD·	72	wood, metal, hard rubber	1846
GOTHA	Go 242/244	ITALERI	H INJ	72		1847
GRANVILLE	GEE BEE	AIRFRAME	H VAC	72		1848
GRANVILLE	GEE BEE	EDISON	H ML· AS	72	w. plastic parts	1849
GREAT LAKES	BT-1	O'NEILL	H VAC	72		1850
GREGOR	FDB-1	CAN-VAC	H VAC	72		1851
GREGOR	FDB-1	EDISON	H ML·	72	w. plastic parts	1852
GRUMMAN	A-6A Intruder	HASEGAWA	H INJ	72		1853
GRUMMAN	A-6A Intruder	MAC VAC CANOPY	H VAC	72		1854
GRUMMAN	EA-6A/KA-6D Intruder	MD	H RSN CV	72		1855
GRUMMAN	A2F-1 (A-6A) Intruder	SETCO	R HR·	72		1856
GRUMMAN	AF-1	O'NEILL	H VAC	72		1857
GRUMMAN	AF-2S/2W Guardian	AIRMODEL	H VAC	72		1858
GRUMMAN	AF-2S/2W Guardian	CRUVER	R HR·	72		1859
GRUMMAN	C-1 Trader	AIRMODEL	H VAC	72	+ Tracker	1860
GRUMMAN	C-1A Trader	FALCON	H VAC CV	72	+ Orion + Banshee	1861
GRUMMAN	C-2A Greyhound	FALCON	H VAC CV	72	+ AD-5W + FJ-3	1862
GRUMMAN	C-2A Greyhound	AIRMODEL	H VAC	72	Test VAC	1863
GRUMMAN	C-2A Greyhound	I.D. MODELS	H VAC CV	72		1864
GRUMMAN	E-1B Tracer	AIRMODEL	H VAC	72		1865
GRUMMAN	E-1B Tracer	FALCON	H VAC CV	72	+ F9F-8P + AP-2H	1866
GRUMMAN	E-2A Hawkeye	FUJIMI	H INJ	72		1867
GRUMMAN	E-2C Hawkeye	FUJIMI	H INJ RM	72		1868
GRUMMAN	E-2C Hawkeye	GRUMMAN	D RSN	72		1869
GRUMMAN	EA-6A/6B Prowler	AIRMODEL	H VAC CV	72		1870
GRUMMAN	EA-6B Prowler	HASEGAWA	H INJ	72		1871
GRUMMAN	EA-6B Prowler	MATCHBOX	H INJ	72		1872
GRUMMAN	F-14A Tomcat	ITALERI	H INJ	72		1873
GRUMMAN	F-14A Tomcat	HASEGAWA	H INJ RM	72		1874
GRUMMAN	F-14A Tomcat	AIRFIX	H INJ	72	w. Phoenix, Sparrow m.	1875
GRUMMAN	F-14A Tomcat	HASEGAWA	H INJ	72	w. Phoenix, Sparrow, Sw m.	1876

GRUMMAN	F-14A Tomcat	MATCHBOX	H INJ	72	w. Phoenix, Sparrow m.	1877
GRUMMAN	F-14A Tomcat	MONOGRAM	H INJ	72	w. Phoenix, Sparrow m.	1878
GRUMMAN	F-14A Tomcat	MONOGRAM	H INJ SN	72	w. Sparrow missile	1879
GRUMMAN	F-14A/B Tomcat	HASEGAWA	H INJ RM	72	remoulded F-14A	1880
GRUMMAN	F2F	O'NEILL	H VAC	72		1881
GRUMMAN	F2F	SKYBIRDS	H WD·	72		1882
GRUMMAN	F2F-1	VP CANADA	H VAC	72	w. RSN parts	1883
GRUMMAN	F3F-1	PRIVATE VENTURE	H RSN	72		1884
GRUMMAN	F3F-1/2	RAREPLANES	H VAC	72		1885
GRUMMAN	F3F-2	PEGASUS	H INJ	72		1886
GRUMMAN	F4F-4 Wildcat	ACADEMY MINICRAFT	H INJ	72		1887
GRUMMAN	F4F-4 Wildcat FM-2	AIRFIX	H INJ	72		1888
GRUMMAN	F4F-4 Wildcat	AOSHIMA	H INJ	72		1889
GRUMMAN	F4F-4 Wildcat	ARISTO CRAFT	H INJ	72		1890
GRUMMAN	F4F-4 Wildcat	CRUVER	R HR·	72		1891
GRUMMAN	F4F-4 Wildcat Mk IV	FROG	H INJ	72		1892
GRUMMAN	F4F-4 Wildcat FM-2	HAWK	H INJ	72		1893
GRUMMAN	F4F-4 Wildcat	MAC VAC CANOPY	H VAC	72		1894
GRUMMAN	F4F-4 Wildcat	PLYCRAFT	H CB·	72		1895
GRUMMAN	F4F-4 Wildcat	REVELL	H INJ	72		1896
GRUMMAN	F6F Hellcat	ARISTO CRAFT	H INJ	72		1897
GRUMMAN	F6F Hellcat	CADET	H WD·	72		1898
GRUMMAN	F6F Hellcat	CRUVER	R HR·	72		1899
GRUMMAN	F6F-3 Hellcat	FROG	H INJ	72		1900
GRUMMAN	F6F-3 Hellcat	FROG PENGUIN	H INJ	72		1901
GRUMMAN	F6F-3 Hellcat	HELLER	H INJ	72		1902
GRUMMAN	F6F-3 Hellcat	MAC VAC CANOPY	H VAC	72		1903
GRUMMAN	F6F-3 Hellcat	MATCHBOX	H INJ	72		1904
GRUMMAN	F6F-3/5 Hellcat	AIRFIX	H INJ	72		1905
GRUMMAN	F6F-3/5 Hellcat	HASEGAWA	H INJ	72		1906
GRUMMAN	F6F-5 Hellcat	FUJIMI	H INJ	70		1907
GRUMMAN	F6F-5 Hellcat	LINDBERG	H INJ	72		1908
GRUMMAN	F6F-5 Hellcat	MIDORI	H INJ	67		1909
GRUMMAN	F6F-5 Hellcat	NITTO	H INJ	77		1910
GRUMMAN	F7F Tigercat	CRUVER	R HR·	72		1911
GRUMMAN	F7F-1 Tigercat	AOSHIMA	H INJ	70		1912
GRUMMAN	F7F-2 Tigercat	CRUVER	R HR·	72		1913
GRUMMAN	F7F-3 Tigercat	MAC VAC CANOPY	H VAC	72		1914
GRUMMAN	F7F-3 Tigercat	MONOGRAM	H INJ	72		1915
GRUMMAN	F8F Bearcat Conquest I	ABORN	H VAC	72	canopy	1916
GRUMMAN	F8F Bearcat	CRUVER	R HR·	72		1917
GRUMMAN	F8F-1 Bearcat	MAC VAC CANOPY	H VAC	72		1918
GRUMMAN	F8F-1/1B Bearcat	MONOGRAM	H INJ	72		1919
GRUMMAN	F8F-1B Bearcat	FROG	H INJ	72		1920
GRUMMAN	F9F-2 Panther	HASEGAWA	H INJ	72		1921
GRUMMAN	F9F-2/4 Panther	AIRMODEL	H VAC	72		1922
GRUMMAN	F9F-4/5 Panther	MATCHBOX	H INJ	72		1923
GRUMMAN	F9F-5 Panther	MICRO SCALE	H INJ CV	72		1924
GRUMMAN	F9F-5 Panther	TOMIYAMA	H INJ	67		1925
GRUMMAN	F9F-6 Cougar	COMET	H INJ	77		1926
GRUMMAN	F9F-6P/8P Cougar	AIRMODEL	H VAC CV	72		1927
GRUMMAN	F9F-8 Cougar	HASEGAWA	H INJ	72	w. Sidewinder missile	1928
GRUMMAN	F9F-8 Cougar	O'NEILL	H VAC	72		1929
GRUMMAN	F9F-8P Cougar	FALCON	H VAC CV	72	+ E-1B + AP-2H	1930
GRUMMAN	F9F-8P Cougar	O'NEILL	H VAC	72		1931
GRUMMAN	F9F-8P/8T Cougar	AIRMODEL	H VAC	72		1932
GRUMMAN	F9F-8T Cougar	FALCON	H VAC CV	72	+ F-106B + Mirage IIID	1933
GRUMMAN	F9F-9 (F11F) Tiger	VERNON	H WD·	72		1934
GRUMMAN	F11F Tiger	NOSE JOBS	H ML· CV	72		1935
GRUMMAN	F11F Tiger	Y.M.C.	H INJ	67		1936
GRUMMAN	F11F-1 Tiger	AIRMODEL	H VAC	72		1937
GRUMMAN	F11F-1 Tiger	CRUVER	R HR·	72		1938
GRUMMAN	F11F-1 Tiger	HASEGAWA	H INJ	72	w. Sidewinder missile	1939
GRUMMAN	F11F-1 Tiger	O'NEILL	H VAC	72		1940
GRUMMAN	FF-1 Goblin	O'NEILL	H VAC	72		1941
GRUMMAN	FF-1 Goblin	RAREPLANES	H VAC	72		1942
GRUMMAN	G-21 Goose	ARNE ANDERSSON	H VAC	72		1943

GRUMMAN	G-21 Goose	ATLANTIC MODELS	D INJ	72		1944
GRUMMAN	G-21 Goose	EXECUTIVE	D —	72		1945
GRUMMAN	G-21 Goose	RAREPLANES	H VAC	72		1946
GRUMMAN	G-21 (JRF) Goose	O'NEILL	H VAC	72		1947
GRUMMAN	G-21 (JRF-1) Goose	DESIGN CENTER	H INJ	72		1948
GRUMMAN	G-73 Mallard	AIR JET ADVANCE	D FG·	72		1949
GRUMMAN	G-73 Mallard	EXECUFORM	H VAC	72		1950
GRUMMAN	Gulfstream II	AIRTEC	D FM·	72		1951
GRUMMAN	Gulfstream II	MICRO-WEST	H INJ	72		1952
GRUMMAN	Gulfstream II	T.W.R.	H VAC	72		1953
GRUMMAN	HU-16B/D/E Albatross	MONOGRAM	H INJ	72		1954
GRUMMAN	SA-16 Albatross	CRUVER	R HR·	72		1955
GRUMMAN	J2F-4 Duck	ARISTO CRAFT	H INJ	72		1956
GRUMMAN	J2F-4 Duck	CRUVER	R HR·	72		1957
GRUMMAN	J2F-6 Duck	AIRFIX	H INJ	72		1958
GRUMMAN	J4F-2 Gosling/Widgeon	AIRFIX	H INJ	72		1959
GRUMMAN	OV-1A/1C Mohawk	HASEGAWA	H INJ	72		1960
GRUMMAN	OV-1B Mohawk	HASEGAWA	H INJ	72		1961
GRUMMAN	S-2F1 (S-2A) Tracker	HASEGAWA	H INJ	72		1962
GRUMMAN	S-2E Tracker	AIRMODEL	H VAC	72	+ Trader	1963
GRUMMAN	S-2F Tracker	UNIQUE SCALE	H RSN	72		1964
GRUMMAN	S-2F3 Tracker	SETCO	R HR·	72		1965
GRUMMAN	TBF Avenger	FUJIMI	H INJ	70		1966
GRUMMAN	TBF Avenger	LINDBERG	H INJ	72		1967
GRUMMAN	TBF Avenger	NITTO	H INJ	77		1968
GRUMMAN	TBF-1 Avenger	ACADEMY MINICRAFT	H INJ	72		1969
GRUMMAN	TBF-1 Avenger	ARISTO CRAFT	H INJ	72		1970
GRUMMAN	TBF-1 Avenger	CRUVER	R HR·	72		1971
GRUMMAN	TBF/TBM-1 Avenger	FROG	H INJ	72		1972
GRUMMAN	TBF/TBM-1 Avenger	MAC VAC CANOPY	H VAC	72	turret	1973
GRUMMAN	TBF/TBM-3 Avenger	AIRFIX	H INJ	72		1974
GRUMMAN	TBF/TBM-3U/3W Avenger	AIRMODEL	H VAC CV	72	+ AD-4W	1975
GRUMMAN	TBF/TBM-3U/3S/3W Avenger	AIRMODEL	H VAC CV	72	+ AD-4W	1976
GRUMMAN	TBM-3W Avenger	FALCON	H VAC CV	72	+ TF-86F + P2V-5	1977
GRUMMAN	WF-2	SETCO	R HR·	72		1978
GRUMMAN	X-29A	HASEGAWA	H INJ	72		1979
GRUMMAN	X-29A	RACCOON	H RSN	72		1980
GRUMMAN	XF5F-1 Skyrocket	AIRFRAME	H VAC	72		1981
GRUMMAN	XF5F-1 Skyrocket	J & L	H VAC	72		1982
GRUMMAN	XF5F-1 Skyrocket	J & L	H VAC	72	long nose	1983
GRUMMAN	XF5F-1 Skyrocket	MAC VAC CANOPY	H VAC	72		1984
GRUMMAN	XF5F-1 Skyrocket	MERLIN	H INJ	72	w. ML parts	1985
GRUMMAN	XF5F-1 Skyrocket	PRIVATE VENTURE	H RSN	72		1986
GRUMMAN	XF5F-1 Skyrocket	RAREPLANES	H VAC	72		1987
GRUMMAN	XP-50	AIRFRAME	H VAC	72		1988
GRUMMAN	XP-50	J & L	H VAC	72		1989
GRUMMAN	XP-50	PRIVATE VENTURE	H RSN	72		1990
HALBERSTADT	CL II	CRAMER	H VAC	72		1991
HALBERSTADT	CL II	FORMAPLANE	H VAC	72		1992
HALBERSTADT	CL IV	JOYSTICK	H VAC	72	w. ML parts	1993
HALBERSTADT	D II	AIRFRAME	H VAC	72		1994
HALBERSTADT	D II	MERLIN	H INJ	72		1995
HALBERSTADT	D III	C.A. ATKINS	H ML·	72		1996
HALL ALUMINIUM	PH-3	O'NEILL	H VAC	72		1997
HANDLEY-PAGE	0/400	AIRFIX	H INJ	72		1998
HANDLEY-PAGE	HP.24 Hyderabad/HP.33 Hinaidi	SUTCLIFFE	H VAC	72	w. ML parts	1999
HANDLEY-PAGE	HP.42/45 Heracles	SUTCLIFFE	H VAC	72		2000
HANDLEY-PAGE	HP.50 Heyford Mk I/II/III	MATCHBOX	H INJ	72		2001
HANDLEY-PAGE	HP.50 Heyford	SKYBIRDS	H WD·	72		2002
HANDLEY-PAGE	HP.50 Heyford	SUTCLIFFE	H VAC	72		2003
HANDLEY-PAGE	HP.52 Hampden B Mk 1	AIRFIX	H INJ	72		2004
HANDLEY-PAGE	HP.52 Hampden	ARISTO CRAFT	H INJ	72		2005
HANDLEY-PAGE	HP.52 Hampden	CRUVER	R HR·	72		2006
HANDLEY-PAGE	HP.52 Hampden	FROG PENGUIN	H INJ	72		2007
HANDLEY-PAGE	HP.52 Hampden	SKYBIRDS	H WD·	72		2008
HANDLEY-PAGE	HP.53 Hereford	MAINTRACK	H RSN CV	72		2009
HANDLEY-PAGE	HP.53 Hereford	SUTCLIFFE	H VAC CV	72	+ Halifax	2010

HANDLEY-PAGE	HP.54 Harrow/Sparrow	SUTCLIFFE	H VAC	72		2011
HANDLEY-PAGE	HP.57 Halifax Mk I	ARISTO CRAFT	H INJ	72		2012
HANDLEY-PAGE	HP.57 Halifax Mk I	CRUVER	R HB·	72		2013
HANDLEY-PAGE	HP.57 Halifax Mk I	FROG	H HR·	72		2014
HANDLEY-PAGE	HP.57 Halifax Mk I/B.II/GR.II	MATCHBOX	H INJ	72		2015
HANDLEY-PAGE	HP.57 Halifax Mk I/B Mk II	SUTCLIFFE	H VAC CV	72	transport v., + Hereford	2016
HANDLEY-PAGE	HP.57 Halifax B Mk III	AIRFIX	H INJ	72		2017
HANDLEY-PAGE	HP.67 Hastings	CRUVER	R HR·	72		2018
HANDLEY-PAGE	HP.67 Hastings	O'NEILL	H VAC	72		2019
HANDLEY-PAGE	HP.67 Hastings C Mk 2	FORMAPLANE	H VAC	72		2020
HANDLEY-PAGE	HP.70 Halifax C Mk VIII/Halton	MAINTRACK	H RSN CV	72		2021
HANDLEY-PAGE	HPR.7 Herald	EXECUTIVE	D FG·	72		2022
HANDLEY-PAGE	HPR.7 Herald Series 200	FROG	H INJ	72		2023
HANDLEY-PAGE	Victor	NOVA MODELS	H VAC	72		2024
HANDLEY-PAGE	Victor K Mk 2	MATCHBOX	H INJ	72		2025
HANDLEY-PAGE	Victor K Mk 2	RAREPLANES	H VAC	72		2026
HANNOVER	CL IIIa	AIRFIX	H INJ	72		2027
HANNOVER	CL IIIa	SKYBIRDS	H WD·	72		2028
HANRIOT	HD.1	CRAMER	H VAC	72		2029
HANRIOT	HD.1	FORMAPLANE	H VAC	72		2030
HANRIOT	HD.1	PEGASUS	H INJ	72		2031
HANRIOT	HD.1	RUDEL	H VAC	72		2032
HANRIOT	HD.1/2	CLASSIC PLANE	H VAC	72		2033
HANRIOT	HD.1/2	MODELPOINT	H INJ	72		2034
HANRIOT	HD.220	CHALLENGE	H VAC	72		2035
HANRIOT	HD.232	ALPHA	H VAC	72		2036
HANSA-BRANDENBURG	C I	CLASSIC PLANE	H VAC	72		2037
HANSA-BRANDENBURG	C I	EAGLES TALON	H VAC	72		2038
HANSA-BRANDENBURG	C I	PRIVATE VENTURE BC	H RSN	72		2039
HANSA-BRANDENBURG	C I	WINGS 72	H VAC	72		2040
HANSA-BRANDENBURG	CC	CLASSIC PLANE	H VAC	72		2041
HANSA-BRANDENBURG	D I	C.A. ATKINS	H ML·	72		2042
HANSA-BRANDENBURG	D I	CLASSIC PLANE	H VAC	72		2043
HANSA-BRANDENBURG	D I	EDISON	H ML· AS	72	w. plastic parts	2044
HANSA-BRANDENBURG	D I	FORMAPLANE	H VAC	72	w. ML parts	2045
HANSA-BRANDENBURG	KDW	FORMAPLANE	H VAC	72		2046
HANSA-BRANDENBURG	W 12	FORMAPLANE	H VAC	72		2047
HANSA-BRANDENBURG	W 12	PRIVATE VENTURE	H RSN	72		2048
HANSA-BRANDENBURG	W 12	WINGS 72	H VAC	72		2049
HANSA-BRANDENBURG	W 12	WINGS 72	H VAC	72	w. ML parts	2050
HANSA-BRANDENBURG	W 12V	PRIVATE VENTURE	H RSN	72		2051
HANSA-BRANDENBURG	W 20	AIRFRAME	H VAC	72		2052
HANSA-BRANDENBURG	W 29	FORMAPLANE	H VAC	72		2053
HANSA-BRANDENBURG	W 29	PRIVATE VENTURE C	H RSN	72		2054
HANSA-BRANDENBURG	W 29	VEEDAY	H INJ	72		2055
HAWKER	Demon	AIRFIX	H INJ	72		2056
HAWKER	Demon	FROG PENGUIN	H INJ	72		2057
HAWKER	Fury	CRUVER	R HR·	72		2058
HAWKER	Fury	FROG PENGUIN	H INJ	72		2059
HAWKER	Fury	GUANO	H INJ CV	72	Yugoslav version	2060
HAWKER	Fury	MATCHBOX	H INJ	72		2061
HAWKER	Fury	RAREPLANES	H VAC	72		2062
HAWKER	Fury	SKYBIRDS	H WD·	72		2063
HAWKER	Hart	AIRFIX	H INJ	72		2064
HAWKER	Hart	FROG PENGUIN	H INJ	72		2065
HAWKER	Hart	MERLIN	H INJ	72	ex-FROG w. ML parts	2066
HAWKER	Hart	SKYBIRDS	H WD·	72		2067
HAWKER	Hector	PRIVATE VENTURE C	H RSN	72		2068
HAWKER	Henley	SKYBIRDS	H WD·	72		2069
HAWKER	Henley T Mk III	FORMAPLANE	H VAC	72		2070
HAWKER	Hind	ATO	H WD·	72		2071
HAWKER	Hind	FROG PENGUIN	H INJ	72		2072
HAWKER	Hind	MERLIN	H INJ	72	ex-FROG w. ML parts	2073
HAWKER	Horsley	SUTCLIFFE	H VAC	72		2074
HAWKER	Hunter	CRUVER	R HR·	72		2075
HAWKER	Hunter F Mk 1	FROG	H INJ	72		2076
HAWKER	Hunter F Mk 6	AEROCLUB MODELS	H VAC CV	72	nose	2077

HAWKER	Hunter F Mk 6	AIRFIX	H INJ	72		2078
HAWKER	Hunter F Mk 6	CENTRAL	H INJ	72	w. Sidewinder missile	2079
HAWKER	Hunter F Mk 6	MAC VAC CANOPY	H VAC	72		2080
HAWKER	Hunter F Mk 6/T Mk 7	MATCHBOX	H INJ	72		2081
HAWKER	Hunter FGA Mk 9	AIRFIX	H INJ RM	72		2082
HAWKER	Hunter FGA Mk 9/Hunter Mk 58	FROG	H INJ RM	72		2083
HAWKER	Hunter T Mk 7	AEROCLUB MODELS	H VAC CV	72	nose	2084
HAWKER	Hunter T Mk 7	AIR CONVERSIONS	H INJ CV	72		2085
HAWKER	Hunter T Mk 7/8	AIRMODEL	H VAC CV	72	canopy, + Lightning	2086
HAWKER	Hurricane (prototype)	C.A. ATKINS	H ML·	72		2087
HAWKER	Hurricane	COMPASS	H WD·	72		2088
HAWKER	Hurricane Mk I	AIRFIX	H INJ	72		2089
HAWKER	Hurricane Mk I	ARISTO CRAFT	H INJ	72		2090
HAWKER	Hurricane Mk I	DANBURY MINT	H ML·	72		2091
HAWKER	Hurricane Mk I	GUANO	H INJ CV	72		2092
HAWKER	Hurricane Mk I	PATHFINDERS	H ML·	72		2093
HAWKER	Hurricane Mk I	REVELL	H INJ	72		2094
HAWKER	Hurricane Mk I	REVELL	H INJ RM	72		2095
HAWKER	Hurricane Mk I	SKYBIRDS	H WD·	72		2096
HAWKER	Hurricane Mk I/IIB/IID/Mk IV	AIRFIX	H INJ RM	72		2097
HAWKER	Hurricane Mk II	CRUVER	R HR·	72		2098
HAWKER	Hurricane Mk II	FROG PENGUIN	H INJ	72		2099
HAWKER	Hurricane Mk II	GEE'S AERO WORKS	H WD·	72		2100
HAWKER	Hurricane Mk II	MAC VAC CANOPY	H VAC	72		2101
HAWKER	Hurricane Mk II	SANWA	H INJ	72		2102
HAWKER	Hurricane Mk IIB/IIC	FROG	H INJ	72	Sea Hurricane Mk IIC	2103
HAWKER	Hurricane Mk IIC	HELLER	H INJ	72		2104
HAWKER	Hurricane Mk IIC	KEIL KRAFT	H INJ	72		2105
HAWKER	Hurricane Mk IIC	MATCHBOX	H INJ	72		2106
HAWKER	Hurricane Mk IID	AOSHIMA	H INJ	72		2107
HAWKER	Hurricane Mk IV	AIRFIX	H INJ	72		2108
HAWKER	Nimrod Mk I/II	ESOTERIC	H VAC	72	w. ML parts	2109
HAWKER	Osprey	FROG PENGUIN	H INJ	72		2110
HAWKER	Osprey Mk IV	MERLIN	H INJ	72	ex-FROG w. ML parts	2111
HAWKER	P.1127 Kestrel	AIRFIX	H INJ	72		2112
HAWKER	Sea Fury	CRUVER	R HR·	72		2113
HAWKER	Sea Fury FB Mk 11	ELLIOTT	H VAC	72	w. ML parts	2114
HAWKER	Sea Fury FB Mk 11	FROG	H INJ	72		2115
HAWKER	Sea Fury FB Mk 11	MAC VAC CANOPY	H VAC	72		2116
HAWKER	Sea Fury T Mk 20	C. SCALE	H ML· CV	72	+ Firefly	2117
HAWKER	Sea Fury T Mk 20	AIRMODEL	H VAC CV	72	+ Typhoon + Spit, + Beauf.	2118
HAWKER	Sea Hawk	CRUVER	R HR·	72		2119
HAWKER	Sea Hawk F Mk 1	FROG	H INJ	72		2120
HAWKER	Sea Hawk FGA Mk 6/Mk 100	AIRFIX	H INJ	72		2121
HAWKER	Tempest	COMPASS	H WD·	72		2122
HAWKER	Tempest Mk II	CRUVER	R HR·	72		2123
HAWKER	Tempest Mk II	FROG PENGUIN	H INJ	72		2124
HAWKER	Tempest Mk II	GEE'S AERO WORKS	H WD·	72		2125
HAWKER	Tempest Mk II	PATHFINDERS	H ML·	72		2126
HAWKER	Tempest Mk II/VI	MATCHBOX	H INJ	72		2127
HAWKER	Tempest Mk V	CRUVER	R HR·	72		2128
HAWKER	Tempest Mk V	HELLER	H INJ	72		2129
HAWKER	Tempest Mk V	MAC VAC CANOPY	H VAC	72		2130
HAWKER	Tempest Mk V	REVELL	H INJ	72		2131
HAWKER	Tempest S Mk V	FROG	H INJ	72		2132
HAWKER	Typhoon	ARISTO CRAFT	H INJ	72		2133
HAWKER	Typhoon	CADET	H WD·	72		2134
HAWKER	Typhoon	CRUVER	R HR·	72		2135
HAWKER	Typhoon	FROG PENGUIN	H INJ	72		2136
HAWKER	Typhoon	PATHFINDERS	H ML·	72		2137
HAWKER	Typhoon Mk IB	AIRFIX	H INJ	72		2138
HAWKER	Typhoon Mk IB	FROG	H INJ	72	bubble canopy	2139
HAWKER	Typhoon Mk IB	FROG	H INJ	72	car door canopy	2140
HAWKER	Typhoon Mk IB	GEE'S AERO WORKS	H WD·	72		2141
HAWKER	Typhoon F Mk IA	AIRMODEL	H VAC CV	72	+ Sea F. + Spit. + Beauf.	2142
HAWKER	Woodcock	MERLIN	H INJ	72	w. ML parts	2143
HAWKER	Woodcock	PRIVATE VENTURE B	H RSN	72		2144

HAWKER SIDDELEY	HS 148	I.D. MODELS	H ML· CV	72		2145
HAWKER SIDDELEY	HS 748 Andover	EXECUTIVE	D —	72		2146
HAWKER SIDDELEY	HS 748 Andover	I.D. MODELS	H VAC	72		2147
HAWKER SIDDELEY	HS 748 Andover	MODELMASTERS	D —	72		2148
HAWKER SIDDELEY	HS 748 Andover	T.W.R.	H VAC	72		2149
HAWKER SIDDELEY/DH/BAe	Trident 3	SKYLAND MODELS	D FG·	72		2150
HEINKEL	He 5	ARNE ANDERSSON	H VAC	72		2151
HEINKEL	He 39	AIRMODEL	H VAC	72		2152
HEINKEL	He 42C-2	AIRMODEL	H VAC	72		2153
HEINKEL	He 45	AIRMODEL	H VAC	72	w. RSN parts	2154
HEINKEL	He 46	AIRMODEL	H VAC	72		2155
HEINKEL	He 46C/D	PRIVATE VENTURE C	H RSN	72		2156
HEINKEL	He 46C/D	WINGS 72	H VAC	72		2157
HEINKEL	He 51B-1	HASEGAWA	H INJ	72		2158
HEINKEL	He 51B-1	RAREPLANES	H VAC	72		2159
HEINKEL	He 51B-2	HASEGAWA	H INJ	72		2160
HEINKEL	He 59B-2	AIRMODEL	H VAC	72		2161
HEINKEL	He 60C	AIRMODEL	H VAC	72		2162
HEINKEL	He 60C	PRIVATE VENTURE A	H RSN	72		2163
HEINKEL	He 70F	AIRMODEL	H VAC	72		2164
HEINKEL	He 70F	PRIVATE VENTURE C	H RSN	72		2165
HEINKEL	He 70	SKYBIRDS	H WD·	72		2166
HEINKEL	He 70F/70G/170	AIRMODEL	H VAC	72		2167
HEINKEL	He 100D	CRUVER	R HR·	72		2168
HEINKEL	He 100D	LINDBERG	R INJ	72		2169
HEINKEL	He 100D	MAC VAC CANOPY	H VAC	72		2170
HEINKEL	He 100D	PRIVATE VENTURE B	H RSN	72		2171
HEINKEL	He 111	ARISTO CRAFT	H INJ	72		2172
HEINKEL	He 111B-2	AIRMODEL	H VAC CV	72		2173
HEINKEL	He 111F-4	AIRMODEL	H VAC CV	72		2174
HEINKEL	He 111H	CRUVER	R HR·	72		2175
HEINKEL	He 111H	MAC VAC CANOPY	H VAC	72		2176
HEINKEL	He 111H-1/6	FROG	H INJ	72		2177
HEINKEL	He 111H-1/6	ITALERI	H INJ	72		2178
HEINKEL	He 111H-4	AIRMODEL	H INJ CV	72		2179
HEINKEL	He 111H-5	MATCHBOX	H INJ	72		2180
HEINKEL	He 111H-20	AIRFIX	H INJ	72		2181
HEINKEL	He 111Z	AIRMODEL	H VAC CV	72		2182
HEINKEL	He 111Z-1	ITALERI	H INJ	72		2183
HEINKEL	He 112	CRUVER	R HR·	72		2184
HEINKEL	He 1112B0	ARISTO CRAFT	H INJ	72		2185
HEINKEL	He 112B0	VEEDAY	H INJ	72		2186
HEINKEL	He 112B0/B1	HELLER	H INJ	72		2187
HEINKEL	He 112B0/V9	RAREPLANES	H VAC	72		2188
HEINKEL	He 113	ARISTO CRAFT	H INJ	72		2189
HEINKEL	He 114A	AIRMODEL	H VAC	72		2190
HEINKEL	He 115	ARISTO CRAFT	H INJ	72		2191
HEINKEL	He 115	CRUVER	R HR·	72		2192
HEINKEL	He 115B-1	AIRMODEL	H VAC	72		2193
HEINKEL	He 115B-1	MATCHBOX	H INJ	72		2194
HEINKEL	He 115C-1	FROG	H INJ	72		2195
HEINKEL	He 116	VACU-SPECIAL	H VAC	72		2196
HEINKEL	He 119	AIRMODEL	H VAC	72		2197
HEINKEL	He 162A Salamander	FROG	H INJ	72		2198
HEINKEL	He 162A Salamander	LINDBERG	H INJ	72		2199
HEINKEL	He 162A Salamander	MAC VAC CANOPY	H VAC	72		2200
HEINKEL	He 162A Salamander	VOLKS	H RSN	72		2201
HEINKEL	He 170	PRIVATE VENTURE	H RSN	72		2202
HEINKEL	He 176	AIRMODEL	H VAC	72		2203
HEINKEL	He 176	CLASSIC PLANE	H VAC	72		2204
HEINKEL	He 176	PRIVATE VENTURE A	H RSN	72		2205
HEINKEL	He 177 Greif	ARISTO CRAFT	H INJ	72		2206
HEINKEL	He 177 Greif	CRUVER	R HR·	72		2207
HEINKEL	He 177A-5 Greif	AIRFIX	H INJ	72	w. Hs 293 missile	2208
HEINKEL	He 178	AIRMODEL	H VAC	72		2209
HEINKEL	He 178	EAGLES TALON	H VAC	72		2210
HEINKEL	He 178	KPM	H VAC	72		2211

HEINKEL	He 178	PRIVATE VENTURE B	H RSN	72		2212
HEINKEL	He 178	WINGS 72	H VAC	72		2213
HEINKEL	He 219 Uhu	VOLKS	H RSN	72		2214
HEINKEL	He 219A Uhu	MAC VAC CANOPY	H VAC	72		2215
HEINKEL	He 219A-2/R4 Uhu	LINDBERG	H INJ	72		2216
HEINKEL	He 219A-2/R4 Uhu	REVELL	H INJ	72		2217
HEINKEL	He 219A-5/R4/B-1 Uhu	FRANK-MODELLBAU	H VAC CV	72		2218
HEINKEL	He 219A-7/R4 Uhu	FROG	H INJ	72		2219
HEINKEL	He 280 V2	PRIVATE VENTURE C	H RSN	72	JUMO engine	2220
HEINKEL	He 280 V1/V7/V8	PRIVATE VENTURE C	H RSN	72	BMW engine	2221
HEINKEL	He 280 V1/V2/V3/V4/V5	FRANK-MODELLBAU	H VAC	72		2222
HEINKEL	He 280 V2/V4/V5/V6/V7/V8/V9	FRANK-MODELLBAU	H VAC	72		2223
HEINKEL	He 280 V3	AIRMODEL	H RSN	72		2224
HEINKEL	He 280 V8	PRIVATE VENTURE C	H RSN	72	glider version	2225
HEINKEL	P.1077 Julia	AIRMODEL	H VAC	72	+ Romeo	2226
HEINKEL	P.1077 Julia 1 & 2	FRANK-MODELLBAU	H VAC	72	+ Romeo	2227
HEINKEL	P.1077 Julia	PRIVATE VENTURE B	R RSN	72		2228
HEINKEL	P.1078 Romeo	AIRMODEL	H VAC	72	+ Julia	2229
HEINKEL	P.1078 Romeo	FRANK-MODELLBAU	H VAC	72	+ Julia	2230
HEINKEL	P.1078 Romeo	PRIVATE VENTURE C	H RSN	72		2231
HENSCHEL	Hs 123A-1	AIRFIX	H INJ	72		2232
HENSCHEL	Hs 126	ARISTO CRAFT	H INJ	72		2233
HENSCHEL	Hs 126	CRUVER	R HR·	72		2234
HENSCHEL	Hs 126A-1/B-1	AIRFIX	H INJ	72		2235
HENSCHEL	Hs 126A-1/B-1	ITALERI	H INJ	72		2236
HENSCHEL	Hs 126A-1/B-1/N-1	RAREPLANES	H VAC	72		2237
HENSCHEL	Hs 126B-1	MATCHBOX	H INJ	72		2238
HENSCHEL	Hs 129	ARISTO CRAFT	H INJ	72		2239
HENSCHEL	Hs 129	CRUVER	R HR·	72		2240
HENSCHEL	Hs 129B-2/B-3	AIRFIX	H INJ	72		2241
HENSCHEL	Hs 129B-2/B-3	LINDBERG	H INJ	72	B-2, w. BK75 gun	2242
HENSCHEL	Hs 132	AIRFRAME	H VAC	72		2243
HENSCHEL	Hs 132V1	FRANK-MODELLBAU	H VAC	72		2244
HESTON	Type 5 Racer	AIRFRAME	H VAC	72		2245
HESTON	Type 5 Racer	SKYBIRDS	H WD·	72		2246
HILLER	X-18	COMET	H INJ	70		2247
HIRD	H4H1 Flying Boat	O'NEILL	H VAC	72		2248
HISPANO	HA-200 Saeta/HA-220 Super Saeta	REPLICA	H RSN	72		2249
HISPANO	HA 1112 Buchon	HISPANO-AVIO-KIT	H VAC	72	Spanish Bf 109	2250
HISPANO	HA 1112 Buchon	PEGASUS	H INJ	72	Spanish Bf 109	2251
HORTEN	Ho 229	DRAGON MPW	H RSN	72	w. VAC, ML parts	2252
HORTEN	Ho 229	PIONEER 2	H INJ	72		2253
HORTEN	Ho 229	PRIVATE VENTURE B	H RSN	72		2254
HORTEN	Ho 229A-1	AIRMODEL	H VAC	72		2255
HORTEN	Ho 229A-1/U-1	JRC	H RSN	72		2256
HORTEN	Ho 229 V3	BOLESLAV	H VAC	72		2257
HOVER	MF-11	ALPHA	H VAC	72		2258
HOWARD	DGA-15	EXECUFORM	H VAC	72		2259
HOWARD	GH-1	DESIGN CENTER	H INJ	72		2260
HUGHES	200 (TH-55A Osage)	PRIVATE VENTURE C	H RSN	72		2261
HUGHES	369 Cayuse (OH-6A)	AIRMODEL	H VAC	72	+ UH-2A Seasprite	2262
HUGHES	500 Cayuse	GAMES	H INJ SN	72	as BELL 206B 1/100 on box	2263
HUGHES	500 Cayuse	HELLER BOBKIT	H INJ SN	72		2264
HUGHES	500 Cayuse	HELLER CLIC CLAC	H INJ SN	72	remoulded	2265
HUGHES	500 Cayuse	PILEN	H INJ	75		2266
HUGHES	500 Cayuse	PRIVATE VENTURE	H RSN	72		2267
HUGHES	500 Cayuse	UDC	H ML·	72		2268
HUGHES	AH-64 Apache	HASEGAWA	H INJ	72	w. Hellfire missile	2269
HUGHES	AH-64 Apache	ITALERI	H INJ	72		2270
HUGHES	XF-11	EXECUFORM	H VAC	72		2271
HUNTING PERCIVAL	Pembroke	AIRMODEL	H VAC	72		2272
HUNTING PERCIVAL	Pembroke	CRUVER	R HR·	72		2273
IAI	1124N Sea Scan	LEOMAN	H RSN	72		2274
IAI	Arava	O'NEILL	H VAC	72		2275
IAI	Kfir-C2	HASEGAWA	H INJ	72	w. Shafrir missile	2276
IAI	Kfir-C2 (F-21)	ITALERI	H INJ	72		2277
IAR	39	ALPHA	H VAC	72		2278

IAR	39	O'NEILL	H VAC	72		2279
IAR	80	AIRMODEL	H VAC	72		2280
IAR	80	FORMAPLANE	H VAC	72		2281
IAR	80	MAC VAC CANOPY	H VAC	72		2282
IAR	80	PRIVATE VENTURE A	H RSN	72		2283
IKARUS	IK-2	ALPHA	H VAC	72		2284
IKARUS	IK-2	GUANO	H RSN	72		2285
IKARUS	IK-2	GUANO	H INJ	72		2286
IKARUS	IK-3	FORMAPLANE	H VAC	72		2287
ILYUSHIN	Il-1	CRUVER	R HR·	72		2288
ILYUSHIN	Il-2 Shturmovik (Bark)	AIRMODEL	H VAC CV	72	c., + MiG-15UTI + MiG-21U	2289
ILYUSHIN	Il-2 Shturmovik (Bark)	CRUVER	R HR·	72		2290
ILYUSHIN	Il-2 Shturmovik (Bark)	MAC VAC CANOPY	H VAC	72		2291
ILYUSHIN	Il-2 Shturmovik (Bark)	MIKRO	H INJ	72	ex-BSh-2	2292
ILYUSHIN	Il-2 Type 3M Shturmovik (Bark)	AIRFIX	H INJ	72		2293
ILYUSHIN	Il-2 Type 3M Shturmovik (Bark)	KOVOZAVODY	H INJ	72		2294
ILYUSHIN	Il-3	CRUVER	R HR·	72		2295
ILYUSHIN	Il-4 (DB-3f) (Bob)	SUTCLIFFE	H VAC	72	w. ML parts	2296
ILYUSHIN	Il-4 (DB-3f) (Bob)	CRUVER	R HR·	72		2297
ILYUSHIN	Il-4 (DB-3f) (Bob)	KPL MODELS	H VAC	72		2298
ILYUSHIN	Il-4 (DB-3/3f) (Bob)	O'NEILL	H VAC	72		2299
ILYUSHIN	Il-4 (DB-3M) (Bob)	VP CANADA	H VAC	72	w. RSN parts	2300
ILYUSHIN	Il-10 (AVIA B-33) (Beast)	KOVOZAVODY	H INJ	72		2301
ILYUSHIN	Il-12 (Coach)	CRUVER	R HR·	72		2302
ILYUSHIN	Il-18 (Coot)	CRUVER	R HR·	72		2303
ILYUSHIN	Il-18 (Coot)	J & L	H VAC	72		2304
ILYUSHIN	Il-20	PRIVATE VENTURE C	H RSN	72		2305
ILYUSHIN	Il-28 (Beagle)	AIRFIX	H INJ	72		2306
ILYUSHIN	Il-28 (Beagle)	CRUVER	R HR·	72		2307
ILYUSHIN	Il-40 (Brawny)	SETCO	R HR·	72		2308
IMAM (MERIDIONALI)	Ro.32	ALPHA	H VAC	72		2309
IMAM (MERIDIONALI)	Ro.37	CHALLENGE	H VAC	72		2310
IMAM (MERIDIONALI)	Ro.37	PRIVATE VENTURE BC	H RSN	72		2311
IMAM (MERIDIONALI)	Ro.37	WINGS 72	H VAC	72		2312
IMAM (MERIDIONALI)	Ro.37/37bis	AIRMODEL	H VAC	72	w. RSN parts	2313
IMAM (MERIDIONALI)	Ro.37/37bis	ALPHA	H VAC	72		2314
IMAM (MERIDIONALI)	Ro.37bis	CRAMER	H VAC	72		2315
IMAM (MERIDIONALI)	Ro.37bis	PRIVATE VENTURE	H RSN	72		2316
IMAM (MERIDIONALI)	Ro.43	PRIVATE VENTURE	H RSN	72		2317
IMAM (MERIDIONALI)	Ro.43/Ro.44	AIRMODEL	H VAC	72	w. RSN parts	2318
IMAM (MERIDIONALI)	Ro.44	PRIVATE VENTURE	H RSN	72		2319
IMAM (MERIDIONALI)	Ro.57	ABORN	H VAC	72	canopy	2320
IMAM (MERIDIONALI)	Ro.57	KPL MODELS	H VAC	72		2321
IMAM (MERIDIONALI)	Ro.57	O'NEILL	H VAC	72		2322
IMAM (MERIDIONALI)	Ro.57	PRIVATE VENTURE	H RSN	72		2323
IMAM (MERIDIONALI)	Ro.57	WINGS 72	H VAC	72		2324
IMAM (MERIDIONALI)	Ro.58	KPL MODELS	H VAC	72	w. INJ parts	2325
JUNKERS	D II	CRAMER	H VAC	72		2326
JUNKERS	F 13	CLASSIC PLANE	H VAC	72		2327
JUNKERS	F 13	PRIVATE VENTURE	H RSN	72		2328
JUNKERS	G 38	AIRMODEL	H VAC	72		2329
JUNKERS	J 9 (D I)	CLASSIC PLANE	H VAC	72		2330
JUNKERS	J 9 (D I)	PEGASUS	H INJ	72		2331
JUNKERS	J 9 (D I)	PRIVATE VENTURE	H RSN	72		2332
JUNKERS	J 9 (D I)	RAREPLANES	H VAC	72		2333
JUNKERS	J 10 (CL I)	CLASSIC PLANE	H VAC	72		2334
JUNKERS	J 10 (CL I)	CRAMER	H VAC	72		2335
JUNKERS	Ju 52	ARISTO CRAFT	H INJ	72		2336
JUNKERS	Ju 52	CRUVER	R HR·	72		2337
JUNKERS	Ju 52/3m	ITALERI	H INJ	72		2338
JUNKERS	Ju 52/3m g3e/4e	AIRFIX	H INJ	72	w. floats	2339
JUNKERS	Ju 52/3m g5e/6e/7e/8e/9e	ITALERI	H INJ	72	w. skis	2340
JUNKERS	Ju 52/3m g5e/9e	ITALERI	H INJ	72	w. DG ring	2341
JUNKERS	Ju 52/3m g5e/9e	ITALERI	H INJ	72	w. floats	2342
JUNKERS	Ju 52/3m g6e	HELLER	H INJ	72		2343
JUNKERS	Ju 52 Dust-Bin	GUANO	H INJ CV	72		2344
JUNKERS	Ju 86D-1	ITALERRI	H INJ	72		2345

JUNKERS	Ju 86D/E	AIRMODEL	H VAC	72		2346
JUNKERS	Ju 86E-2	ITALERI	H INJ	72		2347
JUNKERS	Ju 86K	ARISTO CRAFT	H INJ	72		2348
JUNKERS	Ju 86K	CRUVER	R HR·	72		2349
JUNKERS	Ju 87A Stuka	AIRFRAME	H VAC CV	72		2350
JUNKERS	Ju 87A Stuka	AIRMODEL	H VAC CV	72		2351
JUNKERS	Ju 87A Stuka	SETCO	R HR·	72		2352
JUNKERS	Ju 87B Stuka	AIRFIX	H INJ	72		2353
JUNKERS	Ju 87B Stuka	ARISTO CRAFT	H INJ	72		2354
JUNKERS	Ju 87B Stuka	CRUVER	R HR·	72		2355
JUNKERS	Ju 87B Stuka	DINKY TOYS	T ML· AS	72		2356
JUNKERS	Ju 87B-1 Stuka	HELLER	H INJ	75		2357
JUNKERS	Ju 87B-2 Stuka	AIRFIX	H INJ	72		2358
JUNKERS	Ju 87B/R Stuka	FUJIMI	H INJ	72		2359
JUNKERS	Ju 87B/R Stuka	MAC VAC CANOPY	H VAC	72		2360
JUNKERS	Ju 87B/R Stuka	OTAKI	H INJ	68		2361
JUNKERS	Ju 87B Stuka	POLISTIL	H INJ	72		2362
JUNKERS	Ju 87B/R Stuka	REVELL	H INJ	72		2363
JUNKERS	Ju 87B/R-2 Stuka	AIRFIX	H INJ RM	72	canopy	2364
JUNKERS	Ju 87D-1/D-3/D-7 Stuka	FUJIMI	H INJ	72		2365
JUNKERS	Ju 87D-3 Stuka	AIRMODEL	H VAC CV	72	personnel pod	2366
JUNKERS	Ju 87D-3/G Stuka	MATCHBOX	H INJ	72		2367
JUNKERS	Ju 87D-5/G Stuka	FROG	H INJ	72		2368
JUNKERS	Ju 87D-5-/D-8 Stuka	FUJIMI	H INJ	72		2369
JUNKERS	Ju 87D-5/G Stuka	MAC VAC CANOPY	H VAC	72		2370
JUNKERS	Ju 87D Stuka	REVELL	H INJ	72		2371
JUNKERS	Ju 87G-1 Stuka	FUJIMI	H INJ	72		2372
JUNKERS	Ju 87G-2 Stuka	FUJIMI	H INJ	72		2373
JUNKERS	Ju 88A	ARISTO CRAFT	H INJ	72		2374
JUNKERS	Ju 88A	CRUVER	R HR·	72		2375
JUNKERS	Ju 88A-4	AIRFIX	H INJ	72		2376
JUNKERS	Ju 88A-4	AMT	H INJ RM	72	remoulded FROG kit	2377
JUNKERS	Ju 88A-4	FROG	H INJ	72		2378
JUNKERS	Ju 88A-4/D-1	REVELL	H INJ	72		2379
JUNKERS	Ju 88A-15/P/G	AIRMODEL	H VAC CV	72	+ Do 217M/N	2380
JUNKERS	Ju 88C-6C	REVELL	H INJ	72		2381
JUNKERS	Ju 88G/P/S	AIRMODEL	H VAC CV	72	+ Ki-46-III	2382
JUNKERS	Ju 90	ARISTO CRAFT	H INJ	72		2383
JUNKERS	Ju 90	CRUVER	R HR·	72		2384
JUNKERS	Ju 90V5	AIRMODEL	H VAC	72		2385
JUNKERS	Ju 160A	AIRMODEL	H VAC	72		2386
JUNKERS	Ju 188	CRUVER	R HR·	72		2387
JUNKERS	Ju 188A/E	AIRMODEL	H VAC CV	72	canopy, + Do 217E	2388
JUNKERS	Ju 188E/F	ITALERI	H INJ	72	JUMO/BMW engine	2389
JUNKERS	Ju 188E/F	MATCHBOX	H INJ	72	BMW engine	2390
JUNKERS	Ju 252	AIRMODEL	H VAC	72		2391
JUNKERS	Ju 252	FRANK-MODELLBAU	H VAC	72		2392
JUNKERS	Ju 287V1	AIRMODEL	H VAC	72		2393
JUNKERS	Ju 288V3	AIRMODEL	H VAC	72		2394
JUNKERS	Ju 290A-2/3/4/5/6/7/8/9	FRANK-MODELLBAU	H VAC	72		2395
JUNKERS	Ju 290A-2/A-9	SUTCLIFFE	H VAC	72		2396
JUNKERS	Ju 290V1/V2	FRANK-MODELLBAU	H VAC	72		2397
JUNKERS	Ju 352 Herkules	I.D. MODELS	H VAC	72		2398
JUNKERS	Ju 352A-0/A-1 Herkules	FRANK-MODELLBAU	H VAC	72		2399
JUNKERS	Ju 388J-1/K-1/L-0/V2	AIRMODEL	H VAC CV	72		2400
JUNKERS	Ju 388K-1/L-1	FRANK-MODELLBAU	H VAC CV	72		2401
JUNKERS	Ju 388L-0	FRANK-MODELLBAU	H VAC CV	72		2402
JUNKERS	Ju 388V1/V2	FRANK-MODELLBAU	H VAC	72		2403
JUNKERS	Ju 388V-2 (J-1)	FRANK-MODELLBAU	H VAC CV	72		2404
JUNKERS	Ju 388V-4 (J-1)	FRANK-MODELLBAU	H VAC CV	72		2405
JUNKERS	Ju 390	SUTCLIFFE	H VAC	72		2406
JUNKERS	Mistel 1 (Ju 88A-4/Bf 109F)	AIRMODEL	H INJ CV	72		2407
JUNKERS	Mistel 1 (Ju 88A-4/Bf 109F)	AIRMODEL	H VAC CV	72		2408
JUNKERS	Mistel 2	FALCON	H VAC CV	72	Ju 88A-4 nose	2409
JUNKERS	W.34	AIRMODEL	H VAC	72		2410
KAMAN	H-43B Huskie	AIRMODEL	H VAC	72	+ BELL H-13J	2411
KAMAN	SH-2F Seasprite	AIRFIX	H INJ	72		2412

KAMAN	SH-2F Seasprite	FUJIMI	H INJ	72		2413
KAMAN	UH-2A Seasprite	AIRMODEL	H VAC	72	+ OH-6A Cayuse	2414
KAMAN	YSH-2E Lamps	FUJIMI	H INJ	72		2415
KAMOV	Ka-25 Hormone A/C	AIRFIX	H INJ	72		2416
KAMOV	Ka-25 Hormone A/B/C	MPC	H INJ	72	AIRFIX w. Ka-25 B parts	2417
KAWANISHI	E15K2 Shiun (Violet Cloud)	AOSHIMA	H INJ	72	Norm	2418
KAWANISHI	E7K1	HASEGAWA	H INJ	72	Alf	2419
KAWANISHI	E7K1	HASEGAWA	H INJ	72	Alf, w. catapult	2420
KAWANISHI	H6K type 97 NPB	ARISTO CRAFT	H INJ	72	Mavis	2421
KAWANISHI	H6K	CRUVER	R HR·	72	Mavis	2422
KAWANISHI	H6K5	HASEGAWA	H INJ	72	Mavis	2423
KAWANISHI	H8K	CRUVER	R HR·	72	Emily	2424
KAWANISHI	H8K2	HASEGAWA	H INJ	72	Emily	2425
KAWANISHI	N1K Shidenkai	CRUVER	R HR·	72	George	2426
KAWANISHI	N1K1 Kyofu (Mighty Wind)	EAGLES TALON	H VAC	72	Rex	2427
KAWANISHI	N1K1 Kyofu (Mighty Wind)	O'NEILL	H VAC	72	Rex	2428
KAWANISHI	N1K2-J Shidenkai	AOSHIMA	H INJ	71	George	2429
KAWANISHI	N1K2-J Shidenkai	HASEGAWA	H INJ	72	George	2430
KAWANISHI	N1K2-J Shidenkai	NICHIMO	H INJ	70	George	2431
KAWANISHI	N1K2-J Shidenkai	NITTO	H INJ	73	George	2432
KAWASKI	C-1	RACCOON	H RSN	72		2433
KAWASKI	Ki-3 Type 93	GUNZE SANGYO	H ML·	72		2434
KAWASKI	Ki-3 Type 93	O'NEIL	H VAC	72		2435
KAWASKI	Ki-10	KPM	H VAC	72	Perry	2436
KAWASKI	Ki-10	PRIVATE VENTURE C	H RSN	72	Perry	2437
KAWASKI	Ki-10	WINGS 72	H VAC	72	Perry	2438
KAWASKI	Ki-28	PRIVATE VENTURE	H RSN	72	Bob	2439
KAWASKI	Ki-32	MERLIN	H INJ	72	Mary	2440
KAWASKI	Ki-32	PRIVATE VENTURE	H RSN	72	Mary	2441
KAWASKI	Ki-32	CRUVER	R HR·	72	Mary	2442
KAWASKI	Ki-32	EAGLES TALON	H VAC	72	Mary	2443
KAWASKI	Ki-32	KPM	H VAC	72	Mary	2444
KAWASKI	Ki-32	WINGS 72	H VAC	72	Mary	2445
KAWASKI	Ki-32 Type 97	ARISTO CRAFT	H INJ	72	Mary	2446
KAWASKI	Ki-45 Toryu	CRUVER	R HR·	72	Nick	2447
KAWASKI	Ki-45 Toryu	REVELL	H INJ	72	Nick	2448
KAWASKI	Ki-48	ARISTO CRAFT	H INJ	72	Lily	2449
KAWASKI	Ki-48	CRUVER	R HR·	72	Lily	2450
KAWASKI	Ki-48	MANIA	H INJ	72	Lily	2451
KAWASKI	Ki-60	KPL MODELS	H VAC	72		2452
KAWASKI	Ki-60	PRIVATE VENTURE	H RSN	72		2453
KAWASKI	Ki-60	WINGS 72	H VAC	72	w. ML parts	2454
KAWASKI	Ki-61 Hien	CRUVER	R HR·	72	Tony	2455
KAWASKI	Ki-61-I Hien	HASEGAWA	H INJ	70	Tony	2456
KAWASKI	Ki-61-I Hien	REVELL	H INJ	70	Tony	2457
KAWASKI	Ki-61-II Hien	AOSHIMA	H INJ	72	Tony	2458
KAWASKI	Ki-61-II Hien	FUJIMI	H INJ	70	Tony	2459
KAWASKI	Ki-61-II	NICHIMO	H INJ	70	Tony	2460
KAWASKI	Ki-61-II Hien	TAMIYA	H INJ	75	Tony	2461
KAWASKI	Ki-64 Hien	KPL MODELS	H VAC	72	Rob	2462
KAWASKI	Ki-78	PRIVATE VENTURE C	H RSN	75		2463
KAWASKI	Ki-100 Goshikisen	RED BARON	H RSN	72		2464
KAWASKI	Ki-100-I Goshikisen	FUJIMI	H INJ	70		2465
KAWASKI	Ki-100-Ia Goshikisen	AOSHIMA	H INJ	70		2466
KAWASKI	Ki-100-II Goshikisen	FUJIMI	H INJ	70		2467
KAWASKI	Ki-102	KPL MODELS	H VAC	72	Randy	2468
KAWASKI	Ki-102	PRIVATE VENTURE C	H RSN	72	Randy	2469
KAWASKI	Ki-108	KPL MODELS	H VAC	72		2470
KAWASKI	Type 88 (KDA-2)	O'NEILL	H VAC	72		2471
KAWASKI	Type 92 (KDA-5)	O'NEILL	H VAC	72		2472
KAWASKI (BOEING VERTOL)	KV-107/II-3	FUJIMI	H INJ	72	JMSDF version	2473
KAWASKI (BOEING VERTOL)	KV-107/II-4	FUJIMI	H INJ	72	JGSDF version	2474
KAWASKI (BOEING VERTOL)	KV-107/II-5	FUJIMI	H INJ	72	JASDF version	2475
KAYABA	Ka-1 Kago	EAGLES TALON	H VAC	72		2476
KAYABA	Ka-1 Kago	O'NEILL	H VAC	72		2477
KAYABA	Ka-1 Kago	PRIVATE VENTURE C	H RSN	72		2478
KAYABA	Ka-1 Kago	WINGS 72	H VAC	72		2479

KAYABA	Ka-2	PRIVATE VENTURE	H RSN	72		2480
KELLET	YO-60 Autogiro	O'NEILL	H VAC	72		2481
KEYSTONE	B-4A	O'NEILL	H VAC	72		2482
KLEMM	Kl 35	ARNE ANDERSSON	H VAC	72		2483
KLEMM	Kl 35	HUMA	H INJ	72		2484
KLEMM	Kl 35	PRIVATE VENTURE B	H RSN	72		2485
KLEMM	Kl 35B/BW/D	AIRMODEL	H VAC	72		2486
KLEMM	L 25	AEROCLUB MODELS	H VAC	72	w. ML parts	2487
KOKUSAI	Ki-76	O'NEILL	H VAC	72	Stella	2488
KOKUSAI	Ki-86	EAGLES TALON	H VAC	72	Cypress, id. BUCKER Bü 131	2489
KOKUSAI	Ki-86	PRIVATE VENTURE	H RSN	72	Cypress, id. BUCKER Bü 131	2490
KOKUSAI	Ku-8	O'NEILL	H VAC	72	Glider version of Ki-59	2491
KOOLHOVEN	FK 58	KPL MODELS	H VAC	72		2492
KOOLHOVEN	FK 58	REPLICA	H RSN	72		2493
KOOLHOVEN	FK 58/58A	RUDEL	H VAC	72		2494
KYUSHU	K11W1/2 Shiragiku (White Chrys.)	PRIVATE VENTURE	H RSN	72		2495
KYUSHU	J7W1 Shinden (Magnif. Lightning)	MAC VAC CANOPY	H VAC	72		2496
KYUSHU	J7W1 Shinden (Magnif. Lightning)	TAMIYA	H INJ RM	72		2497
KYUSHU	J7W1 Shinden (Magnif. Lightning)	TAMIYA	H INJ MT	72		2498
KYUSHU	K10W1	O'NEILL	H VAC	72	Oak	2499
KYUSHU	Q1W1 Tokai (Eastern Sea)	ABORN	H VAC	72	Lorna	2500
KYUSHU	Q1W1 Tokai (Eastern Sea)	O'NEILL	H VAC	72	Lorna	2501
KYUSHU	Q1W1 Tokai (Eastern Sea)	WINGS 72	H VAC	72	Lorna	2502
L.G.L.	32	O'NEILL	H VAC	72		2503
LATECOERE	Laté 28-3	REPLICA	H RSN	72		2504
LATECOERE	Laté 298	PRIVATE VENTURE	H RSN	72		2505
LATECOERE	Laté 298	RUDEL	H VAC	72		2506
LAVOCHKIN	La-5	CRUVER	R HR·	72		2507
LAVOCHKIN	La-5	KPM	H VAC	72		2508
LAVOCHKIN	La-5FN	BOLESLAV	H VAC	72		2509
LAVOCHKIN	La-5FN	ITALERI	H INJ	72		2510
LAVOCHKIN	La-5FN	KOVOZAVODY	H INJ	72		2511
LAVOCHKIN	La-5FN	RAREPLANES	H VAC	72		2512
LAVOCHKIN	La-5FN	SDELAND	H ML· WK	72		2513
LAVOCHKIN	La-7 (Fin)	CRUVER	R HR·	72		2514
LAVOCHKIN	La-7 (Fin)	FROG	H INJ	72		2515
LAVOCHKIN	La-7 (Fin)	KOVOZAVODY	H INJ	72		2516
LAVOCHKIN	La-9 (Fritz)	PSC	H VAC	72		2517
LAVOCHKIN	La-9 (Fritz)	VP CANADA	H VAC	72		2518
LAVOCHKIN	La-9 (Fritz)	CRUVER	R HR·	72		2519
LAVOCHKIN	La-9 (Fritz)	KPL MODELS	H VAC	72		2520
LAVOCHKIN	La-9 (Fritz)	O'NEILL	H VAC	72	+ La-11 Fang	2521
LAVOCHKIN	La-11 (Fang)	PSC	H VAC	72		2522
LAVOCHKIN	La-11 (Fang)	CRUVER	R HR·	72		2523
LAVOCHKIN	La-11 (Fang)	KPL MODELS	H VAC	72		2524
LAVOCHKIN	La-15 (Fantail	SUTCLIFFE	H VAC	72		2525
LAVOCHKIN	La-15 (Fantail)	THEATRE SPECIALT.	R HR·	72		2526
LAVOCHKIN	LaGG-3	AIRMODEL	H VAC	72		2527
LAVOCHKIN	LaGG-3	BOLESLAV	H VAC	72		2528
LAVOCHKIN	LaGG-3	FROG	H INJ	72		2529
LAVOCHKIN	LaGG-3	JMK	H VAC	72		2530
LAVOCHKIN	LaGG-3	KPM	H VAC	72		2531
LAVOCHKIN	LaGG-3/35, 3L	LOTNIA	H VAC	72		2532
LEDUC	022	FABULON	H RSN	72		2533
LEDUC	022	FABULON	H RSN RM	72		2534
LETOV	S 16	KOVOZAVODY	H INJ	72		2535
LETOV	S 231	KOVOZAVODY	H INJ	72		2536
LETOV	S 231	PRIVATE VENTURE	H RSN	72		2537
LETOV	S 328	KOVOZAVODY	H INJ	72		2538
LEVASSEUR	PL 8 (Oiseau Blanc)	CLASSIC PLANE	H VAC	72		2539
LEVASSEUR	PL 8 (Oiseau Blanc)	MACH	H RSN	72		2540
LFG ROLAND	C II	AIRFIX	H INJ	72		2541
LFG ROLAND	D II	MERLIN	H INJ	72	w. ML parts	2542
LFG ROLAND	D II	PRIVATE VENTURE	H RSN	72		2543
LFG ROLAND	D II	ROSEPLANE	H VAC	72	w. ML parts	2544
LFG ROLAND	D VI	C.A. ATKINS	H ML·	72		2545
LFG ROLAND	D VI	CRAMER	H VAC	72		2546

LFG ROLAND	D VIb	FORMAPLANE	H VAC	72	w. ML parts	2547
LOIRE ET OLIVIER	LeO C.30	REPLICA	H RSN	72	id. CIERVA C.30	2548
LOIRE ET OLIVIER	LeO 20	O'NEILL	H VAC	72		2549
LOIRE ET OLIVIER	LeO 45	HELLER	H INJ	72		2550
LOIRE ET OLIVIER	LeO 451	HELLER	H INJ	72		2551
LOIRE ET OLIVIER	LeO H-257 bis	O'NEILL	H VAC	72		2552
LIPPISCH	DM-1	AIRMODEL	H VAC	72		2553
LLOYD	C II	CLASSIC PLANE	H VAC	72		2554
LLOYD	C II	FORMAPLANE	H VAC	72	w. ML parts	2555
LLOYD	C II	JOYSTICK	H VAC	72		2556
LOCKHEED	1 Vega	RAREPLANES	H VAC	72		2557
LOCKHEED	1 Vega	SKYBIRDS	H WD·	72		2558
LOCKHEED	9 Orion (UC-85)	MERLIN	H INJ	72	w. ML parts	2559
LOCKHEED	10 Electra	EXECUFORM	H VAC	72		2560
LOCKHEED	10 Electra	SKYBIRDS	H WD·	72		2561
LOCKHEED	10 C-36/C-37 Electra	O'NEILL	H VAC	72		2562
LOCKHEED	12 C-48 Electra Junior	O'NEILL	H VAC	72		2563
LOCKHEED	18 C-60 Lodestar	AIR JET ADVANCE	D FG·	72		2564
LOCKHEED	18 C-60 Lodestar	AIRMODEL	H VAC CV	72		2565
LOCKHEED	18 C-60 Lodestar	ARISTO CRAFT	H INJ	72		2566
LOCKHEED	18 C-60 Lodestar	CRUVER	R HR·	72		2567
LOCKHEED	18 C-60 Lodestar	O'NEILL	H VAC CV	72		2568
LOCKHEED	37 PV-1 Ventura	ACADEMY MINICRAFT	H INJ	72		2569
LOCKHEED	37 PV-1 Ventura	ARISTO CRAFT	H INJ	72		2570
LOCKHEED	37 PV-1 Ventura	FROG	H INJ	72		2571
LOCKHEED	37 PV-1 Ventura	RAREPLANES	H VAC	72		2572
LOCKHEED	37 PV-1 Ventura	SUTCLIFFE	H VAC CV	72		2573
LOCKHEED	37 PV-2 Harpoon	CRUVER	R HR·	72		2574
LOCKHEED	37 PV-2 Harpoon	O'NEILL	H VAC	72		2575
LOCKHEED	37 PV-2 Harpoon	RAREPLANES	H VAC	72	w. INJ parts	2576
LOCKHEED	A-29 Hudson	AIRFIX	H INJ	72		2577
LOCKHEED	A-29 Hudson	ARISTO CRAFT	H INJ	72		2578
LOCKHEED	A-29 Hudson	E.B.B.	H INJ	72		2579
LOCKHEED	AH-56 Cheyenne	AURORA	H INJ	72		2580
LOCKHEED	C-130 Hercules	MODELMASTERS	D —	72		2581
LOCKHEED	HC-130 Hercules	AIRMODEL	H VAC CV	72	+ F-10A/B/C	2582
LOCKHEED	AC-130A Hercules Gunship	AIRFIX	H INJ RM	72		2583
LOCKHEED	AC-130A Hercules Gunship	ITALERI	H INJ	72		2584
LOCKHEED	AC-130A/H/LC-130R/W Mk 2	AIRMODEL	H VAC CV	72		2585
LOCKHEED	DC-130A Hercules	ITALERI	H INJ	72	+ Firebee I drone	2586
LOCKHEED	DC-130A/E Hercules	AIRMODEL	H VAC CV	72	+ Firebee II drone + DP-2E	2587
LOCKHEED	DC-130A/E Hercules	AIRMODEL	H VAC CV	72	+ Firebee I drone	2588
LOCKHEED	C-130B/E Hercules	AIR JET ADVANCE	D FG·	72		2589
LOCKHEED	C-130B/E Hercules	AMERICAN AIRCRAFT	H INJ	72		2590
LOCKHEED	HC-130B/H/N/P JC-130A KC-130F	AIRMODEL	H VAC	72	other versions: cf. below	2591
LOCKHEED	MC-130H YC-130A C-130A/E	AIRMODEL		0		0
LOCKHEED	L-100-20/30 C Mk 3	AIRMODEL		0		0
LOCKHEED	C-130E/K Hercules	AIRFIX	H INJ	72	w. Bloodhound missile in	2592
LOCKHEED		AIRFIX		0	kits 881 and 9001	0
LOCKHEED	KC-130F Hercules	ITALERI	H INJ	72	Blue Angels	2593
LOCKHEED	HC-130H Hercules	AIRMODEL	H VAC CV	72	+ F-80C + F-106B	2594
LOCKHEED	HC-130P Hercules	FALCON	H VAC CV	72	+ F4H-1 + A-10B	2595
LOCKHEED	L-100-20 Hercules	EXECUTIVE	D FG·	72		2596
LOCKHEED	L-100-30 Hercules	EXECUTIVE	D —	72		2597
LOCKHEED	L-100-30 Hercules	MODELMASTERS	D —	72		2598
LOCKHEED	C-140 Jetstar	AIRMODEL	H VAC	72		2599
LOCKHEED	C-140 Jetstar	T.W.R.	H VAC	72		2600
LOCKHEED	C-141A Starlifter	NOVA MODELS	H VAC	72		2601
LOCKHEED	C-141B Starlifter	NOVA MODELS	H VAC	72		2602
LOCKHEED	F-19 Stealth	ITALERI	H INJ	72	TESTOR design	2603
LOCKHEED	F-19 Stealth	MONOGRAM	H INJ SN	72		2604
LOCKHEED	F-19 Stealth	REVELL	H INJ SN	72		2605
LOCKHEED	F-80 Shooting Star	AIRFIX	H INJ	72		2606
LOCKHEED	F-80 Shooting Star	ARISTO CRAFT	H INJ	72		2607
LOCKHEED	F-80 Shooting Star	MAC VAC CANOPY	H VAC	72		2608
LOCKHEED	F-80 Shooting Star	STROMBECKER	H WD·	72		2609
LOCKHEED	F-80A Shooting Star	CRUVER	R HR·	72		2610
LOCKHEED	F-80C Shooting Star	AIRMODEL	H VAC CV	72	canopy, + HC-130H + F-106B	2611
LOCKHEED	F-80C Shooting Star	CRUVER	R HR·	72		2612
LOCKHEED	F-94B Starfire	AIRMODEL	H VAC CV	72		2613

LOCKHEED	F-94 Starfire	STROMBECKER	H WD·	72		2614
LOCKHEED	F-94B Starfire	HELLER	H INJ	72		2615
LOCKHEED	F-94C Starfire	CRUVER	R HR·	72		2616
LOCKHEED	F-104 Starfighter	COMPASS	H WD·	72		2617
LOCKHEED	F-104 Starfighter	EXECUTIVE	D —	72		2618
LOCKHEED	F-104A Starfighter	AIRMODEL	H INJ CV	72	+ TF-104G	2619
LOCKHEED	F-104A Starfighter	CRUVER	R HR·	72		2620
LOCKHEED	F-104A Starfighter	MODELAIR	H INJ	72		2621
LOCKHEED	F-104A Starfighter	Y.M.C.	H INJ	67		2622
LOCKHEED	F-104C Starfighter	ESCI	H INJ	72	w. Sidewinder missile	2623
LOCKHEED	F-104G Starfighter	AIRFIX	H INJ	72	w. Sidewinder missile	2624
LOCKHEED	F-104G Starfighter	HELLER	H INJ	72	+ TF-104G	2625
LOCKHEED	F-104G Starfighter	MATCHBOX	H INJ	72	w. Sidewinder missile	2626
LOCKHEED	F-104G/J Starfighter	HASEGAWA	H INJ	72	w. Sidewinder missile	2627
LOCKHEED	F-104G/S Starfighter	ESCI	H INJ	72	w. Sidewinder missile	2628
LOCKHEED	TF-104G Starfighter	AIRMODEL	H INJ CV	72	+ F-104A	2629
LOCKHEED	TF-104G Starfighter	HELLER	H INJ	72	+ F-104G	2630
LOCKHEED	TF-104G Starfighter	MATCHBOX	H INJ	72		2631
LOCKHEED	L-188 Electra	AIRTEC	H FM·	72		2632
LOCKHEED	L-188 Electra	ATLANTIC MODELS	D INJ	72		2633
LOCKHEED	L-188 Electra	EXECUTIVE	D FG·	72		2634
LOCKHEED	L-188 Electra	J & L	H VAC	72		2635
LOCKHEED	L-188 Electra	MODELMASTERS	D —	72		2636
LOCKHEED	C-69 Constellation	ARISTO CRAFT	H INJ	72		2637
LOCKHEED	C-69 Constellation	CRUVER	R HR·	72		2638
LOCKHEED	L-749 Constellation	EXECUTIVE	D FG·	72		2639
LOCKHEED	L-749 Constellation	HAUSSER	H INJ	72		2640
LOCKHEED	L-749 Constellation	HELLER	H INJ	72		2641
LOCKHEED	L-1049 Super Constellation	MODELMASTERS	D —	72		2642
LOCKHEED	C-121 Super Constellaton	T.W.R.	H VAC	72		2643
LOCKHEED	L-1049 Super Constellaton	T.W.R.	H VAC	72		2644
LOCKHEED	L-1049G Super Constellation	EXECUTIVE	D RSN	72		2645
LOCKHEED	L-1094G Super Constellation	HELLER	H INJ RM	72	remoulded WV-2	2646
LOCKHEED	EC-121K/WV-2 Warning Star	HELLER	H INJ	72		2647
LOCKHEED	EC-121K/WV-2 Warning Star	RAREPLANES	H VAC	72		2648
LOCKHEED	L-1649 Starliner	EXECUTIVE	D FG·	72		2649
LOCKHEED	L-1011 Tristar	WESTWAY	H INJ	72		2650
LOCKHEED	P-3A Orion	HASEGAWA	H INJ	72		2651
LOCKHEED	P-3C Orion Update II	HASEGAWA	H INJ RM	72		2652
LOCKHEED	EP-3E Orion	FALCON	H VAC CV	72	+ Banshee + Trader	2653
LOCKHEED	WP-3D Orion (Hurricane Tracker)	AIR JET ADVANCE	D FG·	72		2654
LOCKHEED	P-38 Lightning	ARISTO CRAFT	H INJ	72		2655
LOCKHEED	P-38F Lightning	AIRFIX	H INJ	72		2656
LOCKHEED	P-38F Lightning	CRUVER	R HR·	72		2657
LOCKHEED	P-38F Lightning	PATHFINDERS	H ML·	72		2658
LOCKHEED	P-38F Lightning	SKYBIRDS	H WD·	72		2659
LOCKHEED	P-38F/F-4C Lightning	REVELL	H INJ	72		2660
LOCKHEED	P-38F/J/L Lightning	HASEGAWA	H INJ	72		2661
LOCKHEED	P-38J/L Lightning	AIRFIX	H INJ	72		2662
LOCKHEED	P-38J/L Lightning	FROG	H INJ	72		2663
LOCKHEED	P-38J/L Lightning	FROG PENGUIN	H INJ	72		2664
LOCKHEED	P-38J/L Lightning	MAC VAC CANOPY	H VAC	72		2665
LOCKHEED	P-38J/L Lightning	MATCHBOX	H INJ	72		2666
LOCKHEED	P-38J/L/M Lightning	REVELL	H INJ	72		2667
LOCKHEED	P-38M Lightning	AIRMODEL	H VAC CV	72	+ T-6G	2668
LOCKHEED	AP-2H Neptune	FALCON	H VAC CV	72	+ E-1B + F9F-8P	2669
LOCKHEED	DP-2E Neptune	AIRMODEL	H VAC CV	72	+ Firebee II + DC-130A/E	2670
LOCKHEED	P2V-2 Neptune	CRUVER	R HR·	72		2671
LOCKHEED	P2V-3 Neptune	O'NEILL	H VAC CV	72		2672
LOCKHEED	P2V-5 Neptune	FALCON	H VAC CV	72	+ TF-86F + TBM-3W	2673
LOCKHEED	P2V-7 (P-2H) Neptune	HASEGAWA	H INJ	72		2674
LOCKHEED	S-3A Viking	AIRFIX	H INJ	72	w. Harpoon missile	2675
LOCKHEED	S-3A Viking	HASEGAWA	H INJ	72		2676
LOCKHEED	US-3A Viking	HASEGAWA	H INJ RM	72		2677
LOCKHEED	SR-71A Blackbird	ACADEMY MINICRAFT	H INJ	72		2678
LOCKHEED	SR-71A Blackbird	HASEGAWA	H INJ RM	72	w. Tagboard	2679
LOCKHEED	SR-71A Blackbird	MONOGRAM	H INJ	72	w. Tagboard	2680

LOCKHEED	SR-71A Blackbird	REVELL	H INJ	72		2681
LOCKHEED	SR-71A Blackbird	RICK'S	D FM·	72	id. TEEPEE	2682
LOCKHEED	SR-71A/B Blackbird	ITALERI	H INJ	72		2683
LOCKHEED	T-33	HASEGAWA	H INJ	72		2684
LOCKHEED	T-33	MAC VAC CANOPY	H VAC	72		2685
LOCKHEED	T-33/RT-33	HELLER	H INJ	72		2686
LOCKHEED	T2V-1 SeaStar	GRIFFIN	H VAC	72		2687
LOCKHEED	U-2	ACADEMY MINICRAFT	H INJ	72		2688
LOCKHEED	TR-1A	RICK'S	D FM·	72	id. TEEPEE	2689
LOCKHEED	U-2A/B/C	RAREPLANES	H VAC	72		2690
LOCKHEED	U-2B/C/D	MPC	H INJ	72	ARIFIX w. U-2C parts	2691
LOCKHEED	U-2B/D	AIRFIX	H INJ	72		2692
LOCKHEED	U-2D	AIRMODEL	H VAC	72		2693
LOCKHEED	XF-90	WINGS 72	H VAC	72	w. ML parts	2694
LOCKHEED	XF-90	KR MODELS	H VAC	72		2695
LOCKHEED	XFV-1	AIRMODEL	H VAC	72	w. RSN parts	2696
LOCKHEED	XFV-1	STROMBECKER	H WD·	72		2697
LOCKHEED	YF-12A	ITALERI	H INJ	72	w. Eagle missile	2698
LOCKHEED	YF-12A	REVELL	H INJ	72	w. Eagle missile	2699
LOCKHEED	YF-97A (YF-94C)	KR MODELS	H VAC	72		2700
LOENING	OA-1A	ESOTERIC	H VAC	72	w. ML parts	2701
LOENING	OL-8/9	ESOTERIC	H VAC	72	w. ML parts	2702
LOHNER	CI	FORMAPLANE	H VAC	72	w. ML parts	2703
LOHNER	L	FORMAPLANE	H VAC	72		2704
LOHNER	L	WINGS 72	H VAC	72	w. ML parts	2705
LOHNER	L-47	PRIVATE VENTURE C	H RSN	72		2706
LOIRE	46	O'NEILL	H VAC	72		2707
LOIRE	46	PRIVATE VENTURE C	H RSN	72		2708
LOIRE	60	PRIVATE VENTURE	H RSN	72		2709
LOIRE	130	O'NEILL	H VAC	72		2710
LOIRE	130	REPLICA	H RSN	72		2711
LOIRE	130	RUDEL	H VAC	72		2712
LOIRE-NIEUPORT	LN.401/411	PRIVATE VENTURE	H RSN	72		2713
LOIRE-NIEUPORT	LN.401/411	RUDEL	H VAC	72		2714
LONG	Midget Mustang	PRIVATE VENTURE C	H RSN	72		2715
LUBLIN	R-XIII	ALPHA	H VAC	72		2716
LUNAK	LF-107	PRIVATE VENTURE A	H RSN	72		2717
LUSCOMBE	8 Silvaire	MAIRCRAFT	H WD·	72		2718
LVG	C V	SKYBIRDS	H WD·	72		2719
LVG	C VI	CLASSIC PLANE	H VAC	72		2720
MACCHI	M.7	LIBRAMODELS	H VAC	72	w. ML parts	2721
MACCHI	M.16	ESOTERIC	H VAC	72	w. ML parts	2722
MACCHI	MC.72 Castoldi	DELTA	H INJ	72		2723
MACCHI	MC.72 Castoldi	SKYBIRDS	H WD·	72		2724
MACCHI	MC.200 Saetta	AIRFORM	H INJ CV	72		2725
MACCHI	MC.200 Saetta	ARISTO CRAFT	H INJ	72		2726
MACCHI	MC.200 Saetta	CRUVER	R HR·	72		2727
MACCHI	MC.200 Saetta	MAC VAC CANOPY	H VAC	72		2728
MACCHI	MC.200 Saetta	REVELL	H INJ	72		2729
MACCHI	MC.202 Folgore	ARISTO CRAFT	H INJ	72		2730
MACCHI	MC.202 Folgore	CRUVER	R HR·	72		2731
MACCHI	MC.202 Folgore	FROG	H INJ	72		2732
MACCHI	MC.202 Folgore	MAC VAC CANOPY	H VAC	72		2733
MACCHI	MC.202 Folgore	SANWA	H INJ	72		2734
MACCHI	MC.202 Folgore	SUPERMODEL	H INJ	72		2735
MACCHI	MC.205 Veltro	DELTA	H INJ	72		2736
MACCHI	MC.205/205 Trop Veltro	SUPERMODEL	H INJ	72		2737
MARTIN	Model 130 China Clipper	ATLANTIC MODELS	D INJ	72		2738
MARTIN	Model 130 China Clipper	COMBAT MODEL	H VAC	72	w. ML parts	2739
MARTIN	167 Maryland	ARISTO CRAFT	H INJ	72		2740
MARTIN	167 Maryland	CRUVER	R HR·	72		2741
MARTIN	167 Maryland	FROG	H INJ	72		2742
MARTIN	187 A-30 Baltimore	ARISTO CRAFT	H INJ	72		2743
MARTIN	187 A-30 Baltimore	CRUVER	R HR·	72		2744
MARTIN	187 A-30 Baltimore	FROG	H INJ	72		2745
MARTIN	4-0-4 Mainliner	AIRTEC	H FM·	72		2746
MARTIN	4-0-4 Mainliner	VICTOR SIXTY-SIX	H VAC	72		2747

MARTIN	AM-1 Mauler	AIRMODEL	H VAC	72		2748
MARTIN	AM-1 Mauler	CRUVER	R HR·	72		2749
MARTIN	B-10	RAREPLANES	H VAC	72		2750
MARTIN	B-10	SUTCLIFFE	H VAC	72		2751
MARTIN	B-10B	WILLIAMS BROTHERS	H INJ	72		2752
MARTIN	B-26 Marauder	ARISTO CRAFT	H INJ	72		2753
MARTIN	B-26 Marauder	CRUVER	R HR·	72		2754
MARTIN	B-26 Marauder	SETCO	R HR·	72		2755
MARTIN	B-26 Marauder	STROMBECKER	H WD·	72		2756
MARTIN	B-26B Marauder	AIRFIX	H INJ	72		2757
MARTIN	B-26B Marauder	MATCHBOX	H INJ	72		2758
MARTIN	B-26B Marauder	MONOGRAM	H INJ SN	72		2759
MARTIN	B-26B Marauder	REVELL	H INJ	72		2760
MARTIN	B-26B Marauder	REVELL	H INJ RM	72		2761
MARTIN	B-26C Marauder	FROG	H INJ	72		2762
MARTIN	B-57B	AIRMODEL	H VAC CV	72		2763
MARTIN	B-57B	ITALERI	H INJ	72		2764
MARTIN	B-57/RB-57E	AIRFIX	H INJ	72		2765
MARTIN	RB-57F	AIRMODEL	H VAC	72		2766
MARTIN	MB-1	O'NEILL	H VAC	72		2767
MARTIN	MB-2	ITC	H INJ	72		2768
MARTIN	P4M-1 Mercator	CRUVER	R HR·	72		2769
MARTIN	P4M-1Q Mercator	O'NEILL	H VAC	72		2770
MARTIN	P6M-2 Seamaster	AIRMODEL	H VAC	72		2771
MARTIN	PBM Mariner	O'NEILL	H VAC CV	72		2772
MARTIN	PBM-3 Mariner	ARISTO CRAFT	H INJ	72		2773
MARTIN	PBM-3/3R/35/5 Mariner	RAREPLANES	H VAC	72		2774
MARTIN	PBM-5 Mariner	EXECUFORM	H VAC	72		2775
MARTIN	PBM-5A Mariner	CRUVER	R HR·	72		2776
MARTIN	SP-5B Marlin	HASEGAWA	H INJ	72		2777
MARTIN	T4M-1	ESOTERIC	H VAC	72	w. ML parts	2778
MARTIN	X-24A	KPM	H VAC	72		2779
MARTIN	X-24A	PRIVATE VENTURE C	H RSN	72		2780
MARTIN	X-24A/B	EAGLES TALON	H VAC	72		2781
MARTIN	X-24B	KPM	H VAC	72		2782
MARTIN	X-24B	PRIVATE VENTURE B	H RSN	72		2783
MARTIN	XB-51 Panther	EXECUFORM	H VAC	72		2784
MARTIN	XB-51 Panther	MAC VAC CANOPY	H VAC	72		2785
MARTIN	XB-51 Panther	O'NEILL	H VAC	72		2786
MARTIN-BAKER	MB.2	AIRFRAME	H VAC	72		2787
MARTIN-BAKER	MB.5	AIRFRAME	H VAC	72		2788
MARTIN-BAKER	MB.5	FALCON	H VAC	72		2789
MARTIN-BAKER	MB.5	PEGASUS	H INJ	72		2790
MARTIN-BAKER	MB.5	PRIVATE VENTURE	H RSN	72		2791
MARTIN-BAKER	MB.5	SKYBIRDS 86	H INJ	72	w. ML parts	2792
MARTINSYDE	F.4 Buzzard	CLASSIC PLANE	H VAC	72		2793
MARTINSYDE	F.4 Buzzard	CRAMER	H VAC	72		2794
MARTINSYDE	G.100/G.102 Elephant	CLASSIC PLANE	H VAC	72		2795
MARTINSYDE	G.100/G.102 Elephant	ROSEPLANE	H VAC	72		2796
MARTINSYDE	S.1	CLASSIC PLANE	H VAC	72		2797
MAX HOLSTE	MH.1521 Broussard	GRAPHY-AIR	H RSN	72	w. EB, ML parts	2798
MAX HOLSTE	MH-260 Super Broussard	HELLER	H INJ	75	mentioned as 1/50 on box	2799
MBB	HFB 320 Hansa	AIRMODEL	H VAC	72		2800
MBB	HFB 320 Hansa	T.W.R.	H VAC	72		2801
MBB	Bö 105M/C	AIRFIX	H INJ	72		2802
MESSERSCHMITT	Bf 108 Taifun	AIRMODEL	H VAC	72		2803
MESSERSCHMITT	Bf 108B Taifun	HELLER	H INJ	72		2804
MESSERSCHMITT	Bf 109	BONUX	H INJ SN	70		2805
MESSERSCHMITT	B 109	COMPASS	H WD·	72		2806
MESSERSCHMITT	Bf 109B-1/C-1	HELLER	H INJ	72		2809
MESSERSCHMITT	Bf 109B/C	AIRMODEL	H VAC CV	72		2807
MESSERSCHMITT	Bf 109B/C	FROG PENGUIN	H INJ	72		2808
MESSERSCHMITT	Bf 109B/C	PRIVATE VENTURE A	H RSN	72		2810
MESSERSCHMITT	Bf 109E	AIRFIX	H INJ	72		2811
MESSERSCHMITT	Bf 109E	ARISTO CRAFT	H INJ	72		2812
MESSERSCHMITT	Bf 109E	CRUVER	R HR·	72		2813
MESSERSCHMITT	Bf 109E	MAC VAC CANOPY	H VAC	72		2814

MESSERSCHMITT	Bf 109E	OTAKI	H INJ	72		2815
MESSERSCHMITT	Bf 109E	REVELL	H INJ	72		2816
MESSERSCHMITT	Bf 109E	SKYBIRDS	H WD·	72		2817
MESSERSCHMITT	Bf 109E-1	JMK	H VAC	72		2818
MESSERSCHMITT	Bf 109E-1/4	HELLER	H INJ	72		2819
MESSERSCHMITT	Bf 109E-3/F/K/G-12	AIRMODEL	H VAC CV	72		2820
MESSERSCHMITT	Bf 109E-3/4 Trop	MATCHBOX	H INJ	72		2821
MESSERSCHMITT	Bf 109E-4	DANBURY MINT	H ML·	72		2822
MESSERSCHMITT	Bf 109E-7b	HASEGAWA	H INJ	72		2823
MESSERSCHMITT	Bf 109E/F/G/K	AIRFORM	H INJ CV	72		2824
MESSERSCHMITT	Bf 109F	ARISTO CRAFT	H INJ	72		2825
MESSERSCHMITT	Bf 109F	CRUVER	R HR·	72		2826
MESSERSCHMITT	Bf 109F	FROG	H INJ	72		2827
MESSERSCHMITT	Bf 109F	HOBBYTIME	H INJ	66		2829
MESSERSCHMITT	Bf 109F	MAC VAC CANOPY	H VAC	72		2830
MESSERSCHMITT	Bf 109F	SKYBIRDS	H WD·	72		2831
MESSERSCHMITT	Bf 109F-2 Trop	HELLER	H INJ	75		2828
MESSERSCHMITT	Bf 109F/G	JO HAN	H INJ	72		2832
MESSERSCHMITT	Bf 109G	AIRFIX	H INJ RM	72		2834
MESSERSCHMITT	Bf 109G	AIRFIX	H INJ SN	72		2835
MESSERSCHMITT	Bf 109G	GLASSLITE	H FG·	72		2836
MESSERSCHMITT	Bf 109G	MAC VAC CANOPY	H VAC	72	GALLAND canopy	2837
MESSERSCHMITT	Bf 109G-2/5/6	HELLER	H INJ	72		2838
MESSERSCHMITT	Bf 109G-6/G-6/R2	AIRFIX	H INJ	72		2833
MESSERSCHMITT	Bf 109G-6	HASEGAWA	H INJ	72		2839
MESSERSCHMITT	Bf 109G-6	HAWK	H INJ	70		2840
MESSERSCHMITT	Bf 109G-6	POLISTIL	H INJ	72		2841
MESSERSCHMITT	Bf 109H	AIRMODEL	H VAC CV	72	+ Bf 109Z	2842
MESSERSCHMITT	Bf 109K-4	HELLER	H INJ RM	72		2843
MESSERSCHMITT	Bf 109Z	AIRMODEL	H VAC CV	72	+ Bf 109H	2844
MESSERSCHMITT	Bf 109Z	PRIVATE VENTURE C	H RSN	72		2845
MESSERSCHMITT	Bf 110	ARISTO CRAFT	H INJ	72		2846
MESSERSCHMITT	Bf 110	CRUVER	R HR·	72		2847
MESSERSCHMITT	Bf 110	FROG PENGUIN	H INJ	72		2848
MESSERSCHMITT	Bf 110C	DANBURY MINT	H ML·	72		2849
MESSERSCHMITT	Bf 110C	FUJIMI	H INJ	72		2850
MESSERSCHMITT	Bf 110C-3/D-2	MATCHBOX	H INJ	72		2851
MESSERSCHMITT	Bf 110D	AIRFIX	H INJ	72		2852
MESSERSCHMITT	Bf 110D	MAC VAC CANOPY	H VAC	72		2854
MESSERSCHMITT	Bf 110D	MIDORI	H INJ	72		2855
MESSERSCHMITT	Bf 110D	SKYBIRDS	H WD·	72		2856
MESSERSCHMITT	Bf 110D-1/R1/D-3	FUJIMI	H INJ	72		2853
MESSERSCHMITT	Bf 110E	MONOGRAM	H INJ	72		2857
MESSERSCHMITT	Bf 110G-2/4	FROG	H INJ	72		2859
MESSERSCHMITT	Bf 110G-4	AIRMODEL	H VAC CV	72		2858
MESSERSCHMITT	M.35b	HUMA	H INJ	72		2860
MESSERSCHMITT	Me 163A Komet	KPM	H VAC	72		2861
MESSERSCHMITT	Me 163A Komet	PRIVATE VENTURE C	H RSN	72		2862
MESSERSCHMITT	Me 163A Komet	VP CANADA	H VAC	72		2863
MESSERSCHMITT	Me 163A V4 Komet	AIRMODEL	H VAC	72		2864
MESSERSCHMITT	Me 163B Komet	LINDBERG	H INJ	72		2865
MESSERSCHMITT	Me 163B Komet	MAC VAC CANOPY	H VAC	72		2866
MESSERSCHMITT	Me 163B-1a Komet	AIRFIX	H INJ	72		2867
MESSERSCHMITT	Me 163B-1a Komet	HELLER	H INJ	72	+ tractor	2868
MESSERSCHMITT	Me 163C-0 Komet	FRANK-MODELLBAU	H VAC	72		2869
MESSERSCHMITT	Me 163S Komet	FRANK-MODELLBAU	H VAC CV	72	+ Me 262V1	2870
MESSERSCHMITT	Me 163S Komet	PRIVATE VENTURE C	H RSN	72		2871
MESSERSCHMITT	Me 209A-1 V5	AIRMODEL	H VAC	72		2872
MESSERSCHMITT	Me 209A-1 V5/A-2 V6	FRANK-MODELLBAU	H VAC	72		2873
MESSERSCHMITT	Me 209 V1	C.A. ATKINS	H ML·	72		2874
MESSERSCHMITT	Me 209 V1	FRANK-MODELLBAU	H VAC	72		2875
MESSERSCHMITT	Me 209 V1/V4	HUMA	H INJ	72		2876
MESSERSCHMITT	Me 209 V4	FRANK-MODELLBAU	H VAC	72		2877
MESSERSCHMITT	Me 209 V5	PRIVATE VENTURE C	H RSN	72		2878
MESSERSCHMITT	Me 209 V6	PRIVATE VENTURE C	H RSN	72		2879
MESSERSCHMITT	Me 210 Hornisse	ARISTO CRAFT	H INJ	72		2880
MESSERSCHMITT	Me 210 Hornisse	CRUVER	R HR·	72		2881

MESSERSCHMITT	Me 210 Hornisse	GEE'S AERO WORKS	H WD·	72		2882
MESSERSCHMITT	Me 262A Schwalbe	AIRFIX	H INJ	72		2883
MESSERSCHMITT	Me 262A Schwalbe	MAC VAC CANOPY	H VAC	72		2884
MESSERSCHMITT	Me 262A Schwalbe	REVELL	H INJ	72		2885
MESSERSCHMITT	Me 262A Schwalbe	SANWA	H INJ	72		2886
MESSERSCHMITT	Me 262A-1a/U3/U4	Z MODEL	H RSN CV	72		2887
MESSERSCHMITT	Me 262A-1a/2a Schwalbe	HASEGAWA	H INJ	72		2888
MESSERSCHMITT	Me 262A-1a/2a Schwalbe	MATCHBOX	H INJ	72		2889
MESSERSCHMITT	Me 262A-1a Schwalbe	REVELL	H INJ RM	72		2890
MESSERSCHMITT	Me 262A-2a Schwalbe	POLISTIL	H INJ	72		2891
MESSERSCHMITT	Me 262A/B Schwalbe	FROG	H INJ	72		2892
MESSERSCHMITT	Me 262A/B-1a Schwalbe	JO HAN	H INJ	72		2893
MESSERSCHMITT	Me 262B Schwalbe	MAC VAC CANOPY	H VAC	72		2894
MESSERSCHMITT	Me 262B-1/2 Schwalbe	FRANK-MODELLBAU	H VAC CV	72		2895
MESSERSCHMITT	Me 262B-1a/U1 Schwalbe	AIRMODEL	H VAC CV	72		2896
MESSERSCHMITT	Me 262B-1a/U1 Schwalbe	HASEGAWA	H INJ	72		2897
MESSERSCHMITT	Me 262B-1a/U1 Schwalbe	HELLER	H INJ	72		2898
MESSERSCHMITT	Me 262 V1	PRIVATE VENTURE B	H RSN	72		2899
MESSERSCHMITT	Me 262 V1	AIRMODEL	H VAC	72		2900
MESSERSCHMITT	Me 262 V1	FRANK-MODELLBAU	H VAC	72	+ Me 262A	2901
MESSERSCHMITT	Me 262 V1	FRANK-MODELLBAU	H VAC CV	72	+ Me 163S	2902
MESSERSCHMITT	Me 263 (Ju 248)	PRIVATE VENTURE	H RSN	72		2903
MESSERSCHMITT	Me 263 V1	FRANK-MODELLBAU	H VAC	72		2904
MESSERSCHMITT	Me 264	AIRMODEL	H VAC	72		2905
MESSERSCHMITT	Me 264 V1/2/3	FRANK-MODELLBAU	H VAC	72		2906
MESSERSCHMITT	Me 309 V1/4	FRANK-MODELLBAU	H VAC	72		2907
MESSERSCHMITT	Me 321 Gigant	AIRMODEL	H VAC	72	+ Me 323D-1	2908
MESSERSCHMITT	Me 321B-1 Gigant	ITALERI	H INJ	72		2909
MESSERSCHMITT	Me 323D-1 Gigant	AIRMODEL	H VAC	72	+ Me 321	2910
MESSERSCHMITT	Me 323D Gigant	ITALERI	H INJ	72		2911
MESSERSCHMITT	Me 328A/B	FRANK-MODELLBAU	H VAC CV	72		2912
MESSERSCHMITT	Me 410A	LINDBERG	H INJ	72		2913
MESSERSCHMITT	Me 410A-2/U4/B-1	FROG	H INJ	72		2914
MESSERSCHMITT	Me 410A/B	MAC VAC CANOPY	H VAC	72		2915
MESSERSCHMITT	Me 410A-2/U4/B-1	MATCHBOX	H INJ	72		2916
MESSERSCHMITT	Me 463	FRANK-MODELLBAU	H VAC	72		2917
MESSERSCHMITT	P.1101	FRANK-MODELLBAU	H VAC	72		2918
MIKOYAN-GURYEVICH	MiG-3	CAP CROIX DU SUD	H INJ	72		2919
MIKOYAN-GURYEVICH	MiG-3	CRUVER	R HR·	72		2920
MIKOYAN-GURYEVICH	MiG-3	EAGLES TALON	H VAC	72		2921
MIKOYAN-GURYEVICH	MiG-3	FORMAPLANE	H VAC	72		2922
MIKOYAN-GURYEVICH	MiG-3	FROG	H INJ	72		2923
MIKOYAN-GURYEVICH	MiG-3	KPL MODELS	H VAC	72		2924
MIKOYAN-GURYEVICH	MiG-3	KPM	H VAC	72		2925
MIKOYAN-GURYEVICH	MiG-3	PRIVATE VENTURE A	H RSN	72		2926
MIKOYAN-GURYEVICH	MiG-3	SKYBIRDS	H WD·	72		2927
MIKOYAN-GURYEVICH	MiG-3	WINGS 72	H VAC	72		2928
MIKOYAN-GURYEVICH	MiG-7	KPL MODELS	H VAC	72		2929
MIKOYAN-GURYEVICH	MiG-9 (Fargo)	AIRMODEL	H VAC	72		2930
MIKOYAN-GURYEVICH	MiG-9 (Fargo)	CRUVER	R HR·	72		2931
MIKOYAN-GURYEVICH	MiG-9 (Fargo)	PRIVATE VENTURE A	H RSN	72		2932
MIKOYAN-GURYEVICH	MiG-9 (Fargo)	SUTCLIFFE	H VAC	72		2933
MIKOYAN-GURYEVICH	MiG-15bis (Fagot)	AIRFIX	H INJ	72		2934
MIKOYAN-GURYEVICH	MiG-15bis (Fagot)	CHARMORE	H INJ	72		2935
MIKOYAN-GURYEVICH	MiG-15bis (Fagot)	COMA	H INJ	72		2936
MIKOYAN-GURYEVICH	MiG-15bis (Fagot)	CRUVER	R HR·	72		2937
MIKOYAN-GURYEVICH	MiG-15bis (Fagot)	KOVOZAVODY	H INJ	72		2938
MIKOYAN-GURYEVICH	MiG-15bis (Fagot)	M.C.C.N.E.	H INJ	72		2939
MIKOYAN-GURYEVICH	MiG-15bis (Fagot)	NITTO	H INJ	72		2940
MIKOYAN-GURYEVICH	MiG-15bis (Fagot)	NOVOEXPORT	H INJ	72		2941
MIKOYAN-GURYEVICH	MiG-15bis (Fagot)	RUCH	H INJ	72		2942
MIKOYAN-GURYEVICH	MiG-15bis (Fagot)	SDELAND	H ML· WK	72		2943
MIKOYAN-GURYEVICH	MiG-15UTI (Midget)	AIRMODEL	H VAC CV	72	canopy, + MiG-21U + Il-2	2944
MIKOYAN-GURYEVICH	MiG-15UTI (Midget)	KOVOZAVODY	H INJ	72		2945
MIKOYAN-GURYEVICH	MiG-15UTI (Midget)	LFI	H INJ	72		2946
MIKOYAN-GURYEVICH	MiG-15UTI (Midget)	MAC VAC CANOPY	H VAC	72		2947
MIKOYAN-GURYEVICH	MiG-17 (Fresco A)	AEROCLUB MODELS	H VAC CV	72		2948

MIKOYAN-GURYEVICH	MiG-17 (Fresco A)	CRUVER	R HR·	72		2949
MIKOYAN-GURYEVICH	MiG-17 (Fresco A)	E.D.H.	H FM·	72		2950
MIKOYAN-GURYEVICH	MiG-17 (Fresco A)	M.C.C.N.E.	H INJ	72		2951
MIKOYAN-GURYEVICH	MiG-17F (Fresco C)	AEROCLUB MODELS	H VAC CV	72		2952
MIKOYAN-GURYEVICH	MiG-17F (Fresco C)	LFI	H INJ	72		2953
MIKOYAN-GURYEVICH	MiG-17PF (Fresco D/E)	HASEGAWA	H INJ	72	w. Alkali missile	2954
MIKOYAN-GURYEVICH	MiG-17PF (Fresco D)	KOVOZAVODY	H INJ	72		2955
MIKOYAN-GURYEVICH	MiG-17PFU (Fresco E)	AEROCLUB MODELS	H VAC CV	72		2956
MIKOYAN-GURYEVICH	MiG-19 (Farmer)	SETCO	R HR·	72		2957
MIKOYAN-GURYEVICH	MiG-19PM (Farmer E)	CENTRAL	H INJ	72	w. Alkali missile	2958
MIKOYAN-GURYEVICH	MiG-19PM (Farmer E)	HELLER	H INJ	72	w. Alkali missile	2959
MIKOYAN-GURYEVICH	MiG-19PM (Farmer E)	LFI	H INJ	72	w. Alkali missile	2960
MIKOYAN-GURYEVICH	MiG-19SF (Farmer C)	KOVOZAVODY	H INJ	72		2961
MIKOYAN-GURYEVICH	Ye-8A (MiG-21Sht prototype)	AIRMODEL	H VAC	72	w. RSN parts	2962
MIKOYAN-GURYEVICH	Ye-8A (MiG-21Sht prototype)	PRIVATE VENTURE	H RSN	72		2963
MIKOYAN-GURYEVICH	MiG-21 (Fishbed)	SETCO	R HR·	72		2964
MIKOYAN-GURYEVICH	MiG-21F (Fishbed C)	AIRFIX	H INJ	73	w. Atoll missile	2965
MIKOYAN-GURYEVICH	MiG-21F (Fishbed C)	HASEGAWA	H INJ	68	w. Atoll missile	2966
MIKOYAN-GURYEVICH	MiG-21F (Fishbed C)	HELLER	H INJ	72	w. Atoll missile	2967
MIKOYAN-GURYEVICH	MiG-21F (Fishbed C)	IMC	H INJ	70	w. Atoll missile	2968
MIKOYAN-GURYEVICH	MiG-21F (Fishbed C)	MAC VAC CANOPY	H VAC	72		2969
MIKOYAN-GURYEVICH	MiG-21MF (Fishbed J)	KOVOZAVODY	H INJ	72	w. Atoll missile	2970
MIKOYAN-GURYEVICH	MiG-21MF (Fishbed J)	MALKA	H INJ	72		2971
MIKOYAN-GURYEVICH	MiG-21MF (Fishbed J)	MATCHBOX	H INJ RM	72	remoulded PF	2972
MIKOYAN-GURYEVICH	MiG-21PF (Fishbed E)	MATCHBOX	H INJ	72		2973
MIKOYAN-GURYEVICH	MiG-21SMT (Fishbed K)	MIR	H INJ	72		2974
MIKOYAN-GURYEVICH	MiG-21U (Mongol A)	AIRMODEL	H VAC CV	72	canopy, + MiG-15UTI + Il-2	2975
MIKOYAN-GURYEVICH	MiG-23S (Flogger B)	AIRFIX	H INJ	72	w. Atoll, Apex missile	2976
MIKOYAN-GURYEVICH	MiG-23S (Flogger B)	HASEGAWA	H INJ	72	w. Apex, Aphid missile	2977
MIKOYAN-GURYEVICH	MiG-25 (Foxbat A)	HASEGAWA	H INJ	72	w. Acrid missile	2978
MIKOYAN-GURYEVICH	MiG-27 (Flogger D)	ACADEMY MINICRAFT	H INJ	72		2979
MIKOYAN-GURYEVICH	MiG-27 (Flogger D)	HASEGAWA	H INJ	72	w. Atoll missile	2980
MIKOYAN-GURYEVICH	MiG-29 (Fulcrum)	FUJIMI	H INJ	72		2981
MIKOYAN-GURYEVICH	MiG-29 (Fulcrum)	HASEGAWA	H INJ	72		2982
MIKOYAN-GURYEVICH	MiG-29 (Fulcrum)	HOBBY SHOP WORK	H VAC	72		2983
MIKOYAN-GURYEVICH	MiG-I-224	PRIVATE VENTURE C	H RSN	72	id 4a, MiG-7	2984
MIKOYAN-GURYEVICH	MiG-I-270	AIRMODEL	H RSN	72	Russian Me 263	2985
MIKOYAN-GURYEVICH	MiG-I-270/Zh	VP CANADA	H VAC	72	Russian Me 263, w. RSN p.	2986
MIL	Mi-1/1M Moskvich (Hare)	MAI	H RSN	72		2987
MIL	Mi-4 (Hound)	CRUVER	R HR·	72		2988
MIL	Mi-6 (Hook)	AIRMODEL	R HR·	72		2989
MIL	Mi-6 (Hook)	VEB PLASTICART	H INJ	73		2990
MIL	Mi-24 (Hind A)	FORMAPLANE	H VAC	72		2991
MIL	Mi-24 (Hind A)	HASEGAWA	H INJ	72	w. EB parts	2992
MIL	Mi-24 (Hind A/D)	MPC	H INJ	72	AIRFIX w. Mi-24A parts	2993
MIL	Mi-24 (Hind D)	AIRFIX	H INJ	72	w. Swatter missile	2994
MIL	Mi-24 (Hind D)	HASEGAWA	H INJ	72	w. EB parts	2995
MIL	Mi-24 (Hind E)	HASEGAWA	H INJ	72	w. EB parts	2996
MILES	M.3 Falcon	ARNE ANDERSSON	H VAC	72		2997
MILES	M.9A Master Mk I	AIRMODEL	H VAC CV	72		2998
MILES	M.9A Master Mk I	FALCON	H VAC CV	72		2999
MILES	M.9A Master Mk I	SKYBIRDS	H WD·	72		3000
MILES	M14 Magister	FROG	H INJ	72		3001
MILES	M.14 Magister	FROG PENGUIN	H INJ	72		3002
MILES	M.25 Martinet	AIRMODEL	H VAC CV	72	canopy, + Battle + Defiant	3003
MILES	M.27 Master Mk III	FROG	H INJ	72		3004
MILES	M.33 Monitor	SUTCLIFFE	H VAC	72		3005
MILES	M.38 Messenger	AEROCLUB MODELS	H VAC	72	w. ML parts	3006
MILES	M.39B Libellula	AIRFRAME	H VAC	72		3007
MILES	M.52	AIRVAC	H VAC	72		3008
MILES	M.60 Marathon	SUTCLIFFE	H VAC	72		3009
MITSUBISHI	A5M4	ARISTO CRAFT	H INJ	72	Claude	3010
MITSUBISHI	A5M4	COMET	H WD·	72	Claude	3011
MITSUBISHI	A5M4	CRUVER	R HR·	72	Claude	3012
MITSUBISHI	A5M4	NICHIMO	H INJ	72	Claude	3013
MITSUBISHI	A6M2 Reisen (Zero Fighter)	AIRFIX	H INJ	72	Zeke	3014
MITSUBISHI	A6M2 Reisen (Zero Fighter)	AOSHIMA	H INJ	72	Zeke	3015

MITSUBISHI	A6M2 Reisen (Zero Fighter)	ARISTO CRAFT	H INJ	72	Zeke	3016
MITSUBISHI	A6M2 Reisen (Zero Fighter)	CRUVER	R HR·	72	Zeke	3017
MITSUBISHI	A6M2 Reisen (Zero Fighter)	FUJIMI	H INJ	70	Zeke	3018
MITSUBISHI	A6M2 Reisen (Zero Fighter)	HASEGAWA	H INJ	72	Zeke	3019
MITSUBISHI	A6M2 Reisen (Zero Fighter)	JO HAN	H INJ	72	Zeke, + Rufe	3020
MITSUBISHI	A6M2 Reisen (Zero Fighter)	L.S.	H INJ	75	Zeke	3021
MITSUBISHI	A6M2 Reisen (Zero Fighter)	NICHIMO	H INJ	69	Zeke	3022
MITSUBISHI	A6M2 Reisen (Zero Fighter)	POLISTIL	H INJ	72	Zeke	3023
MITSUBISHI	A6M3 Reisen (Zero Fighter)	ARISTO CRAFT	H INJ	72	Hamp (ex-Zeke 32)	3024
MITSUBISHI	A6M3 Reisen (Zero Fighter)	CRUVER	R HR·	72	Hamp (ex-Zeke 32)	3025
MITSUBISHI	A6M3 Reisen (Zero Fighter)	FUJIMI	H INJ	70	Hamp (ex-Zeke 32)	3026
MITSUBISHI	A6M3 Reisen (Zero Fighter)	HASEGAWA	H INJ	72	Hamp (ex-Zeke 32)	3027
MITSUBISHI	A6M3 Reisen (Zero Fighter)	HASEGAWA	H INJ	72	Hamp (ex-Zeke 32)	3028
MITSUBISHI	A6M3 Reisen (Zero Fighter)	MATCHBOX	H INJ	72	Hamp (ex-Zeke 32)	3029
MITSUBISHI	A6M3 Reisen (Zero Fighter)	TAMIYA	H INJ	72	Hamp (ex-Zeke 32)	3030
MITSUBISHI	A6M5 Reisen (Zero Fighter)	DESIGN CENTER	H INJ	72	Zeke	3031
MITSUBISHI	A6M5 Reisen (Zero Fighter)	FROG	H INJ	72	Zeke	3032
MITSUBISHI	A6M5 Reisen (Zero Fighter)	FUJIMI	H INJ	70	Zeke	3033
MITSUBISHI	A6M5 Reisen (Zero Fighter)	GLASSLITE	H FG·	72	Zeke	3034
MITSUBISHI	A6M5 Reisen (Zero Fighter)	HASEGAWA	H INJ	75	Zeke	3035
MITSUBISHI	A6M5 Reisen (Zero Fighter)	HASEGAWA	H INJ	75	Zeke, transparent model	3036
MITSUBISHI	A6M5 Reisen (Zero Fighter)	HAWK	H INJ	72	Zeke	3037
MITSUBISHI	A6M5 Reisen (Zero Fighter)	HELLER	H INJ	72	Zeke	3038
MITSUBISHI	A6M5 Reisen (Zero Fighter)	L.S.	H INJ	75	Zeke	3039
MITSUBISHI	A6M5 Reisen (Zero Fighter)	MAC VAC CANOPY	H VAC	72	Zeke	3040
MITSUBISHI	A6M5 Reisen (Zero Fighter)	NICHIMO	H INJ	70	Zeke	3041
MITSUBISHI	A6M5 Reisen (Zero Fighter)	REVELL	H INJ	72	Zeke	3042
MITSUBISHI	A6M5 Reisen (Zero Fighter)	STARFIX	H INJ	72	Zeke	3043
MITSUBISHI	A6M5 Reisen (Zero Fighter)	ZA	AH INJ	70	Zeke	3044
MITSUBISHI	A6M8 Reisen (Zero Fighter)	FUJIMI	H INJ	70	Zeke	3045
MITSUBISHI	A7M2 Reppu (Hurricane)	AOSHIMA	H INJ	72	Sam	3046
MITSUBISHI	B2M Type 89	O'NEILL	H VAC	72		3047
MITSUBISHI	B5M	O'NEILL	H VAC	72		3048
MITSUBISHI	C5M	ARISTO CRAFT	H INJ	72	Babs (Ki-15 Navy version)	3049
MITSUBISHI	C5M	CRUVER	R HR·	72	Babs (Ki-15 Navy version)	3050
MITSUBISHI	C5M2	L.S.	H INJ	72	Babs (Ki-15 Navy version)	3051
MITSUBISHI	C5M2 Karigane (Long Range)	L.S.	H INJ	72	(Ki-15 civil version)	3052
MITSUBISHI	F-1	HASEGAWA	H INJ	72		3053
MITSUBISHI	F1M Sasebo "O"	ARISTO CRAFT	H INJ	72	Pete, built at Sasebo	3054
MITSUBISHI	F1M	CRUVER	R HR·	72	Pete	3055
MITSUBISHI	F1M2	HASEGAWA	H INJ	75	Pete	3056
MITSUBISHI	F1M2	WINGS 72	H VAC	72	Pete	3057
MITSUBISHI	G3M	CRUVER	R HR·	72	Nell	3058
MITSUBISHI	G3M1/2 Model 21	L.S.	H INJ	75	Nell	3059
MITSUBISHI	G3M1 Nippon Go	L.S.	H INJ	75	Nell	3060
MITSUBISHI	G3M3	L.S.	H INJ	75	Nell	3061
MITSUBISHI	G4M	ARISTO CRAFT	H INJ	72	Betty	3062
MITSUBISHI	G4M	CRUVER	R HR·	72	Betty	3063
MITSUBISHI	G4M1	HASEGAWA	H INJ	72	Betty, + Ohka	3064
MITSUBISHI	G4M2	LINDBERG	H INJ	72	Betty	3065
MITSUBISHI	J2M Raiden (Thunderbolt)	CRUVER	R HR·	72	Jack	3066
MITSUBISHI	J2M3 Raiden (Thunderbolt)	HASEGAWA	H INJ	72	Jack	3067
MITSUBISHI	J2M3 Raiden (Thunderbolt)	MAC VAC CANOPY	H VAC	72	Jack	3068
MITSUBISHI	J2M3 Raiden (Thunderbolt)	NICHIMO	H INJ	72	Jack	3069
MITSUBISHI	J2M3 Raiden (Thunderbolt)	OTAKI	H INJ	72	Jack	3070
MITSUBISHI	J2M3 Raiden (Thunderbolt)	TAMIYA	H INJ	72	Jack	3071
MITSUBISHI	J8M1 Shusui (Sword Stroke)	PRIVATE VENTURE C	H RSN	72		3072
MITSUBISHI	J8M1 Shusui (Sword Stroke)	WINGS 72	H VAC	72		3073
MITSUBISHI	K3M	PRIVATE VENTURE	H RSN	72	Pine	3074
MITSUBISHI	K3M3	O'NEILL	H VAC	72	Pine	3075
MITSUBISHI	Ki-2	O'NEILL	H VAC	72		3076
MITSUBISHI	Ki-2	PRIVATE VENTURE	H RSN	72		3077
MITSUBISHI	Ki-15 Kamikaze (Divine Wind)	L.S.	H INJ	72	civil version	3078
MITSUBISHI	Ki-15	MANIA	H INJ	72	Babs	3079
MITSUBISHI	Ki-15-I	L.S.	H INJ	72	Babs	3080
MITSUBISHI	Ki-15-II	L.S.	H INJ	72	Babs	3081
MITSUBISHI	Ki-15-II Kamikaze (Divine Wind)	MANIA	H INJ	72	civil version	3082

MITSUBISHI	Ki-21	ARISTO CRAFT	H INJ	72	Sally	3083
MITSUBISHI	Ki-21	CRUVER	R HR·	72	Sally	3084
MITSUBISHI	Ki-21	REVELL	H INJ	72	Sally	3085
MITSUBISHI	Ki-30	CRUVER	R HR·	72	Ann	3086
MITSUBISHI	Ki-30	PRIVATE VENTURE C	H VAC	72	Ann	3087
MITSUBISHI	Ki-30	WINGS 72	H VAC	72	Ann	3088
MITSUBISHI	Ki-46-II	AIRFIX	H INJ	72	Dinah	3089
MITSUBISHI	Ki-46-II	CRUVER	R HR·	72	Dinah	3090
MITSUBISHI	Ki-46-II	L.S.	H INJ	72	Dinah	3091
MITSUBISHI	Ki-46-II	NAKAMURA	H INJ	75	Dinah	3092
MITSUBISHI	Ki-46-II	OTAKI	H INJ	71	Dinah	3093
MITSUBISHI	Ki-46-II Kai	L.S.	H INJ	72	Dinah (Kai = Trainer v.)	3094
MITSUBISHI	Ki-46-III	AIRMODEL	H VAC CV	72	Dinah, c. + Ju-88G/P/S	3095
MITSUBISHI	Ki-46-III	L.S.	H INJ	72	Dinah	3096
MITSUBISHI	Ki-46-III Kai	L.S.	H INJ	72	Dinah (Kai = Trainer v.)	3097
MITSUBISHI	Ki-51	ARISTO CRAFT	H INJ	72	Sonia	3098
MITSUBISHI	Ki-51	CRUVER	R HR·	72	Sonia	3099
MITSUBISHI	Ki-51	MANIA	H INJ	72	Sonia	3100
MITSUBISHI	Ki-57	ARISTO CRAFT	H INJ	72	Topsy	3101
MITSUBISHI	Ki-57	CRUVER	R HR·	72	Topsy	3102
MITSUBISHI	Ki-57	O'NEILL	H VAC CV	72	Topsy	3103
MITSUBISHI	Ki-67-I Hiryu (Flying Dragon)	L.S.	H INJ	75	Peggy	3104
MITSUBISHI	Ki-67-Ib Yasukuni	L.S.	H INJ	75	Peggy	3105
MITSUBISHI	Ki-83	KPL MODELS	H VAC	72	Steve	3106
MITSUBISHI	Ki-83	RED BARON	H RSN	72	Steve	3107
MITSUBISHI	Ki-109B	L.S.	H INJ	75		3108
MITSUBISHI	MU2-A	OTAKI	H INJ	71		3109
MITSUBISHI	MU2-J	HASEGAWA	H INJ	72	w. tractor	3110
MITSUBISHI	MU2-S	HASEGAWA	H INJ	72	w. tractor	3111
MITSUBISHI	T-2	HASEGAWA	H INJ	72	w. Sidewinder missile	3112
MITSUBISHI	T-2 CCV	HASEGAWA	H INJ RM	72	w. Sidewinder missile	3113
MORANE-SAULNIER	Type AI	CLASSIC PLANE	H VAC	72		3114
MORANE-SAULNIER	Type AI	CRAMER	H VAC	72		3115
MORANE-SAULNIER	Type AI	FORMAPLANE	H VAC	72		3116
MORANE-SAULNIER	Type L	AIRFRAME	H VAC	72		3117
MORANE-SAULNIER	Type L	SCALEPLANES	H VAC	72		3118
MORANE-SAULNIER	Type N	REVELL	H INJ	72		3119
MORANE-SAULNIER	MS.225	HELLER	H INJ	72		3120
MORANE-SAULNIER	MS.230	HELLER	H INJ	72		3121
MORANE-SAULNIER	MS.406	FROG	H INJ	72		3122
MORANE-SAULNIER	MS.406	HELLER	H INJ	72		3123
MORANE-SAULNIER	MS.406	SKYBIRDS	H WD·	72		3124
MORANE-SAULNIER	MS.540	O'NEILL	H VAC	72		3125
MYASISHCHYEV	M-4 (Bison)	SUTCLIFFE	H VAC	72	w. INJ parts	3126
McDONNELL	FH-1 Phantom	AIRMODEL	H VAC	72		3127
McDONNELL	FH-1 Phantom	GRIFFIN	H VAC	72		3128
McDONNELL	FH-1 Phantom	LVGD	H ML·	72		3129
McDONNELL	FH-1 Phantom	O'NEILL	H VAC	72		3130
McDONNELL	FH-1 Phantom	PRIVATE VENTURE C	H RSN	72		3131
McDONNELL	F2H-1 Banshee	CRUVER	R HR·	72		3132
McDONNELL	F2H-2 Banshee	O'NEILL	H VAC	72		3133
McDONNELL	F2H-2/2P Banshee	AIRFIX	H INJ	72		3134
McDONNELL	F2H-2/2P Banshee	AIRMODEL	H VAC	72		3135
McDONNELL	F2H-3 Banshee	FALCON	H VAC CV	72	+ Orion + Trader	3136
McDONNELL	F2H-3/4 Banshee	EXECUFORM	H VAC	72		3137
McDONNELL	F2H-4 Banshee	O'NEILL	H VAC	72		3138
McDONNELL	F3H-1 Demon	CRUVER	R HR·	72		3139
McDONNELL	F3H-1 Demon	McDONNELL	H RSN	72		3140
McDONNELL	F3H-1 Demon	RAREPLANES	H VAC	72	w. ML parts	3141
McDONNELL	F3H-2 Demon	AIRMODEL	H VAC	72		3142
McDONNELL	F3H-2 Demon	O'NEILL	H VAC	72		3143
McDONNELL	F3H-2 Demon	VOLKS	H RSN	72		3144
McDONNELL	F4H-1 Phantom II	FALCON	H VAC CV	72	+ A-10B + HC-130P	3145
McDONNELL	F4H-1 Phantom II	SETCO	R HR·	72		3146
McDONNELL	F-4 Phantom II	AMERICAN AIRCRAFT	H INJ	72		3147
McDONNELL	F-4 Phantom II	EXECUTIVE	D —	72		3148
McDONNELL	F-4 Phantom II	MODELAIR	H INJ	72		3149

McDONNELL	F-4B Phantom II	AIRFIX	H INJ	72		3150
McDONNELL	F-4B Phantom II	FUJIMI	H INJ	72		3151
McDONNELL	F-4B Phantom II	HASEGAWA	H INJ	72	w. Sparrow missile	3152
McDONNELL	F-4B/C/D/E/J Phantom II	AIRFIX	H INJ RM	72	w. Sparrow missile	3153
McDONNELL	RF-4B Phantom II	FUJIMI	H INJ	72		3154
McDONNELL	RF-4B Phantom II	IMC	H INJ	72		3155
McDONNELL	RF-4B/C/E/ Phantom II	AIRFRAME	H VAC CV	72		3156
McDONNELL	F-4C Phantom II	HASEGAWA	H INJ	72	w. Sparrow missile	3157
McDONNELL	F-4C Phantom II	REVELL	H INJ	72		3158
McDONNELL	F-4C/D Phantom II	FUJIMI	H INJ	72	w. Sidewinder, Sparrow m.	3159
McDONNELL	F-4C/D Phantom II	MONOGRAM	H INJ	72		3160
McDONNELL	F-4C/J Phantom II	ESCI	H INJ	72	w. Sparrow, Sidewinder m.	3161
McDONNELL	RF-4C Phantom II	FUJIMI	H INJ	72		3162
McDONNELL	RF-4C/E Phantom II	ESCI	H INJ	72		3163
McDONNELL	RF-4C/E Phantom II	ITALERI	H INJ	72		3164
McDONNELL	F-4D Phantom II	EXECUTIVE	D —	72		3165
McDONNELL	F-4D/J Phantom II	HASEGAWA	H INJ	72	w. Sparrow missile	3166
McDONNELL	F-4E Phantom II	FUJIMI	H INJ	72		3167
McDONNELL	F-4E Phantom II	HELLER BOBCAT	H INJ	72		3168
McDONNELL	F-4E Phantom II	MONOGRAM	H INJ SN	72	w. Sidewinder missile	3169
McDONNELL	F-4E/F Phantom II	ESCI	H INJ	72	w. Sparrow, Sidewinder m.	3170
McDONNELL	F-4E/F/G Phantom II	ITALERI	H INJ	72	w. AGM-78B, Shrike m.	3171
McDONNELL	F-4E/J Phantom II	EXECUTIVE	D —	72		3172
McDONNELL	F-4E/J Phantom II	FUJIMI	H INJ	72		3173
McDONNELL	F-4E/J Phantom II	HASEGAWA	H INJ	72	w. Falcon, Sparrow, Sw m.	3174
McDONNELL	F-4E/J Phantom II	REVELL	H INJ	72	w. Sparrow, Sidewinder m.	3175
McDONNELL	RF-4E Phantom II	AIRMODEL	H VAC CV	72		3176
McDONNELL	RF-4E Phantom II	AIRMODEL	H VAC CV	72	+ S-58 (H-34)	3177
McDONNELL	RF-4E Phantom II	AIRTEC	H INJ CV	72		3178
McDONNELL	RF-4E Phantom II	FUJIMI	H INJ	72		3179
McDONNELL	RF-4E Phantom II	REVELL	H INJ	72		3180
McDONNELL	F-4F Phantom II	FUJIMI	H INJ	72		3181
McDONNELL	F-4G Phantom II	FUJIMI	H INJ	72		3182
McDONNELL	F-4H Phantom II	HASEGAWA	H INJ	72		3183
McDONNELL	F-4J Phantom II	FUJIMI	H INJ	72		3184
McDONNELL	F-4J Phantom II	GUILLOW	H WD·	72		3185
McDONNELL	F-4J Phantom II	MONOGRAM	H INJ	72		3186
McDONNELL	F-4K Phantom II	FUJIMI	H INJ	72		3187
McDONNELL	Phantom FG Mk 1 (F-4K)	FUJIMI	H INJ	72		3188
McDONNELL	F-4K/M Phantom II	FROG	H INJ	72		3189
McDONNELL	F-4K/M Phantom II	HASEGAWA	H INJ	72	w. Bullpup missile	3190
McDONNELL	F-4K/M Phantom II	MATCHBOX	H INJ	72	w. Sparrow, Sidewinder m.	3191
McDONNELL	F-4K/M Phantom II	MATCHBOX	H INJ RM	72		3192
McDONNELL	F-4K/M Phantom II	REVELL	H INJ	72	w. Sparrow missile	3193
McDONNELL	F-4M Phantom II	FUJIMI	H INJ	72		3194
McDONNELL	Phantom FGR Mk 2 (F-4M)	FUJIMI	H INJ	72		3195
McDONNELL	F-4N Phantom II	FUJIMI	H INJ	72	w. Sidewinder, Sparrow m.	3196
McDONNELL	F-4S Phantom II	ESCI	H INJ	72		3197
McDONNELL	F-4S Phantom II	ESCI	H INJ	72		3198
McDONNELL	F-4S Phantom II	FUJIMI	H INJ	72	w. Sidewinder, Sparrow m.	3199
McDONNELL	RF-4X	TWELVE SQUARED	H INJ CV	72	HIAC pod, nose, camera	3200
McDONNELL	F-101 Voodoo	AIRTEC	H INJ CV	72		3201
McDONNELL	F-101A Voodoo	CRUVER	R HR·	72		3202
McDONNELL	F-101A Voodoo	NITTO	H INJ	77		3203
McDONNELL	F101A Voodoo	REVELL	H INJ	76		3204
McDONNELL	F-101A/B/C	AIRMODEL	H VAC CV	72	+ HC-130	3205
McDONNELL	F-101A/C Voodoo	MICRO SCALE	H INJ	72		3206
McDONNELL	F-101B Voodoo	AIRMODEL	H VAC CV	72	+ F-100F + F-105F	3207
McDONNELL	F-101B Voodoo	ARMTEC	H INJ CV	72		3208
McDONNELL	F101B/F/RF-101B Voodoo	MATCHBOX	H INJ	72		3209
McDONNELL	RF-101C Voodoo	HASEGAWA	H INJ	72		3210
McDONNELL	RF-101C Voodoo	MAC VAC CANOPY	H VAC	72		3211
McDONNELL	XF-85 Goblin	AIRMODEL	H VAC	72		3212
McDONNELL	XF-85 Goblin	MAC VAC CANOPY	H VAC	72		3213
McDONNELL	XF-85 Goblin	PRIVATE VENTURE B	H RSN	72		3214
McDONNELL	XF-88 Voodoo	KR MODELS	H VAC	72		3215
McDONNELL	XHJH-1 Whirlaway	O'NEILL	H VAC	72		3216

McDONNELL	XP-67 Bat	MAC VAC CANOPY	H VAC	72		3217
McDONNELL	XP-67 Bat	PRIVATE VENTURE C	H RSN	72		3218
McDONNELL	XP-67 Bat	RAREPLANES	H VAC	72		3219
McDONNELL DOUGLAS	A4D-1 (A-4A) Skyhawk	AIRFIX	H INJ	72		3220
McDONNELL DOUGLAS	A4D-1 (A-4A) Skyhawk	SETCO	R HR·	72		3221
McDONNELL DOUGLAS	A-4A/B/C/ Skyhawk	IMPS USA	H INJ CV	72		3222
McDONNELL DOUGLAS	A-4B Skyhawk	HELLER CADET	H INJ	72		3223
McDONNELL DOUGLAS	A-4C Skyhawk	NOSE JOBS	H ML· CV	72		3224
McDONNELL DOUGLAS	A-4B/C Skyhawk	NOSE JOBS	H ML· CV	72		3225
McDONNELL DOUGLAS	A-4D Skyhawk	CENTRAL	H INJ	72	w. Sidewinder missile	3226
McDONNELL DOUGLAS	A-4E Skyhawk	ESCI	H INJ	72		3227
McDONNELL DOUGLAS	A-4E Skyhawk	IMC	H INJ	72		3228
McDONNELL DOUGLAS	A-4E Skyhawk	OTAKI	H INJ	78		3229
McDONNELL DOUGLAS	A-4E/F Skyhawk	HASEGAWA	H INJ	72	w. Bullpup, Sparrow, Sw m.	3230
McDONNELL DOUGLAS	A-4E/F Skyhawk	MAC VAC CANOPY	H VAC	72		3231
McDONNELL DOUGLAS	A-4F Skyhawk	ESCI	H INJ	72		3232
McDONNELL DOUGLAS	A-4M Skyhawk	FUJIMI	H INJ	72		3233
McDONNELL DOUGLAS	A-4M Skyhawk	ITALERI	H INJ	72		3234
McDONNELL DOUGLAS	A-4M Skyhawk	MATCHBOX	H INJ	72	w. Bullpup missile	3235
McDONNELL DOUGLAS	OA-4M Skyhawk	FUJIMI	H INJ	72		3236
McDONNELL DOUGLAS	OA-4M Skyhawk	HASEGAWA	H INJ RM	72	remoulded TA-4J	3237
McDONNELL DOUGLAS	TA-4 Skyhawk	MAC VAC CANOPY	H VAC	72		3238
McDONNELL DOUGLAS	TA-4F Skyhawk	AIRMODEL	H VAC CV	72	canopy, + TA-7C + PBY	3239
McDONNELL DOUGLAS	TA-4J Skyhawk	HASEGAWA	H INJ RM	72	remoulded A-4E, w. Sparrow	3240
McDONNELL DOUGLAS	DC-9-10	EXECUTIVE	D FG·	72		3241
McDONNELL DOUGLAS	DC-9-15	AURORA	H INJ	72		3242
McDONNELL DOUGLAS	DC-9-15	AURORA	H INJ RM	72		3243
McDONNELL DOUGLAS	DC-9-30	EXECUTIVE	D FG·	72		3244
McDONNELL DOUGLAS	C-9A Nightingale	AMERICAN AIRCRAFT	H INJ	72		3245
McDONNELL DOUGLAS	DC-9-51	EXECUTIVE	D FG·	72		3246
McDONNELL DOUGLAS	MD-80 (ex-DC-9 Super 80)	EXECUTIVE	D FG·	72	renamed MD-80 in 1983	3247
McDONNELL DOUGLAS	MD-80 (ex-DC-9 Super 80)	SKYLAND MODELS	D FG·	72		3248
McDONNELL DOUGLAS	DC-10	MODELMASTERS	D —	72		3249
McDONNELL DOUGLAS	DC-10-30	EXECUTIVE	D FG·	72		3250
McDONNELL DOUGLAS	DC-10-30	SKYLAND MODELS	D FG·	72		3251
McDONNELL DOUGLAS	KC-10A Extender	AMERICAN AIRCRAFT	H INJ	72		3252
McDONNELL DOUGLAS	F-15A Eagle	AMERICAN AIRCRAFT	H INJ	72		3253
McDONNELL DOUGLAS	F-15A Eagle	ESCI	H INJ	72		3254
McDONNELL DOUGLAS	F-15A Eagle	EXECUTIVE	D —	72		3255
McDONNELL DOUGLAS	F-15A Eagle	HASEGAWA	H INJ	72	w. Sparrow missile	3256
McDONNELL DOUGLAS	F-15A Eagle	MONOGRAM	H INJ	72	w. Sparrow, Sidewinder m.	3257
McDONNELL DOUGLAS	F-15A Eagle	REVELL	H INJ	72	w. Sidewinder missile	3258
McDONNELL DOUGLAS	F-15A Eagle	REVELL	H INJ RM	72	w. Sparrow, Sidewinder m.	3259
McDONNELL DOUGLAS	F-15A Eagle	RICK'S	D FM·	72	id. TEEPEE	3260
McDONNELL DOUGLAS	F-15A/B Eagle	AIRFIX	H INJ	72	w. Sparrow, Sidewinder m.	3261
McDONNELL DOUGLAS	F-15A/C Eagle	ESCI	H INJ	72		3262
McDONNELL DOUGLAS	F-15B Eagle	ESCI	H INJ	72		3263
McDONNELL DOUGLAS	F-15B/D Eagle	HASEGAWA	H INJ	72	w. Sparrow missile	3264
McDONNELL DOUGLAS	F-15C Eagle	HASEGAWA	H INJ	72	w. Sparrow, Sidewinder m.	3265
McDONNELL DOUGLAS	F-15D/DJ Eagle	HASEGAWA	H INJ	72		3266
McDONNELL DOUGLAS	F-15E Eagle	ESCI	H INJ	72		3267
McDONNELL DOUGLAS	F-15E Eagle	HASEGAWA	H INJ	72	w. Sparrow, Sidewinder m.	3268
McDONNELL DOUGLAS	F-15E Eagle	MONOGRAM	H INJ	72	w. Sidewinder missile	3269
McDONNELL DOUGLAS	F-15J Eagle	HASEGAWA	H INJ RM	72	remoulded F-15C, w. Sp, Sw	3270
McDONNELL DOUGLAS	F/A-18 Hornet	AIRFIX	H INJ	72	w. Sparrow, Sidewinder m.	3271
McDONNELL DOUGLAS	F/A-18 Hornet	ENTEX	H INJ	72	w. Sparrow, Sidewinder m.	3272
McDONNELL DOUGLAS	F/A-18 Hornet	ESCI	H INJ	72	w. Sidewinder missile	3273
McDONNELL DOUGLAS	F/A-18 Hornet	EXECUTIVE	D —	72		3274
McDONNELL DOUGLAS	F/A-18 Hornet	HASEGAWA	H INJ	72	w. Sparrow, Sidewinder m.	3275
McDONNELL DOUGLAS	F/A-18 Hornet	MODELAIR	H INJ	72		3276
McDONNELL DOUGLAS	F/A-18 Hornet	MONOGRAM	H INJ SN	72	w. Sparrow, Sidewinder m.	3277
McDONNELL DOUGLAS	F/A-18A Hornet	HASEGAWA	H INJ RM	72		3278
McDONNELL DOUGLAS	RF-18A Hornet	ITALERI	H INJ	72		3279
McDONNELL DOUGLAS	TF/A-18A Hornet	HASEGAWA	H INJ	72		3280
McDONNELL DOUGLAS	TF/A-18A Hornet	ITALERI	H INJ	72	w. Sparrow, AIM-92 missile	3281
McDONNELL DOUGLAS	TF/A-18A Hornet	ITALERI	H INJ	72	+ F-18A	3282
McDONNELL DOUGLAS/BAe	AV-8B Harrier II	ITALERI	H INJ	72	w. Sidewinder missile	3283

McDONNELL DOUGLAS/BAe	TAV-8B Harrier II/Harrier GR.5	MAINTRACK	H RSN CV	72		3284
NAKAJIMA	A2N1	O'NEILL	H VAC	72		3285
NAKAJIMA	A2N1	PRIVATE VENTURE	H RSN	72		3286
NAKAJIMA	Type 91	O'NEILL	H VAC	72		3287
NAKAJIMA	Type 91	PRIVATE VENTURE	H RSN	72		3288
NAKAJIMA	Type 91	RAREPLANES	H VAC	72		3289
NAKAJIMA	A4N1	O'NEILL	H VAC	72		3290
NAKAJIMA	A6M2-N (A6M2 seaplane version)	ARISTO CRAFT	H INJ	72	Rufe	3291
NAKAJIMA	A6M2-N (A6M2 seaplane version)	CRUVER	R HR·	72	Rufe	3292
NAKAJIMA	A6M2-N (A6M2 seaplane version)	FROG	H INJ	72	Rufe	3293
NAKAJIMA	A6M2-N (A6M2 seaplane version)	JO HAN	H INJ	72	Rufe, + A6M2	3294
NAKAJIMA	A6M2-N (A6M2 seaplane version)	L.S.	H INJ	75	Rufe	3295
NAKAJIMA	A6M2-N (A6M2 seaplane version)	YODEL	H INJ	72	Rufe	3296
NAKAJIMA	B5N1 Type 97	NITTO	H INJ	72	Kate	3297
NAKAJIMA	B5N1/2 Type 97	MANIA	H INJ	72	Kate	3298
NAKAJIMA	B5N2 Type 97	ARISTO CRAFT	H INJ	72	Kate	3299
NAKAJIMA	B5N2 Type 97	CRUVER	R HR·	72	Kate	3300
NAKAJIMA	B5N2 Type 97	NITTO	H INJ	75	Kate	3301
NAKAJIMA	B6N Tenzan (Heavenly Mountain)	DESIGN CENTER	H INJ	72	Jill	3302
NAKAJIMA	B6N1 Tenzan (Heavenly Mountain)	FUJIMI	H INJ	72	Jill	3303
NAKAJIMA	B6N2 Tenzan (Heavenly Mountain)	EAGLES TALON	H VAC	72	Jill	3304
NAKAJIMA	B6N2 Tenzan (Heavenly Mountain)	FUJIMI	H INJ	72	Jill	3305
NAKAJIMA	B6N2 Tenzan (Heavenly Mountain)	IKKO	H INJ	67	Jill	3306
NAKAJIMA	B6N2 Tenzan (Heavenly Mountain)	L.S.	H INJ	67	Jill	3307
NAKAJIMA	B6N2 Tenzan (Heavenly Mountain)	NITTO	H INJ	75	Jill	3308
NAKAJIMA	B6N2 Tenzan (Heavenly Mountain)	WINGS 72	H VAC	72	Jill	3309
NAKAJIMA	C6N Saiun (Painted Cloud)	RED BARON	H RSN	72	Myrt	3310
NAKAJIMA	C6N Saiun (Painted Cloud)	CRUVER	R HR·	72	Myrt	3311
NAKAJIMA	C6N1 Saiun (Painted Cloud)	AOSHIMA	H INJ	73	Myrt	3312
NAKAJIMA	C6N1 Saiun (Painted Cloud)	NITTO	H INJ	75	Myrt	3313
NAKAJIMA	E8N Type 95	PRIVATE VENTURE	H RSN	72	Dave	3314
NAKAJIMA	E8N Type 95	ARISTO CRAFT	H INJ	72	Dave	3315
NAKAJIMA	E8N Type 95	CRUVER	R HR·	72	Dave	3316
NAKAJIMA	E8N Type 95	DESIGN CENTER	H INJ	72	Dave	3317
NAKAJIMA	E8N Type 95	O'NEILL	H VAC	72	Dave	3318
NAKAJIMA	E8N1/2 Type 95	WINGS 72	H VAC	72	Dave	3319
NAKAJIMA	G5N Shinzan (Mountain Recess)	O'NEILL	H VAC	72	Liz	3320
NAKAJIMA	G8N1 Renzan (Mountain Range)	HASEGAWA	H INJ	72	Rita	3321
NAKAJIMA	J1N1 Gekko (Moonlight)	DESIGN CENTER	H INJ	72	Irving	3322
NAKAJIMA	J1N1 Gekko (Moonlight)	O.D.K.	H INJ	71	Irving	3323
NAKAJIMA	J1N1 Gekko (Moonlight)	REVELL	H INJ	72	Irving	3324
NAKAJIMA	Ki-4 Type 94	O'NEILL	H VAC	72		3325
NAKAJIMA	Ki-11	PRIVATE VENTURE	H RSN	72		3326
NAKAJIMA	Ki-27 Type 97 Fighter	ARISTO CRAFT	H INJ	72	Nate	3327
NAKAJIMA	Ki-27 Type 97 Fighter	CRUVER	R HR·	72	Nate	3328
NAKAJIMA	Ki-27 Type 97 Fighter	MANIA	H INJ	72	Nate	3329
NAKAJIMA	Ki-34 Type 97 T	O'NEILL	H VAC	72	Thora	3330
NAKAJIMA	Ki-43-I Hayabusa (Peregrine)	ARISTO CRAFT	H INJ	72	Oscar	3331
NAKAJIMA	Ki-43-I Hayabusa (Peregrine)	CRUVER	R HR·	72	Oscar	3332
NAKAJIMA	Ki-43-I Hayabusa (Peregrine)	L.S.	H INJ	75	Oscar	3333
NAKAJIMA	Ki-43-I Hayabusa (Peregrine)	REVELL	H INJ	72	Oscar	3334
NAKAJIMA	Ki-43-I Hayabusa (Peregrine)	ZA	H INJ	70	Oscar	3335
NAKAJIMA	Ki-43-II Hayabusa (Peregrine)	AOSHIMA	H INJ	78	Oscar	3336
NAKAJIMA	Ki-43-II Hayabusa (Peregrine)	CRUVER	R HR·	72	Oscar	3337
NAKAJIMA	Ki-43-II Hayabusa (Peregrine)	FUJIMI	H INJ	70	Oscar	3338
NAKAJIMA	Ki-43-II Hayabusa (Peregrine)	HASEGAWA	H INJ	72	Oscar (type IIa/b)	3339
NAKAJIMA	Ki-43-II Hayabusa (Peregrine)	L.S.	H INJ	75	Oscar	3340
NAKAJIMA	Ki-44 Shoki (Devil-Queller)	CRUVER	R HR·	72	Tojo	3341
NAKAJIMA	Ki-44 Shoki (Devil-Queller)	TAMIYA	H INJ	72	Tojo	3342
NAKAJIMA	Ki-44-I/II Shoki (Devil-Queller)	HASEGAWA	H INJ	72	Tojo	3343
NAKAJIMA	Ki-44-II Shoki (Devil-Queller)	FUJIMI	H INJ	70	Tojo	3344
NAKAJIMA	Ki-49 Donryu (Storm Dragon)	CRUVER	R HR·	72	Helen	3345
NAKAJIMA	Ki-49 Donryu (Storm Dragon)	HELLER	H INJ	72	Helen	3346
NAKAJIMA	Ki-84 Hayate (Gale)	AOSHIMA	H INJ	76	Frank	3347
NAKAJIMA	Ki-84 Hayate (Gale)	CRUVER	R HR·	72	Frank	3348
NAKAJIMA	Ki-84 Hayate (Gale)	FUJIMI	H INJ	70	Frank	3349
NAKAJIMA	Ki-84 Hayate (Gale)	REVELL	H INJ	72	Frank	3350

NAKAJIMA	Ki-84-I Hayate (Gale)	HASEGAWA	H INJ	72	Frank	3351
NAKAJIMA	Ki-84-I Hayate (Gale)	TAMIYA	H INJ	72	Frank	3352
NAKAJIMA	Ki-115 Tsurugi (Sabre)	D & R	H VAC	72		3353
NAKAJIMA	Ki-115 Tsurugi (Sabre)	KPL MODELS	H VAC	72		3354
NAKAJIMA	Ki-115 Tsurugi (Sabre)	PRIVATE VENTURE B	H RSN	72		3355
NAKAJIMA	Kikka (Orange Blossom)	BOLESLAV	H VAC	72		3356
NAKAJIMA	Kikka (Orange Blossom)	EAGLES TALON	H VAC	72		3357
NAKAJIMA	Kikka (Orange Blossom)	O'NEILL	H VAC	72		3358
NAKAJIMA	Kikka (Orange Blossom)	PRIVATE VENTURE Č	H RSN	72		3359
NAKAJIMA	Kikka (Orange Blossom)	WINGS 72	H VAC	72		3360
NAMC	YS-11	IMAI	H INJ	72		3361
NAMC	YS-11	MODELMASTERS	D —	72		3362
NANCHANG	Q-5 Fantan A	PRIVATE VENTURE B	H RSN	72		3363
NIEUPORT	Monoplan 1912	SCALEPLANES	H VAC	72		3364
NIEUPORT	Type 10/Type 12	CLASSIC PLANE	H VAC	72		3365
NIEUPORT	Type 11 Bébé Nieuport	CLASSIC PLANE	H VAC	72		3366
NIEUPORT	Type 11 Bébé Nieuport	EDISON	H ML· AS	72	w. plastsic parts	3367
NIEUPORT	Type 12	FORMAPLANE	H VAC	72		3368
NIEUPORT	Type 17C	ELDON	H INJ	72		3369
NIEUPORT	Type 17	PLASTIQUES DERMATT	H INJ	72		3370
NIEUPORT	Type 17	RENWAL	H INJ	72		3371
NIEUPORT	Type 17	REVELL	H INJ	72		3372
NIEUPORT	Type 17	SKYBIRDS	H WD·	72		3373
NIEUPORT	Type 28	REVELL	H INJ	72		3374
NIEUPORT-DELAGE	Ni-D 29	CRAMER	H VAC	72		3375
NIEUPORT-DELAGE	Ni-D 52	REPLICA	H RSN	72	HISPANO SUIZA engine	3376
NIEUPORT-DELAGE	Ni-D 52C1	PRIVATE VENTURE C	H VAC CV	72		3377
NIEUPORT-DELAGE	Ni-D 622	HELLER	H INJ	72		3378
NOORDUYN	UC-64A Norseman	FORMAPLANE	H VAC	72		3379
NOORDUYN	UC-64A Norseman	MATCHBOX	H INJ	72		3380
NOORDUYN	UC-64A Norseman	O'NEILL	H VAC	72		3381
NORD	1500 Griffon II	FANAMODELE	H RSN	72	w. EB, ML parts	3382
NORD	1500 Griffon II	PRIVATE VENTURE	H RSN	72		3383
NORD	2601 Noratlas	HELLER	H INJ	72		3384
NORD	2502 Noratlas	HELLER	H INJ RM	72	remoulded NORD 2501	3385
NORTH AMERICAN	A3J Vigilante	MONOGRAM	H INJ WK	76		3386
NORTH AMERICAN	A3J-1 Vigilante	SETCO	R HR·	72		3387
NORTH AMERICAN	A-5A Vigilante	MONOGRAM	H INJ RM	76		3388
NORTH AMERICAN	RA-5C Vigilante	AIRFIX	H INJ	72		3389
NORTH AMERICAN	RA-5C Vigilante	HASEGAWA	H INJ	72		3390
NORTH AMERICAN	AJ-1 Savage	AIRMODEL	H VAC	72		3391
NORTH AMERICAN	AJ-1 Savage	CRUVER	R HR·	72		3392
NORTH AMERICAN	AJ-1 Savage	O'NEILL	H VAC	72		3393
NORTH AMERICAN	B-25 Mitchell	ARISTO CRAFT	H INJ	72		3394
NORTH AMERICAN	B-25B/C Mitchell	ITALERI	H INJ	72		3395
NORTH AMERICAN	B-25C Mitchell	CRUVER	R HR·	72		3396
NORTH AMERICAN	B-25D Mitchell	FROG	H INJ	72		3397
NORTH AMERICAN	B-25H Mitchell	MONOGRAM	H INJ	70		3398
NORTH AMERICAN	B-25H/J Mitchell	AIRFIX	H INJ	72		3399
NORTH AMERICAN	B-25H/J Mitchell	ITALERI	H INJ	72		3400
NORTH AMERICAN	B-25H/J Mitchell	MATCHBOX	H INJ	72		3401
NORTH AMERICAN	B-25J Mitchell	MONOGRAM	H INJ SN	72		3402
NORTH AMERICAN	B-45A Tornado	CRUVER	R HR·	72		3403
NORTH AMERICAN	B-45A Tornado	O'NEILL	H VAC	72		3404
NORTH AMERICAN	B-45A/B/C Tornado	ELLIOTT	H VAC	72	w. ML parts	3405
NORTH AMERICAN	B-45C/RB-45C Tornado	AEROFORM	H VAC	72		3406
NORTH AMERICAN	RB-45 Tornado	AEROSPACE CASTING	H RSN	72		3407
NORTH AMERICAN	RB-45C Tornado	ELLIOTT	H VAC	72	w. ML parts	3408
NORTH AMERICAN	F-82 Twin Mustang	CRUVER	R HR·	72		3409
NORTH AMERICAN	F-82 Twin Mustang	FROG	H INJ	72		3410
NORTH AMERICAN	F-82 Twin Mustang	MAC VAC CANOPY	H VAC	72		3411
NORTH AMERICAN	F-82 Twin Mustang	NITTO	H INJ	77		3412
NORTH AMERICAN	F-82E/G Twin Mustang	MONOGRAM	H INJ	72		3413
NORTH AMERICAN	F-82F Twin Mustang	CRUVER	R HR·	72		3414
NORTH AMERICAN	F-86A/E Sabre	MATCHBOX	H INJ	72		3415
NORTH AMERICAN	F-86D Sabre	AIRFIX	H INJ	72		3416
NORTH AMERICAN	F-86D Sabre	AIRMODEL	H VAC CV	72		3417

NORTH AMERICAN	F-86D Sabre	CRUVER	R HR·	72		3418
NORTH AMERICAN	F-86D Sabre	RAREPLANES	H VAC	72		3419
NORTH AMERICAN	F-86E Sabre	CRUVER	R HR·	72		3420
NORTH AMERICAN	F-86E Sabre	FROG	H INJ	72		3421
NORTH AMERICAN	F-86F Sabre	HASEGAWA	H INJ	72	w. Sidewinder missile	3422
NORTH AMERICAN	F-86F Sabre	HELLER	H INJ	72		3423
NORTH AMERICAN	F-86F Sabre	MAC VAC CANOPY	H VAC	72		3424
NORTH AMERICAN	F-86F Sabre	STROMBECKER	H WD·	72		3425
NORTH AMERICAN	F-86F-30 Sabre	FUJIMI	H INJ	72		3426
NORTH AMERICAN	F86F-40 Sabre	FUJIMI	H INJ	72		3427
NORTH AMERICAN	RF-86F Sabre	FUJIMI	H INJ	72		3428
NORTH AMERICAN	TF-86F Sabre	AIRMODEL	H VAC CV	72	+ F-86H/K + CA-27	3429
NORTH AMERICAN	TF-86F Sabre	FALCON	H VAC CV	72	+ P2V-5 + TBM-3W	3430
NORTH AMERICAN	F-86H Sabre	RAREPLANES	H VAC CV	72		3431
NORTH AMERICAN	F-86H Sabre	VENTURA	H INJ CV	72		3432
NORTH AMERICAN	F-86H/K Sabre	AIRMODEL	H VAC CV	72	+ TF-86F + CA-27	3433
NORTH AMERICAN	F-86K Sabre	MODELMARKET	H VAC CV	72		3434
NORTH AMERICAN	F-100A Super Sabre	HOBBYTIME	H INJ	71		3435
NORTH AMERICAN	F-100C Super Sabre	AGRES POLY	H INJ	72		3436
NORTH AMERICAN	F-100C Super Sabre	AURORA	H INJ	77		3437
NORTH AMERICAN	F-100C Super Sabre	IMC	H INJ	72		3438
NORTH AMERICAN	F-100C Super Sabre	PIONEER 2	H INJ	72		3439
NORTH AMERICAN	F-100C Super Sabre	REVELL	H INJ	70		3440
NORTH AMERICAN	F-100C Super Sabre	SETCO	R HR·	72		3441
NORTH AMERICAN	F-100D Super Sabre	ESCI	H INJ	72	w. Bullpup, Sidwinder m.	3442
NORTH AMERICAN	F-100D Super Sabre	HASEGAWA	H INJ	72	w. Bullpup, Sidewinder m.	3443
NORTH AMERICAN	F-100D Super Sabre	MAC VAC CANOPY	H VAC	72		3444
NORTH AMERICAN	F-100F Super Sabre	AIRMODEL	H VAC CV	72	canopy, + F-101B + F-105F	3445
NORTH AMERICAN	F-100F Super Sabre	FALCON	H VAC	72	+ TA-7C + RF-8G	3446
NORTH AMERICAN	F-100F Super Sabre	MAINTRACK	H RSN CV	72		3447
NORTH AMERICAN	F-107A	AIRMODEL	H VAC	72		3448
NORTH AMERICAN	F-107A	KR MODELS	H VAC	72		3449
NORTH AMERICAN	F-107A	O'NEILL	H VAC	72		3450
NORTH AMERICAN	F-107A	RED BARON	H RSN	72		3451
NORTH AMERICAN	F-108A Rapier	KR MODELS	H VAC	72		3452
NORTH AMERICAN	DJ-1 Fury	CRUVER	R HR·	72		3453
NORTH AMERICAN	FJ-1 Fury	MERLIN	H INJ	72	w. ML parts	3454
NORTH AMERICAN	FJ-1 Fury	O'NEILL	H VAC	72		3455
NORTH AMERICAN	FJ-1 Fury	PRIVATE VENTURE	H RSN	72		3456
NORTH AMERICAN	FJ-1 Fury	RAREPLANES	H VAC	72		3457
NORTH AMERICAN	FJ-2 Fury	STROMBECKER	H WD·	72		3458
NORTH AMERICAN	FJ-3 Fury	FALCON	H VAC CV	72	+ AD-5W + C-2A	3459
NORTH AMERICAN	FJ-3 Fury	O'NEILL	H VAC	72		3460
NORTH AMERICAN	FJ-4 Fury	SETCO	R HR·	72		3461
NORTH AMERICAN	FJ-4B Fury	AIRMODEL	H VAC	72		3462
NORTH AMERICAN	FJ-4B Fury	MERLIN	H INJ	72	w. ML parts	3463
NORTH AMERICAN	FJ-4B Fury	RAREPLANES	H VAC	72	w. Bullpup	3464
NORTH AMERICAN	O-47	RAREPLANES	H VAC	72		3465
NORTH AMERICAN	O-47B	EXECUFORM	H VAC	72		3466
NORTH AMERICAN	O-47B	O'NEILL	H VAC	72		3467
NORTH AMERICAN	OV-10A Bronco	AIRFIX	H INJ	72	w. Sidewinder missile	3468
NORTH AMERICAN	OV-10A Bronco	HASEGAWA	H INJ	72	w. Sidewinder missile	3469
NORTH AMERICAN	OV-10A Bronco	MAC VAC CANOPY	H VAC	72		3470
NORTH AMERICAN	OV-10A Bronco	REVELL	H INJ	72	w. Sidewinder missile	3471
NORTH AMERICAN	OV-10B Bronco	REVELL	H INJ RM	72	w. Sidewinder missile	3472
NORTH AMERICAN	OV-10D Bronco	AIRFIX	H INJ RM	72	w. Hellfire, Sidewinder m.	3473
NORTH AMERICAN	P-51A Mustang	CRUVER	R HR·	72		3474
NORTH AMERICAN	P-51A Mustang	FROG	H INJ	72		3475
NORTH AMERICAN	P-51B Mustang	AIRFIX	H INJ	72		3476
NORTH AMERICAN	P-51B Mustang	ARISTO CRAFT	H INJ	72		3477
NORTH AMERICAN	P-51B Mustang	LINDBERG	H INJ	72		3478
NORTH AMERICAN	P-51B Mustang	MAC VAC CANOPY	H VAC	72		3479
NORTH AMERICAN	P-51B Mustang	MONOGRAM	H INJ	72		3480
NORTH AMERICAN	P-51B Mustang	PATHFINDERS	H ML·	72		3481
NORTH AMERICAN	P-51B/C Mustang	JMK	H RSN	72		3482
NORTH AMERICAN	P-51D Mustang	AIRFIX	H INJ	72		3483
NORTH AMERICAN	P-51D Mustang	AIRMODEL	H VAC CV	72	+ P-40N + GOODYEAR FG-1A	3484

NORTH AMERICAN	P-51D Mustang	BANDAI	H INJ	72		3485
NORTH AMERICAN	P-51D Mustang	BELL	H INJ	72		3486
NORTH AMERICAN	P-51D Mustang	CADET	H WD·	72		3487
NORTH AMERICAN	P-51D Mustang	CRUVER	R HR·	72		3488
NORTH AMERICAN	P-51d Mustang	FARMTEX	H VAC	72		3489
NORTH AMERICAN	P-51D Mustang	FROG PENGUIN	H INJ	72		3490
NORTH AMERICAN	P-51D Mustang	GEE'S AERO WORKS	H WD·	72		3491
NORTH AMERICAN	P-51D Mustang	GLASSLITE	H FG·	72		3493
NORTH AMERICAN	P-51D Mustang	HASEGAWA	H INJ	70		3493
NORTH AMERICAN	P-51D Mustang	HASEGAWA	H INJ	70	transparent model	3494
NORTH AMERICAN	P-51D Mustang	HASEGAWA	H INJ RM	72		3495
NORTH AMERICAN	P-51D Mustang	HELLER	H INJ	72		3496
NORTH AMERICAN	P-51D Mustang	HOBBYTIME	H INJ	74		3497
NORTH AMERICAN	P-51D Mustang	LINDBERG	H INJ	74		3498
NORTH AMERICAN	P-51D Mustang	MAC VAC CANOPY	H VAC	72		3499
NORTH AMERICAN	P-51D Mustang	MATCHBOX	H INJ	72		3500
NORTH AMERICAN	P-51D Mustang	NICHIMO	H INJ	75		3501
NORTH AMERICAN	P-51D Mustang	REVELL	H INJ	72		3502
NORTH AMERICAN	P-51D/K Mustang	AIRFIX	H INJ RM	72		3503
NORTH AMERICAN	P-51H Mustang	O'NEILL	H VAC CV	72		3504
NORTH AMERICAN	P-51H Mustang	RAREPLANES	H VAC CV	72		3505
NORTH AMERICAN	P-51H Mustang	WINGS 72	H VAC	72		3506
NORTH AMERICAN	TP-51D Mustang	MAC VAC CANOPY	H VAC	72		3507
NORTH AMERICAN	T-2A/B/C Buckeye	AIRMODEL	H VAC	72		3508
NORTH AMERICAN	T-2C/E Buckeye	MATCHBOX	H INJ	72		3509
NORTH AMERICAN	T-6D Texan	AIRFIX	H INJ	72		3510
NORTH AMERICAN	T-6D Texan	AIRFIX	H INJ RM	72		3511
NORTH AMERICAN	T-6D Texan	MAC VAC CANOPY	H VAC	72		3512
NORTH AMERICAN	T-6G Texan	AIRMODEL	H VAC CV	72	canopy, + P-38M	3513
NORTH AMERICAN	T-6G Texan	HAWK	H INJ	72		3514
NORTH AMERICAN	T-6G Texan	HELLER	H INJ	72		3515
NORTH AMERICAN	SNJ-2 Texan	ARISTO CRAFT	H INJ	72		3516
NORTH AMERICAN	SNJ-2 Texan	CRUVER	R HR·	72		3517
NORTH AMERICAN	SNJ-3 Texan	ARISTO CRAFT	H INJ	72		3518
NORTH AMERICAN	SNJ-3 Texan	CRUVER	R HR·	72		3519
NORTH AMERICAN	T-28 Trojan	MAC VAC CANOPY	H VAC	72		3520
NORTH AMERICAN	T-28B/C/D Trojan	AIRMODEL	H VAC	72		3521
NORTH AMERICAN	T-28D Fennec	HELLER	H INJ	72		3522
NORTH AMERICAN	T-39A/D Sabreliner	AIRMODEL	H VAC	72		3523
NORTH AMERICAN	T-39 Sabreliner	FOWLER	H FM·	72		3524
NORTH AMERICAN	T-39 Sabreliner	O'NEILL	H VAC	72		3525
NORTH AMERICAN	T-39 Sabreliner	T.W.R.	H VAC	72		3526
NORTH AMERICAN	T-39-40 Sabreliner	AIRTEC	H FM·	72		3527
NORTH AMERICAN	T-39-40 Sabreliner	MICRO-WEST	H INJ	72		3528
NORTH AMERICAN	T-39-60/65 Sabreliner	AIRTEC	H FM·	72		3529
NORTH AMERICAN	T-39-60/65 Sabreliner	MICRO-WEST	H INJ	72		3530
NORTH AMERICAN	T-39-75A Sabreliner	AIRTEC	H FM·	72		3531
NORTH AMERICAN	T-39-75A Sabreliner	MICRO-WEST	H INJ	72		3532
NORTH AMERICAN	X-15	ESTES	T INJ	71		3533
NORTH AMERICAN	X-15	MIYAUCHI	H INJ	70		3534
NORTH AMERICAN	X-15A-2	FRANK-MODELLBAU	H VAC	72		3535
NORTH AMERICAN	X-15A-2	MONOGRAM	H INJ	72		3536
NORTH AMERICAN	X-15A-2	SA	H RSN	72		3537
NORTH AMERICAN	XB-70 Valkyrie	SUTCLIFFE	H VAC	72		3538
NORTH AMERICAN	YF-93A	KR MODELS	H VAC	72	flush inlets	3539
NORTH AMERICAN	YF-93A	KR MODELS	H VAC	72	lateral inlets	3540
NORTH AMERICAN	YF-95	KR MODELS	H VAC	72	F-86D prototype	3541
NORTHROP	3-A	MAC VAC CANOPY	H VAC	72		3542
NORTHROP	A-17	RAREPLANES	H VAC	72		3543
NORTHROP	BT-1	O'NEILL	H VAC CV	72		3544
NORTHROP	C-125 Raider	O'NEILL	H VAC	72		3545
NORTHROP	Delta	O'NEILL	H VAC CV	72		3546
NORTHROP	T-38 Talon	HASEGAWA	H INJ	72	F-5A/B air intakes	3547
NORTHROP	F-5A Freedom Fighter	AIRFIX	H INJ	72	w. Sidewinder missile	3548
NORTHROP	F-5A Freedom Fighter	ESCI	H INJ	72	w. Sidewinder missile	3549
NORTHROP	F-5A Freedom Fighter	HASEGAWA	H INJ	72	w. Bullpup, Sidewinder m.	3550
NORTHROP	F-5A Freedom Fighter	MATCHBOX	H INJ	72	w. Sidewinder missile	3551

NORTHROP	F-5A Freedom Fighter	P.M.S.	H INJ	72		3552
NORTHROP	F-5B	ESCI	H INJ	72		3553
NORTHROP	F-5B	MATCHBOX	H INJ RM	72		3554
NORTHROP	F-5B	P.M.S.	H INJ	72		3555
NORTHROP	F-5C/RF-5C	ESCI	H INJ	72	w. Sidewinder missile	3556
NORTHROP	F-5E Tiger II	AIRFIX	H INJ RM	72	w. Maverick, Sidewinder m.	3557
NORTHROP	F-5E Tiger II	ITALERI	H INJ	72	w. Sidewinder missile	3558
NORTHROP	F-5F Tiger II	ITALERI	H INJ	72	w. Sidewinder missile	3559
NORTHROP	F-15A Reporter	AIRMODEL	H VAC CV	72		3560
NORTHROP	F-20 Tigershark	HASEGAWA	H INJ	72	w. Sidewinder missile	3561
NORTHROP	F-89C Scorpion	CRUVER	R HR·	72		3562
NORTHROP	F-89C Scorpion	WAR EAGLE	H VAC	72		3563
NORTHROP	F-89C/H Scorpion	AIRMODEL	H VAC	72		3564
NORTHROP	F-89D/J Scorpion	WAR EAGLE	H VAC	72		3565
NORTHROP	Gamma	WILLIAMS BROTHERS	H INJ	72		3566
NORTHROP	HL-10	EAGLES TALON	H VAC	72		3567
NORTHROP	M2-F2/M2-F3	EAGLES TALON	H VAC	72		3568
NORTHROP	N-1M Jeep	EXECUFORM	H VAC	72		3569
NORTHROP	N-1M Jeep	PRIVATE VENTURE C	H RSN	72		3570
NORTHROP	N-9M Flying Wing	EAGLES TALON	H VAC	72		3571
NORTHROP	N-9M Flying Wing	PRIVATE VENTURE C	H RSN	72		3572
NORTHROP	N-9M Flying Wing	WINGS 72	H VAC	72		3573
NORTHROP	P-61 Black Widow	ARISTO CRAFT	H INJ	72		3574
NORTHROP	P-61 Black Widow	CRUVER	R HR·	72		3575
NORTHROP	P-61 Black Widow	FROG	H INJ	72		3576
NORTHROP	P-61 Black Widow	MAC VAC CANOPY	H VAC	72		3577
NORTHROP	P-61A/B Black Widow	AIRFIX	H INJ	72		3578
NORTHROP	P-61C Black Widow	STROMBECKER	H WD·	72		3579
NORTHROP	X-4 Bantam	DRAGON	H VAC	72	+ BELL X-5	3580
NORTHROP	X-4 Bantam	PRIVATE VENTURE C	H RSN	72		3581
NORTHROP	XB-35 Flying Wing	NOVA MODELS	H VAC	72		3582
NORTHROP	XB-35 Flying Wing	NOVA MODELS	H VAC RM	72	w. ML parts	3583
NORTHROP	XP-56 #1 Black Bullet	EXECUFORM	H VAC	72		3584
NORTHROP	XP-56 #1 Black Bullet	PRIVATE VENTURE C	H RSN	72		3585
NORTHROP	XP-56 #2 Black Bullet	PRIVATE VENTURE C	H RSN	72		3586
NORTHROP	XP-79A/B Flying Ram	KR MODELS	H VAC	72		3587
NORTHROP	YB-49 Flying Wing	AIRMODEL	H VAC	72		3588
NORTHROP/BOEING	B-2 Stealth Bomber	MODEL TECHNOLOGIES	H VAC	72	w. EB, ML, RSN parts	3589
NORTHROP/BOEING	B-2 Stealth Bomber	REVELL	H INJ	72	w. ALCM AGM-86B	3590
PACKARD-LE PERE	LUSAC-11	CLASSIC PLANE	H VAC	72		3591
PACKARD-LE PERE	LUSAC-11	CRAMER	H VAC	72		3592
PACKARD-LE PERE	LUSAC-11	ROSEPLANE	H VAC	72		3593
PANAVIA	Tornado (prototype)	AIRFIX	H INJ	72	w. Martel, Skyflash, Sp m.	3594
PANAVIA	Tornado (prototype)	ESCI	H INJ	72	w. Kormoran missile	3595
PANAVIA	Tornado (prototype)	ITALERI	H INJ	72	w. Martel, Skyflash m.	3596
PANAVIA	Tornado	EXECUTIVE	D —	72		3597
PANAVIA	Tornado F Mk 2	C. SCALE	H ML· CV	72		3598
PANAVIA	Tornado F Mk 3	MATCHBOX	H INJ	72		3599
PANAVIA	Tornado GR Mk 1	AIRFIX	H INJ RM	72	w. Sidewinder missile	3600
PANAVIA	Tornado GR Mk 1	ESCI	H INJ RM	72		3601
PANAVIA	Tornado GR Mk 1	ITALERI	H INJ RM	72		3602
PANAVIA	Tornado GR Mk 1	MONOGRAM	H INJ	72	w. Kormoran, Sidewinder m.	3603
PANAVIA	Tornado GR Mk 1	REVELL	H INJ	72	w. Kormoran, Sidewinder m.	3604
PAYEN	PA.22	PRIVATE VENTURE C	H RSN	72		3605
PERCIVAL	Gull	FROG PENGUIN	H INJ	72		3606
PERCIVAL	Gull	SKYBIRDS	H WD·	72		3607
PERCIVAL	Mew Gull	AIRFRAME	H VAC	72		3608
PERCIVAL	Mew Gull	SKYBIRDS	H ML·	72		3609
PERCIVAL	P.40 Prentice	ELLIOTT	H VAC	72	w. ML parts	3610
PERCIVAL	Proctor IV	FROG	H INJ	72		3611
PERCIVAL	Provost	AIRFRAME	H VAC	72		3612
PERCIVAL	Provost T Mk I	MATCHBOX	H INJ	72		3613
PERCIVAL	Vega Gull	SKYBIRDS	H WD·	72		3614
PESCO	Special Racer	AIRFRAME	H VAC	72		3615
PETLYAKOV	Pe-2 (Buck)	AIRFIX	H INJ	72		3616
PETLYAKOV	Pe-2 (Buck)	CRUVER	R HR·	72		3617
PETLYAKOV	Pe-8	AIRMODEL	H VAC	72	id. ANTONOV ANT-42 (TB-7)	3618

PETLYAKOV	Pe-8	CRUVER	R HR·	72	in-line engine	3619
PETLYAKOV	Pe-8	CRUVER	R HR·	72	radial engine	3620
PETLYAKOV	Pe-8	SUTCLIFFE	H VAC	72		3621
PFALZ	A II	CRAMER	H VAC	72		3622
PFALZ	D III	RAREPLANES	H VAC	72		3623
PFALZ	D III	RENWAL	H INJ	72		3624
PFALZ	D III	VEEDAY	H INJ	72	+ Albatros D XI	3625
PFALZ	D XII	CLASSIC PLANE	H VAC	72		3626
PFALZ	D XII	CRAMER	H VAC	72		3627
PFALZ	D XII	VEEDAY	H INJ	72	+ Dolphin	3628
PFALZ	Dr I	C.A. ATKINS	H ML·	72		3629
PFALZ	Dr I	CRAMER	H VAC	72		3630
PFALZ	Dr I	FORMAPLANE	H VAC	72	w. ML parts	3631
PFALZ	Dr I	MERLIN	H INJ	72	w. ML parts	3632
PHöNIX	A	JOYSTICK	H VAC	72		3633
PHöNIX	D I	AIRFRAME	H VAC	72		3634
PHöNIX	D I	J & L	H VAC	72		3635
PHöNIX	D I/D II	C.A. ATKINS	H ML·	72		3636
PHöNIX	J I	SPECIALTRYCK	H CB·	72		3637
PHöNIX	Scout	FORMAPLANE	H VAC	72		3638
PIAGGIO	P.32	ARISTO CRAFT	H INJ	72		3639
PIAGGIO	P.32	CHALLENGE	H VAC	72		3640
PIAGGIO	P.32	CRUVER	R HR·	72		3641
PIAGGIO	P.108B	CHALLENGE	H VAC	72		3642
PIAGGIO	P.108B	O'NEILL	H VAC	72		3643
PIAGGIO	P.148	VETROMODELLI	H FG·	72		3644
PIAGGIO	P.149FD	HELL PLANES	H INJ	72		3645
PIAGGIO	P.149D	VACU-SPECIAL	H VAC	72		3646
PIAGGIO	P.149D	VAMI	H RSN	72	w. ML parts	3647
PIAGGIO	P.1001	PIAGGIO	D ML·	72		3648
PIASECKI	H-21 Work Horse	AIRMODEL	H VAC	72		3649
PIASECKI	H-21 Work Horse	RUDEL	H VAC	72		3650
PIASECKI	HUP Retreiver (UH-25)	AIRMODEL	H VAC	72	H-25A Army Mule/+UH-1B	3651
PILATUS	PC-6A	VACU-SPECIAL	H VAC	72		3652
PILATUS	Turbo-porter	FORMAPLANE	H VAC	72		3653
PIPER	J-3 Cub	C.A. ATKINS	H ML·	72		3654
PIPER	J-3 Cub	FORMAPLANE	H VAC	72		3655
PIPER	J-3 Cub	MAIRCRAFT	H WD·	72		3656
PIPER	J-3 Cub	PRIVATE VENTURE A	H RSN	72		3657
PIPER	J-3 Cub	RAREPLANES	H VAC	72		3658
PIPER	J-3 Cub	RUDEL	H VAC	72		3659
PIPER	J-3 Cub/Super Cub L-18	AIRMODEL	H VAC	72		3660
PIPER	L-4 Grasshopper	ARISTO CRAFT	H INJ	72		3661
PIPER	L-4 Grasshopper	CRUVER	R HR·	72		3662
PIPER	L-21A	CRUVER	R HR·	72		3663
PIPER	PA-23 Aztec	AURORA	H INJ	72		3664
PIPER	PA-28 Cherokee Arrow II	AIRFIX	H INJ	72		3665
PIPER	PA-28 Cherokee 180C	AURORA	H INJ	72		3666
PIPER	PA-32 Cherokee Six	BANDAI	H INJ	72		3667
PITTS	S-1 Special	KPM	H VAC	72		3668
PITTS	S-2A Special	L.S.	H INJ	72		3669
POLIKARPOV	I-15 Chaika	PRIVATE VENTURE	H RSN	72		3670
POLIKARPOV	I-15/15bis Chaika	AIRMODEL	H VAC	72		3671
POLIKARPOV	I-15bis Chaika	PRIVATE VENTURE C	H RSN	72		3672
POLIKARPOV	I-153 Chaika	HELLER	H INJ	72		3673
POLIKARPOV	I-153 Chaika	PRIVATE VENTURE	H RSN	72		3674
POLIKARPOV	I-153 Chaika	RAREPLANES	H VAC	72		3675
POLIKARPOV	I-16 Mosca	GUANO	H INJ	72	also dubbed Rata	3676
POLIKARPOV	I-16 Mosca	SDELAND	H ML· WK	72	also dubbed Rata	3677
POLIKARPOV	I-16 tip-5/6 Mosca	REPLICA	H RSN	72	also dubbed Rata	3678
POLIKARPOV	I-16 tip-24 Mosca	REVELL	H INJ	72	also dubbed Rata	3679
POLIKARPOV	I-17	AIRMODEL	H RSN	72		3680
POLIKARPOV	I-17	KPL MODELS	H VAC	72		3681
POLIKARPOV	I-17	KPM	H VAC	72		3682
POLIKARPOV	Po-2 (U-2) Kukuruznik	KOVOZAVODY	H INJ	72	Mule	3683
POLIKARPOV	R-5	KPM	H VAC	72		3684
POLIKARPOV	R-5	O'NEILL	H VAC	72		3685

POLIKARPOV	R-5	VICTOR SIXTY-SIX	H VAC	72		3686
POLIKARPOV	R-5	VP CANADA	H VAC	72		3687
POLIKARPOV	R-Z (R-Zet)	PRIVATE VENTURE	H RSN	72	dubbed Rasante in Spain	3688
POLIKARPOV	R-Z (R-Zet)	VACUKIT	H VAC	72	dubbed Rasante in Spain	3689
POMILIO	PE	LIBRAMODELS	H VAC	72	w. ML parts	3690
POTEZ	25	ALPHA	H VAC	72		3691
POTEZ	25	REPLICA	H RSN	72	Jupiter engine	3692
POTEZ	25 A.2	REPLICA	H RSN	72	Lorraine engine	3693
POTEZ	33	ALPHA	H VAC	72		3694
POTEZ	540	HELLER	H INJ	72		3695
POTEZ	63.11	HELLER	H INJ	72		3696
POTEZ	631	HELLER	H INJ	72		3697
POTEZ	650	O'NEILL	H VAC CV	72		3698
POTEZ	650	RUDEL	H VAC CV	72		3699
PZL	130 Orlik	SABAWKARSTWO	H VAC	72		3700
PZL	P.11C	HELLER	H INJ	72		3701
PZL	P.11C	REVELL	H INJ	72		3702
PZL	P.11C	RUCH	H INJ	72		3703
PZL	P.23A Karas	RUCH	H INJ	72		3704
PZL	P.23A/B Karas	HELLER	H INJ	72		3705
PZL	P.24	ABORN	H VAC	72	canopy	3706
PZL	P.24	AIRMODEL	H VAC	72		3707
PZL	P.24	PRIVATE VENTURE A	H RSN	72		3708
PZL	P.37 Los	ALPHA	H VAC	72		3709
PZL	P.37 Los	KPL MODELS	H VAC	72		3710
PZL	P.37 Los	O'NEILL	H VAC	72		3711
PZL	P.37A/B Los	MIKRO	H INJ	72		3712
PZL	P.50	KPL MODELS	H VAC	72		3713
PZL	P.50	PRIVATE VENTURE	H RSN	72		3714
PZL MIELEC	TS-11 Iskra	RUCH	H INJ	72		3715
REGGIANE	Re.2000 Falco I	ARISTO CRAFT	H INJ	72		3716
REGGIANE	Re.2000 Falco I	CRUVER	R HR·	72		3717
REGGIANE	Re.2000 Falco I	SUPERMODEL	H INJ	72		3718
REGGIANE	Re.2001 Falco II	ALIPLAST	H INJ	72		3719
REGGIANE	Re.2001 Falco II	ARISTO CRAFT	H INJ	72		3720
REGGIANE	Re.2001 Falco II	CRUVER	R HR·	72		3721
REGGIANE	Re.2002 Ariete	SUPERMODEL	H INJ	72		3722
REGGIANE	Re.2005 Sagittario	KPL MODELS	H VAC	72		3723
REGGIANE	Re.2005 Sagittario	VETROMEDLLI	H FG·	72		3724
REGGIANE	Re.5000	PENZANI	H VAC	72		3725
RENARD	R.31	ALPHA	H VAC	72		3726
RENARD	R.31	O'NEILL	H VAC	72		3727
RENARD	R.31	REPLICA	H RSN	72		3728
REPUBLIC	F-84E Thunderjet	CRUVER	R HR·	72		3729
REPUBLIC	F-84F Thunderstreak	AIRFIX	H INJ	72		3730
REPUBLIC	F-84F Thunderstreak	CRUVER	R HR·	72		3731
REPUBLIC	F-84F Thunderstreak	HAWK	H INJ	75		3732
REPUBLIC	F-84F Thunderstreak	HOBBYTIME	H INJ	67		3733
REPUBLIC	F-84F Thunderstreak	ITALERI	H INJ	72		3734
REPUBLIC	F-84F Thunderstreak	MAC VAC CANOPY	H VAC	72		3735
REPUBLIC	F-84F Thunderstreak	STROMBECKER	H WD·	72		3736
REPUBLIC	RF-84F Thunderflash	ITALERI	H INJ	72		3737
REPUBLIC	F-84G Thunderjet	CRUVER	R HR·	72		3738
REPUBLIC	F-84G Thunderjet	FROG	H INJ	72		3739
REPUBLIC	F-84G Thunderjet	HELLER	H INJ	72		3740
REPUBLIC	F-84G Thunderjet	RAREPLANES	H VAC	72		3741
REPUBLIC	F-105A Thunderchief	AURORA	H INJ	78		3742
REPUBLIC	F-105A Thunderchief	REVELL	H INJ	77		3743
REPUBLIC	F-105B Thunderchief	CRUVER	R HR·	72		3744
REPUBLIC	F-105B Thunderchief	HASEGAWA	H INJ	72		3745
REPUBLIC	F-105D Thunderchief	HASEGAWA	H INJ	72	w. Bullpup missile	3746
REPUBLIC	F-105D Thunderchief	IMC	H INJ	73		3747
REPUBLIC	F-105D Thunderchief	MONOGRAM	H INJ	73		3748
REPUBLIC	F-105F Thunderchief	AIRFIX	H INJ	72	w. Shrike missile	3749
REPUBLIC	F-105F Thunderchief	AIRMODEL	H VAC CV	72	canopy, + F-100F + F-101b	3750
REPUBLIC	F-105F Thunderchief	MONOGRAM	H INJ	72		3751
REPUBLIC	F-105G Thunderchief	MONOGRAM	H INJ	72	w. AGM-78B, Shrike missile	3752

REPUBLIC	F-105G Thunderchief	NOVA MODELS	H VAC CV	72	w. Shrike missile	3753
REPUBLIC	P-43 Lancer	ARISTO CRAFT	H VAC CV	72		3754
REPUBLIC	P-43 Lancer	CRUVER	R HR·	72		3755
REPUBLIC	P-43A Lancer	RAREPLANES	H VAC	72		3756
REPUBLIC	P-47 Thunderbolt	ARISTO CRAFT	H INJ	72		3757
REPUBLIC	P-47B Thunderbolt	CRUVER	R HR·	72		3758
REPUBLIC	P-47B Thunderbolt	LINDBERG	H INJ	72		3759
REPUBLIC	P-47B/D-20 Thunderbolt	MAC VAC CANOPY	H VAC	72		3760
REPUBLIC	P-47D-20 Thunderbolt	AIRFIX	H INJ	72		3761
REPUBLIC	P-47D-20 Thunderbolt	CADET	H WD·	72		3762
REPUBLIC	P-47D-20 Thunderbolt	CRUVER	R HR·	72		3763
REPUBLIC	P-47D-20 Thunderbolt	DANBURY MINT	H ML·	72		3764
REPUBLIC	P-47D-20 Thunderbolt	DESIGN CENTER	H INJ	72		3765
REPUBLIC	P-47D-20 Thunderbolt	FROG	H INJ	72		3766
REPUBLIC	P-47D-20 Thunderbolt	FROG PENGUIN	H INJ	72		3767
REPUBLIC	P-47D-20 Thunderbolt	GEE'S AERO WORKS	H WD·	72		3768
REPUBLIC	P-47D-20 Thunderbolt	HASEGAWA	H INJ	72		3769
REPUBLIC	P-47D-20 Thunderbolt	MAC VAC CANOPY	H VAC	72		3770
REPUBLIC	P-47D-20 Thunderbolt	MATCHBOX	H INJ	72		3771
REPUBLIC	P-47D-20 Thunderbolt	PATHFINDERS	H ML·	72		3772
REPUBLIC	P-47D-20/25 Thunderbolt	JO HAN	H INJ	72		3773
REPUBLIC	P-47D-25 Thunderbolt	FROG	H INJ	72		3774
REPUBLIC	P-47D-25 Thunderbolt	FUJIMI	H INJ	72		3775
REPUBLIC	P-47D-25 Thunderbolt	HASEGAWA	H INJ	72		3776
REPUBLIC	P-47D-25 Thunderbolt	MAC VAC CANOPY	H VAC	72		3777
REPUBLIC	P-47D-25 Thunderbolt	REVELL	H INJ	72		3778
REPUBLIC	P-47N Thunderbolt	CRUVER	R HR·	72		3779
REPUBLIC	P-47N Thunderbolt	HELLER	H INJ	72		3780
REPUBLIC	P-47N Thunderbolt	RAREPLANES	H VAC	72		3781
REPUBLIC	RC-3 Seabee	PRIVATE VENTURE	H RSN	72		3782
REPUBLIC	XF-12 Rainbow	RICK'S	H FM·	72	w. ML parts	3783
REPUBLIC	XF-12 Rainbow	GRIFFIN	H VAC	72		3784
REPUBLIC	XF-91 Thunderceptor	PRIVATE VENTURE	H RSN RM	72		3785
REPUBLIC	XF-91 Thunderceptor	KR MODELS	H VAC	72	butterfly tail	3786
REPUBLIC	XF-91 Thunderceptor	KR MODELS	H VAC	72	radar nose	3787
REPUBLIC	XF-91 Thunderceptor	KR MODELS	H VAC	72		3788
REPUBLIC	XF-91 Thunderceptor	PRIVATE VENTURE B	H RSN	72		3789
REPUBLIC	XF-103	KR MODELS	H VAC	72		3790
REPUBLIC	XF-103	MATH	H RSN	72		3791
REPUBLIC	XP-47H Thunderbolt	AIRMODEL	H VAC CV	72		3792
REPUBLIC	XP-47H Thunderbolt	PRIVATE VENTURE	H RSN	72		3793
REPUBLIC	YF-96 Thunderstreak	KR MODELS	H VAC	72		3794
ROCKWELL	B-1B	AIRFIX	H INJ	72	w. AGM-86B ALCM	3795
ROCKWELL	B-1B	MONOGRAM	H INJ	72	W. AGM-86B ALCM	3796
ROCKWELL	Shrike Commander	MICRO-WEST	H INJ	72		3797
ROGOZARSKI	IK-2	O'NEILL	H VAC	72		3798
ROGOZARSKI	IK-3	O'NEILL	H VAC	72		3799
ROGOZARSKI	SIM-XIV-H	O'NEILL	H VAC	72		3800
ROYAL AIRCRAFT FACTORY	BE.2/12	FORMAPLANE	H VAC	72	BE: Blériot Experimental	3801
ROYAL AIRCRAFT FACTORY	BE.2c	FORMAPLANE	H VAC	72		3802
ROYAL AIRCRAFT FACTORY	BE.2c	SKYBIRDS	H WD·	72		3803
ROYAL AIRCRAFT FACTORY	BE.2c	VEEDAY	H INJ	72		3804
ROYAL AIRCRAFT FACTORY	FE.2b	CRAMER	H VAC	72	FE : Fighter Experimental	3805
ROYAL AIRCRAFT FACTORY	FE.2b	FORMAPLANE	H VAC	72		3806
ROYAL AIRCRAFT FACTORY	FE.8	AIRFRAME	H VAC	72		3807
ROYAL AIRCRAFT FACTORY	FE.8	SCALEPLANES	H VAC	72		3808
ROYAL AIRCRAFT FACTORY	FE.8	SKYBIRDS	H WD·	72		3809
ROYAL AIRCRAFT FACTORY	RE.8	AIRFIX	H INJ	72	RE : Reconnaissance Exp.	3810
ROYAL AIRCRAFT FACTORY	RE.8	SKYBIRDS	H WD·	72		3811
ROYAL AIRCRAFT FACTORY	SE.2a	CRAMER	H VAC	72	SE : Scout Experimental	3812
ROYAL AIRCRAFT FACTORY	SE.5	SCALEPLANES	H VAC	72	SE : Scout Experimental	3813
ROYAL AIRCRAFT FACTORY	SE.5a	ATO	H WD·	72		3814
ROYAL AIRCRAFT FACTORY	SE.5a	EDISON	H ML· AS	72	w. plastic parts	3815
ROYAL AIRCRAFT FACTORY	SE.5a	ELDON	H INJ	72		3816
ROYAL AIRCRAFT FACTORY	SE.5a	JOY	H INJ	72		3817
ROYAL AIRCRAFT FACTORY	SE.5a	RENWAL	H INJ	72		3818
ROYAL AIRCRAFT FACTORY	SE.5a	REVELL	H INJ	72		3819

ROYAL AIRCRAFT FACTORY	SE.5a	SKYBIRDS	H WD·	72		3820
RUMPLER	6B 1	FORMAPLANE	H VAC	72		3821
RUMPLER	C I	JOYSTICK	H VAC	72		3822
RUMPLER	D I	CRAMER	H VAC	72		3823
RWD	5/5 bis	MIKRO	H INJ	72		3824
RWD	14b Czapla	MIKRO	H INJ	72		3825
RYAN	FR-1 Fireball	AIRMODEL	H VAC	72		3826
RYAN	FR-1 Fireball	EAGLES TALON	H VAC	72		3827
RYAN	FR-1 Fireball	EXECUFORM	H VAC	72		3828
RYAN	FR-1 Fireball	MAC VAC CANOPY	H VAC	72		3829
RYAN	FR-1 Fireball	PEGASUS	H INJ	72		3830
RYAN	FR-1 Fireball	PRIVATE VENTURE	H RSN	72		3831
RYAN	L-17A Navion	O'NEILL	H VAC	72	NORTH AMERICAN design	3832
RYAN	M.1 Mailplane	GREENBANK CASTLE	H INJ	72		3833
RYAN	NYP Spirit of Saint Louis	FROG	H INJ	72		3834
RYAN	NYP Spirit of Saint Louis	HAWK	H INJ	76		3835
RYAN	PT-20/20A/STM-22	H.D.H.	H VAC	72		3836
RYAN	PT-20/20A/21/22	MAI	H RSN	72		3837
RYAN	PT-20/20A/21/22	RAREPLANES	H VAC	72		3838
RYAN	VZ-3RY	PRIVATE VENTURE C	H RSN	72		3839
RYAN	X-13 Vertijet	AIRMODEL	H VAC	72	w. RSN parts	3840
RYAN	X-13 Vertijet	EAGLES TALON	H VAC	72		3841
RYAN	X-13 Vertijet	PRIVATE VENTURE	H RSN	72		3842
RYAN	X-13 Vertijet	RACCOON	H RSN	72		3843
RYAN	X-13 Vertijet	EXECUFORM	H VAC	72		3844
RYAN	XF2R-1 Dark Shark	EAGLES TALON	H VAC	72		3845
RYAN	XF2R-1 Dark Shark	PRIVATE VENTURE	H RSN	72		3846
SAAB	B.17A	ARNE ANDERSSON	H VAC	72		3847
SAAB	B.17A	FORMAPLANE	H VAC	72		3848
SAAB	B.18	ARNE ANDERSSON	H VAC	72		3849
SAAB	B.18	KPL MODELS	H VAC	72		3850
SAAB	105	ARNE ANDERSSON	H VAC	72		3851
SAAB	105C	PEGASUS	H INJ	72		3852
SAAB	105C	PRIVATE VENTURE B	H RSN	72		3853
SAAB	91 Safir	ARNE ANDERSSON	H VAC	72		3854
SAAB	91 Safir	HELLER	H INJ	72		3855
SAAB	AJ-37 Viggen	AIRFIX	H INJ	72	w. Robotbyran missile	3856
SAAB	AJ-37 Viggen	HASEGAWA	H INJ	72	w. Robotbyran missile	3857
SAAB	AJ-37 Viggen	MATCHBOX	H INJ	72	w. Robotbyran missile	3858
SAAB	AJ/SF/SK-37 Viggen	HELLER	H INJ	72		3859
SAAB	SK-37 Viggen	MATCHBOX	H INJ	72		3860
SAAB	J.21	O'NEILL	H VAC	72		3861
SAAB	J.21A	ARNE ANDERSSON	H VAC	72		3862
SAAB	J.21A	HELLER	H INJ	72		3863
SAAB	J.21R	ARNE ANDERSSON	H VAC	72		3864
SAAB	J.29A Tunnan	J & L	H VAC	72		3865
SAAB	J.29A Tunnan	MAC VAC CANOPY	H VAC	72		3866
SAAB	J.29A Tunnan	SETCO	R HR·	72		3867
SAAB	J.29E/S.29C Tunnan	HELLER	H INJ	72		3868
SAAB	J.29F Tunnan	ARNE ANDERSSON	H VAC	72		3869
SAAB	J.29F Tunnan	MATCHBOX	H INJ	72		3870
SAAB	J.32 Lansen	ARNE ANDERSSON	H VAC	72		3871
SAAB	J.32 Lansen	ASTRA	H VAC CV	72		3872
SAAB	J.32 Lansen	O'NEILL	H VAC	72		3873
SAAB	J.32 Lansen	SETCO	R HR·	72		3874
SAAB	A.32A/S.32C Lansen	HELLER	H INJ	72		3875
SAAB	J.35B Draken	MAC VAC CANOPY	H VAC	72		3876
SAAB	J.35B Draken	REVELL	H INJ	72		3877
SAAB	J.35B Draken	SETCO	R HR·	72		3878
SAAB	J.33F Draken	AIRFIX	H INJ	72	w. Falcon, Robotbyran m.	3879
SAAB	J.35F Draken	MAC VAC CANOPY	H VAC	72		3880
SAAB	J.35F/RF/TF.35 Draken	HELLER	H INJ	72		3881
SAAB	TF.35 Draken	MAC VAC CANOPY	H VAC	72		3882
SAAB FAIRCHILD	144	AIR JET ADVANCE	D RSN	72		3883
SABLATING	SF5	AIRFRAME	H VAC	72		3884
SAI	207	KPL MODELS	H VAC	72		3885
SAI	403	KPL MODELS	H VAC	72		3886

SALMSON	2.A2	CRAMER	H VAC	72		3887
SALMSON	2.A2	PRIVATE VENTURE C	H RSN	72		3888
SALMSON	2.A2	WINGS 72	H VAC	72	w. ML parts	3889
SARO	A.27 London	O'NEILL	H VAC	72		3890
SARO	A.27 London	SUTCLIFFE	H VAC	72		3891
SARO	S.36 Lerwick	CRUVER	R HR·	72		3892
SARO	S.36 Lerwick	SUTCLIFFE	H VAC	72		3893
SARO	SR.53	AIRFIX	H INJ	72		3894
SARO	SR.A/1	DRAGON	H VAC	72		3895
SARO	SR.A/1	I.D. MODELS	H VAC	72		3896
SARO	SR.A/1	PRIVATE VENTURE	H RSN	72		3897
SARO	Skeeter	PRIVATE VENTURE	H RSN	72	id. CIERVA Skeeter	3898
SAVOIA-MARCHETTI	S.55X	CHALLENGE	H VAC	72		3899
SAVOIA-MARCHETTI	S.55X	DELTA	H INJ	72		3900
SAVOIA-MARCHETTI	SM.79 Sparviero	AIRFIX	H INJ	72		3901
SAVOIA-MARCHETTI	SM.79 Sparviero	ARISTO CRAFT	H INJ	72		3902
SAVOIA-MARCHETTI	SM.79 Sparviero	CRUVER	R HR·	72		3903
SAVOIA-MARCHETTI	SM.79B Sparviero	ALPHA	H VAC	72	2-engine	3904
SAVOIA-MARCHETTI	SM.79B Sparviero	CHALLENGE	H VAC	72	2-engine	3905
SAVOIA-MARCHETTI	SM.79C/T Sparviero	CHALLENGE	H VAC	72		3906
SAVOIA-MARCHETTI	SM.79K Sparviero	CHALLENGE	H VAC	72		3907
SAVOIA-MARCHETTI	SM.81 Pipistrello	ARSITO CRAFT	H INJ	72		3908
SAVOIA-MARCHETTI	SM.81 Pipistrello	CRUVER	R HR·	72		3909
SAVOIA-MARCHETTI	SM.81 Pipistrello	SUPERMODEL	H INJ	72		3910
SAVOIA-MARCHETTI	SM.82 Canguru	ARISTO CRAFT	H INJ	72		3911
SAVOIA-MARCHETTI	SM.82 Canguru	CHALLENGE	H VAC	72		3912
SAVOIA-MARCHETTI	SM.82 Canguru	CRUVER	R HR·	72		3913
SAVOIA-MARCHETTI	SM.82 Canguru	O'NEILL	H VAC	72		3914
SAVOIA-MARCHETTI	SM.84	ARISTO CRAFT	H INJ	72		3915
SAVOIA-MARCHETTI	SM.84	CRUVER	R HR·	72		3916
SAVOIA-MARCHETTI	SM.84	O'NEILL	H VAC CV	72		3917
SAVOIA-MARCHETTI	SM.84 Bis	CHALLENGE	H VAC	72		3918
SAVOIA-MARCHETTI	SM.85	O'NEILL	H VAC	72		3919
SAVOIA-MARCHETTI	SM.91	KPL MODELS	H VAC	72		3920
SAVOIA-MARCHETTI	SM.92	KPL MODELS	H VAC	72		3921
SCHEIBE	Bergfalke	ARNE ANDERSSON	H VAC	72		3922
SCHNEIDER	Grunau Baby IIB	AIRMODEL	H VAC	72		3923
SCHNEIDER	Grunau Baby	PRIVATE VENTURE X	H RSN	72	id. NORD 1300	3924
SCHNEIDER	Grunau 9	HUMA	H INJ	72	+ SG-38	3925
SCHNEIDER	SG-38	HUMA	H INJ	72	+ Grunau 9	3926
SCHNEIDER	SG-38	PRIVATE VENTURE C	H RSN	72		3927
SCOTTISH AVIATION	Bulldog T Mk I/101	AIRFIX	H INJ	72		3928
SCOTTISH AVIATION	Twin Pioneer	AIRMODEL	H VAC	72		3929
SCOTTISH AVIATION	Twin Pioneer	HALLAM-VAC	H VAC	72	w. ML parts	3930
SEDBURGH	Mk 1	PHOENIX	H VAC	72		3931
SEPECAT	Jaguar A	AIRFIX	H INJ	72	w. AS.30 missile	3932
SEPECAT	Jaguar A	MAC VAC CANOPY	H VAC	72		3933
SEPECAT	Jaguar ACT	MAINTRACK	H RSN CV	72		3934
SEPECAT	Jaguar A/E	FROG	H INJ	72	w. Martel missile	3935
SEPECAT	Jaguar A/E	HELLER	H INJ	72		3936
SEPECAT	Jaguar A/GR Mk 1	HASEGAWA	H INJ	72	w. Magic missile	3937
SEPECAT	Jaguar E	AIRMODEL	H VAC CV	72	canopy, + G-91T + Mir. III	3938
SEPECAT	Jaguar E	MAC VAC CANOPY	H VAC	72		3939
SEPECAT	Jaguar E/T Mk 2	HASEGAWA	H INJ	72		3940
SEPECAT	Jaguar GR Mk 1	AIRFIX	H INJ RM	72		3941
SEPECAT	Jaguar GR Mk 1	MATCHBOX	H INJ	72	w. AS.30L missile	3942
SEPECAT	Jaguar T Mk 2	MATCHBOX	H INJ	72		3943
SEVERSKY	AT-12 (2PA Guardsman)	RAREPLANES	H VAC	72	2-seat P-35	3944
SEVERSKY	P-35	RAREPLANES	H VAC	72		3945
SEVERSKY	P-35	RAREPLANES	H VAC RM	72		3946
SEVERSKY	P-35	VEEDAY	H INJ	72		3947
SHAVROV	Sh-2	PSC	H VAC	72		3948
SHIN MEIWA	PS-1	HASEGAWA	H INJ	72		3949
SHORT	184	AIRFRAME	H VAC	72		3950
SHORT	S.8 Rangoon	SUTCLIFFE	H VAC	72	+ S8/8 Calcutta	3951
SHORT	S.19 Singapore Mk III	FROG PENGUIN	H INJ	72		3952
SHORT	S.19 Singapore	O'NEILL	H VAC	72		3953

SHORT	S.19 Singapore	SUTCLIFFE	H VAC	72		3954
SHORT	S.20 Mercury	AIRFRAME	H VAC	72		3955
SHORT	S.21 Maia	SUTCLIFFE	H VAC	72		3956
SHORT	S.23 Empire	EXECUTIVE	D FG·	72		3957
SHORT	S.25 Solent/Sendringham	EXECUTIVE	D FG·	72		3958
SHORT	S.25 Sunderland	ARISTO CRAFT	H INJ	72		3959
SHORT	S.25 Sunderland Mk III	AIRFIX	H INJ	72		3960
SHORT	S.25 Sunderland Mk III	CRUVER	R HR·	72		3961
SHORT	S.29 Stirling	ARISTO CRAFT	H INJ	72		3962
SHORT	S.29 Stirling	CRUVER	R HR·	72		3963
SHORT	S.29 Stirling	SUTCLIFFE	H VAC CV	72		3964
SHORT	S.29 Stirling Mk I/III	AIRFIX	H INJ	72		3965
SHORT	S.33 Empire	FROG PENGUIN	H INJ	72		3966
SHORT	S.33 Empire	FROG PENGUIN	H INJ TR	72		3967
SHORT	SA.2 Sturgeon	SUTCLIFFE	H VAC	72		3968
SHORT	SB.6 Seamew	CRUVER	R HR·	72		3969
SHORT	SB.6 Seamew	SUTCLIFFE	H VAC	72		3970
SHORT	SC.5 Belfast	EXECUTIVE	D FG·	72		3971
SHORT	SC.5 Belfast	MODELMASTERS	D —	72		3972
SHORT	SC.7 Skyvan	AIRFIX	H INJ	72		3973
SHORT	SC.7 Skyvan	T.W.R.	H VAC	72		3974
SHORT	Shetland	SUTCLIFFE	H VAC	72		3975
SHORT-BRISTOW	Crusader	C.A. ATKINS	H ML·	72		3976
SHORTS	360	EXECUTIVE	D FG·	72		3977
SIAI-MARCHETTI	S.211	VETROMODELLI	H FG·	72		3978
SIAI-MARCHETTI	SF.260	CHALLENGE	H VAC	72		3979
SIAI-MARCHETTI	SF.260	PENZANI	H VAC	72		3980
SIAI-MARCHETTI	SF.260	PRIVATE VENTURE	H RSN	72		3981
SIAI-MARCHETTI	SF.260	VETROMODELLI	H FG·	72		3982
SIAI-MARCHETTI	SF.260 Turbo	VETROMODELLI	H FG·	72		3983
SIAI-MARCHETTI	SF.260M	RUDEL	H VAC	72		3984
SIAI-MARCHETTI	SM.1019	CHALLENGE	H VAC	72		3985
SIAI-MARCHETTI	SM.1019	VETROMODELLI	H FG· CV	72		3986
SIEBEL	Fh 104 Hallore	VACU-SPECIAL	H VAC	72		3987
SIEBEL	Si 204A	AIRMODEL	H VAC CV	72		3988
SIEBEL	Si 204D	KOVOZAVODY	H INJ	72	id. AERO C-3A	3989
SIEMENS-SCHUCKERT	D III	AIRFRAME	H VAC	72		3990
SIEMENS-SCHUCKERT	D III	CLASSIC PLANE	H VAC	72		3991
SIEMENS-SCHUCKERT	D III	PEGASUS	H INJ	72		3992
SIEMENS-SCHUCKERT	D III	PEGASUS	H INJ RM	72		3992
SIEMENS-SCHUCKERT	D III	PRIVATE VENTURE	H RSN	72		3994
SIEMENS-SCHUCKERT	D III/D IV	AIRFRAME	H VAC RM	72		3995
SIKORSKY	R-4	O'NEILL	H VAC	72		3996
SIKORSKY	R-4	PRIVATE VENTURE C	H RSN	72		3997
SIKORSKY	R-6	O'NEILL	H VAC	72	Delalio mould	3998
SIKORSKY	S-39B	O'NEILL	H VAC	72		3999
SIKORSKY	S-40	AIR JET ADVANCE	D FG·	72		4000
SIKORSKY	S-42	AIR JET ADVANCE	D FG·	72		4001
SIKORSKY	S-42	ATLANTIC MODELS	D INJ	72		4002
SIKORSKY	S-42	COMBAT MODEL	H VAC	72	w. ML parts	4003
SIKORSKY	S-43 Baby Clipper	AIR JET ADVANCE	D FG·	72		4004
SIKORSKY	S-43 Baby Clipper	EXECUFORM	H VAC	72		4005
SIKORSKY	S-43 Baby Clipper	EXECUTIVE	D FG·	72		4006
SIKORSKY	S-43 JRS-1 Baby Clipper	CRUVER	R HR·	72		4007
SIKORSKY	S-43 JR2S-1 Baby Clipper	CRUVER	R HR·	72		4008
SIKORSKY	S-43 JRS/OA-8 Baby Clipper	O'NEILL	H VAC	72		4009
SIKORSKY	S-51 Dragonfly H-5	AIRMODEL	H VAC	72		4010
SIKORSKY	S-51 Dragonfly H-5	BRITAVIA MODELS	H VAC	72		4011
SIKORSKY	S-51 Dragonfly H-5	PRIVATE VENTURE C	H RSN	72		4012
SIKORSKY	S-56 Mojave CH-37	AIRMODEL	H VAC	72		4013
SIKORSKY	S-58 Choctaw H-34	AIRMODEL	H VAC CV	72		4014
SIKORSKY	S-58 Choctaw H-34	AIRMODEL	H VAC CV	72	+ RF-4E	4015
SIKORSKY	S-58 H-34 Choctaw, Seabat	MAINTRACK	H RSN CV	72	+ Seahorse, w. ML parts	4016
SIKORSKY	S-61 HH-3 Jolly Green Giant	LINDBERG	H INJ SN	72		4017
SIKORSKY	S-61 HH-3 Jolly Green Giant	REVELL	H INJ	72		4018
SIKORSKY	S-61 HH-3E Jolly Green Giant	AURORA	H INJ	72		4019
SIKORSKY	S-61 HH-3E Jolly Green Giant	STARFIX	H INJ	72		4020

SIKORSKY	S-61 HH-3F Pelican	AIRFRAME	H VAC CV	72		4021
SIKORSKY	S-61 Sea King	REVELL	H INJ	72		4022
SIKORSKY	S-61 HSS-2B Sea King	FUJIMI	H INJ	72		4023
SIKORSKY	S-61 SH-3D Sea King	AIRFIX	H INJ	72		4024
SIKORSKY	S-61 SH-3D Sea King	LINDBERG	H INJ SN	72		4025
SIKORSKY	S-61 SH-3H Sea King	FUJIMI	H INJ	72		4026
SIKORSKY	S-64 CH-54 Tarhe (Skycrane)	AURORA	H INJ	72		4027
SIKORSKY	S-64 CH-54 Tarhe (Skycrane)	REVELL	H INJ	72		4028
SIKORSKY	S-65 CH-53 Sea Stallion	AIRMODEL	H VAC	72		4029
SIKORSKY	S-65 CH-53D/G Sea Stallion	AIRFIX	H INJ	72		4030
SIKORSKY	S-65 CH-53D Super Jolly Green G.	FUJIMI	H INJ	72		4031
SIKORSKY	S-65 HH-53C Super Jolly Green G.	AIRFIX	H INJ	72		4032
SIKORSKY	S-65 HH-53C Super Jolly Green G.	FUJIMI	H INJ	72		4033
SIKORSKY	S-65 RH-53D Super Jolly Green G.	FUJIMI	H INJ	72		4034
SIKORSKY	S-70 EH-60A Quick Fix	FUJIMI	H INJ	72		4035
SIKORSKY	S-70 HH-60D Night Hawk	FUJIMI	H INJ	72		4036
SIKORSKY	S-70 HH-60D Night Hawk	HASEGAWA	H INJ	72		4037
SIKORSKY	S-70 SH-60D Sea Hawk	HASEGAWA	H INJ	72		4038
SIKORSKY	S-70 UH-60A Black Hawk	FUJIMI	H INJ	72		4039
SIKORSKY	S-70 UH-60A Rescue Hawk	FUJIMI	H INJ	72		4040
SIKORSKY	S-70 UH-60A Black Hawk	HASEGAWA	H INJ	72		4041
SIKORSKY	S-70 UH-60A/HH-60A	REVELL	H INJ	72	ex-FUJIMI w. HH-60A parts	4042
SIKORSKY	VS-44 Excalibur	EXECUTIVE	D FG·	72		4043
SKODA-KAUBA	SK V4/SK 257	EAGLES TALON	H VAC	72		4044
SKODA-KAUBA	SK V4/SK 257	KPM	H VAC	72		4045
SKODA-KAUBA	SK V4/SK 257	PRIVATE VENTURE C	H RSN	72		4046
SKODA-KAUBA	SK V4/SK 257	WINGS 72	H VAC	72		4047
SLINGSBY	Cadet Mk 1	PHOENIX	H VAC	72		4048
SLINGSBY	Cadet Mk 2	PHOENIX	H VAC	72		4049
SLINGSBY	Cadet Mk 3	PHOENIX	H VAC	72		4050
SLINGSBY	Type 21B Sedbergh	ARNE ANDERSSON	H VAC	72		4051
SNECMA	C-450 Coléoptère	AIRMODEL	H VAC	72		4052
SNECMA	C-450 Coléoptère	RUDEL	H VAC	72		4053
SOPWITH	1 ½ Strutter	AIRFRAME	H VAC	72		4054
SOPWITH	1 ½ Strutter	CLASSIC PLANE	H VAC	72		4055
SOPWITH	5F.1 Dolphin	CRAMER	H VAC	72		4056
SOPWITH	5F.1 Dolphin	PEGASUS	H INJ	72		4057
SOPWITH	5F.1 Dolphin	PRIVATE VENTURE C	H RSN	72		4058
SOPWITH	5F.1 Dolphin	VEEDAY	H INJ	72	+ PFALZ D.XII	4059
SOPWITH	Baby	AIRFRAME	H VAC	72		4060
SOPWITH	Baby	EDISON	H ML· AS	72	w. plastic parts	4061
SOPWITH	Bat Boat	JOYSTICK	H VAC	72	w. ML parts	4062
SOPWITH	Camel 2F.1	AIRFIX	H INJ	72		4063
SOPWITH	Camel F.1	ATO	H WD·	72		4064
SOPWITH	Camel F.1	ELDON	H INJ	72		4065
SOPWITH	Camel F.1	GUNZE SANGYO	H ML·	72		4066
SOPWITH	Camel F.1	KEIL KRAFT	H INJ	72		4067
SOPWITH	Camel F.1	RENWAL	H INJ	72		4068
SOPWITH	Camel F.1	REVELL	H INJ	72		4069
SOPWITH	Camel F.1	SKYBIRDS	H WD·	72		4070
SOPWITH	Dove	AIRFRAME	H VAC CV	72	+ Swallow	4071
SOPWITH	Pup	AIRFIX	H INJ	72		4072
SOPWITH	Schneider	AIRFRAME	H VAC	72	+ Tabloid	4073
SOPWITH	Schneider	SKYBIRDS	H WD·	72		4074
SOPWITH	Snipe	PEGASUS	H INJ	72		4075
SOPWITH	Snipe	PRIVATE VENTURE	H RSN	72		4076
SOPWITH	Snipe	RAREPLANES	H VAC	72		4077
SOPWITH	Swallow	AIRFRAME	H VAC	72	+ Dove	4078
SOPWITH	Tabloid	AIRFAME	H VAC	72	+ Schneider	4079
SOPWITH	Triplane	RENWAL	H INJ	72		4080
SOPWITH	Triplane	REVELL	H INJ	72		4081
SOPWITH	Triplane	REVELL	H INJ RM	72		4082
SPAD	510	O'NEILL	H VAC	72		4083
SPAD	S.VII	AIRFIX	H INJ	72		4084
SPAD	S.VII	SKYBIRDS	H WD·	72		4085
SPAD	S.XIII	EDISON	H ML· AS	72	w. plastic parts	4086
SPAD	S.XIII	ELDON	H INJ	72		4087

SPAD	S.XIII	RENWAL	H INJ	72		4088
SPAD	S.XIII	REVELL	H INJ	72		4089
SPARTAN	7W Executive	EXECUFORM	H VAC	72		4090
SPARTAN	7W Executive	O'NEILL	H VAC	72		4091
STAMPE	RSV.32/90	ALPHA	H VAC	72		4092
STAMPE	SV.4B	REPLICA	H RSN	72		4093
STAMPE	SV.4B/C	RUDEL	H VAC	72		4094
STAMPE	SV.5	RUDEL	H VAC	72		4095
STANDARD	E-1	CRAMER	H VAC	72		4096
STINSON	L-1 Vigilant	ARISTO CRAFT	H INJ	72		4097
STINSON	L-1 Vigilant	CRUVER	R HR·	72		4098
STINSON	L-1 Vigilant	EXECUFORM	H VAC	72		4099
STINSON	L-1 Vigilant	GEE'S AERO WORKS	H WD·	72		4100
STINSON	L-1 Vigilant	O'NEILL	H VAC	72		4101
STINSON	L-5A Sentinel	ARISTO CRAFT	H INJ	72		4102
STINSON	L-5A Sentinel	CRUVER	R HR·	72		4103
STINSON	L-5A Sentinel	RAREPLANES	H VAC	72		4104
STINSON	Reliant	CRUVER	R HR·	72		4105
STINSON	SR-10B Reliant	ARISTO CRAFT	H INJ	72		4016
STINSON	SR-10B Reliant	EXECUFORM	H VAC	72		4107
STINSON	Trimotor Model A	J & L	H VAC	72		4108
STINSON	Trimotor Model T	J & L	H VAC	72		4109
STINSON	Trimotor Model U	J & L	H VAC	72		4110
SUD-EST	SE.117 Voltigeur	REDUCTA	H WD·	75	w. RSN parts	4111
SUD-EST	SE.5003 Baroudeur	REPLICA	H RSN	72	w. trailer	4112
SUD-EST	SE.535 Mistral	HELLER	H INJ	72		4113
SUD-OUEST	SO.4050 Vautour	AIRMODEL	H VAC	72		4114
SUD-OUEST	SO.4050 Vautour	BEVELITE	H INJ	72		4115
SUD-OUEST	SO.4050 Vautour	O'NEILL	H VAC	72		4116
SUD-OUEST	SO.4050 Vautour IIA	REPLICA	H RSN	72		4117
SUD-OUEST	SO.4050 Vautour IIB	REPLICA	H RSN	72		4118
SUD-OUEST	SO.4050 Vautour IIN	MACH	H INJ	72		4119
SUD-OUEST	SO.4050 Vautour IIN	REPLICA	H RSN	72		4120
SUD-OUEST	SO.6000 Triton	RUDEL	H VAC	72		4121
SUD-OUEST	SO.6001 Triton	RUDEL	H VAC	72		4122
SUD-OUEST	SO.9050 Trident II	AIRMODEL	H VAC	72	w. RSN parts	4123
SUD-OUEST	SO.9050 Trident	NEW-MAQUETTES	H WD·	75		4124
SUD-OUEST	SO.9050 Trident II	PRIVATE VENTURE	H RSN	72		4125
SUKHOI	Su-2	ALFA	H INJ	72		4126
SUKHOI	Su-2	BOLESLAV	H VAC	72		4127
SUKHOI	Su-2	EAGLES TALON	H VAC	72		4128
SUKHOI	Su-2	KPM	H VAC	72		4129
SUKHOI	Su-2	PRIVATE VENTURE	H RSN	72		4130
SUKHOI	Su-2	SUTCLIFFE	H VAC	72		4131
SUKHOI	Su-2	WINGS 72	H VAC	72		4132
SUKHOI	Su-5	BOLESLAV	H VAC	72		4133
SUKHOI	Su-5	PRIVATE VENTURE C	H RSN	72		4134
SUKHOI	Su-5	WINGS 72	H VAC	72		4135
SUKHOI	Su-7B/U (Fitter A/Moujik)	ELLIOTT	H VAC	72	w. ML parts	4136
SUKHOI	Su-7 (Fitter A)	SETCO	R HR·	72		4137
SUKHOI	Su-7B (Fitter A)	VEB PLASTICART	H INJ	72		4138
SUKHOI	Su-7B/M (Fitter A)	AIRMODEL	H VAC	72		4139
SUKHOI	Su-9 (Fishpot B)	CRAMER	H VAC	72		4140
SUKHOI	Su-11 (Fishpot C)	AAA MODELS	H VAC	72	w. INJ parts	4141
SUKHOI	Su-11UTI (Maiden)	CRAMER	H VAC	72		4142
SUKHOI	Su-15 (Flagon)	CRAMER	H VC	72		4143
SUKHOI	Su-15 (Flagon)	I.D. MODELS	H VAC	72		4144
SUKHOI	Su-15 (Flagon)	LEOMAN	H RSN	72		4145
SUKHOI	Su-15 (Flagon F)	NOVA MODELS	H VAC	72	w. ML parts	4146
SUKHOI	Su-17 (Fitter)	AAA MODELS	H VAC	72	w. INJ parts	4147
SUKHOI	Su-17/20/22 (Fitter)	ELLIOTT	H VAC	72	w. ML parts	4148
SUKHOI	Su-22 (Fitter)	AAA MODELS	H VAC	72	w. INJ parts	4149
SUKHOI	Su-22 (Fitter F)	LEOMAN	H RSN	72		4150
SUKHOI	Su-22 (Fitter H/J)	MD	H RSN	72		4151
SUKHOI	Su-24 (Fencer)	ELLIOTT	H VAC	72	w. ML parts	4152
SUKHOI	Su-25 (Frogfoot)	AIRMODEL	H VAC	72	w. RSN parts	4153
SUKHOI	Su-25 (Frogfoot)	PRIVATE VENTURE	H RSN	72		4154

SUKHOI	Su-25 (Frogfoot)	SUTCLIFFE	H VAC	72		4155
SUPERMARINE	Attacker	ELLIOTT	H VAC	72	w. ML parts	4156
SUPERMARINE	Attacker FB Mk 2	CRUVER	R HR·	72		4157
SUPERMARINE	Attacker FB Mk 2	FROG	H INJ	72		4158
SUPERMARINE	Attacker FB Mk 2	VERNON	H WD·	72		4159
SUPERMARINE	S.4	AIRFRAME	H VAC	72		4160
SUPERMARINE	S.5	EDISON	H ML· AS	72	w. plastic parts	4161
SUPERMARINE	S.6B	AIRFIX	H INJ	72		4162
SUPERMARINE	S.6B	FROG	H INJ	72		4163
SUPERMARINE	Scapa	SUTCLIFFE	H VAC	72		4164
SUPERMARINE	Scimitar	FROG	H INJ	72		4165
SUPERMARINE	Scimitar	SETCO	R HR·	72		4166
SUPERMARINE	Scimitar	SUTCLIFFE	H VAC	72		4167
SUPERMARINE	Scimitar F Mk 1	MERLIN	H INJ	72		4168
SUPERMARINE	Seafire FR Mk 17	AEROCLUB MODELS	H VAC CV	72		4169
SUPERMARINE	Seafire FR Mk 47	PEGASUS	H INJ	72		4170
SUPERMARINE	Seafire FR Mk 47	PRIVATE VENTURE	H RSN	72		4171
SUPERMARINE	Seafire FR Mk 47	RAREPLANES	H VAC	72		4172
SUPERMARINE	Sea Otter	O'NEILL	H VAC	72		4173
SUPERMARINE	Seafang	CLARKE	H VAC	72	canopy, + Spiteful canopy	4174
SUPERMARINE	Seafang	RAREPLANES	H VAC	72	+ Spiteful	4175
SUPERMARINE	Southampton	SUTCLIFFE	H VAC	72		4176
SUPERMARINE	Spitfire (prototype)	C.A. ATKINS	H ML·	72		4177
SUPERMARINE	Spitfire (prototype)	FRANKLIN	D ML·	72		4178
SUPERMARINE	Type 224	RAREPLANES	H VAC	72	Spitfire prototype	4179
SUPERMARINE	Spitfire Mk I	ARISTO CRAFT	H INJ	72		4180
SUPERMARINE	Spitfire Mk I	CRUVER	R HR·	72		4181
SUPERMARINE	Spitfire Mk I	FROG PENGUIN	H INJ	72		4182
SUPERMARINE	Spitfire Mk I	GEE'S AERO WORKS	H WD·	72		4183
SUPERMARINE	Spitfire Mk I	HASEGAWA	H INJ	72		4184
SUPERMARINE	Spitfire Mk I	HELLER	H INJ	75		4185
SUPERMARINE	Spitfire Mk I	PATHFINDERS	H ML·	72		4186
SUPERMARINE	Spitfire Mk I	POLISTIL	H INJ	72		4187
SUPERMARINE	Spitfire Mk I	SKYBIRDS	H WD·	72		4188
SUPERMARINE	Spitfire Mk I/II	REVELL	H INJ RM	72		4189
SUPERMARINE	Spitfire Mk I/II/V	MAC VAC CANOPY	H VAC	72		4190
SUPERMARINE	Spitfire Mk I/II/V/VI	ARMTEC	H INJ CV	72		4191
SUPERMARINE	Spitfire Mk I/II/V Tropical/VII	AIRFORM	H INJ CV	72		4192
SUPERMARINE	Spitfire Mk IA	AIRFIX	H INJ	72		4193
SUPERMARINE	Spitfire Mk IA	AIRFIX	H INJ RM	72		4194
SUPERMARINE	Spitfire Mk IA	AIRFIX	H INJ SN	72		4195
SUPERMARINE	Spitfire Mk IA/5A	FROG	H INJ	72		4196
SUPERMARINE	Spitfire Mk II	FROG	H INJ	72		4197
SUPERMARINE	Spitfire Mk IIA	REVELL	H INJ	72		4198
SUPERMARINE	Spitfire Mk V	ARISTO CRAFT	H INJ	72		4199
SUPERMARINE	Spitfire Mk V	HOBBYTIME	H INJ	75		4200
SUPERMARINE	Spitfire Mk V	NICHIMO	H INJ	70		4201
SUPERMARINE	Spitfire Mk V/IX	I.D. MODELS	H VAC CV	72		4202
SUPERMARINE	Spitfire Mk VB	AIRFIX	H INJ	72		4203
SUPERMARINE	Spitfire LF Mk VB/VB Tropical	HELLER	H INJ	72		4204
SUPERMARINE	Spitfire Mk VB Tropical	P.M.S.	H INJ	72		4205
SUPERMARINE	Spitfire Mk VC Tropical	PIONEER 2	H INJ	72		4206
SUPERMARINE	Spitfire Mk VII	PRIVATE VENTURE C	H RSN	72		4207
SUPERMARINE	Spitfire Mk VIII/IX	FROG	H INJ	72		4208
SUPERMARINE	Spitfire Mk IX	CADET	H WD·	72		4209
SUPERMARINE	Spitfire Mk IX	CRUVER	R HR·	72		4210
SUPERMARINE	Spitfire Mk IX	DANBURY MINT	H ML·	72		4211
SUPERMARINE	Spitfire Mk IX	LINDBERG	H INJ	75		4212
SUPERMARINE	Spitfire Mk IX	LOTNIA	H INJ	72		4213
SUPERMARINE	Spitfire Mk IXA	CRUVER	R HR·	72		4214
SUPERMARINE	Spitfire Mk IXB	CRUVER	R HR·	72		4215
SUPERMARINE	Spitfire Mk IXC	AIRFIX	H INJ	72		4216
SUPERMARINE	Spitfire Mk IXC/E	MATCHBOX	H INJ	72		4217
SUPERMARINE	Spitfire LF Mk IXE	KOVOZAVODY	H INJ	72		4218
SUPERMARINE	Spitfire Mk IX Trainer	M & E	H INJ CV	72		4219
SUPERMARINE	Spitfire Mk IX UTI	LOTNIA	H INJ	72		4220
SUPERMARINE	Spitfire Mk XII	FROG PENGUIN	H INJ	72		4221

SUPERMARINE	Spitfire Mk XII	GEE'S AERO WORKS	H WD·	72		4222
SUPERMARINE	Spitfire Mk XII	JMK	H VAC	72		4223
SUPERMARINE	Spitfire Mk XII	MERLIN	H INJ	72	w. ML parts	4224
SUPERMARINE	Spitfire F Mk XII	AEROCLUB MODELS	H VAC CV	72		4225
SUPERMARINE	Spitfire Mk XIII	PRIVATE VENTURE A	H RSN	72		4226
SUPERMARINE	Spitfire Mk XIV	FROG	H INJ	72	w. Fi 103 (V-1)	4227
SUPERMARINE	Spitfire Mk XIV	MAC VAC CANOPY	H VAC	72		4228
SUPERMARINE	Spitfire F Mk XIVC	AEROCLUB MODELS	H VAC CV	72		4229
SUPERMARINE	Spitfire F Mk XIV	FALCON	H VAC	72		4230
SUPERMARINE	Spitfire F Mk XIV	PRIVATE VENTURE	H RSN	72		4231
SUPERMARINE	Spitfire Mk XVI	AIRMODEL	H VAC CV	72	+ Beauf. + Sea F. + Typh.	4232
SUPERMARINE	Spitfire Mk XVIE	HELLER	H INJ	72		4233
SUPERMARINE	Spitfire FR Mk XVIII	AEROCLUB MODELS	H VAC CV	72		4234
SUPERMARINE	Spitfire Mk 22	CRUVER	R HR·	72		4235
SUPERMARINE	Spitfire Mk 22	HAWK	H INJ	72		4236
SUPERMARINE	Spitfire Mk 22	MAC VAC CANOPY	H VAC	72		4237
SUPERMARINE	Spitfire Mk 22	PRIVATE VENTURE	H RSN	72		4238
SUPERMARINE	Spitfire Mk 22	SKYBIRDS	H WD·	72		4239
SUPERMARINE	Spitfire Mk 22/24	PEGASUS	H INJ	72		4240
SUPERMARINE	Spitfire Mk 24	PRIVATE VENTURE	H RSN	72		4241
SUPERMARINE	Spitfire Mk 24	SABRE	H VAC	72		4242
SUPERMARINE	Spitfire Floatplane	I.D. MODELS	H VAC CV	72		4243
SUPERMARINE	Spiteful	CLARKE	H VAC	72	canopy, + Seafang canopy	4244
SUPERMARINE	Spiteful	PEGASUS	H INJ	72		4245
SUPERMARINE	Spiteful	RAREPLANES	H VAC	72	+ Seafang	4246
SUPERMARINE	Spiteful F Mk 14	PRIVATE VENTURE	H RSN	72		4247
SUPERMARINE	Stranraer	O'NEILL	H VAC	72		4248
SUPERMARINE	Stranraer	SUTCLIFFE	H VAC	72		4249
SUPERMARINE	Stranraer Mk I/II/III	MATCHBOX	H INJ	72		4250
SUPERMARINE	Swift F Mk 4	HAWK	H HR·	72		4251
SUPERMARINE	Swift F Mk 4	HAWK	H INJ RM	72		4252
SUPERMARINE	Swift FR Mk 5	I.D. MODELS	H VAC	72		4253
SUPERMARINE	Swift FR Mk 5	MERLIN	H INJ	72		4254
SUPERMARINE	Swift FR Mk 5	PEGASUS	H INJ	72		4255
SUPERMARINE	Swift FR Mk 5	PRIVATE VENTURE	H RSN	72		4256
SUPERMARINE	Swift FR Mk 5	RAREPLANES	H VAC	72	w. ML parts	4257
SUPERMARINE	Walrus Mk I/II	MATCHBOX	H INJ	72		4258
SUPERMARINE	Walrus Mk II	AIRFIX	H INJ	72		4259
SUPERMARINE	Walrus Mk II	ARISTO CRAFT	H INJ	72		4260
SUPERMARINE	Walrus Mk II	CRUVER	R HR·	72		4261
SUPERMARINE	Walrus Mk II	SKYBIRDS	H WD·	72		4262
SZD	10 Bocian Bis	P.Z.W. SIEDLCE	H RSN	72		4263
SZD	16 Gil	P.Z.W. SIEDLCE	H RSN CV	72		4264
SZD	19 Zefir 2	PLASTIK	H INJ	75		4265
SZD	24 Foka 5	PRIVATE VENTURE C	H RSN	72		4266
SZD	41 Jantar-Standard	P.Z.W. SIEDLCE	H INJ	72		4267
SZD	IS-1 SEP Bis	P.Z.W. SIEDLCE	H INJ	72		4268
SZD	8 Jaskolka	PLASTIK	H INJ	75		4269
SZD	Mucha-Standard	P.Z.W. SIEDLCE	H INJ	72		4270
TACHIKAWA	Ki-9	PRIVATE VENTURE	H RSN	72	Spruce	4271
TACHIKAWA	Ki-9	O'NEILL	H VAC	72	Spruce	4272
TACHIKAWA	Ki-36/Ki-55	CRUVER	R HR·	72	Ida	4273
TACHIKAWA	Ki-36 Kisaragi	FUJIMI	H INJ	72		4274
TACHIKAWA	Ki-36 Kisaragi Type 98	FUJIMI	H INJ	72		4275
TACHIKAWA	Ki-36/Ki-55	MAIRCRAFT	H WD·	72	Ida	4276
TACHIKAWA	Ki-36/Ki-55	PRIVATE VENTURE C	H RSN	72	Ida	4277
TACHIKAWA	Ki-36/Ki-55	TAYLORCRAFT	H WD·	72	Ida	4278
TACHIKAWA	Ki-36/Ki-55	WINGS 72	H VAC	72	Ida	4279
TACHIKAWA	Ki-54	O'NEILL	H VAC	72	Hickory	4280
TACHIKAWA	Ki-55 Type 99	FUJIMI	H INJ	72	Ida	4281
TACHIKAWA	Ki-74	O'NEILL	H VAC	72	Patsy	4282
TACHIKAWA	Ki-74	PRIVATE VENTURE	H RSN	72	Patsy	4283
TACHIKAWA	Ki-77	O'NEILL	H VAC	72		4284
TAYLORCRAFT	Cabin Monoplane	MAIRCRAFT	H WD·	72		4285
TAYLORCRAFT	L-2 Grasshopper	CRUVER	R HR·	72		4286
TEMCO	TT-1 Pinto	ARTCRAFT AIRCRAFT	H VAC	72		4287
TEMCO	TT-1 Pinto	EAGLES TALON	H VAC	72		4288

TEMCO	TT-1 Pinto	KPM	H VAC	72		4289
THOMAS-MORSE	O-19	O'NEILL	H VAC	72		4290
THOMAS-MORSE	S-4C Scout	RAREPLANES	H VAC	72		4291
TRANSALL	C-160	HELLER BOBKIT	H INJ	72	Aéropostale	4292
TRANSALL	C.160	AIRMODEL	H VAC	72		4293
TRANSALL	C.160 NG	HELLER BOBCAT	H INJ	72		4294
TUPOLEV	ANT-6 (TB-3)	CRUVER	R HR·	72		4295
TUPOLEV	ANT-40 (SB-2) Katyushka	FROG	H INJ	72		4296
TUPOLEV	ANT-42 (TB-7)	DESIGN CENTER	H INJ	72	id. PETLYAKOV Pe-8	4297
TUPOLEV	Tu-2 (Bat)	CRUVER	R HR·	72		4298
TUPOLEV	Tu-2 (Bat)	VEB PLASTICART	H INJ	72		4299
TUPOLEV	Tu-14 (Bosun)	CRUVER	R HR·	72		4300
TUPOLEV	Tu-14T (Bosun)	SUTCLIFFE	H VAC	72		4301
TUPOLEV	Tu-16 (Badger)	AIRMODEL	H VAC	72		4302
TUPOLEV	Tu-16 (Badger)	CRUVER	R HR·	72		4303
TUPOLEV	Tu-20 (Bear)	SUTCLIFFE	H VAC	72	w. Kangaroo missile	4304
TUPOLEV	Tu-22 (Blinder)	EXECUFORM	H VAC	72		4305
TUPOLEV	Tu-22 (Blinder)	NOVA MODELS	H VAC	72	w. Kitchen missile	4306
TUPOLEV	Tu-22M (Tu-26) (Backfire-B)	I.D. MODELS	H VAC	72		4307
TUPOLEV	Tu-22M (Tu-26) (Backfire-B)	NOVA MODELS	H VAC	72	w. ML parts	4308
TUPOLEV	Tu-70 (Cart)	CRUVER	R HR·	72		4309
TUPOLEV	Tu-73	SUTCLIFFE	H VAC	72		4310
TUPOLEV	Tu-114 (Cleat)	SUTCLIFFE	H VAC	72	+ Tu.126, w. INJ parts	4311
TUPOLEV	Tu-126 (Moss)	SUTCLIFFE	H VAC	72	+ Tu.114, w. INJ parts	4312
UFAG	C I	EAGLES TALON	H VAC	72		4313
UFAG	C I	PRIVATE VENTURE BC	H RSN	72		4314
UFAG	C I	WINGS 72	H VAC	72		4315
VEF	I-16 Irbitis	PRIVATE VENTURE	H RSN	72		4316
VFW-FOKKER	614	AIRMODEL	H VAC	72		4317
VFW-FOKKER	614	EXECUTIVE	D —	72		4318
VICKERS	54 Viking	MODELMASTERS	D —	72		4319
VICKERS	56 Victoria	SUTCLIFFE	H VAC	72	+ Virginia + Valentia	4320
VICKERS	57 Virginia	SUTCLIFFE	H VAC	72	+ Victoria + Valentia	4321
VICKERS	132 Vildebeest	O'NEILL	H VAC	72		4322
VICKERS	132 Vildebeest	SUTCLIFFE	H VAC	72	+ Vincent	4323
VICKERS	246 Wellesley Mk I	AIRFRAME	H VAC	72		4324
VICKERS	246 Wellesley	FROG PENGUIN	H INJ	72		4325
VICKERS	246 Wellesley Mk I/Mk I LRDF	MATCHBOX	H INJ	72		4326
VICKERS	264 Valentia	SUTCLIFFE	H VAC	72	+ Victoria + Virginia	4327
VICKERS	266 Vincent	SUTCLIFFE	H VAC	72	+ Vildebeest	4328
VICKERS	271 Wellington Mk I/GR Mk XIV	AIRMODEL	H VAC CV	72		4329
VICKERS	271 Wellington Mk I	FROG	H INJ	72		4330
VICKERS	271 Wellington Mk I	FROG	H WD·	72		4331
VICKERS	271 Wellington Mk I	FROG PENGUIN	H INJ	72		4332
VICKERS	271 Wellington B Mk II	ARISTO CRAFT	H INJ	72		4333
VICKERS	271 Wellington B Mk II	CRUVER	R HR·	72		4334
VICKERS	271 Wellington B Mk II	SUTCLIFFE	H VAC CV	72		4335
VICKERS	271 Wellington B Mk II	AIRFIX	H INJ	72		4336
VICKERS	271 Wellington B Mk III	ARISTO CRAFT	H INJ	72		4337
VICKERS	271 Wellington B Mk III	CRUVER	R HR·	72		4338
VICKERS	271 Wellington B Mk X/GR Mk XIV	MATCHBOX	H INJ	72		4339
VICKERS	284 Warwick	SUTCLIFFE	H VAC	72		4340
VICKERS	607 Valetta	AIRMODEL	H VAC	72		4341
VICKERS	630 Viscount	AIR JET ADVANCE	D FG·	72		4342
VICKERS	630 Viscount	CRUVER	R HR·	72		4343
VICKERS	630 Viscount	MODELAIR	H INJ	72		4344
VICKERS	630 Viscount	UNIQUE SCALE	H RSN	72		4345
VICKERS	630 Viscount 700	AIRTEC	H FG·	72		4346
VICKERS	630 Viscount 700	EXECUTIVE	D FG·	72		4347
VICKERS	630 Viscount 700	MODELMASTERS	D —	72		4348
VICKERS	630 Viscount 800	AVF	H VAC	72		4349
VICKERS	630 Viscount 800	EXECUTIVE	D FG·	72		4350
VICKERS	630 Viscount 800	MIAMI AIRPLANE	D FM·	72		4351
VICKERS	630 Viscount 800	MODELMASTERS	D —	72		4352
VICKERS	648 Varsity	SABRE	H VAC	72		4353
VICKERS	648 Varsity T Mk 1	AIRMODEL	H VAC	72		4354
VICKERS	648 Varsity T Mk 1	I.D. MODELS	H VAC	72		4355

VICKERS	667 Valiant B.1	SUTCLIFFE	H VAC	72		4356
VICKERS	950 Vanguard	EXECUTIVE	D FG·	72		4357
VICKERS	950 Vanguard	MODELMASTERS	D —	72		4358
VICKERS	950 Vanguard	RICK'S	H VAC	72		4359
VICKERS	FB.5 Gunbus	AIRFRAME	H VAC	72		4360
VICKERS	FB.12C	CRAMER	H VAC	72		4361
VICKERS	FB.19	CRAMER	H VAC	72		4362
VICKERS	FB.19	SCALEPLANES	H VAC	72		4363
VICKERS	FB.27 Vernon	SUTCLIFFE	H VAC CV	72		4364
VICKERS	FB.27 Vimy (Alcock & Brown)	FROG	H INJ	72		4365
VICKERS	FB.27 Vimy Mk IV	FROG	H INJ RM	72		4366
VICKERS	VC10	AVF	H VAC	72		4367
VICKERS	VC10	EXECUTIVE	D FG·	72		4368
VICKERS	Super VC10	EXECUTIVE	D FG·	72		4369
VICKERS	Warwick	SUTCLIFFE	H VAC	72		4370
VL	Myrsky	O'NEILL	H VAC	72		4371
VL	Myrsky II	ALPHA	H VAC	72		4372
VL	Myrsky II	FAIREY	H RSN	72	w. ML parts	4373
VL	Myrsky II	KPL MODELS	H VAC	72		4374
VL	Myrsky II	PRIVATE VENTURE	H RSN	72		4375
VL	Pyörremysky	KPL MODELS	H VAC	72	Finnish Bf 109	4376
VOISIN	V	CRAMER	H VAC	72		4377
VOISIN-FARMAN	1908	RENWAL	H INJ	72		4378
VOUGHT	A-7A Corsair II	FUJIMI	H INJ	72		4379
VOUGHT	A-7A Corsair II	HASEGAWA	H INJ	72	w. Sidewinder missile	4380
VOUGHT	A-7A Corsair II	HASEGAWA	H INJ RM	72	w. Sidewinder missile	4381
VOUGHT	A-7A Corsair II	REVELL	H INJ	72	w. Sidewinder missile	4382
VOUGHT	A-7B Corsair II	FUJIMI	H INJ	72		4383
VOUGHT	TA-7C Corsair II	AIRMODEL	H VAC CV	72	canopy, + TA-4F + PBY	4384
VOUGHT	TA-7C Corsair II	FALCON	H VAC	72	+ F-100F + RF-8G	4385
VOUGHT	TA-7C/A-7L Corsair II	MAINTRACK	H RSN CV	72		4386
VOUGHT	A-7D Corsair II	FUJIMI	H INJ	72		4387
VOUGHT	A-7D Corsair II	MATCHBOX	H INJ	72	w. Sidewinder missile	4388
VOUGHT	A-7D Corsair II	REVELL	H INJ	72	w. Sidewinder missile	4389
VOUGHT	A-7D/E Corsair II	AIRFIX	H INJ	72	w. Sidewinder missile	4390
VOUGHT	A-7E Corsair II	FUJIMI	H INJ	72		4391
VOUGHT	A-7E Corsair II	TESTOR	H INJ	72		4392
VOUGHT	F8U-1 Crusader	CRUVER	R HR·	72		4393
VOUGHT	F8U-1 Crusader	SETCO	R HR·	72		4394
VOUGHT	F-8A/B Crusader	NOSE JOBS	H ML· CV	72		4395
VOUGHT	TF-8A Crusader	AIRMODEL	H VAC CV	72	+ RF-8G	4396
VOUGHT	F-8D Crusader	FUJIMI	H INJ	70		4397
VOUGHT	F-8D Crusader	REVELL	H INJ	67	w. Sidewinder missile	4398
VOUGHT	F-8E Crusader	HASEGAWA	H INJ	72	w. Sidewinder missile	4399
VOUGHT	F-8E Crusader	REVELL	H INJ RM	67		4400
VOUGHT	F-8E/J/E(FN) Crusader	HELLER	H INJ	72	w. R.530, Sidewinder missile	4401
VOUGHT	RF-8G Crusader	AIRMODEL	H VAC CV	72	+ TF-8A	4402
VOUGHT	RF-8G Crusader	FALCON	H VAC CV	72	+ F-100F + TA-7C	4403
VOUGHT	F8U-3 Crusader III	EAGLES TALON	H VAC	72		4404
VOUGHT	O2U-1 Corsair	ESOTERIC	H VAC	72	w. ML parts	4405
VOUGHT	OS2U-1 Kingfisher	ARISTO CRAFT	H INJ	72		4406
VOUGHT	OS2U-1 Kingfisher	CRUVER	R HR·	72		4407
VOUGHT	OS2U-1 Kingfisher	DESIGN CENTER	H INJ	72	float version	4408
VOUGHT	OS2U-1 Kingfisher	DESIGN CENTER	H INJ	72	wheel version	4409
VOUGHT	OS2U-3 Kingfisher	AIRFIX	H INJ	72	w. wheel, floats	4410
VOUGHT	OS2U-3 Kingfisher	LINDBERG	H INJ	72		4411
VOUGHT	OS2U-3 Kingfisher	MAC VAC CANOPY	H VAC	72		4412
VOUGHT	SB2U Vindicator	MAC VAC CANOPY	H VAC	72		4413
VOUGHT	SB2U Vindicator	RAREPLANES	H VAC	72		4414
VOUGHT	SB2U-3 Vindicator	RAREPLANES	H VAC RM	72		4415
VOUGHT	SB2U-3 Vindicator	ARISTO CRAFT	H INJ	72		4416
VOUGHT	SB2U-3 Vindicator	CRUVER	R HR·	72		4417
VOUGHT	SBU-1	ESOTERIC	H VAC	72	w. ML parts	4418
VOUGHT	SBU-1	MAC VAC CANOPY	H VAC	72		4419
VOUGHT	SBU-1	O'NEILL	H VAC	72		4420
VSO	10	ALPHA	H VAC	72		4421
VSO	10	PRIVATE VENTURE AB	H RSN	72		4422

VULTEE	A-31 Vengeance	ARISTO CRAFT	H VAC	72		4423
VULTEE	A-31 Vengeance	CRUVER	R HR·	72		4424
VULTEE	A-35 Vengeance	CRUVER	R HR·	72		4425
VULTEE	A-35 Vengeance	MAC VAC CANOPY	H VAC	72		4426
VULTEE	A-35 Vengeance Mk.2	FROG	H INJ	72		4427
VULTEE	BT-13 Valiant	EXECUFORM	H VAC	72		4428
VULTEE	BT-13 Valiant	MAI	H RSN	72		4429
VULTEE	BT-13 Valiant	O'NEILL	H VAC	72		4430
VULTEE	P-66 Vanguard	AIRFRAME	H VAC	72		4431
VULTEE	P-66 Vanguard	MAC VAC CANOPY	H VAC	72		4432
VULTEE	V-1A	EXECUFORM	H VAC	72		4433
VULTEE	V-11GB	O'NEILL	H VAC	72		4434
VULTEE	XP-54 Swoose Goose	EXECUFORM	H VAC	72		4435
VULTEE	XP-54 Swoose Goose	MAC VAC CANOPY	H VAC	72		4436
VULTEE	XP-54 Swoose Goose	PRIVATE VENTURE C	H RSN	72		4437
WACO	CG-4A	ARISTO CRAFT	H INJ	72		4438
WACO	CG-4A	CRUVER	R HR·	72		4439
WACO	CG-4A	ITALERI	H INJ	72		4440
WACO	CG-4A	SUTCLIFFE	H VAC	72		4441
WACO	CG-13A	SUTCLIFFE	H VAC	72		4442
WACO	UC-72	EXECUFORM	H VAC	72		4443
WESTLAND	Lynx WG 13	FROG	H INJ	72	Army/Navy proto. versions	4444
WESTLAND	Lynx	MATCHBOX	H INJ	72	Army/Navy proto. versions	4445
WESTLAND	Lynx AH Mk 1	AIRFIX	H INJ	72	Army version, w. Hot m.	4446
WESTLAND	Lynx AH Mk 1	FUJIMI	H INJ	72	Army version, w. Hot m.	4447
WESTLAND	Lynx HAS Mk 2	AIRFIX	H INJ	72	Navy version	4448
WESTLAND	Lynx HAS Mk 2	FUJIMI	H INJ	72	Navy version	4449
WESTLAND	Lynx HAS Mk 2/3	C. SCALE	H ML· CV	72	w. Sea Skua missile	4450
WESTLAND	Lysander	AIRMODEL	H VAC CV	72	Tandem Wing version	4451
WESTLAND	Lysander	ARISTO CRAFT	H INJ	72		4452
WESTLAND	Lysander	FROG PENGUIN	H INJ	72		4453
WESTLAND	Lysander	MAC VAC CANOPY	H VAC	72		4454
WESTLAND	Lysander	SKYBIRDS	H WD·	72		4455
WESTLAND	Lysander Mk I	AIRFIX	H INJ	72		4456
WESTLAND	Lysander Mk I	CRUVER	R HR·	72		4457
WESTLAND	Lysander Mk I/II	FROG	H INJ	72		4458
WESTLAND	Lysander Mk I/II	MATCHBOX	H INJ	72		4459
WESTLAND	Lysander Mk II/III	AIRFIX	H INJ RM	72		4460
WESTLAND	Scout AH Mk 1	AIRFIX	H INJ	72		4461
WESTLAND	Sea King Mk 41	FUJIMI	H INJ	72		4462
WESTLAND	Sea King AEW Mk 2	C. SCALE	H ML· CV	72		4463
WESTLAND	Sea King HAR Mk 3	AIRFIX	H INJ RM	72		4464
WESTLAND	Sea King HAR Mk 3	FUJIMI	H INJ	72		4465
WESTLAND	Sea King HAS Mk 5	C. SCALE	H ML· CV	72		4466
WESTLAND	Sea King HC Mk 4	C. SCALE	H ML· CV	72		4467
WESTLAND	Wallace	FROG	H INJ	72		4468
WESTLAND	Wallace	SKYBIRDS	H —	72		4469
WESTLAND	Welkin	ARISTO CRAFT	H INJ	72		4470
WESTLAND	Welkin	CRUVER	R HR·	72		4471
WESTLAND	Welkin	SUTCLIFFE	H VAC	72		4472
WESTLAND	Welkin Mk I	HALLAM-VAC	H VAC	72	w. ML parts	4473
WESTLAND	Wessex	SCALECRAFT	H INJ SN	72	Police v., w. electr. eng.	4474
WESTLAND	Wessex HAS Mk 1/31	FROG	H INJ	72		4475
WESTLAND	Wessex HAS Mk 3	SCALECRAFT	H INJ SN	72	Royal Navy v., w. el. eng.	4476
WESTLAND	Wessex HAS Mk 1	MAINTRACK	H RSN	72	w. ML parts	4477
WESTLAND	Wessex HC Mk 2/HU Mk 5	MAINTRACK	H RSN	72	w. ML parts	4478
WESTLAND	Whirlwind Mk I	AIRFIX	H INJ	72	(airplane)	4479
WESTLAND	Whirlwind Mk I	ARISTO CRAFT	H INJ	72	(airplane)	4480
WESTLAND	Whirlwind Mk I	CRUVER	R HR·	72	(airplane)	4481
WESTLAND	Whirlwind Mk I	MAC VAC CANOPY	H VAC	72	(airplane)	4482
WESTLAND	Whirlwind Mk I	POLISTIL	H INJ	72	(airplane)	4483
WESTLAND	Whirlwind Mk I	AIRFIX	H INJ RM	72	(airplane)	4484
WESTLAND	Whirlwind	FROG	H INJ	67	(helicopter)	4485
WESTLAND	Whirlwind	RUCH	H INJ	72	(helicopter)	4486
WESTLAND	Whirlwind	SANWA	H INJ	72	(helicopter)	4487
WESTLAND	Whirlwind HAR Mk 1	AIRFIX	H INJ	72	(helicopter)	4488
WESTLAND	Whirlwind HAR Mk 9	MAINTRACK	H RSN	72	(helicopter) w. ML parts	4489

WESTLAND	Whirlwind HAR Mk 10	AIRMODEL	H VAC CV	72	(helicopter)	4490
WESTLAND	Whirlwind HAR Mk 10	MAINTRACK	H RSN	72	(helicopter) w. ML parts	4491
WESTLAND	Whirlwind HAS Mk 22	AIRFIX	H INJ RM	72	(helicopter)	4492
WESTLAND	Widgeon Mk II/III	AIRFRAME	H VAC	72	w. ML parts	4493
WESTLAND	Wyvern	MAC VAC CANOPY	H VAC	72		4494
WESTLAND	Wyvern S Mk 4	FROG	H INJ	72		4495
WESTLAND-HILL	Pterodactyl	PRIVATE VENTURE	H RSN	72		4496
WESTLAND-HILL	Pterodactyl Mk I	AIRFRAME	H VAC	72		4497
WESTLAND-HILL	Pterodactyl Mk V	AIRFRAME	H VAC	72		4498
WIBAULT	72	O'NEILL	H VAC	72		4499
WRIGHT	Flyer 1903	RENWAL	H INJ	72		4500
YAKOVLEV	UT-1 (AIR-14)	PSC	H VAC	72		4501
YAKOVLEV	Yak-1	KPM	H VAC	72		4502
YAKOVLEV	Yak-1M	KPM	H VAC	72		4503
YAKOVLEV	Yak-1/1M	MIKRO	H INJ	72		4504
YAKOVLEV	Yak-3	CRUVER	R HR·	72		4505
YAKOVLEV	Yak-3	FROG	H INJ	72		4506
YAKOVLEV	Yak-3	HELLER	H INJ	72		4507
YAKOVLEV	Yak-3	SDELAND	H ML· WK	72		4508
YAKOVLEV	Yak-4	ALFA	H INJ	72		4509
YAKOVLEV	Yak-4	KPL MODELS	H VAC	72		4510
YAKOVLEV	Yak-4	O'NEILL	H VAC	72		4511
YAKOVLEV	Yak-6	ALFA	H INJ	72		4512
YAKOVLEV	Yak-6	PRIVATE VENTURE C	H RSN	72		4513
YAKOVLEV	Yak-6	WINGS 72	H VAC	72	w. ML parts	4514
YAKOVLEV	Yak-7/7U (Mark)	PRIVATE VENTURE A	H RSN	72		4515
YAKOVLEV	Yak-7/7U (Mark)	AIRMODEL	H VAC	72		4516
YAKOVLEV	Yak-9D (Frank)	AIRFIX	H INJ	72		4517
YAKOVLEV	Yak-9D (Frank)	CRUVER	R HR·	72		4518
YAKOVLEV	Yak-9D (Frank)	DANBURY MINT	H ML·	72		4519
YAKOVLEV	Yak-11 (Moose)	ABORN	H VAC	72	canopy	4520
YAKOVLEV	Yak-11 (Moose)	AIRMODEL	H VAC	72		4521
YAKOVLEV	Yak-11 (Moose)	MAI	H RSN	72		4522
YAKOVLEV	Yak-11 (Moose)	PRIVATE VENTURE C	H RSN	72		4523
YAKOVLEV	Yak-11 (Moose)	WAKU	H VAC	72		4524
YAKOVLEV	Yak-14	O'NEILL	H VAC	72		4525
YAKOVLEV	Yak-15	AIRMODEL	H VAC	72		4526
YAKOVLEV	Yak-15	BOLESLAV	H VAC	72		4527
YAKOVLEV	Yak-15	CRAMER	H VAC	72		4528
YAKOVLEV	Yak-15	CRUVER	R HR·	72		4529
YAKOVLEV	Yak-15	DUBENA CESKY DUB	H VAC	72		4530
YAKOVLEV	Yak-15	PIONEER 2	H INJ	72		4531
YAKOVLEV	Yak-15	PRIVATE VENTURE X	H RSN	72		4532
YAKOVLEV	Yak-15	SUTCLIFFE	H VAC	72		4533
YAKOVLEV	Yak-15	VEEDAY	H INJ	72		4534
YAKOVLEV	Yak-15	WAKU	H VAC	72		4535
YAKOVLEV	Yak-17 (Feather)	BOLESLAV	H VAC	72		4536
YAKOVLEV	Yak-17 (Feather)	DUBENA CESKY DUB	H VAC	72		4537
YAKOVLEV	Yak-17 (Feather)	WAKU	H VAC	72		4538
YAKOVLEV	Yak-17 UTI (Magnet)	PSC	H VAC	72		4539
YAKOVLEV	Yak-21	PSC	H VAC	72	2-seat Yak-15	4540
YAKOVLEV	Yak-23/23UTI (Flora)	AIRMODEL	H VAC	72		4541
YAKOVLEV	Yak-23 (Flora)	CRAMER	H VAC	72		4542
YAKOVLEV	Yak-23 (Flora)	CRUVER	R HR·	72		4543
YAKOVLEV	Yak-23 (Flora)	KOVOZAVODY	H INJ	72		4544
YAKOVLEV	Yak-23 (Flora)	PRIVATE VENTURE A	H RSN	74		4545
YAKOVLEV	Yak-25 (Flashlight)	AIRMODEL	H VAC	72		4546
YAKOVLEV	Yak-25 (Flashlight)	EAGLES TALON	H VAC	72		4547
YAKOVLEV	Yak-25 (Flashlight)	SETCO	R HR·	72		4548
YAKOVLEV	Yak-25 (Flashlight)	SUTCLIFFE	H VAC	72		4549
YAKOVLEV	Yak-25 (Flashlight)	WK	H VAC	72	w. RSN parts	4550
YAKOVLEV	Yak-28 (Brewer)	CRAMER	H VAC	72		4551
YAKOVLEV	Yak-28B/C (Brewer)	SUTCLIFFE	H VAC	72	w. INJ, ML p., + Yak-28P	4552
YAKOVLEV	Yak-28P (Firebar)	AIRMODEL	H VAC	72	w. RSN parts	4553
YAKOVLEV	Yak-28P (Firebar)	SUTCLIFFE	H VAC	72	w. INJ, ML p., + Yak-28B/C	4554
YAKOVLEV	Yak-38 (Yak-36MP) (Forger A)	CRAMER	H VAC	72		4555
YAKOVLEV	Yak-38 (Yak-36MP) (Forger A)	I.D. MODELS	H VAC	72		4556

YAKOVLEV	Yak-38 (Yak-36MP) (Forger A)	ELLIOTT	H VAC	72	w. ML parts	4557
YAKOVLEV	Yak-38 (Yak-36MP) (Forger A)	WINGS 72	H VAC	72	w. ML parts	4558
YAKOVLEV	Yak-40 (Codling)	EXECUTIVE	D FG·	72		4559
YAKOVLEV	Yak-40 (Codling)	J & L	H VAC	72		4560
YAKOVLEV	Yak-1000	AIRMODEL	H VAC	72		4561
YAKOVLEV	Yak-1000	PRIVATE VENTURE	H RSN	72		4562
YOKOSUKA	BAY1	O'NEILL	H VAC	72	Jean	4563
YOKOSUKA	D4Y2 Suisei (Comet)	CRUVER	R HR·	72	Judy	4564
YOKOSUKA	D4Y2 Suisei (Comet)	FUJIMI	H INJ	72	Judy	4565
YOKOSUKA	D4Y2 Suisei (Comet)	L.S.	H INJ	75	Judy	4566
YOKOSUKA	D4Y2 Suisei (Comet)	L.S.	H INJ RM	72	Judy	4567
YOKOSUKA	D4Y2 Suisei (Comet)	Y.M.C.	H INJ	72	Judy	4568
YOKOSUKA	D4Y3 Suisei (Comet)	FUJIMI	H INJ	72	Judy	4569
YOKOSUKA	D4Y3 Suisei (Comet)	L.S.	H INJ	72	Judy	4570
YOKOSUKA	E14Y1	AIRFRAME	H VAC	72	Glen	4571
YOKOSUKA	E14Y1	EAGLES TALON	H VAC	72	Glen	4572
YOKOSUKA	E14Y1	KPM	H VAC	72	Glen	4573
YOKOSUKA	E14Y1	PRIVATE VENTURE C	H RSN	72	Glen	4574
YOKOSUKA	E14Y1	WINGS 72	H VAC	72	Glen	4575
YOKOSUKA	E16A1	O'NEILL	H VAC	72	Glen	4576
YOKOSUKA	H5Y	O'NEILL	H VAC	72	Cherry	4577
YOKOSUKA	K5Y	BANDAI	H INJ	70	Willow	4578
YOKOSUKA	K5Y1 Type 93	L.S.	H INJ	72	Willow	4579
YOKOSUKA	K5Y1 Type 93	GUNZE SANGYO	H ML·	72	Willow	4580
YOKOSUKA	K5Y2 Type 93	L.S.	H INJ	72	Willow, float version	4581
YOKOSUKA	MXY7 Ohka (Cherry Blossom)	AIRFRAME	H VAC	72	Baka	4582
YOKOSUKA	MXY7 Ohka (Cherry Blossom)	GEE'S AERO WORKS	H WD·	72	Baka	4583
YOKOSUKA	MXY7 Ohka (Cherry Blossom)	HASEGAWA	H INJ	72	Baka, + G4M	4584
YOKOSUKA	P1Y Ginga (Milky Way)	CRUVER	R HR·	72	Frances	4585
YOKOSUKA	P1Y1 Ginga (Milky Way)	REVELL	H INJ	72	Frances	4586
YOKOSUKA	R2Y1 Keiun (Beautiful Cloud)	EAGLES TALON	H VAC	72		4587
YOKOSUKA	R2Y1 Keiun (Beautiful Cloud)	PRIVATE VENTURE C	H RSN	72		4588
YOKOSUKA	R2Y1 Keiun (Beautiful Cloud)	WINGS 72	H VAC	72		4589
ZEPPELIN-LINDAU	D.I	AIRFRAME	H VAC	72		4590
ZEPPELIN-STAAKEN	E.4/20	CLASSIC PLANE	H VAC	72		4591
ZEPPELIN-STAAKEN	R VI/L	SUTCLIFFE	H VAC	72		4592
ZLIN	Z.50L	PRIVATE VENTURE X	H RSN	72		4593
ZMC-2	Rigid Airship (US Navy)	AIRMODEL	H VAC	72		4594

MISSILES

AEROJET GENERAL	X-8 Aerobee	RACCOON	H RSN	72	w. X-7A, X-7A-3 and X-9	1
AERONCA	GB-1	PRIVATE VENTURE C	H RSN	72		2
AEROSPATIALE	AM.39 Exocet	HASEGAWA	H INJ	72	w. Super Etendard	3
AEROSPATIALE	AM.39 Exocet	HELLER	H INJ	72	w. Super Etendard	4
AEROSPATIALE	AM.39 Exocet	HELLER BOBKIT	H INJ	72	w. AS 332B Super Puma	5
AEROSPATIALE	AM.39 Exocet	PRIVATE VENTURE	H RSN	72	w. Super Etendard	6
AEROSPATIALE	AS.30	AIRFIX	H INJ	72	w. Jaguar A (first issue)	7
AEROSPATIALE	AS.30L	MATCHBOX	H INJ	72	w. Jaguar GR.	8
BAC	P3T Sea Eagle	HASEGAWA	H INJ	72	w. FRS.1 Sea Harrier	9
BAC	Sea Skua	C. SCALE	H ML·	72	w. Lynx HAS.2/3	10
BAC	Skyflash	AIRFIX	H INJ	72	w. Tornado	11
BAC	Skyflash	ITALERI	H INJ	72	w. Tornado	12
BELL	X-9 Shrike	RACCOON	H RSN	72	w. X-7A, X-7A-3 and X-8	13
BOEING	AGM-86B	AIRFIX	H INJ	72	w. B-1B	14
BOEING	AGM-86B	MONOGRAM	H INJ	72	w. B-1B	15
BOEING	AGM-86B	PROJEKTS	H INJ	72		16
BOEING	AGM-86B	REVELL	H INJ	72	w. B-2	17
BRISTOL	Bloodhound	AIRFIX	H INJ	72	w. Land Rover & launcher	18
BRISTOL	Bloodhound	AIRFIX	H INJ	72	w. C-130K Hercules kit	19
BRISTOL-SIDDELEY	Blue Steel	AIRFIX	H INJ	72	w. Vulcan B.2	20
BRISTOL-SIDDELEY	Blue Steel	NOVA	H VAC	72	w. Vulcan	21
CANADAIR	CL-227	PRIVATE VENTURE C	H RSN	72		22
CONVAIR	X-11	RACCOON	H RSN	72	w. X-12	23
CONVAIR	X-12	RACCOON	H RSN	72	w. X-11	24
DE HAVILLAND	Firestreak	AIRFIX	H INJ	72	w. Lightning F.1A	25
DE HAVILLAND	Firestreak	AIRFIX	H INJ	72	w. SR.53	26
DE HAVILLAND	Firestreak	FROG	H INJ	72	w. remoulded Javelin FAW.9	27
DE HAVILLAND	Firestreak	MATCHBOX	H INJ	72	w. Lightning F.2A/F.6	28
DE HAVILLAND	Firestreak	MATCHBOX	H INJ	72	w. Lightning T.55	29
DOUGLAS	Skybolt GAM-87	NOVA	H VAC	72	w. Vulcan	30
DOUGLAS	Thor-Delta	TOPPING	H INJ	72		31
DOUGLAS	Thor (Lunar probe launcher)	AURORA	H INJ	72	w. platform, tower	32
DOUGLAS	Thor SM-75	AURORA	H INJ	72	w. platform, tower	33
EUROMISSILE	Hot	AHKETON	H ML·	72	w. AMX 10	34
EUROMISSILE	Hot	AIRFIX	H INJ	72	w. Lynx (Army version)	35
EUROMISSILE	Hot	FUJIMI	H INJ	72	w. Lynx (Army version)	36
FIESELER	Fi 103 (V-1)	FROG	H INJ	72	w. Ar 234	37
FIESELER	Fi 103 (V-1)	FROG	H INJ	72	w. Spitfire XIV	38
FIESELER	Fi 103 (V-1)	GEE'S AERO WORKS	H WD·	72		39
FIESELER	Fi 103 (V-1)	SMDC	H INJ	72		40
FRITZ	X	GUANO	H INJ	72		41
FRITZ	X	GUANO	H INJ	72	w. DORNIER Do 217K-2	42
FRITZ	X	PRIVATE VENTURE B	H RSN	72		43
GENERAL DYNAMICS	Standard Arm AGM-78B	HASEGAWA	H RSN	72	w. Air Weapon Set III	44
GENERAL DYNAMICS	Standard Arm AGM-78B	ITALERI	H INJ	72	W. F-4E/F/6 Phantom II	45
GENERAL DYNAMICS	Standard Arm AGM-78B	MONOGRAM	H INJ	72	w. F-105G Thunderchief	46
GENERAL DYNAMICS	Tomahawk AGM-109	TWELVE SQUARED	H INJ	72		47
GERMAN	V-2	GRIP	H INJ	76	w. launcher, radar vehicle	48
GERMAN	V-2	REVELL	H INJ	69	w. launcher	49
GRUMMAN	LEM (Lunar Excursion Module)	AIRFIX	H INJ	72		50
GRUMMAN	LEM (Lunar Excursion Module)	TAMIYA	H INJ	70		51
GRUMMAN/ROCKWELL	Apollo Spacecraft	TAMIYA	H INJ	70		52
HAWKER-SIDDELEY	Red Top	FROG	H INJ	72	w. Lightning F.6	53
HAWKER-SIDDELEY	Red Top	FROG	H INJ	72	w. remoulded Sea Vixen	54
HAWKER-SIDDELEY	Red Top	MATCHBOX	H INJ	72	w. Lightning F.2A/F.6	55
HAWKER-SIDDELEY	Red Top	MATCHBOX	H INJ	72	w. Lightning T.55	56
HENSCHEL	Hs 246 Hagelkorn	PRIVATE VENTURE C	H RSN	72		57
HENSCHEL	Hs 293	AIRFIX	H INJ	72	w. He 177A-5 Greif	58
HUGHES	Maverick AGM-65	AIRFIX	H INJ	72	w. F-5E Tiger II	59
HUGHES	Maverick AGM-65	AIRFIX	H INJ	72	w. F-16A/B Fighting Falcon	60
HUGHES	Maverick AGM-65	FUJIMI	H INJ	72	w. A-7E Corsair II	61
HUGHES	Maverick AGM-65	HASEGAWA	H INJ	72	w. Air Weapon Set III	62
HUGHES	Maverick AGM-65C	HASEGAWA	H INJ	72	w. A-10A Thunderbolt	63
HUGHES	AIM-120A AMRAAM	HASEGAWA	H INJ	72	w. Air Weapon Set II	64
HUGHES	AIM-120A AMRAAM	MONOGRAM	H INJ	72	w. F-16XL	65

HUGHES	Eagle AIM-47A	ITALERI	H INJ	72	w. YF-12A Blackbird	66
HUGHES	Eagle AIM-47A	REVELL	H INJ	72	w. YF-12A Blackbird	67
HUGHES	Falcon AIM-4C/D	AIRFIX	H INJ	72	w. J.35F Draken	68
HUGHES	Falcon AIM-4C/D	HASEGAWA	H INJ	72	w. F-4E/J Phantom II	69
HUGHES	Falcon AIM-4D	HASEGAWA	H INJ	72	w. Air Weapon Set II	70
HUGHES	Falcon AIM-4F	AIRFIX	H INJ	72	w. J.35F Draken	71
HUGHES	Falcon AIM-4F	HASEGAWA	H INJ	72	W. F-106 Delta Dart	72
HUGHES	Falcon AIM-4G	HASEGAWA	H INJ	72	w. Air Weapon Set II	73
HUGHES	Falcon AIM-4G	HASEGAWA	H INJ	72	w. F-102 Delta Dagger	74
HUGHES	Phoenix AIM-54A	AIRFIX	H INJ	72	w. F-14 Tomcat	75
HUGHES	Phoenix AIM-54A	HASEGAWA	H INJ	72	w. Air Weapon Set II	76
HUGHES	Phoenix AIM-54A	HASEGAWA	H INJ	72	w. F-14 Tomcat	77
HUGHES	Phoenix AIM-54A	MATCHBOX	H INJ	72	w. F-14 Tomcat	78
HUGHES	Phoenix AIM-54A	MONOGRAM	H INJ	72	w. F-14 Tomcat	79
HUGHES	Tow BGM-71A	FUJIMI	H INJ	72	w. AH-1S Huey Cobra	80
IGO	IA/IB	PRIVATE VENTURE	H RSN	72		81
KONGSBERG	Penguin Mk.3	FUJIMI	H INJ	72	w. F-16A (Norway)	82
LOCKHEED	GTD-21 Tagboard	HASEGAWA	H INJ	72	w. SR-71 Blackbird	83
LOCKHEED	GTD-21B Tagboard	AIRMODEL	H VAC	72		84
LOCKHEED	GTD-21B Tagboard	EAGLES TALON	H VA	72		85
LOCKHEED	GTD-21B Tagboard	ITALERI	H INJ	72	w. SR-71A/B Blackbird	86
LOCKHEED	GTD-21B Tagboard	MONOGRAM	H INJ	72	w. SR-71A Blackbird	87
LOCKHEED	GTD-21B Tagboard	PRIVATE VENTURE	H RSN	72		88
LOCKHEED	X-7A/X-7A-3	RACCOON	H RSN	72	w. X-8 and X-9	89
MARTIN MARIETTA	Bullpup A AGM-12A/B	ESCI	H INJ	72	w. F-100D Super Sabre	90
MARTIN MARIETTA	Bullpup A AGM-12A/B	HASEGAWA	H INJ	72	w. Air Weapon Set III	91
MARTIN MARIETTA	Bullpup A AGM-12A/B	HASEGAWA	H INJ	72	w. A-4F Skyhawk	92
MARTIN MARIETTA	Bullpup A AGM-12A/B	HASEGAWA	H INJ	72	w. F-100D Super Sabre	93
MARTIN MARIETTA	Bullpup A AGM-12A/B	HASEGAWA	H INJ	72	w. F-5A Freedom Fighter	94
MARTIN MARIETTA	Bullpup A AGM-12A/B	HASEGAWA	H INJ	72	w. F-105D Thunderchief	95
MARTIN MARIETTA	Bullpup A AGM-12A/B	HASEGAWA	H INJ	72	w. F-4K/M Phantom II	96
MARTIN MARIETTA	Bullpup A AGM-12A/B	MATCHBOX	H INJ	72	w. A-4M Skyhawk	97
MARTIN MARIETTA	Bullpup A AGM-12A/B	RAREPLANES	H INJ	72	w. FJ-4B Fury	98
MARTIN MARIETTA	Bullpup A AGM-12A/B	SMDC	H INJ	72		99
MARTIN MARIETTA	Bullpup AGM-12C	HASEGAWA	H INJ	72	w. Air Weapon Set III	100
MARTIN MARIETTA	SM-68 Titan I	TOPPING	H INJ	66	version w. AVCO Mk 4	101
MATRA	R.440 Crotale	TRAME	H RSN	72	w. EB parts, firing unit	102
MATRA	R.511	AIRFIX	H INJ	72	w. Mirage IIIC	103
MATRA	R.530	AIRFIX	H INJ	72	w. Mirage F.1C	104
MATRA	R.530	CENTRAL	H INJ	72	w. Mirage IIIC	105
MATRA	R.530	HASEGAWA	H INJ	72	w. Mirage F.1C	106
MATRA	R.530	HELLER	H INJ	72	w. Mirage F.1B/C	107
MATRA	R.530	HELLER	H INJ	72	w. F-8 Crusader	108
MATRA	R.530	UNIKIT	H INJ	72	w. Mirage F.1C (SN)	109
MATRA	Super 530	HELLER	H INJ	72	w. Mirage 2000	110
MATRA	R.550 Magic	AIRFIX	H INJ	72	w. Mirage F.1C	111
MATRA	R.550 Magic	HASEGAWA	H INJ	72	w. Mirage F.1C	112
MATRA	R.550 Magic	HASEGAWA	H INJ	72	w. Jaguar A/GR.1	113
MATRA	R.550 Magic	HELLER	H INJ	72	w. Mirage 2000	114
MATRA	R.550 Magic	SUNNY	H INJ	72	w. Super Etendard	115
MATRA	R.550 Magic	UNIKIT	H INJ	72	w. Mirage F.1C (SN)	116
MATRA/HAWKER-SIDDELEY	Martel AS.37	AIRFIX	H INJ	72	w. Tornado	117
MATRA/HAWKER-SIDDELEY	Martel AS.37	AIRFIX	H INJ	72	w. Buccaneer	118
MATRA/HAWKER-SIDDELEY	Martel AS.37	AIRFIX	H INJ	72	w. Jaguar A/E	119
MATRA/HAWKER-SIDDELEY	Martel AS.37	FUJIMI	H INJ	72	w. Harrier GR.3	120
MATRA/HAWKER-SIDDELEY	Martel AS.37	FUJIMI	H INJ	72	w. Sea Harrier FRS.1	121
MATRA/HAWKER-SIDDELEY	Martel AS.37	ITALERI	H INJ	72	w. Tornado	122
MBB/AEROSPATIALE	Kormoran AS.34	ESCI	H INJ	72	w. Tornado	123
MBB/AEROSPATIALE	Kormoran AS.34	ITALERI	H INJ	72	w. Tornado	124
MBB/AEROSPATIALE	Kormoran AS.34	REVELL	H INJ	72	w. Tornado	125
McDONNELL	GAM-72 Quail	MAI	H RSN	72		126
McDONNELL DOUGLAS	Harpoon AGM-84A	AIRFIX	H INJ	72	w. S-3 Viking	127
McDONNELL DOUGLAS	Harpoon AGM-84	HASEGAWA	H INJ	72	w. Air Weapon Set III	128
McDONNELL DOUGLAS	Saturn 1B	ESTES	H— WK	70	flying rocket model	129
MIKOYAN-GURYEVICH	Kangaroo AS-3	SUTCLIFFE	H VAC	72	w. Tu-20	130
MIKOYAN-GURYEVICH	Kitchen AS-4	NOVA	H VAC	72	w. Tu-22	131

NORTH AMERICAN	Hound Dog AGM-28	MAI	H RSN	72		132
PHILCO/FORD	Sidewinder AIM-9A/B	AIRFIX	H INJ	72	w. A-7D/E Corsair II	133
PHILCO/FORD	Sidewinder AIM-9A/B	AIRFIX	H INJ	72	w. F4D-1 Skyray	134
PHILCO/FORD	Sidewinder AIM-9A/B	AIRFIX	H INJ	72	w. F-104G Starfighter	135
PHILCO/FORD	Sidewinder AIM-9A/B	AIRFIX	H INJ	72	w. OV-10A/D Bronco	136
PHILCO/FORD	Sidewinder AIM-9A/B	CENTRAL	H INJ	72	w. A-4D Skyhawk	137
PHILCO/FORD	Sidewinder AIM-9A/B	CENTRAL	H INJ	72	w. Hunter	138
PHILCO/FORD	Sidewinder AIM-9A/B	FROG	H INJ	72	w. Mirage IIIE/O	139
PHILCO/FORD	Sidewinder AIM-9A/B	HASEGAWA	H INJ	72	w. A-4E/F Skyhawk	140
PHILCO/FORD	Sidewinder AIM-9A/B	HASEGAWA	H INJ	72	w. A-7A Corsair II	141
PHILCO/FORD	Sidewinder AIM-9A/B	HASEGAWA	H INJ	72	w. Mirage F.1C	142
PHILCO/FORD	Sidewinder AIM-9A/B	HASEGAWA	H INJ	72	w. F-4E/J Phantom II	143
PHILCO/FORD	Sidewinder AIM-9A/B	HASEGAWA	H INJ	72	w. F-5A Freedom Fighter	144
PHILCO/FORD	Sidewinder AIM-9A/B	HASEGAWA	H INJ	72	w. F9F-8 Cougar	145
PHILCO/FORD	Sidewinder AIM-9A/B	HASEGAWA	H INJ	72	w. F11-1 Tiger	146
PHILCO/FORD	Sidewinder AIM-9A/B	HASEGAWA	H INJ	72	w. F-86F Sabre	147
PHILCO/FORD	Sidewinder AIM-9A/B	HASEGAWA	H INJ	72	w. F-100D Super Sabre	148
PHILCO/FORD	Sidewinder AIM-9A/B	HASEGAWA	H INJ	72	w. F-104J Starfighter	149
PHILCO/FORD	Sidewinder AIM-9A/B	HASEGAWA	H INJ	72	w. OV-10A Bronco	150
PHILCO/FORD	Sidewinder AIM-9A/B	HASEGAWA	H INJ	72	w. T-2	151
PHILCO/FORD	Sidewinder AIM-9A/B	HASEGAWA	H INJ	72	w. T-2 CCV	152
PHILCO/FORD	Sidewinder AIM-9A/B	MATCHBOX	H INJ	72	w. A-7D Corsair II	153
PHILCO/FORD	Sidewinder AIM-9A/B	MATCHBOX	H INJ	72	w. F-4K/M Phantom II	154
PHILCO/FORD	Sidewinder AIM-9A/B	MATCHBOX	H INJ	72	w. Sea Harrier FRS.1	155
PHILCO/FORD	Sidewinder AIM-9A/B	MONOGRAM	H INJ	72	w. F-4J Phantom II	156
PHILCO/FORD	Sidewinder AIM-9A/B	REVELL	H INJ	72	w. A-7A/D Corsair II	157
PHILCO/FORD	Sidewinder AIM-9A/B	REVELL	H INJ	72	w. F-15A Eagle	158
PHILCO/FORD	Sidewinder AIM-9A/B	REVELL	H INJ	72	w. OV-10 Bronco	159
PHILCO/FORD	Sidewinder AIM-9A/B	SMDC	H INJ	72		160
PHILCO/FORD	Sidewinder AIM-9B	AIRFIX	H INJ	72	w. F-5A Freedom Fighter	161
PHILCO/FORD	Sidewinder AIM-9B	AIRFIX	H INJ	72	w. Jaguar A (first issue)	162
PHILCO/FORD	Sidewinder AIM-9B	ESCI	H INJ	72	w. F-100D Super Sabre	163
PHILCO/FORD	Sidewinder AIM-9B	ESCI	H INJ	72	w. F-104C/G/S Starfighter	164
PHILCO/FORD	Sidewinder AIM-9B	ESCI	H INJ	72	w. F-5A Freedom Fighter	165
PHILCO/FORD	Sidewinder AIM-9B	ESCI	H INJ	72	w. F-5C/RF-5C	166
PHILCO/FORD	Sidewinder AIM-9B	FUJIMI	H INJ	72	w. F-4C/D Phantom II	167
PHILCO/FORD	Sidewinder AIM-9B	FUJKIMI	H INJ	72	w. F-4N Phantom II	168
PHILCO/FORD	Sidewinder AIM-9B	FUJIMI	H INJ	72	w. F-4S Phantom II	168
PHILCO/FORD	Sidewinder AIM-9B	FUJIMI	H INJ	72	w. A-7E Corsair II	170
PHILCO/FORD	Sidewinder AIM-9B	FUJIMI	H INJ	72	w. F-86F Sabre	171
PHILCO/FORD	Sidewinder AIM-9B	HASEGAWA	H INJ	72	w. Air Weapon Set II	172
PHILCO/FORD	Sidewinder AIM-9B	HASEGAWA	H INJ	72	w. F-16A Fighting Falcon	173
PHILCO/FORD	Sidewinder AIM-9B	MATCHBOX	H INJ	72	w. F-194G Starfighter	174
PHILCO/FORD	Sidewinder AIM-9B	MATCHBOX	H INJ	72	w. F-5A Freedom Fighter	175
PHILCO/FORD	Sidewinder AIM-9B	MONOGRAM	H INJ	72	w. F-15A Eagle	176
PHILCO/FORD	Sidewinder AIM-9B	MONOGRAM	H INJ	72	w. F-16A Fighting Falcon	177
PHILCO/FORD	Sidewinder AIM-9B	REVELL	H INJ	72	w. Mirage IIIE/R/RS/S	178
PHILCO/FORD	Sidewinder AIM-9B	REVELL	H INJ	72	w. Tornado	179
PHILCO/FORD	Sidewinder AIM-9C	HASEGAWA	H INJ	72	w. F-8E Crusader	180
PHILCO/FORD	Sidewinder AIM-9C	HELLER	H INJ	72	w. F-8E/J Crusader	181
PHILCO/FORD	Sidewinder AIM-9C	REVELL	H INJ	72	w. F-8D Crusader	182
PHILCO/FORD	Sidewinder AIM-9C	SMDC	H INJ	72		183
PHILCO/FORD	Sidewinder AIM-9D	HASEGAWA	H INJ	72	w. Air Weapon Set II	184
PHILCO/FORD	Sidewinder AIM-9D/E	SMDC	H INJ	72		185
PHILCO/FORD	Sidewinder AIM-9E	ENTEX	H INJ	72	w. F/A-18 Hornet	186
PHILCO/FORD	Sidewinder AIM-9E	HASEGAWA	H INJ	72	w. F-14A Tomcat	187
PHILCO/FORD	Sidewinder AIM-9E	HASEGAWA	H INJ	72	w. YF-16 CCV	188
PHILCO/FORD	Sidewinder AIM-9E	HASEGAWA	H INJ	72	w. F-16A (Thunderbirds)	189
PHILCO/FORD	Sidewinder AIM-9E	MATCHBOX	H INJ	72	w. F-16A/B Fighting Falcon	190
PHILCO/FORD	Sidewinder AIM-9E	MONOGRAM	H INJ	72	w. F-4E/J Phantom II (SN)	191
PHILCO/FORD	Sidewinder AIM-9E	REVELL	H INJ	72	w. F-4E/J Phantom II	192
PHILCO/FORD	Sidewinder AIM-9E	SMDC	H INJ	72	w. Air Weapon Set II	193
PHILCO/FORD	Sidewinder AIM-9J	AIRFIX	H INJ	72	w. F-5E Tiger II	194
PHILCO/FORD	Sidewinder AIM-9J	ESCI	H INJ	72	w. F-4E/F Phantom II	195
PHILCO/FORD	Sidewinder AIM-9J	ESCI	H INJ	72	w. F-4C/J Phantom II	196
PHILCO/FORD	Sidewinder AIM-9J	ESCI	H INJ	72	w. F-16A Fighting Falcon	197

PHILCO/FORD	Sidewinder AIM-9J	ESCI	H INJ	72	w. F-16B Fighting Falcon	198
PHILCO/FORD	Sidewinder AIM-9J	ESCI	H INJ	72	w. F/A-18 Hornet	199
PHILCO/FORD	Sidewinder AIM-9J	FUJIMI	H INJ	72	w. AV-8A Harrier/Matador	200
PHILCO/FORD	Sidewinder AIM-9J	FUJIMI	H INJ	72	w. GR.3 Harrier	201
PHILCO/FORD	Sidewinder AIM-9J	FUJIMI	H INJ	72	w. FRS.1 Sea Harrier	202
PHILCO/FORD	Sidewinder AIM-9J	FUJIMI	H INJ	72	F-16A (USA/Norway)	203
PHILCO/FORD	Sidewinder AIM-9J	HASEGAWA	H INJ	72	w. Air Weapon Set II	204
PHILCO/FORD	Sidewinder AIM-9J	HASEGAWA	H INJ	72	w. F-20A Tigershark	205
PHILCO/FORD	Sidewinder AIM-9J	ITALERI	H INJ	72	w. AV-8B Harrier II	206
PHILCO/FORD	Sidewinder AIM-9J	ITALERI	H INJ	72	w. F-5E Tiger II	207
PHILCO/FORD	Sidewinder AIM-9J	ITALERI	H INJ	72	w. F-5F Tiger II	208
PHILCO/FORD	Sidewinder AIM-9J	ITALERI	H INJ	72	w. F-16A/B Fighting Falcon	209
PHILCO/FORD	Sidewinder AIM-9J	REVELL	H INJ	72	w. F-16A Fighting Falcon	210
PHILCO/FORD	Sidewinder AIM-9J	SMDC	H INJ	72		211
PHILCO/FORD	Sidewinder AIM-9L	AIRFIX	H INJ	72	w. F-15A/B Eagle	212
PHILCO/FORD	Sidewinder AIM-9L	AIRFIX	H INJ	72	w. F-16A/B Fighting Falcon	213
PHILCO/FORD	Sidewinder AIM-9L	AIRFIX	H INJ	72	w. F/A-18A Hornet	214
PHILCO/FORD	Sidewinder AIM-9L	AIRFIX	H INJ	72	w. Tornado GR.1	215
PHILCO/FORD	Sidewinder AIM-9L	ESCI	H INJ	72	w. AV-8A Harrier/Matador	216
PHILCO/FORD	Sidewinder AIM-9L	ESCI	H INJ	72	w. FRS.1 Sea Harrier	217
PHILCO/FORD	Sidewinder AIM-9L	ESCI	H INJ	72	w. GR.3 Harrier	218
PHILCO/FORD	Sidewinder AIM-9L	HASEGAWA	H INJ	72	w. Air Weapon Set II	219
PHILCO/FORD	Sidewinder AIM-9L	HASEGAWA	H INJ	72	w. FRS.1 Sea Harrier	220
PHILCO/FORD	Sidewinder AIM-9L	HASEGAWA	H INJ	72	w. F-15C Eagle	221
PHILCO/FORD	Sidewinder AIM-9L	HASEGAWA	H INJ	72	w. F-15E Eagle	222
PHILCO/FORD	Sidewinder AIM-9L	HASEGAWA	H INJ	72	w. F-15J Eagle	223
PHILCO/FORD	Sidewinder AIM-9L	HASEGAWA	H INJ	72	w. F/A-18 Hornet	224
PHILCO/FORD	Sidewinder AIM-9L	HASEGAWA	H INJ	72	w. F/A-18 Hornet remoulded	225
PHILCO/FORD	Sidewinder AIM-9L	ITALERI	H INJ	72	w. F/A-18 Hornet	226
PHILCO/FORD	Sidewinder AIM-9L	MONOGRAM	H INJ	72	w. F-15E Eagle	227
PHILCO/FORD	Sidewinder AIM-9L	MONOGRAM	H INJ	72	w. F-16XL Fighting Falcon	228
PHILCO/FORD	Sidewinder AIM-9L	MONOGRAM	H INJ	72	w. F/A-18 Hornet (SN)	229
PHILCO/FORD	Sidewinder AIM-9L	MONOGRAM	H INJ	72	w. Tornado	230
*PHILCO/FORD	Sidewinder AIM-9L	REVELL	H INJ	72	w. F-18 Hornet	231
PHILCO/FORD	Sidewinder AIM-9L	SMDC	H INJ	72		232
RAPHAEL ARMAMENT	Shafrir	HASEGAWA	H INJ	72	w. Kfir C.2	233
REPUBLIC	JB-2 Loon	SMDC	H INJ	72		234
ROBOTAVDELNINGEN	Robotbyran RB 04C	AIRFIX	H INJ	72	w. AJ.37 Viggen	235
ROBOTAVDELNINGEN	Robotbyran RB 04C	HASEGAWA	H INJ	72	w. AJ.37 Viggen	236
ROBOTAVDELNINGEN	Robotbyran RB 04C	MATCHBOX	H INJ	72	w. AJ.37 Viggen	237
ROBOTAVDELNINGEN	Robotbyran RB 05A	AIRFIX	H INJ	72	w. AJ.37 Viggen	238
ROBOTAVDELNINGEN	Robotbyran RB 05A	MATCHBOX	H INJ	72	w. AJ.37 Viggen	239
ROBOTAVDELNINGEN	Robotbyran RB 28	AIRFIX	H INJ	72	w. J.35F Draken	240
ROCKWELL	AGM-114A Hellfire	AIRFIX	H INJ	72	w. OV-10D Bronco	241
ROCKWELL	AGM-114A Hellfire	HASEGAWA	H INJ	72	w. UH-60A Black Hawk	242
ROCKWELL	AGM-114A Hellfire	ITALERI	H INJ	72	w. AH-1W Super Cobra	243
ROCKWELL	AGM-114A Hellfire	ITALERI	H INJ	72	w. AH-64 Apache	244
ROCKWELL	Apollo Command Module	TAMIYA	H INJ	70		245
ROCKWELL	Apollo Space Capsule	ESTES	H -	70		246
ROCKWELL	Hellfire AGM-11A	HASEGAWA	H INJ	72	w. AH-64 Apache	247
ROCKWELL	Space Shuttle	MONOGRAM	H INJ	72	w. Spacelab	248
ROCKWELL	Space Shuttle	MONOGRAM	H INJ	72	w. tank and boosters	249
ROCKWELL	Space Shuttle	REVELL	H INJ	72	w. Spacelab	250
RYAN	Firebee I AQM-34	AIRMODEL	H VAC	72	w. DC-130A/E Hercules	251
RYAN	Firebee I AQM-34	PRIVATE VENTURE B	H RSN	72		252
RYAN	Firebee I BQM-34A	ITALERI	H INJ	72	w. DC-130 Hercules	253
RYAN	Firebee II BQM-34E	PRIVATE VENTURE C	H RSN	72		254
RYAN	Firebee II BQM-34E/S/T	AIRMODEL	H VAC	72	w. DC-130A/E & DP-2E (CV)	255
RYAN	Compass Cope YQM-98A	AIRMODEL	H VAC	72		256
RYAN	Compass Arrow AQM-91	PRIVATE VENTURE C	H RSN	72		257
RYAN	Compass Cope YQM-98A	PRIVATE VENTURE	H RSN	72		258
SAAB-SCANIA	RB-04	MATCHBOX	H INJ	72	w. SK-37 Viggen	259
SATELLITE	Pioneer I Lunar satellite	AURORA	H INJ	72	"USAF ROCKET" w. Launcher	260
SATELLITE	Bio & Medical	MONOGRAM	H INJ	72	w. Space Shuttle	261
SOVIET	AA-1 Alkali	CENTRAL	H INJ	72	w. MiG-19PM	262
SOVIET	AA-1 Alkali	HASEGAWA	H INJ	72	w. MiG-17PF	263

SOVIET	AA-1 Alkali	HELLER	H INJ	72	w. MiG-19PM	264
SOVIET	AA-1 Alkali	LFI	H INJ	72	w. MiG-19PM	265
SOVIET	AA-2 Atoll	AIRFIX	H INJ	72	w. MiG-21	266
SOVIET	AA-2 Atoll	AIRFIX	H INJ	72	w. MiG-23 (Flogger B)	267
SOVIET	AA-2 Atoll	HASEGAWA	H INJ	72	w. MiG-21F	268
SOVIET	AA-2 Atoll	HASEGAWA	H INJ	72	w. MiG-27 (Flogger D)	269
SOVIET	AA-2 Atoll	HELLER	H INJ	72	w. MiG-21F	270
SOVIET	AA-2 Atoll	IMC	H INJ	72	w. MiG-21PF	271
SOVIET	AA-2 Atoll	KOVOZAVODY	H INJ	72	w. MiG-21MF	272
SOVIET	AA-2 Atoll	MD	H RSN	72	w. Su-22 (Fitter)	273
SOVIET	AA-6 Acrid IR	HASEGAWA	H INJ	72	w. MiG-25 (Foxbat)	274
SOVIET	AA-6 Acrid SARH	HASEGAWA	H INJ	72	w. MiG-25 (Foxbat)	275
SOVIET	AA-7 Apex IR	AIRFIX	H INJ	72	w. MiG-23 (Flogger B)	276
SOVIET	AA-7 Apex IR	HASEGAWA	H INJ	72	w. MiG-23S (Flogger B)	277
SOVIET	AA-7 Apex IR	SUTCLIFFE	H ML	72	w. Yak-28B/C/P	278
SOVIET	AA-7 Apex SARH	AIRFIX	H INJ	72	w. MiG-23 (Flogger B)	279
SOVIET	AA-8 Aphid	FUJIMI	H INJ	72	w. MiG-29 (Fulcrum)	280
SOVIET	AA-8 Aphid	HASEGAWA	H INJ	72	w. MiG-23S (Flogger B)	281
SOVIET	AA-10 Alamo	FUJIMI	H INJ	72	w. MiG-29 (Fulcrum)	282
SOVIET	AS-4 Kitchen	NOVA	H VAC	72	w. Tu-22M (Backfire B)	283
SOVIET	AT-2 Swatter	AIRFIX	H INJ	72	w. Mi-24 (Hind A/D)	284
SOVIET	AT-2 Swatter	HASEGAWA	H INJ	72	w. Mi-24 (Hind A/D/E)	285
SOVIET	SA-2 Guideline	AIRFIX	H INJ	76	w. ZIL 157	286
SPERRY	Sparrow I AIM-7A	FUJIMI	H INJ	72	w. F7U-3M Cutlass	287
SPERRY	Sparrow I AIM-7A	HAWK	H INJ	72	w. Javelin FAW.1	288
SPERRY	Sparrow I AIM-7A	HAWK	H INJ	72	w. XF-92A	289
SPERRY	Sparrow I AIM-7A	MONOGRAM	H INJ	72	w. F-4J Phantom II	290
SPERRY	Sparrow I AIM-7A	SMDC	H INJ	72		291
SPERRY	Sparrow II/III AIM-7B/C/D/E/F	ENTEX	H INJ	72	w. F-18/A-18 Hornet	292
SPERRY	Sparrow II/III AIM-7B/C/D/E/F	FUJIMI	H INJ	72	w. F-4C/D Phantom II	293
SPERRY	Sparrow II/III AIM-7B/C/D/E/F	FUJIMI	H INJ	72	w. F-4N Phantom II	294
SPERRY	Sparrow II/III AIM-7B/C/D/E/F	FUJIMI	H INJ	72	w. F-4S Phantom II	295
SPERRY	Sparrow II/III AIM-7B/C/D/E/F	AIRFIX	H INJ	72	w. F-4B/C/D/E/J Phantom II	296
SPERRY	Sparrow II/III AIM-7B/C/D/E/F	AIRFIX	H INJ	72	w. F-14A Tomcat	297
SPERRY	Sparrow II/III AIM-7B/C/D/E/F	AIRFIX	H INJ	72	w. F-15A/B Eagle	298
SPERRY	Sparrow II/III AIM-7B/C/D/E/F	AIRFIX	H INJ	72	w. F/A-18A Hornet	299
SPERRY	Sparrow II/III AIM-7B/C/D/E/F	AIRFIX	H INJ	72	w. Tornado	300
SPERRY	Sparrow II/III AIM-7B/C/D/E/F	ESCI	H INJ	72	w. F-4C/J Phantom II	301
SPERRY	Sparrow II/III AIM-7B/C/D/E/F	ESCI	H INJ	72	w. F-4E/F Phantom II	302
SPERRY	Sparrow II/III AIM-7B/C/D/E/F	HASEGAWA	H INJ	72	w. Air Weapon Set II	303
SPERRY	Sparrow II/III AIM-7B/C/D/E/F	HASEGAWA	H INJ	72	w. A-4F Skyhawk	304
SPERRY	Sparrow II/III AIM-7B/C/D/E/F	HASEGAWA	H INJ	72	w. F-4B/C/D/E/H/J/K Ph. II	305
SPERRY	Sparrow II/III AIM-7B/C/D/E/F	HASEGAWA	H INJ	72	w. F-14A Tomcat	306
SPERRY	Sparrow II/III AIM-7B/C/D/E/F	HASEGAWA	H INJ	72	w. F-15A Eagle	307
SPERRY	Sparrow II/III AIM-7B/C/D/E/F	HASEGAWA	H INJ	72	w. F-15B/D Eagle	308
SPERRY	Sparrow II/III AIM-7B/C/D/E/F	HASEGAWA	H INJ	72	w. F-15C Eagle	309
SPERRY	Sparrow II/III AIM-7B/C/D/E/F	HASEGAWA	H INJ	72	w. F-15J Eagle	310
SPERRY	Sparrow II/III AIM-7B/C/D/E/F	HASEGAWA	H INJ	72	w. F-15E Eagle	311
SPERRY	Sparrow II/III AIM-7B/C/D/E/F	HASEGAWA	H INJ	72	w. F/A-18 Hornet	312
SPERRY	Sparrow II/III AIM-7B/C/D/E/F	HASEGAWA	H INJ	72	w. TA-4J Skyhawk	313
SPERRY	Sparrow II/III AIM-7B/C/D/E/F	ITALERI	H INJ	72	w. F-16A/B Fighting Falcon	314
SPERRY	Sparrow II/III AIM-7B/C/D/E/F	ITALERI	H INJ	72	w. F/A-18 Hornet	315
SPERRY	Sparrow II/III AIM-7B/C/D/E/F	MATCHBOX	H INJ	72	w. F-4K/M Phantom II	316
SPERRY	Sparrow II/III AIM-7B/C/D/E/F	MATCHBOX	H INJ	72	w. F-14 Tomcat	317
SPERRY	Sparrow II/III AIM-7B/C/D/E/F	MONOGRAM	H INJ	72	w. F-4E Phantom II (SN)	318
SPERRY	Sparrow II/III AIM-7B/C/D/E/F	MONOGRAM	H INJ	72	w. F-14A Tomcat	319
SPERRY	Sparrow II/III AIM-7B/C/D/E/F	MONOGRAM	H INJ	72	w. F-14A Tomcat (SN)	320
SPERRY	Sparrow II/III AIM-7B/C/D/E/F	MONOGRAM	H INJ	72	w. F-15A Eagle	321
SPERRY	Sparrow II/III AIM-7B/C/D/E/F	MONOGRAM	H INJ	72	w. F/A-18 Hornet (SN)	322
SPERRY	Sparrow II/III AIM-7B/C/D/E/F	REVELL	H INJ	72	w. F-4C/E/J Phantom II	323
SPERRY	Sparrow II/III AIM-7B/C/D/E/F	REVELL	H INJ	72	w. F-4K/M Phantom II	324
SPERRY	Sparrow II/III AIM-7B/C/D/E/F	REVELL	H INJ	72	w. F-15A Eagle	325
SPERRY	Sparrow II/III AIM-7B/C/D/E/F	REVELL	H INJ	72	w. F/A-18 Hornet	326
SPERRY	Sparrow II/III AIM-7B/C/D/E/F	SMDC	H INJ	72		327
SPERRY	Sparrow AIM-7F	HASEGAWA	H INJ	72	w. F/A-18 Hornet remoulded	328
TI/SPERRY/UNIVAC	Harm AGM-88A	HASEGAWA	H INJ	72	w. Air Weapon Set III	320

Macross Destroid Spartan	IMAI	INJ		72		66
Macross Destroid Tomahawk	ARII	INJ		72		67
Macross Tactical Pod Glaug	ARII	INJ		72		68
Macross Tactical Pod Regult	IMAI	INJ		72		69
Martian's War Machine WW-1	GENERAL PRODUCTS	VAC		72		70
Martian's War Machine WW-1	SFMA	VAC		72		71
Mugen Calibur VV-54AR Robot	GUNZE SANGYO	INJ		72		72
Nausicaa Adv. Ganshjuf Flyer	TSUKUDA	INJ		72		73
Orguss Flyer	IMAI	INJ		72		74
Orguss Gerwalk	IMAI	INJ		72		75
Orguss Nikick Commander	IMAI	INJ		72		76
Orguss Orgroid Robot	IMAI	INJ		72		77
Orguss Tank	IMAI	INJ		72		78
Pirate Ship "Peter Pan"	REVELL	INJ		72		79
Proteus Sub	MARUSAN	INJ		72		80
Soltic AG9 Nicollfe Robot	TAKARA	INJ		72		81
Soltic Duey Copter MP2	TAKARA	INJ		72		82
Soltic H102 Buschman Robot	TAKARA	INJ		72		83
Soltic H4045 Robot	TAKARA	INJ		72		84
Soltic H8 Handglider Roundfacer	TAKARA	INJ		72		85
Soltic HB Roundfacer Dual	TAKARA	ML		72	w. plastic parts	86
Soltic H8 Roundfacer Robot #Z-17	TAKARA	INJ		72		87
Soltic H8 Roundfacer Robot #Z-24	TAKARA	INJ		72		88
Soltic Korchima SPL Robot	TAKARA	INJ		72		89
Soltic Mavellic Copter	TAKARA	INJ		72		90
Space 1999 Eagle	AIRFIX	INJ		76		91
Space 1999 Hawk Spaceship	AIRFIX	INJ		76		92
Star Wars Tie Fighter	TAKARA	INJ		72		93
Star Wars X-Wing	AIRFIX	INJ	SN	72		94
Stingray Sub	MIDORI	INJ		72		95
The Animage Bisson	ARII	INJ		76		96
The Animage Camui	ARII	INJ		76		97
The Animage Gaspal	ARII	INJ		76		98
The Animage Zarigu	ARII	INJ		76		99
The Hitch-Hicker #1	DENIZEN	INJ		72		100
The Hitch-Hicker #2	DENIZEN	INJ		72		101
The Hitch-Hicker Robot	DENIZEN	INJ		72		102
The Hitch-Hicker Trillian Figure	DENIZEN	INJ		72		103
The Hitch-Hicker Two-Heads Alien	DENIZEN	INJ		72		104
The Invaders UFO	AURORA	INJ		72		105
The Invaders UFO	MONOGRAM	INJ	RM	72	ex-AURORA mould	106
The Time Tunnel Diorama	FUJIMI	INJ		72		107
Thunderbirds 4 Sub #36188	BANDAI	INJ		72		108
Thunderbirds 4 Sub #B-073-300	IMAI	INJ	MT	72	w. clear parts	109
Thunderbirds 4 Sub Secret Base Diorama	BANDAI	INJ	MT	72		110
Ultraman Spacecraft #1 Jet VTOL	GENERAL PRODUCTS	VAC		72		111
Ultraman Spacecraft #2 Sub VTOL	GENERAL PRODUCTS	VAC		72		112
Ultraman Spacecraft #3	GENERAL PRODUCTS	VAC		72		113
Ultraman Spacecraft #4	GENERAL PRODUCTS	VAC		72		114
Zoids Big Tyrannosaurus Vehicule	TOMY	INJ		72		115
Zoids Brontosaurus Vehicule	TOMY	INJ		72		116
Zoids Diplodocus Vehicule	TOMY	INJ		72		117
Zoids Elefant Vehicule	TOMY	INJ		72		118
Zoids Flap-Wing Flyier	TOMY	INJ		72		119
Zoids Flap-Wing Vehicule	TOMY	INJ		72		120
Zoids Frog Vehicule	TOMY	INJ		72		121
Zoids King-Size Tyrannosaurus Vehicule	TOMY	INJ		72		122
Zoids Mammoth Vehicule	TOMY	INJ		72		123
Zoids Mantis Vehicule	TOMY	INJ		72		124
Zoids Plesiosaurus Vehicule	TOMY	INJ		72		125
Zoids Scorpio Vehicule	TOMY	INJ		72		126
Zoids Small Tyrannosaurus Vehicule	TOMY	INJ		72		127
Zoids Spider Vehicule	TOMY	INJ		72		128
Zoids Stegosaur Vehicule	TOMY	INJ		72		129
Zoids Terrestrial Soldiers	TOMY	INJ		72		130
Zoids Tyrannosaurus Vehicule	TOMY	INJ		72		131

ACCESSORIES

1 POWER PLANT

IDENTIFICATION	MODEL	MAT	SC	REF	COMMENT	RANK
ARMSTRONG SIDDELEY Cheetah 7-cylinder (Anson)	AEROCLUB	ML·	72	E006		1
ARMSTRONG SIDDELEY Genet 5-cylinder (Widgeon)	AEROCLUB	ML·	72	E003		2
ARMSTRONG SIDDELEY Genet 7-cylinder (Cadet)	AEROCLUB	ML·	72	E004		3
ARMSTRONG SIDDELEY Jaguar 14-cylinder (Atlas)	AEROCLUB	ML·	72	E007		4
ARMSTRONG SIDDELEY Lynx 7-cylinder (Tutor)	AEROCLUB	ML·	72	E005		5
ARMSTRONG SIDDELEY Panther 14-cylinder (Gordon)	AEROCLUB	ML·	72	E008		6
BENTLEY rotary 9-cylinder (many WWI aircraft)	AEROCLUB	ML·	72	E016		7
BRISTOL Hercules engine and front ring (Lancaster II)	AEROCLUB	ML·	72	E030		8
BRISTOL Jupiter IV/VI (Gamecock, Woodcock)	AEROCLUB	ML·	72	E033		9
BRISTOL Jupiter/Pegasus 9-cylinder (Baffin)	AEROCLUB	ML·	72	E011		10
BRISTOL Jupiter/Pegasus 9-cylinder (HP42)	AEROCLUB	ML·	72	E010	w. 4-blade propeller	11
BRISTOL Pegasus	AEROCLUB	ML·	72	E032		12
CLERGET rotary 9-cylinder (many WW I aircraft)	AEROCLUB	ML·	72	E013		13
DE HAVILLAND Gipsy cowl and propeller (Moth)	AEROCLUB	ML·	72	E001		14
GNOME rotary single-valve 9-cylinder (many WWI aircraft)	AEROCLUB	ML·	72	E019		15
Kestrel Elephant heat exhaust stubs	AEROCLUB	ML·	72	V009		16
LE RHONE rotary 9-cylinder 110 HP (many WWI aircraft)	AEROCLUB	ML·	72	E015		17
LE RHONE rotary 9-cylinder 80 HP (many WWI aircraft)	AEROCLUB	ML·	72	E014		18
MERCEDES in line 160 HP (German WWI aircraft)	AEROCLUB	ML·	72	E020		19
NAPIER Lion 11B	AEROCLUB	ML·	72	E031		20
Pipe exhaust stubs	AEROCLUB	ML·	72	V010		21
PRATT & WHITNEY Hornet 1640 (DOUGLAS 0-38B)	AEROCLUB	ML·	72	E023		22
PRATT & WHITNEY Hornet 1690 (SIKORSKY S-43)	AEROCLUB	ML·	72	E026	id. BMW	23
PRATT & WHITNEY Wasp 1340	AEROCLUB	ML·	72	E022		24
PRATT & WHITNEY Wasp 1340 (BOEING 247)	AEROCLUB	ML·	72	E024		25
PRATT & WHITNEY Wasp Junior 9-cylinder (BEECH 17)	AEROCLUB	ML·	72	E012		26
ROLLS-ROYCE Merlin Mk 85 (Lincoln, Argonaut)	NEWARK	RSN	72			27
ROYAL AIRCRAFT FACTORY 4a cylinders and exhaust (BE.12)	AEROCLUB	ML·	72	E027		28
ROYAL AIRCRAFT FACTORY 4a cylinders and exhaust (RE.8L)	AEROCLUB	ML·	72	E028		29
SALMSON Pobjoy 9-cylinder 9AD (KLEMM)	AEROCLUB	ML·	72	E002		30
SIEMENS Halske rotary 11-cylinder (German WWI aircraft)	AEROCLUB	ML·	72	E029		31
SIEMENS SH14 7-cylinder (Stieglitz)	AEROCLUB	ML·	72	E009		32
Stack exhaust	AEROCLUB	ML·	72	V021		33
TURBOMECO Astazou front cowl and propeller (Pucara)	AEROCLUB	ML·	72	E018		34
WRIGHT 1820F Cyclone (Condor, LOCKHEED 14)	AEROCLUB	ML·	72	E021		35
WRIGHT 1820G Cyclone (CURTISS SC-1)	AEROCLUB	ML·	72	EO25		36
WRIGHT R3350 (EC-121)	K.MODELS	RSN	72		w. radome and propellers	37
WRIGHT Whirlwind J.5 9-cylinder (American pre-WWII)	AEROCLUB	ML·	72	E017		38

2 PROPELLERS

IDENTIFICATION	MODEL	MAT	SC	REF	COMMENT	RANK
AIRSCREW Co GP 11′ 2-blade wooden (Gordon, Baffin)	AEROCLUB	ML·	72	P009		1
ARGUS Schwarz 8′ 2-blade (PILATUS P-2)	AEROCLUB	ML·	72	P019		2
CURTISS Electric 11′ 3-blade (Hawk 75, CURTISS A-18)	AEROCLUB	ML·	72	P026		3
CURTISS Electric 16′ 4-blade (B-29, B-32)	AEROCLUB	ML·	72	P023		4
DE HAVILLAND (HAMILTON STANDARD) 12′ 3-blade (Botha, Skua)	AEROCLUB	ML·	72	P021		5
DE HAVILLAND 12′ 3-blade (Botha, Skua, Harrow, Albacore)	AEROCLUB	ML·	72	P025	w. small spinner	6
DE HAVILLAND 3-blade (Dove, Marathon)	AEROCLUB	ML·	72	P011		7
DE HAVILLAND 3-blade (Lancaster B.II)	AEROCLUB	ML·	72	P020		8
DE HAVILLAND 6′ 2-blade (Mew Gull)	AEROCLUB	ML·	72	P008	w. spinner	9
DE HAVILLAND 6′ 2-blade wooden (Moths)	AEROCLUB	ML·	72	P005		10
DE HAVILLAND Hydromatic 12′6″ 4-blade (Sea Mosquito)	AEROCLUB	ML·	72	P032	w. spinner	11
DE HAVILLAND Hydromatic 13′ 4-blade (Lincoln, Tudor)	AEROCLUB	ML·	72	P030		12
DE HAVILLAND Hydromatic 14′ 3-blade (Albermarle)	AEROCLUB	ML·	72	P013		13
FAIREY REED 3-blade 12′ (Swordfish, London, Hendon)	AEROCLUB	ML·	72	P016		14
FAIREY REED 7′6″ 2-blade (Anson, CIERVA, C.30)	AEROCLUB	ML·	72	P024		15
General purpose 8′ 2-blade wooden	AEROCLUB	ML·	72	P015		36
General purpose WWI wooden	AEROCLUB	ML·	72	P014		17
HAMILTON STANDARD 12′ 3-blade (DC-2)	AEROCLUB	ML·	72	P017		18
HAMILTON STANDARD 15′2″ 3-blade (EC-121)	K.MODELS	RSN	72		w. radome and engines	19
HAMILTON STANDARD 3-blade ground adjustable (pre-War US/AC)	AEROCLUB	ML·	72	P035		20
HAMILTON STANDARD 8′ 2-blade ground adjustable (BT-9)	AEROCLUB	ML·	72	P031		21
HAMILTON STANDARD 8′6″ 2-blade (BEECH 17/18, Goblin)	AEROCLUB	ML·	72	P007		22
HAMILTON STANDARD 9′ 2-blade (Harvard, BT-13)	AEROCLUB	ML·	72	P027		23
HAMILTON STANDARD 9′6″ 2-blade ground adjustable (P-12, 0-38B)	AEROCLUB	ML·	72	P028		24
HAMILTON STANDARD 9′6″ 3-blade (F3F, Shrike)	AEROCLUB	ML·	72	P003		25
HAMILTON STANDARD Hydromatic 11′ 3-blade (DC-3, Ventura)	AEROCLUB	ML·	72	P002		26
HAMILTON STANDARD Hydromatic 13′6″ 3-blade (B-18A)	AEROCLUB	ML·	72	P033	DOUGLAS B-18A Bolo	27
HAMILTON STANDARD Hydromatic 14′ 3-blade (CONVAIR 340)	AEROCLUB	ML·	72	P022		28
HARTZELL 3-blade (Turbo Porter)	AEROCLUB	ML·	72	P010		29
HEINE 8′ 2-blade wooden (Storch)	AEROCLUB	ML·	72	P029		30
HOFFMAN 6′6″ 2-blade (Stieglitz)	AEROCLUB	ML·	72	P006		31
ROTOL 13′ 4-blade (Hastings, Solent, Ambassador, Viking)	AEROCLUB	ML·	72	P004		32
ROTOL contra rotating	AEROCLUB	ML·	72	P034		33
ROTOL Dart 10′ 4-blade (Viscount, Dart Dakota)	AEROCLUB	ML·	72	P018		34
ROTOL Dart 14′ 4-blade (HS 748)	AEROCLUB	ML·	72	P001		35
WATTS 10′6″ 2-blade (Demon, Hart)	AEROCLUB	ML·	72	P012		36

3 COCKPIT LAYOUT

3.1 EJECTION SEATS

IDENTIFICATION	MODEL	MAT	SC	REF	COMMENT	RANK
Ejection seat handles	P.P. AEROPARTS	EB·	72	AC701	w. canopy mirrors	1
Ejection seat handles	MD	EB·	72	PH 72-75	high & low configuration	2
ESCAPAC	AEROCLUB	ML·	72	EJ012		3
LW-3B	HARRIER	ML·	72		Bronco	4
MARTIN-BAKER Aces II	AEROCLUB	ML·	72	EJ005	F-15, A-10	5
MARTIN-BAKER ejection seat handles	MODEL TECHNOLOGIES	EB·	72	MT0015	w. F-15 Head Up Display	6
MARTIN-BAKER GRU7	AEROCLUB	ML·	72	EJ014	Tomcat, Intruder	7
MARTIN-BAKER Mk 1	AEROCLUB	ML·	72	EJ016		8
MARTIN-BAKER Mk 2	AEROCLUB	ML·	72	EJ001		9
MARTIN-BAKER Mk 3	AEROCLUB	ML·	72	EJ008	Canberra	10
MARTIN-BAKER Mk 4	AEROCLUB	ML·	72	EJ010	Hunter	11
MARTIN-BAKER Mk 4bs	AEROCLUB	ML·	72	EJ002	Lightning	12
MARTIN-BAKER Mk 5	AEROCLUB	ML·	72	EJ003	US aircraft	13
MARTIN-BAKER Mk 6/7	AEROCLUB	ML·	72	EJ004	RAF Phantom II	14
MARTIN-BAKER Mk 6MSB	HARRIER	ML·	72		Buccaneer	15
MARTIN-BAKER Mk 9	AEROCLUB	ML·	72	EJ006	Harrier, Jaguar	16
MARTIN-BAKER Mk 10	AEROCLUB	ML·	72	EJ007	Hawk, Alpha Jet	17
MARTIN-BAKER Mk 10	AEROCLUB	ML·	72	EJ011	Sea Harrier	18
MARTIN-BAKER Mk 10b	HARRIER	ML·	72		Hawk	19
MARTIN-BAKER Mk 10c	AEROCLUB	ML·	72	EJ015		20
MARTIN-BAKER Mk 10h	HARRIER	ML·	72			21
SOVIET VS-IBRI	AEROCLUB	ML·	72	EJ013		22
STENCEL	AEROCLUB	ML·	72	EJ009	AV-8A, German Alpha Jet	23

3.2 COCKPIT and CANOPY EQUIPMENT

IDENTIFICATION	MODEL	MAT	SC	REF	RANK
GENERAL DYNAMICS F-16 Fighting Falcon canopy detail set	MODEL TECHNOLOGIES	EB·	72	MT0047	1
GENERAL DYNAMICS F-16A Fighting Falcon interior placard set	MODEL TECHNOLOGIES	EB·	72	MT1003	2
GENERAL DYNAMICS F-16A/C Fighting Falcon canopy detail superset	MODEL TECHNOLOGIES	EB·	72	MT0065	3
GRUMMAN F-14 Tomcat canopy detail set	MODEL TECHNOLOGIES	EB·	72	MT0038	4
HUGHES AH-64A Apache interior placard set	MODEL TECHNOLOGIES	EB·	72	MT1007	5
LOCKHEED F-104 Starfighter canopy detail set	MODEL TECHNOLOGIES	EB·	72	MT0053	6
LOCKHEED F-19 Stealth canopy detail set	MODEL TECHNOLOGIES	EB·	72	MT0062	7
LOCKHEED SR-71 Blackbird canopy detail set	MODEL TECHNOLOGIES	EB·	72	MT0055	8
McDONNELL DOUGLAS F-15A Eagle interior placard set	MODEL TECHNOLOGIES	EB·	72	MT1004	9
McDONNELL DOUGLAS F-15C Eagle canopy detail set	MODEL TECHNOLOGIES	EB·	72	MT0041	10
McDONNELL DOUGLAS F-15E Eagle canopy detail set	MODEL TECHNOLOGIES	EB·	72	MT0044	11
McDONNELL DOUGLAS F/A-18 Hornet canopy detail set	MODEL TECHNOLOGIES	EB·	72	MT0050	12
McDONNELL F-4 Phantom II canopy detail set	MODEL TECHNOLOGIES	EB·	72	MT0026	13
MIKOYAN-GURYEVICH MiG-29 (Fulcrum) canopy detail set	MODEL TECHNOLOGIES	EB·	72	MT0066	14
MIL Mi-24 (Hind) interior detail set	P.P. AEROPARTS	EB·	72	AC 705	15
Mirrors (Jet aircraft)	MODEL TECHNOLOGIES	EB·	72	MT0012	16
Mirrors (US jet carrier)	WALDRON	EB·	72		17
NORTHROP F-5E Tiger II/F-20 Tigershark/X-29 canopy detail set	MODEL TECHNOLOGIES	EB·	72	MT0058	18
Seat belt and harness buckles	WALDRON	EB·	72		19
Seat belt buckles (1930 aircraft)	MODEL TECHNOLOGIES	EB·	72	MT0034	20
Seat belt buckles (Jet aircraft)	MODEL TECHNOLOGIES	EB·	72	MT0009	21
Seat belt buckles (WWII British aircraft)	MODEL TECHNOLOGIES	EB·	72	MT0023	22
Seat belt buckles (WWII Japanese aircraft)	MODEL TECHNOLOGIES	EB·	72	MT0020	23
Seat belt buckles (WWII US aircraft)	MODEL TECHNOLOGIES	EB·	72	MT0006	24
Seat belt buckles, rudder pedals (WWII German aircraft)	MODEL TECHNOLOGIES	EB·	72	MT0003	25

3.3 CANOPY SETS

IDENTIFICATION	MODEL	MAT	SC	REF	RANK
TBM/Avenger, SBC/SB2C Helldiver, OS2U Kingfisher, TBD Devastator, F4F Wildcat, J2F Duck, F8F Bearcat, SBD Dauntless, SOC Seagull, F4U-1 Corsair "Birdcage", F4U-1D Corsair.	FALCON CLEAR-VAX	VAC	72	1	1

4 AIRCRAFT and MISSILES DETAIL PARTS

IDENTIFICATION	MODEL	MAT	SC	REF	COMMENT	RANK
Aileron control horns, fuel dump vents, windscreen wipers	P.P. AEROPARTS	EB·	72	AL722	w. access ladders	1
Arrestor hooks	AEROCLUB	ML·	72	V003		2
General purpose flight refuelling probe	AEROCLUB	ML·	72			3
General purpose tailwheels, oil coolers etc	AEROCLUB	ML·	72			4
SEPECAT Jaguar air brakes panels	P.P. AEROPARTS	EB·	72	AC 704		5
Sidewinder AIM-9 missile fins	P.P. AEROPARTS	EB·	72	AC 702		6
Smoke system for Hawk Red Arrows	HARRIER	ML·	72			7
Wheels (WWI type)	P.P. AEROPARTS	EB·	72	MT 0060		8
Wheels, 10mm diameter (WWI type)	AEROCLUB	ML·	72	V008		9

5 EXTERNAL STORES and WEAPONS

5.1 EXTERNAL STORES

IDENTIFICATION	MODEL	MAT	SC	REF	COMMENT	RANK
BLACKBURN Buccaneer drop tank	ID MODELS	VAC	72			1
BLACKBURN torpedo	SKYBIRDS	INJ	72			2
CBLS (Carrier Bomb Light Stores)	HARRIER	ML·	72		4 different types	3
DASSAULT Mirage III, Jaguar pylons	MD	RSN	72	AC 72003		4
DASSAULT Mirage IIE/V, Jaguar stores	MD	RSN	72	AC 72001	Martel m. + cluster bombs + rockets pods	5
DOUGLAS refuelling pod	GRAPHY-AIR	RSN	72		w. Etendard conversion	6
ECM pods (French aircraft)	MD	RSN	72	AC 72002		7
SEPECAT Jaguar external stores	C.SCALE	ML·	72			8
US Navy D-704 refuelling stores	PRIVATEER	RSN	72		A-4 Skyhawk, A-6 Intruder, A-7 Corsair II	9
WEAPON SET 1	HASEGAWA	INJ	72	X72:1		10
WEAPON SET 2	HASEGAWA	INJ	72	X72:2		11
WEAPON SET 3	HASEGAWA	INJ	72	X72:3		12
WEAPON SET 4	HASEGAWA	INJ	72	X72:4		13

5.2 WEAPONS

IDENTIFICATION	MODEL	MAT	SC	REF	RANK
Anti-aircraft gun	SKYBIRDS	INJ	72		1
Anti-aircraft gun with crew	SKYBIRDS	INJ	72		2
German MG.34/MG.42 machine gun	ARMTEC	INJ	76		3
LEWIS gun	SKYBIRDS	INJ	72		4
LEWIS WWI	AEROCLUB	ML·	72	G002	5
LEWIS WWI (Jacket type)	AEROCLUB	ML·	72	G012	6
Luftwaffe MG.131	AEROCLUB	ML·	72	G010	7
Luftwaffe MG.15	AEROCLUB	ML·	72	G009	8
Luftwaffe MG.81	AEROCLUB	ML·	72	G011	9
Machine gun (50 cal.) & ammo box	ARMTEC	INJ	76		10
OERLIKON 20mm cannon	AEROCLUB	ML·	72	G008	11
PARABELLUM gun	SKYBIRDS	INJ	72		12
PARABELLUM machine gun	AEROCLUB	ML·	72	AG004	13
SCHWARLOSE WWI machine gun	AEROCLUB	ML·	72		14
SPANDAU WWI	AEROCLUB	ML·	72	G003	15
VICKERS 1930 machine gun	AEROCLUB	ML·	72		16
VICKERS gun (modern)	SKYBIRDS	INJ	72		17
VICKERS gun (wartime)	SKYBIRDS	INJ	72		18
VICKERS K 1930	AEROCLUB	ML·	72	G005	19
VICKERS WWI machine gun	AEROCLUB	INJ	72	AG001	20
VICKERS WWII machine gun	AEROCLUB	ML·	72	AG007	21

6 GROUND SUPPORT EQUIPMENT

6.1 ACCESS LADDERS

IDENTIFICATION	MODEL	MAT	SC	REF	COMMENT	RANK
AVRO Vulcan	P.P AEROPARTS	EB·	72	AL720		1
BAC Lightning	P.P. AEROPARTS	EB·	72	AL718		2
BLACKBURN Buccaneer	P.P. AEROPARTS	EB·	72	AL722	w. aircraft detail parts	3
BRITISH AEROSPACE Harrier GR.1/3	P.P. AEROPARTS	EB·	72	AL713		4
BRITISH AEROSPACE Harrier T.4	P.P. AEROPARTS	EB·	72	AL714		5
BRITISH AEROSPACE Hawk	P.P. AEROPARTS	EB·	72	AL716		6
BRITISH AEROSPACE Sea Harrier FRS.1	P.P. AEROPARTS	EB·	72	AL712		7
CONVAIR F-106 Delta Dart	P.P. AEROPARTS	EB·	72	AL731		8
DASSAULT Etendard/Super Etendard	MD	EB·	72	PH 72-72		9
DASSAULT Mirage III/V/F.1	MD	EB·	72	PH 72-71		10
DOUGLAS A-4 Skyhawk	P.P. AEROPARTS	EB·	72	AL707		11
GENERAL DYNAMICS F-111 Aardvark	P.P. AEROPARTS	EB·	72	AL719		12
GENERAL DYNAMICS F-16 Fighting Falcon	P.P. AEROPARTS	EB·	72	AL704		13
GRUMMAN A-6 Intruder/EA-6B Prowler	P.P. AEROPARTS	EB·	72	AL727		14
GRUMMAN F-14 Tomcat	P.P. AEROPARTS	EB·	71	AL726		15
HAWKER Hunter	P.P. AEROPARTS	EB·	72	AL717		16
LOCKHEED CF-104 Starfighter	P.P. AEROPARTS	EB·	72	AL724		17
LOCKHEED F-104 Starfighter	P.P. AEROPARTS	EB·	72	AL706		18
LOCKHEED F-19 Stealth	P.P. AEROPARTS	EB·	72	AL732		19
LOCKHEED T-33/F-94 Starfire	P.P. AEROPARTS	EB·	72	AL725		20
McDONNELL F-15 Eagle	P.P. AEROPARTS	EB·	72	AL703		21
McDONNELL F-18 Hornet	P.P. AEROPARTS	EB·	72	AL710		22
McDONNELL F-4 Phantom II	P.P. AEROPARTS	EB·	72	AL701	front ladder	23
McDONNELL F-4 Phantom II	P.P. AEROPARTS	EB·	72	AL728	front ladders	23
McDONNELL F-4M (FGR.2) Phantom II	P.P. AEROPARTS	EB·	72	AL721	front and rear ladders	25
MIKOYAN MiG-21/MiG-23/Finnish Hawk	P.P. AEROPARTS	EB·	72	AL708		26
NORTH AMERICAN F-100 Super Sabre	P.P. AEROPARTS	EB·	72	AL705		27
NORTHROP F-5 Tiger II/T-38/F-20/X-29	P.P. AEROPARTS	EB·	72	AL702		28
PANAVIA Tornado GR.1	P.P. AEROPARTS	EB·	72	AL723		29
RAF general purpose stepladder	P.P. AEROPARTS	EB·	72	AL709		30
REPUBLIC Thunderchief	P.P. AEROPARTS	EB·	72	AL711		31
SEPECAT Jaguar	P.P. AEROPARTS	EB·	72	AL715		32
SEPECAT Jaguar (French version)	P.P. AEROPARTS	EB·	72	AL729		33
SIKORSKY S-61 Sea King	P.P. AEROPARTS	EB·	72	AL730		34

6.2 VEHICLES

IDENTIFICATION	MODEL	MAT	SC	REF	COMMENT	RANK
Airport air/ground crew and vehicles	HELLER BOBKIT	INJ	72			1
CHEVROLET bomb lift truck (US aircraft)	MD	RSN	72	VM 72203		2
CHEVROLET flight crew vehicle	HASEGAWA	INJ	72	X72:7	w. US pilot/ground crew set	3
DODGE 4x4 Command Car	CLARK	INJ	72			4
DODGE 4x4 Command Car	RENOWN	ML·	72			5
DODGE 4x4 Command Car	ALBY	RSN	72			6
DODGE 4x4 truck	ESCI	INJ	72		w. 37mm gun	7
DODGE 4x4 truck	ESCI	INJ	72			8
DODGE 6x6	ALBY	RSN	72		ESCI conversion set	9
DODGE M880 (US Air Force)	MD	RSN	72	VM 72201		10
DODGE WC 54	ALBY	INJ	72			11
Eager Beaver	P.P. AEROPARTS	ML·	72	GA708	w. ML parts	12
Eager Beaver fork lift truck	P.P. AEROPARTS	ML·	72	GA707	w. ML parts	13
Fire tractor (US Navy carrier)	VERLINDEN	RSN	72	267 (VLS)		14
Fire tractor (US Navy)	MD	RSN	72	VM 72200		15
Fire truck VLEP (French)	MD	RSN	72	VM 72202		16
FORD tractor (US aircraft)	HASEGAWA	INJ	72	X72:5	US AIRCRAFT WEAPON LOADING SET	17
GFE caterpillar tractor	MONOGRAM	INJ	72		w. Regulus II missile	18
LAND ROVER LWD	GRAMODEL	RSN	72			19
LAND ROVER Light lorry	AIRFIX	INJ	72		w. Bloodhound missile	20
LAND ROVER light lorry	GRAMODEL	RSN	72			21
LAND ROVER soft top	J.B. MODELS	INJ	72			22
LAND ROVER strike lorry	AIRFIX	INJ	72		w. C-130 Hercules	23
Lift truck (French)	MD	RSN	72	AC 72013		24
Lift truck (US aircraft)	HASEGAWA	INJ	72	X72:5	US AIRCRAFT WEAPON LOADING SET	25
MASSEY FERGUSSON aircraft tractor	P.P. AEROPARTS	ML·	72	GA706	w. ML parts	26
TOYOTA aircraft tractor	HASEGAWA	INJ	72		w. BEECH T-34	27
TOYOTA aircraft tractor	IMAI	INJ	72		w. NAMC YS-11	28
TOYOTA GB starter truck	HASEGAWA	INJ	72			29
Tow tractor	TRAME	RSN	72	TD 31	w. EB parts	30
Tow tractor (French Air Force)	MD	RSN	72	AC 72004	w. EB parts	31
Tow tractor (French Navy)	MD	RSN	72	AC 72005		32
Tow tractor (Royal Navy)	MD	RSN	72	AC 72009		33
Tow tractor (US Navy)	MD	RSN	72	AC 72006	w. starting unit	34
Tow tractor (US Navy)	MD	RSN	72	AC 72007		35
Tractor (US Navy carrier)	VERLINDEN	RSN	72	ACDA 72003		36
Tractor (US Navy carrier)	VERLINDEN	RSN	72	ACDA 72004		37
WILLYS Jeep	HASEGAWA	INJ	72		w. 37mm gun	38
WILLYS Jeep	MATCHBOX	INJ	72		w. CHEVROLET GS truck	39
WILLYS Jeep	AIRFIX	INJ	72		w. LVT-4	40
WILLYS Jeep	NITTO	INJ	72		w. M4 Half-truck	41
WILLYS Jeep	HASEGAWA	INJ	72		w. MITSUBISHI MU-2S	42
WILLYS Jeep	MATCHBOX	INJ	72		w. MORRIS C8	43
WILLYS Jeep	NITTO	INJ	72		w. SHERMAN tank	44
WILLYS Jeep	GRAMODEL	RSN	72			45
ZIL 157 missile transporter	AIRFIX	INJ	72		w. SAM-2	46

6.3 MISCELLANEOUS

IDENTIFICATION	MODEL	MAT	SC	REF	COMMENT	RANK
Air conditioner A/M32C-10 (US aircraft)	HASEGAWA	INJ	72	X72:6	US AEROSPACE GROUND EQUIPMENT SET	1
Airport geteways with barricades	PREISER	INJ	72			2
Ammo trailer MHU-12M (US aircraft)	HASEGAWA	INJ	72	X72:5	US AIRCRAFT WEAPON LOADING SET	3
Bomb handling trolley (Luftwaffe WWII)	LEAD SLED MODELS	ML·	72			4
Crowd barriers	P.P. AEROPARTS	EB·	72	GA701		5
Drop tank dolly (F-4 370 Gallons)	HASEGAWA	INJ	72	X72:5	US AIRCRAFT WEAPON LOADING SET	6
Fire extinguisher (French Air Force)	MD	RSN	72	AC 72010	w. EB parts	7
Fire extinguisher (USAF)	MD	RSN	72	AC 72011	w. EB parts	8
Fire extinguisher trolley (RAF)	P.P. AEROPARTS	EB·	72	GA702		9
Fire extinguisher, engine crank, jack (German)	ARMTEC	INJ	76			10
Fire extinguisher, tool wagon (US aircraft)	HASEGAWA	INJ	72	X72:6	US AEROSPACE GROUND EQUIPMENT SET	11
Firestreak/Redtop missile trolley	P.P. AEROPARTS	EB·	72	GA712	w. ML parts	12
General purpose dolly (US aircraft)	HASEGAWA	INJ	72	X72:5	US AIRCRAFT WEAPON LOADING SET	13
Generator set A/M32A-60A (US aircraft)	HASEGAWA	INJ	72	X72:6	US AEROSPACE GROUND EQUIPMENT SET	14
Ground power unit	P.P. AEROPARTS	EB·	72	GA705	w. ML parts	15
Ground power unit (French)	MD	RSN	72	AC 72014		16
Ground power unit (Mirage 2000)	TRAME	RSN	72	TD 32	w. EB parts	17

High pressure compressor MC-1A (US aircraft)	HASEGAWA	INJ	72	X72:6	US AEROSPACE GROUND EQUIPMENT SET	18
Hydraulic lift trailer (US aircraft)	HASEGAWA	INJ	72	X72:5	US AIRCRAFT WEAPON LOADING SET	19
Hydraulic test stand TTU-288/E (US aircraft)	HASEGAWA	INJ	72	X72:6	US AEROSPACE GROUND EQUIPMENT SET	20
Jerry cans	ARMTEC	INJ	76			21
Jerry cans	H & S	RSN	76			22
Jerry cans (German)	MODEL MASTER	RSN	72			23
Lighting unit NF-2 (US aircraft)	HASEGAWA	INJ	72	X72:6	US AEROSPACE GROUND EQUIPMENT SET	24
Maintenance platform	MD	EB·	72	PH 72-73		25
Materials for medium-sized biplanes	SKYBIRDS	INJ	72	30		26
Materials for modern fighters	SKYBIRDS	INJ	72	29		27
Materials for wartime models	SKYBIRDS	INJ	72	28		28
Motorcycle, despatch rider, machine gun, crews	SKYBIRDS	INJ	72			29
Nitrogen trolley	P.P. AEROPARTS	EB·	72	GA704	w. ML parts	30
Oil drums	VERLINDEN	IND	72	ACDA72001		31
Oil drums and accessories (German)	PREISER	INJ	72			32
Oxygen trolley	P.P. AEROPARTS	EB·	72	GA703	w. ML parts	33
Petrol pump	SKYBIRDS	INJ	72			34
Pneumatic service trolley (RAF)	G.E.F.	ML·	72			35
Runway control caravan	G.E.F.	ML·	72			36
Tool box	TRAME	EB·	72	TD 39		37
Tool box	MD	EB·	72	PH 72-74	w. 8 tools	38
Tools-shovel, axe, sledge, crowbar, etc (US)	ARMTEC	INJ	76			39
Torpedo handling trolley and torpedo (RAF)	LEAD SLED MODELS	ML·	72	4		40
Tow bar set (RAF/NATO)	P.P. AEROPARTS	EB·	72	GA709	w. ML parts	41
Trolley accumulators	LEAD SLED MODELS	ML·	72			42
Wheel chocks	TRAME	EB·	72	TD 37		43
Wheel chocks (French aviation)	MD	EB·	72	PH 72-70	3 Pairs	44
Wheel chocks (RAF)	P.P. AEROPARTS	EB·	72	AC 703	2 pairs	45
Wheel chocks (US aircraft)	HASEGAWA	INJ	72	X72:6	US AEROSPACE GROUND EQUIPMENT SET	46

7 DIORAMA ENVIRONMENT

7.1 AIRFIELD BUILDINGS and INSTALLATIONS

IDENTIFICATION	MODEL	MAT	SC	RANK
Airport gateways	SKYBIRDS	INJ	72	1
Airport office	SKYBIRDS	INJ	72	2
Club buildings	SKYBIRDS	INJ	72	3
Control tower (Brookland type)	SKYBIRDS	INJ	72	4
Hangar (large hangar Air Travel Ltd.)	SKYBIRDS	INJ	72	5
Hangar (wartime)	SKYBIRDS	INJ	72	6
Hangar (workshop hangar)	SKYBIRDS	INJ	72	7
House and look-out tower	NITTO	INJ	76	8
Modern hangar with working doors	PREISER	CB·	72	9

7.2 TAXIWAYS, RUNWAYS and FLIGHT DECKS

IDENTIFICATION	MODEL	MAT	SC	REF	RANK
Airfield beacon lights	VERLINDEN	RSN	72		1
Anti armour wall (US Air Force)	MD	RSN	72	AC 72012	2
Catapult (US Navy)	UNIQUE SCALE	INJ	72		3
Flight deck (modern aircraft carrier type)	VERLINDEN	CB·	72	PCDA 72003	4
Flight deck (WWII aircraft carrier type)	VERLINDEN	CB·	72	PCDA 72005	5
Helicopter runway	VERLINDEN	CB·	72	PCDA 72002	6
Perforated steel plate (PSP)	VERLINDEN	CB·	72	PCDA 72004	7
Perforated steel plate (PSP)	MD	RSN	72	AC 72008	8
Revetment (Vietnam aircraft)	VERLINDEN	INJ	72	ACDA 72005	9
Runway	VERLINDEN	CB·	72	PCDA 72001	10
Runway end section	PREISER	INJ	72		11
Runway section	PREISER	INJ	72		12
Runway section ground sheet	SKYBIRDS	INJ	72		13
Taxiway	PREISER	INJ	72		14
Taxiway right turn section	PREISER	INJ	72		15

7.3 VEGETATION

IDENTIFICATION	MODEL	SC	RANK
Ornamental tree (2.5″)	WOODLAND SCENICS	76	1
Straight trunk tree (2.5″)	WOODLAND SCENICS	76	2
Hardwood forest (2″-4″)	WOODLAND SCENICS	76	3
Pine (2″-4″)	WOODLAND SCENICS	76	4

Shade trees (4")	WOODLAND SCENICS		76		5
Columnar pine	WOODLAND SCENICS		76		6
Dead trees	WOODLAND SCENICS		76		7
Tree stumps	WOODLAND SCENICS		76		8

7.4 MISCELLANEOUS

IDENTIFICATION	MODEL	MAT	SC	REF	RANK
Accessories, barricades, tower, pillboxes (German)	FUJIMI	INJ	72		1
Accessories, oil drums, cans, tents, etc (German)	FUJIMI	INJ	72		2
Anti-tank emplacement, dragon teeth, observation tower	FUJIMI	INJ	76		3
Barracks (German, large)	PREISER	INJ	72		4
Barracks (German, small)	PREISER	INJ	72		5
Battlefield accessories	ESCI	INJ	72		6
Bicycle	TRAME	EB·	72	TD 35	7
Bridge and checkpoint	NITTO	INJ	76		8
Bus shelter	PIRATE	ML·	72		9
Checkpoint	HASEGAWA	INJ	72		10
Concrete slab	PREISER	INJ	72		11
Country mansion	SKYBIRDS	INJ	72		12
Fencing	SKYBIRDS		72		13
Field accessories	NITTO	INJ	76		14
Field camp equipment	HASEGAWA	INJ	72		15
Garage (German military vehicles)	PREISER	INJ	72		16
Inn	SKYBIRDS	INJ	72		17
Military hospital with ambulance and Jeep	ATLANTIC	INJ	72		18
Military hospital with ambulance and Jeep	ATLANTIC	INJ	72		19
Oil drums	VERLINDEN	IND	72	ACDA72001	20
Radio station, wireless cabin, pylons etc	SKYBIRDS	INJ	72		21
Sand bags	ARMTEC	INJ	76		22
Sand bags, barricades, etc.	ESCI	INJ	72		23
Searchlights	SKYBIRDS	INJ	72		24
Telegraph poles	PREISER	INJ	72		25
Tents, oil drums and sand bags	FUJIMI	INJ	76		26
Tools (British)	ARMTEC	INJ	76		27
Tools-shovel, axe, sledge, crowbar, etc (German)	ARMTEC	INJ	76		28
Tow chains	ARMTEC	INJ	76		29
Zoo animal box 1	AIRFIX	INJ	76		30
Zoo animal box 2	AIRFIX	INJ	76		31

SHIPS

IDENTIFICATION	MODEL	MAT	XT	SC	COMMENT	RANK
Aberdovey-Type Tender	WOODCRAFT	WD·		72		1
Air-Sea Rescue Launch	WATERCRAFT	WD·		72		2
Anna Dordrecht Clipper	AMERANG	WD·		75		3
Bireme Imperator	HELLER	INJ		75		4
Blue Nose Fishing-Boat	AMERANG	WD·		75		5
Bounty	IMAI	INJ		75		6
Broadsword Boat	WOODCRAFT	WD·		75		7
Catalan Sailing Ship	IMAI	INJ		75		8
Charles W. Morgan	REVELL	INJ		66		9
Chinese Junk	AURORA	INJ		72		10
Corvette Flower Class	MATCHBOX	INJ		72		11
Cutty Sark Clipper	AMERANG	WD·		75		12
Denmark School-Ship	AMERANG	WD·		75		13
Gato Class US Navy Submarine	COMBAT	VAC		72		14
German E-Boat	AIRFIX	INJ		72		15
German U-Boat Type IXA/B/C	COMBAT	VAC		72		16
German U-Boat Type IXD	COMBAT	VAC		72		17
German WWI U-35	COMBAT	VAC		72		18
German WWII U-Boat Type IIIC	COMBAT	VAC		72		19
German WWII U-Boat Type VIIC	COMBAT	VAC		72		20
German WWII U-Boat Type XXI	COMBAT	VAC		72		21
Golden Hind Galleon	IMAI	INJ		70		22
HMS Victory	MANTUA	WD·		78		23
Japanese Torpedo Boat	TAMIYA	INJ	MT	72		24
Kairu Midget Submarine	L.S.	INJ		72		25
La Pomone 1690 Corsair Fregate	STEINGRAEBER	INJ		70		26
La Réale de France	HELLER	INJ		75		27
LCM III	AIRFIX	INJ		76		28
Mataro	HELLER	INJ		75		29
Mayflower	IMAI	INJ		70		30
MTB	SCALECRAFT	INJ	MT	72		31
Nina	HELLER	INJ		75		32
Pinta	HELLER	INJ		75		33
PT 109/PT 167 Torpedo Boat	REVELL	INJ		72		34
RAF Rescue Launch	AIRFIX	INJ		72		35
S. Felipe Spanish Vessel	MANTUA	WD·		75		36
SARO (Saunders-Roe) SR.N1 Hovercraft	AIRFIX	INJ		72		37
San Juan Nepomucemo	CONSTRUCTO MODRISA	INJ		75		38
Santa Maria	HELLER	INJ		75		39
Sir Winston Churchill	IMAI	INJ		75		40
Smit/Rotterdam Tugboat	AMERANG	WD·	MT	75		41
Soleil Royal	MANTUA	WD·		75		42
Sovereign of the Seas	MANTUA	WD·		75		43
Spansk Galleon	AMERANG	WD·		66		44
SSN Skipjack Nuclear Submarine	COMBAT	VAC		72		45
The Golden Hind Galleon	WATERCRAFT	INJ		72		46
Torpedo Boat	WATERCRAFT	INJ	MT	72		47
US Navy S Boat	COMBAT	VAC		72		48
USS Constitution Frigate	MANTUA	WD·		78		49
USS Nimitz Nuclear Aircraft Carrier	SUPER SHIPS	FB·		72		50
USS Ward Destroyer	COMBAT	VAC		72		51
Victory Prow Cross Section	MANTUA	WD·		78		52
Vosper Fast Patrol Boat	TAMIYA	INJ	MT	72		53
Vosper MTB	AIRFIX	INJ		72		54
Vosper MTB	REVELL	INJ		72		55
Wasa Swedish Royal Vessel	AMERANG	WD·		75		56

NOTES

NOTES

NOTES